A HELL OF A REGIMENT

To Gettysburg and Beyond with the Twentieth Maine

JARED PEATMAN

Stackpole Books

Essex, Connecticut

STACKPOLE BOOKS

An imprint of The Globe Pequot Publishing Group, Inc.
64 South Main Street
Essex, CT 06426
www.globepequot.com

Copyright © 2026 by Jared Peatman
Maps by Hal Jespersen

British Library Cataloguing in Publication Information available

Library of Congress Cataloging-in-Publication Data
Names: Peatman, Jared author
Title: A hell of a regiment : to Gettysburg and beyond with the Twentieth Maine / Jared Peatman.
Other titles: To Gettysburg and beyond with the Twentieth Maine
Description: Essex, Connecticut : Stackpole Books, 2026. | Includes bibliographical references. | Summary: "Drawing on previously unknown or inaccessible sources, this book is the first major account of the Twentieth Maine's stand at Gettysburg in more than three decades, a fresh telling for a new era. It sheds new light on the battle and explains just how a ragtag group of soldiers, led by a colonel trained in rhetoric and religion instead of military drill and tactics, became an effective fighting force"— Provided by publisher.
Identifiers: LCCN 2025049926 (print) | LCCN 2025049927 (ebook) | ISBN 9780811778152 cloth | ISBN 9780811778169 epub
Subjects: LCSH: Gettysburg, Battle of, Gettysburg, Pa., 1863 | United States. Army. Maine Infantry Regiment, 20th (1862–1865) | Chamberlain, Joshua Lawrence, 1828–1914—Leadership | Maine—History—Civil War, 1861–1865—Regimental histories | United States—History—Civil War, 1861–1865—Regimental histories
Classification: LCC E475.51 .P383 2026 (print) | LCC E475.51 (ebook) | DDC 973.7/349—dc23/eng/20260131
LC record available at https://lccn.loc.gov/2025049926
LC ebook record available at https://lccn.loc.gov/2025049927

"It was without local pride. No county claimed them. No city gave them a flag. They received no words of farewell on leaving your State, no words of welcome on their return. But their name is known in other climes, and their fame is owned by their enemies. In the hour of battle they knew the meaning of 'Dirigo' on your State escutcheon, and their record is as unsullied as your fame; may their memory be as green as your Pines."[1]

—*Joshua Chamberlain on the Twentieth Maine (1865)*

Contents

List of Maps vii
Acknowledgments ix

Introduction 1

CHAPTER 1: "A hell of a regiment": Becoming the
Twentieth Maine. 9

CHAPTER 2: The Professor's Education: Joshua Chamberlain's
Rise to Leadership 57

CHAPTER 3: "So clumsily done": The Second Maine Mutineers 89

CHAPTER 4: "With fixed bayonets and a yell": Gettysburg 121

CHAPTER 5: "Almost worn out": From War to Peace 185

CHAPTER 6: "What you did, the world knows": From
History to Memory 243

Conclusion. 297

Notes. 299

Bibliography 331

LIST OF MAPS

Twentieth Maine Men at Gettysburg: By Home Counties 12

Theater of War: 1862. 28

Battle of Fredericksburg: December 13, 1862 44

Battle of Fredericksburg: Twentieth Maine, December 13–16, 1862 . . 47

The March North: May 20–July 1, 1863. 126

Battle of Upperville: June 21, 1863 132

Gettysburg Battlefield: July 1–3, 1863 142

Battle of Gettysburg: Lee's Plan for July 2, 1863 144

Little Round Top: Vincent's Brigade Arrives 148

Little Round Top: Approach of the Fifteenth Alabama 157

Little Round Top: Twentieth Maine Refuses Their Flank 159

Little Round Top: Twentieth Maine Bayonet Charge 170

Battle of the Wilderness: May 5, 1864. 191

Twentieth Maine Battles: 1864 194

ACKNOWLEDGMENTS

A TREMENDOUS NUMBER OF PEOPLE HAVE HELPED WITH THIS PROJECT since I first became interested in the Civil War and the Twentieth Maine as a twelve-year-old. When I was in the sixth grade, my mother, Kathy, agreed to make the 650-mile drive to visit Gettysburg during our annual April vacation. She then brought me back every April vacation for the next six years and put up with me spending inordinate amounts of time exploring the battlefield. My father, Bernie, brought me to the annual summer reenactments multiple times. Their support laid the foundation for everything in this book and far beyond.

A series of academic mentors supported my study of the Civil War and the Twentieth Maine. Jim Ramsey oversaw an entire independent study on the Twentieth Maine when I was in high school. At Gettysburg College, I was able to keep thinking about the unit and its place in the Civil War while working at the Civil War Institute as a research assistant for Gabor Boritt. On Dr. Boritt's retirement from Gettysburg, he was replaced by Pete Carmichael, whom I met while attending the college's annual summer conference on the Civil War. Pete encouraged me to publish my dissertation on the Gettysburg Address and then introduced me to the folks at Southern Illinois University Press. Without his assistance, it is very likely that my first book would never have been published. Then Pete did what all academics do and said, "So . . . what's next?" When I told him I was interested in publishing a collection of accounts from the Twentieth Maine, he suggested I go a step further and write my own story of the unit. A dozen years later, this book is the result of that suggestion. It says everything about Pete that he took the time to advance the career of someone he barely knew and over the years gave me opportunities to present both tours and talks to ensure that I kept moving forward with the project.

Friends have listened to me drone on about the Twentieth Maine and Joshua Chamberlain for far too long. At Gettysburg, I was fortunate to have as friends Tim Parry and Ian Harkness, who both indulged me in many hours of rants about the Twentieth and Joshua Chamberlain. At Texas A&M, I became fast friends with Bill Collopy, and we have spent countless hours talking about history. Around fifteen years ago, I met Joe Mieczkowski, one of Gettysburg's premier Licensed Battlefield Guides. Despite his unrelenting "dad jokes," I always gain valuable insights from our conversations. More recently, Fran Feyock's observations and questions have been helpful, as were his not-infrequent admonitions to finish the project and not be someone who was always "working on" a book.

Many people and organizations have offered opportunities to test out portions of the book. I always enjoy speaking to the Joshua Chamberlain Civil War Round Table and appreciate Bill Attick's many invitations to do so. In 2019, Larissa Vigue Picard of the Pejepscot History Center asked me to be the keynote speaker at their Chamberlain Days program. I attended the event as a teenager in the 1990s, and it was a great honor to be on the other side of the lectern. Melissa Winn and Dana Shoaf invited me to write a piece about Andrew Tozier for *Civil War Times*. The article was immensely fun to write and advanced the overall project.

In my day job, I provide leadership development events that use history as a teaching tool. In addition to frequent programs in Gettysburg that focus on the overall battle, I have developed a presentation that explores team building via the Twentieth Maine, and another one that uses the story of the Second Maine mutineers to study employee engagement. I appreciate the thousands of people who have listened to those sessions and offered questions and insights that have further shaped my thinking about leadership challenges in 1863 and today. My thanks to Steve Wiley and the Lincoln Leadership Institute at Gettysburg for giving me the opportunity to be on the battlefield with their programs on a frequent basis. At George Washington University's Center for Excellence in Public Leadership, Natalie Houghtby-Haddon has become a dear friend as we have worked together on various leadership development programs and has been a constant sounding board for this project.

I have visited many places that hold collections related to the Twentieth Maine and have universally found the folks working at those institutions to be exceptionally gracious and helpful. As a fourteen-year-old, I began visiting the Maine State Archives, and the staff always treated me like a seasoned historian. A newer generation has recently responded to email requests quickly and comprehensively. The Maine Historical Society is always helpful, and Mia Sigler in particular provided critical information via email. At the Pejepscot History Center, Larissa Vigue Picard has been most helpful on many occasions. The Gettysburg National Military Park Library, Library of Congress, and National Archives all hold vast amounts of information and are lovely places to spend time with old records. I especially appreciate the hundreds upon hundreds of files that the workers at the National Archives made available. Allen Monroe at the Milo Historical Society digitized an entire collection and then sent it to me electronically, which is the definition of going above and beyond. At Gettysburg College, I was fortunate to have the assistance of Meggan Smith and Amy Lucadamo in tracking down some hard-to-find materials.

When I finished the rough draft of this book, I asked my dear friend Pete Vermilyea whether he could read the entire thing in ten days and make edits and suggestions. Over Christmas. And, unbeknownst to me, when he already had personal commitments to another project and would be celebrating his thirtieth wedding anniversary. He said yes without hesitation and offered suggestions both big and small that have vastly improved the manuscript.

I was thrilled when Dave Reisch at Stackpole said they were interested in the project. Dave has been wonderful to work with, and I look forward to our continuing partnership. The talented Hal Jespersen made the maps for the book and did his usual excellent work.

Lastly, two people have lived with me over the last five years as I have written most of this book and have put up with the time it has taken as well as my constant rambling about some facet of the Twentieth or another. My son, Dawes, has grown up with this project and sings along when "The Ballad of the 20th Maine" comes up on my playlist. For the last year that I was working on the project, he would ask me almost every afternoon, "Did you work on your book today?" If I admitted I had not, he would give me a disapproving look, and I would promise to do better the next day. My wife, Melinda, has supported me throughout the process, especially when

I have become discouraged or hit a roadblock, and has kept me focused on the important part of this story: the men in the unit. More than once we have played the "Who would you invite to dinner?" game. She says Andrew Tozier. I might go for Will Livermore. Either way, it is a gift to have a spouse with whom you can have such debates.

INTRODUCTION

IT WAS ONE OF THE CIVIL WAR'S SINGULAR MOMENTS. NEARING SUNDOWN on July 2, 1863, the second day of the Battle of Gettysburg, a massive Confederate assault threatened to expel the Yankees from their defensive position and compel the luckless Army of the Potomac to retreat once again. Confederate general Robert E. Lee and his men sensed that this could be the decisive battle, the one that would convince the northern populace the war was unwinnable and force President Abraham Lincoln to the negotiating table. But first they had to drive the Army of the Potomac off the high ground south of Gettysburg.

The most vulnerable position for any defending army lies on the flanks—or ends—of its line, and it was seemingly the great misfortune of the Union army that the regiment hastily placed on its extreme left flank was the Twentieth Maine. The unit was inexperienced: It had been in the army for just ten months, had engaged in only one major battle previously, and played but a small role there. Its commander was untested: Joshua Chamberlain was not a career military man with a West Point education; he was a college professor who had been teaching modern languages just a year earlier and had only recently been promoted to colonel and given command of the regiment. Lastly, seventy-two of the men present had mutinied in May—half a dozen remained under arrest—and their level of commitment to the cause and their comrades was unclear. As he put the Mainers into position, brigade commander Strong Vincent implored Chamberlain to "hold that ground at all hazards."[1]

"Imagine, if you can," one of the event's chroniclers wrote, "nine small companies of infantry, numbering perhaps three hundred men, in the form of a right angle, on the extreme left of an army of eighty thousand men, put there to hold the key of the entire position." For more than an hour, the men of the Twentieth Maine clung to that critical ground despite a half dozen attacks by a larger and vastly more experienced regiment from Alabama. Now "hardly more than a strong skirmish line" remained, Lieutenant Holman Melcher admitted, "and the 60 rounds of cartridges each man carried into the fight had been fired." Without the ability to defend their position any longer, the decisive moment arrived.[2]

"At that crisis," Chamberlain reported, "I ordered the bayonet." What ensued was perhaps the most famous bayonet charge in the Civil War. William T. Livermore of the color guard wrote, "With fixed bayonets and a yell we rushed on them, which so frightened them, that not another shot was fired on us. Some threw down their arms and ran, but many rose up, begging to be spared." The Mainers captured more than three hundred Confederates from five different regiments, Chamberlain reported, clearing the enemy in front of their position and securing the Union's left flank. Livermore concluded, "Ours was an important position and had we been driven from it, the tide of battle would have been turned against us and what the result might have been we cannot tell." Theodore Gerrish went further than his more measured comrade: "Not once in a century are men permitted to bear such responsibility for freedom and justice, for God and humanity." Over time it became clear that Gettysburg was a turning point in the war that the Union eventually won, a turning point that might not have been possible had the Twentieth Maine faltered.[3]

The high stakes, the improbable unit and leader, the surprising action of the bayonet charge, and the extreme success of the maneuver in such a critical battle combine all the elements of a compelling story, and within a day, the tale of the Twentieth Maine's charge was spreading throughout the army. Some incidents of thrilling action and great importance fade away once the moment has passed, but not this one. At first, it was the veterans who penned accounts of Gettysburg, seeking to better understand what had happened on the wooded, smoke-filled hill they had defended with their life's blood and to share those accounts with family, friends, and the interested public. But then, even before the last veteran who stood on Little Round Top passed away in 1939, men who had not been there and had no connection to the unit took up the story.

The regiment's exploits at Gettysburg have featured prominently in groundbreaking works of nonfiction, novels, and cinema. John Pullen's *The Twentieth Maine*, published in 1957, was the first significant Civil War unit history written by a non-veteran and inaugurated a new genre. In his 1975 Pulitzer Prize–winning novel on the battle, *The Killer Angels*, author Michael Shaara positions the story of Joshua Chamberlain, the Twentieth Maine, and their fight on Little Round Top as the centerpiece of the second day of the Battle of Gettysburg. *Gettysburg*, the 1993 film adaptation of that novel, solidified the standing of the Twentieth Maine and its colonel among the most famous regiments and small-unit commanders in the Civil War and brought forth numerous publications dedicated to more fully telling its story. By the decade's end, there were more than a dozen new books covering the regiment or its colonel. Two standouts—both inaugurated before the movie *Gettysburg*—were a compelling biography of Chamberlain penned by Alice Rains Trulock and an insightful study of the Twentieth Maine at Gettysburg by Thomas Desjardin titled *Stand Firm Ye Boys from Maine*.

In the years since Pullen and Desjardin published their books on the Twentieth Maine, historians have developed new questions and lines of inquiry to guide their studies into the lives of Civil War soldiers and have advanced innumerable new ways to understand the soldier experience before, during, and after the war. New sources also have come to light over those decades. *A Hell of a Regiment* utilizes those new approaches, lines of inquiry, and sources to tell the story of the Twentieth Maine at Gettysburg and beyond in a new and deeper way. Rather than following a strict chronological approach, each chapter investigates a central question that helps readers understand not only *what* happened to the unit before, during, and after Gettysburg but also *how* and *why*.

The question at the heart of chapter 1 is: How did the Twentieth Maine go from a bunch of civilians in the summer of 1862 to the highly effective fighting force that performed so well at Gettysburg just ten months later? This chapter does not recount every incident during the period. Instead, the chapter investigates key events and themes that reveal what motivated the men to enlist, how they adjusted to military life, the training that prepared them for their actions at Gettysburg, and their experiences during the first ten months of their service that both bonded them as a unit and motivated them to prove themselves at Gettysburg. A theme emerges in chapter 1 that is carried throughout the rest of the book: the desire of the men in the Twentieth to earn the respect of their commander as well as the folks back at home and to build a reputation that would persist throughout the war and in its aftermath. While each subsequent chapter has its own focus, the themes of earning respect as well as building and defending a reputation flow throughout.

What the first chapter did for the men of the Twentieth Maine, the second does for Joshua Chamberlain. How did Chamberlain transform from a college professor with no military training in 1862 to one of the army's most capable small-unit commanders less than a year later, one who was awarded the Congressional Medal of Honor for his actions at Gettysburg? This chapter goes back to Chamberlain's earliest years to unearth his life experiences and the skills and mindsets he developed that propelled him from outstanding college professor to exemplary military leader. Chamberlain's own words reveal the extent to which his attempt to both build and be worthy of a reputation drove his actions as a civilian and as a soldier.

Chapter 3 covers a vital part of the Twentieth Maine's story—the integration of the "mutineers" of the Second Maine in May 1863. The same basic story has been told by nearly every previous writer on the subject in a page or two: When eager men volunteered for the Second Maine in 1861, some mistakenly signed three-year enlistment papers and then mutinied when their comrades who had signed two-year enlistments went home in May 1863. The traditional story concludes that Joshua Chamberlain's leadership ultimately led all but one mutineer to drop their protest and agree to serve in the Twentieth Maine. The full story is far more complex and offers a window into the volunteers' views of their rights and responsibilities as soldiers, the ways they responded when they felt they were disrespected, and the dynamics of effective small-unit leadership. Following the mutineers onto Little Round Top and beyond highlights the tremendous contributions the former mutineers made to the Twentieth Maine's success at Gettysburg, as well as the full gravity of that extra year of service.

Chapter 4 covers the Gettysburg Campaign and the fight on Little Round Top, offering the most comprehensive story of that action yet published. Recent works have examined separately the tactics, the weaponry, the psychology of taking another's life, and the human experience during battle. Bringing all of those insights to bear on the various accounts by the men of the Twentieth Maine allows a deep exploration of the soldier experience of Civil War combat at the regimental level with conclusions that go beyond one unit and its ninety-minute struggle on Little Round Top.

Since Vietnam, there has been increasing interest in how veterans navigate the postwar adjustments in returning home, a field of study that has taken on even more urgency in the wake of the wars in Iraq and Afghanistan. Chapter 5 examines the postwar lives of the Twentieth's Gettysburg veterans. Striking vignettes and stories lost for a century or more emerge from the soldiers' pension files, census records, and buried newspaper accounts. These paint dramatic pictures of postwar exploits that are as fascinating as their wartime experiences and reveal the multiplicity of ways the men adjusted to their return home and how their wartime service shaped the rest of their lives.

The final chapter explores how the men remembered and commemorated their actions at Gettysburg and sought to ensure that the reputation they had won at such great cost was not diminished or overshadowed by those they deemed less worthy. Examining the accounts in order of their appearance allows the reader to see each narrative not as singular but as part of an ongoing, public conversation among the veterans that evolved their collective understanding of the fight on Little Round Top. This chapter refutes the notion that the Twentieth Maine's reputation was a late twentieth-century creation, demonstrating instead that it was firmly established by the soldiers during their lifetimes.

At the center of this story are the 506 men from the Twentieth Maine who were at Gettysburg. Though 1,621 men served in the unit at one point or another before the war's end, Gettysburg was ever after their reference point, and thus this book focuses on the men present at the great battle. The roster of those 506 men was both painstakingly created and assuredly inaccurate. In 1898, the state published *Maine at Gettysburg*, containing histories and complete rosters of each unit that fought at Gettysburg. Three veterans of the Twentieth compiled the unit's list of "PARTICIPANTS": Joshua Chamberlain, Holman Melcher, and Samuel Miller. They based the preliminary list on the June 30, 1863, muster roll and then made adjustments. Ultimately, their list contained the names of 509 men. Three of those names should not have been on the list: Records show that Verano Bryant, Theodore Gerrish, and Daniel Morton were sick at the time of the battle and not present. Some of the men on the list were at Gettysburg but not on Little Round Top (such as Quartermaster Alden Litchfield and Quartermaster Sergeant Howard Prince) or were not engaged in combat (such as Chaplain Luther French or three men under arrest for mutiny). Some would argue to remove those men from the list, but such a judgment was not made in 1898, and thus they are left in the sample. To better understand those 506 men as individuals and as a group, I created a database with twenty-five pieces of information on each man, including name, rank, company, where and when they were born, both their stated and their real age on enlistment, their marital status and occupation at enlistment, their height, when they enlisted and were mustered in, any wounds they received, whether they reenlisted, if they transferred to another unit, when and how they left the service, when they died, their age at death, and where they are buried. The basis of this information came from the soldier data cards at the Maine State Archives, with additional information pulled from the Maine Adjutant General's Reports, the soldier's Compiled Military Service Records and Pension Files at the National Archives, and—for the death dates and burial locations—FindaGrave.com. The simple act of compiling this database revealed many fruitful lines of inquiry and allowed for broad statistical statements about the men as a whole. Ultimately, only a dozen of the 506 men proved unfindable in the postwar years.[4]

Many of the sources central to a project such as this are well known and have been accessible to the public for fifty years or more, including the magnificent document collections at the Maine State Archives, the Pejepscot History Center, and the National Archives. Others have been known but difficult to access or utilize until recently. Digitization projects are making myriad sources available in a searchable electronic format. Of particular use for this project was the digitized *Lincoln County News*, a clearinghouse for all things related to the Twentieth Maine in the 1880s and 1890s and the local outlet in which many accounts were first published. Additionally, various census, military, and cemetery records that are digitized and searchable through places like Ancestry.com, Fold3.com, and FindaGrave.com allow a researcher to discover connections and deeper stories that previously would have been nearly impossible to pursue through paper or on microfilmed records. But of all the records, the pension files in the National Archives are perhaps the greatest underutilized resource. Nearly all the soldiers who served in the Twentieth Maine became eligible for a pension at some point in their postwar lives, and the paperwork generated through their application process offers tremendous insights into their lives before the war, the challenges they faced during their time in the service, and the nature of their postwar lives. A small percentage of these files have been digitized, but most are still available only in their original paper format. It is these files, many running one hundred pages or more in length, that truly bring these men to life.

Maine's state seal, then and now, features the Latin word *Dirigo*, which means "I lead." The story of the Twentieth Maine is one of leadership, from the brash young colonel who trained and developed a crack unit, to the former college professor who led one of the war's most famous bayonet charges, to the men themselves who faced up to a moment of crisis and did not turn away from danger, instead lunging toward it. This is the story of *Dirigo*'s sons and what they did on a hot summer day in July 1863 when the fate of the nation hung in the balance.

I

"A hell of a regiment"

Becoming the Twentieth Maine

ELLIS SPEAR, A CAPTAIN IN 1862, LATER ADMITTED THE INAUSPICIOUS beginnings of the Twentieth Maine, noting that, when Colonel Adelbert Ames arrived to take command of the unit, he "proceeded to express his opinion of the conditions of affairs in which the only thing clear to my mind was that the condition was [a] highly unsatisfactory one. He summed the matter up by saying that it was a 'hell of a regiment.'" Proving that the judgment was not a fleeting one rendered in a moment of ill humor, Private Nathan Clark of Company H reported that the colonel reiterated his feelings two weeks later when the unit had arrived in Virginia: "Colonel Ames was disgusted with our appearance and gave us a brief speech as he halted us, saying if we could not do better than that we had better desert."[1]

At Gettysburg—just ten months later—these men changed formations and positions while under fire and undertook a famous bayonet charge—some of the hardest things to do on a battlefield. As a result of these maneuvers, the unit held its critical position on Little Round Top against an experienced, numerically superior foe. They had become one of the Union's most effective regiments, and Brigadier General Joseph Bartlett commented in 1864 that the Mainers had "a reputation second to no Regt. in the service."[2] But how, exactly, did that transformation take place?

This chapter traces the evolution of the Twentieth Maine from a ragtag collection of individuals in the summer of 1862 into the highly effective fighting force that so distinguished itself on July 2, 1863. It is the story of how "a hell of a regiment" became a *hell* of a regiment.

When the Civil War began, most people expected a quick, relatively bloodless affair that would result in victory for their side. The Battle of Bull Run, fought on July 21, 1861, showed the folly of such thinking. The magnitude of nearly five thousand casualties in a single day was shocking. The entire War of 1812 had seen just sixty-seven hundred American battle casualties, and the more recent war with Mexico just fifty-nine hundred. Further, Bull Run had been far from decisive and suggested that the nation was in for a protracted conflict.

With hopes of a quick victory dashed, the leaders of the eastern armies spent much of the next six months training their citizen soldiers. On the Union side, the man overseeing that work was George B. McClellan, a thirty-four-year-old West Pointer and former railroad executive. It was not until early 1862 that McClellan was ready to put his troops back into the field. His plan was to use the Union's superior navy and engineering capabilities to transport his army down the Chesapeake Bay, flanking the Confederate defenses, and land southeast of Richmond on the peninsula formed by the York and James Rivers. He would then trek up the peninsula and in the backdoor of Richmond. Getting underway on March 17, McClellan made slow progress but finally reached the outskirts of the Confederate capital by mid-May. Northern recruiting offices closed in anticipation of the war's imminent end.

At the Battle of Seven Pines on May 31, 1862, Confederate commanding general Joseph Johnston was hit in the shoulder with a rifle bullet and in the chest with a fragment from an artillery shell, necessitating his removal from the battlefield. Confederate president Jefferson Davis replaced Johnston with one of his advisors, Robert E. Lee, and, in so doing, transformed the war. After a pause to plan an offensive, the aggressive Lee inaugurated six battles over seven days from June 25 to July 1, 1862. Those battles drove the Union forces back down the peninsula, ended the threat to Richmond, and gave birth to Lee's reputation as one of the war's great generals.

The following day, July 2, 1862, in a sign of desperation, the United States called for three hundred thousand new volunteers to join the army. Men in Maine were anxious to join the fight. Ellis Spear would always "remember well the strain of the war in that first year, upon those who remained at home, the eager interest for news from the front, the vague rumors, the false reports, the hopes fondly cherished." Thus, "It was a relief to take part in the struggle after the bitter disappointment and grief caused by [the Peninsula Campaign]." Nathan Clark, a twenty-four-year-old married farmer from Masardis and soon to be a member of Company H, remained happily at home "untill after [General Nathaniel] Bankses retreat in West Va the summer of 62 where the 1st Me Cavalry was intirely broken to fragments by a surprise from the Reb Cavalry. Then I told my friends the time had come for me to take a part in the strife."[3]

Maine adjutant general John Hodsdon contended that these volunteers of 1862 were not reluctant soldiers who had dodged enlisting in 1861 but enthusiastic patriots waiting for their chance. When the war broke out in April 1861, Maine had raised ten infantry regiments in just three and a half weeks, and on May 17, 1861, the governor sent home thousands of men who were eager to join the war effort but belonged to units that had not yet been mustered into federal service. Many of those units continued to drill in their towns throughout the fall of 1861 and into 1862, leading Hodsdon to conclude that, by late 1861, "Maine can now be relied upon for twenty thousand militia at three days' notice, unarmed and unorganized, it is true, but in mental and physical power unsurpassed by any like number on the globe." Patriotism and martial spirit, perhaps in excessive quantities, led Hodsdon to lament, "It would indeed be unfortunate if in the present emergency no occasion should require the thousands of reserved, unorganized forces to be called upon for active service, who are so capable of doing honor to themselves and to the government." The failed Peninsula Campaign offered just that "occasion."[4]

On Independence Day in 1862, Maine governor Israel Washburn called for four new regiments of volunteers so "that the Constitution and the Union, which have been to us all the source of unmeasured blessings, may be preserved; that Liberty, of which they were the inspiration and are the selected guardians, may be saved; and that the light of one great example may shine brighter and brighter to guide, to cheer and to bless the nations." The Sixteenth Maine was already forming, and now the Seventeenth, Eighteenth, and Nineteenth were organized. In early August, the federal government asked for a twentieth regiment of Maine infantry, and on August 7, General Hodsdon ordered all companies not yet assigned to one of the previous regiments to rendezvous at Island Park in Portland.[5]

In response to Governor Washburn's call, prominent men throughout the state had begun enlisting volunteers, hoping their work would earn them commissions as officers. Selecting officers in such a way would not necessarily yield the best stock, but the way the men were recruited and the fees paid to recruiters also left something to be

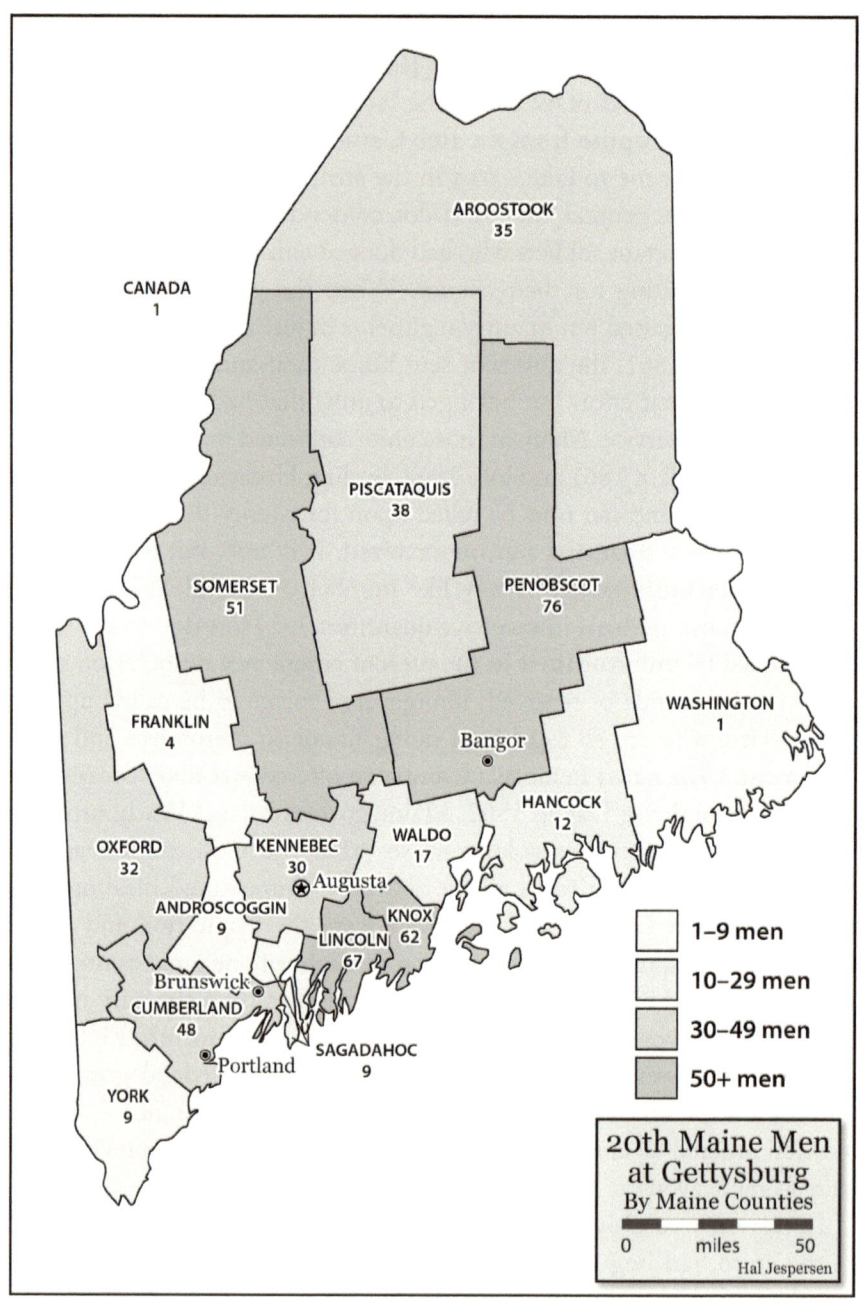

CANADA
1

AROOSTOOK
35

PISCATAQUIS
38

SOMERSET
51

PENOBSCOT
76

FRANKLIN
4

WASHINGTON
1

Bangor

OXFORD
32

KENNEBEC
30

WALDO
17

HANCOCK
12

ANDROSCOGGIN
9

Augusta

KNOX
62

LINCOLN
67

Brunswick

CUMBERLAND
48

SAGADAHOC
9

Portland

YORK
9

1–9 men

10–29 men

30–49 men

50+ men

20th Maine Men
at Gettysburg
By Maine Counties

0   miles   50

Hal Jespersen

desired. Lysander Hill, appointed captain of Company I by the governor, wrote to his benefactor:

> *Lieutenant P. M. Fogler, whom you assigned to my Co. with his squad of men, made an arrangement with one Hiram Bliss Jr., Esq. to furnish him with 25 men and assign them to him, and to put their enlistment papers in his possession on or before Monday, Aug. 18th, in consideration of which, Mr. Fogler agreed to pay him $3.00 apiece for the men, relieving him of the trouble of looking to the State for his pay,—and was to pay him a bonus besides. Mr. Fogler paid Bliss $40.00 down, in cash.—Bliss has not sent, and will not send a single recruiting paper, nor will he transfer one in any way to the possession of Fogler. . . . The supposition is that this Hiram Bliss intends to speculate at Mr. Fogler's expense, by retaining the $40.00, and then putting the enlistment papers into the Adjt Gen's office in his own name and claiming the $3.00 apiece from the State—or else by selling them to somebody else and making another $40.00.*
>
> *This same Bliss has been engaging men to enlist in the town of Washington, to go on the quota of Thomaston, telling them that Thomaston paid a bounty of $100.00.—Thomaston pays a bounty of $130.00—Bliss was, in this way, pocketing $30 a piece for the volunteers enlisted by him, and cheating these poor men, whom everybody that has a soul in him is trying to reward for their service in the country's defense, out of the same amount.*[6]

Unfortunately, such activity was all too common. Chester Greenleaf (later a captain in the Twenty-Fifth Maine) wrote to the governor on August 21, 1862, accusing Company K's Lieutenant James Nichols of trying to sell him the position of company orderly for the sum of $50. Greenleaf was particularly irked as he had recruited fourteen men for the company, helping Nichols achieve his own rank as a lieutenant.[7]

As might be suspected given the incentives to sign up recruits, the supposed physical standards the men were required to meet were often overlooked. Men were supposed to be over eighteen, under forty-five, and at least 5'3" tall; have sufficient teeth to tear open paper cartridges; and be free from any obvious signs of illness or disease. Samuel Keene wrote on August 13, 1862, "Took a squad of 25 men downtown to be examined all passed." That all twenty-five were fit for military service seems unlikely, but given the pressing need for soldiers, anyone who volunteered was likely to be accepted barring an obvious physical infirmity. In his landmark history of the regiment, John Pullen wrote, "Examining physicians could be persuaded that patriotism was sufficient evidence of physical fitness." Ellis Spear recollected some of the tricks employed to fill up the regiment—tricks by both the recruiting officers and the recruits themselves: "One stout little fellow [Henry Pero, of Wiscasset] who wanted to enlist was a trifle too short and I had an extra pair of taps put on his boots, a pious fraud I fear, but it caused him to pass unchallenged. He served until the close of the war and became an excellent soldier." Pero's enlistment papers give his height as 5'7", but postwar medical exams recorded a mere 5'3½"! Pero was far from the only man to get creative. "I remember another fraud," Spear wrote, "not perpetrated by the enlisting officer, and not discovered by him, until after organization of the regiment. This was a man with a very black beard, which turned gray by degrees after we got into camp." The lax standards resulted in hundreds of discharges and even deaths over the ensuing months as unfit men broke down under the burdens of army life and the diseases that swept through the camps.[8]

Ellis Spear (Library of Congress)

Despite the previous anecdote, it was a young man's war. The mean age of the Twentieth's enlistees was 25.6 years, and the median was 23. The most common age was 18. An age is known for 966 of the 979 men who originally joined the unit, and of those, 73.5 percent were in their teens or twenties. Just 7 percent were in their forties. This age distribution also explains why some of these men joined the war effort in 1862: They had been too young in 1861. The 155 eighteen-year-olds, and approximately a third of the 88 nineteen-year-olds, would have been seventeen when the war broke out. Of course, the previous numbers are all the "official" ages provided on enlistment. Pension records and gravestones reveal that of the 506 men with the unit at Gettysburg, five had been just fifteen years old when they enlisted, twelve had been sixteen, and thirty had been seventeen. Those numbers align with a new estimate from historians Frances Clarke and Rebecca Jo Plant that approximately 10 percent of Union soldiers were underage at the time of their enlistment. On the other end of the spectrum, five men had been between forty-five and forty-nine and thus had also lied about their ages so they could enlist.[9]

It was also a single man's war. Of all the unit's enlistees, 62 percent were single, while 38 percent were married. All but three of the 244 teen-agers were single, while 81.7 percent of the thirty-year-olds had wives at home. Those twenty-six and younger were more likely to be single than married, with the twenty-seven-year-olds reversing that trend.[10]

And it was a farmer's war: Two-thirds of the soldiers had worked the fields before enlisting, around twice the number as the average Civil War regiment in the Army of the Potomac. Roughly 3 percent of the men identified themselves as seamen, sailors, or mariners, the second most common profession. Other categories, such as clerks, laborers, mechanics, millers, shoemakers, students, and teachers, each claimed around 2 percent of the unit's members. In the average Union regiment in the Army of the Potomac, 42 percent of the men were unskilled workers—likely hailing from more populous areas—but in the Twentieth, it was less than half that many.[11]

Representative of the men who joined the unit is William T. Livermore, the keeper of a tremendously detailed diary that shapes much of what we know about the daily life of the Twentieth Maine. A single farmer from Milo, Livermore was born in May 1840, making him twenty-two at

William T. Livermore (From John Pullen's *The Twentieth Maine*)

the time of enlistment. He stood 5'9" tall and was a Republican who held strong religious beliefs. He lived at home at the time of his enlistment, as did 40 percent of Union soldiers in the Army of the Potomac.[12]

The officers were a different story. First, they were five years older than the men, with an average age of 30.4 and a median age of 28. Due to their older age, they were also more likely to be married, with 47 percent having wives at home. Professionally, only 15 percent made their living through farming, while 15 percent were merchants, 15 percent were teachers or professors, and 8 percent were lawyers. Lastly, in keeping with modern studies on the social advantages of height, the officers stood just over 5'9" on average, two-thirds of an inch taller than the privates. Typical of the officers was Samuel Keene, a twenty-nine-year-old recently married lawyer from Rockland who helped raise a company and mustered in as a lieutenant before rising to captain and then major.[13]

Samuel Keene (Maine State Archives)

The demographic differences between these men who enlisted in the late summer of 1862 and those who had joined on the outbreak of war a year earlier are illuminating. The average 1861 volunteers who had joined the Second Maine—a unit soon to be associated with the Twentieth—were just 24.7 years old at the time of their enlistment in April or May 1861, with a median age of 22. Only 23 percent of the Second Mainers were married, in contrast to the 38 percent of the men in the Twentieth who left wives behind. In short, the typical recruit in 1862 was both older than those who had rushed off to war in 1861 and much more likely to be married, which helps explain why some may have been more reluctant to join the war effort until the Union's setbacks in the summer of 1862 demanded a more significant commitment from all. The men who joined at this moment were well aware of the war's stakes and seriousness.[14]

Writing a half century later, Joshua Chamberlain recollected, "The motive under which they first sprung to the front was an impulse of sentiment,—the honor of the old flag and love of Country. All that the former stood for, and all that the latter held undetermined, they did not stop to question. They would settle the fact that they had a country and then consider the reasons and rights of it." Historian Gary Gallagher contends, "From the perspective of loyal Americans, their republic stood as the only hope for democracy in a western world that had fallen more deeply into the stifling embrace of oligarchy since the failed European revolutions of the 1840s." Governor Israel Washburn's call for volunteers, with its emphasis on the Constitution and serving as an example of democracy for other nations, reinforces Gallagher's argument. In the spring of 1863, William Owen of Company B wrote to his sister about the transformation of his country that had led up to war, lamenting the existence of "traitors, dough-faced office seekers, slave holders, etc." Like his president, Owen believed that the preservation of the Union and the end of slavery were inextricably linked: "If President Lincoln had, in his slave Proclamation, said that all slaves were forever free, it would have been something done towards gaining the great end which we should all strive for: Freedom, Right, and Humanity. But now if we should conquer, enough of slavery will be left to breed another rebellion. . . . I say put down slavery or let the south go."[15]

Owen's antislavery sentiments stand out as an exception, for most of the diaries, letters, and postwar recollections of the men in the Twentieth Maine focus solely on the preservation of the Union as their driving motivation. In a twist of fate, ten enlistees hailed from the town of Union, Maine. The men made rare references to ending slavery even though 62 percent of Maine voters had backed Abraham Lincoln and the Republican platform pledging to stop slavery from spreading into the territories. But opposing slavery's extension and advocating for its immediate end were two separate things. As Adam Goodheart notes, the moniker *abolitionist* "was still an ugly epithet for most people, connoting dubious patriotism and, perhaps worse, a most un-American tendency to trespass upon affairs of one's fellow citizens."[16]

Most of these men from Maine had no experience with slavery—which had been illegal in the region since the 1700s—or even with African Americans. In 1860, just 1,327 of Maine's 628,279 residents were African American, barely 0.2 percent of the population. Of the 634 towns in Maine in 1860, African Americans were present in just 101. The day the Twentieth arrived in Washington, William T. Livermore wrote, "There I am sitting about 20 feet from a dozen Negroes and I made an errand or an excuse to Sharpen my pencil to get into Conversation with them and I was Surprised to find them So Intelligent there conversation was about the war." He continued, "One of them seemed more frank than the rest and as we were talking about Stonewall Jackson I asked him if he would Shoot him if he could get a chance. 'My God' said he 'I would shoot him before I could get time to get sight of him' They all seemed to understand about affairs as well as the whites There are thousands of them in Washington a great many came in with the Army." The curiosity that drove Livermore's attempt to "get into Conversation with them" and his surprise in finding them "So Intelligent" suggests that this encounter may have been his first interaction with African Americans, which is plausible considering that the 1860 Census taker found not a single African American among the 15,032 people living in Piscataquis County, the location of Livermore's hometown of Milo. No wonder, then, that for the men of the Twentieth the impulse to save the Union took primacy in their consciousness.[17]

In addition to preserving the Union, there were financial incentives to enlist. Joseph Glatthaar found that 90 percent of the soldiers in the Army of the Potomac had a net worth of $400 or less, while the median personal and family wealth of farmers who enlisted stood at $0. Private soldiers received $13 a month, an amount very close to the $14.34 per month (plus board) that the 1860 Census reveals was the average for a farmhand in Maine. On top of that monthly remuneration, the recruits received a state bounty of $45, a federal bounty of $100 ($25 paid up front, the remaining $75 on mustering out), a month's pay in advance, plus a $2 premium from the federal government. Most towns also offered bounties that ranged as high as $400 but averaged around $100. Will Livermore received $145 on mustering in and was owed $75 more on his eventual muster-out. Additionally, towns provided assistance to soldiers' families, with the state reimbursing each town for their remittances up to $0.75 per week for the wife or parent of a soldier, plus an additional $0.50 per week for each child. If disabled, the soldier would receive up to $8 per month. If the soldier was killed, that money went to his family, along with a one-time payment of $100.[18]

Adjutant General Hodsdon touted the benefits offered the soldiers: "Their enlistment with the government, insures them a home in sickness as well as in health, an abundance of comfortable clothing, and an amount of wholesome food of the best description that can be furnished, greater than they can consume, the surplus of which they can realize in cash." Predictably, Hodsdon was far too optimistic about the efficiency of the government. Infrequent paydays and inadequate food would be a constant complaint. In the spring of 1863, Hezekiah Long, a thirty-eight-year-old prison guard who became a sergeant in Company F, wrote to his wife, "We have been living in hopes for some time passed that the greatest of all strangers, the Paymaster, would make his appearance amongst us, but he has not yet." As Long's comment suggests, the men would have been well served to ignore Hodsdon's blue sky promises and remember the more realistic forecast of Italian general Giuseppe Garibaldi, who told his men, "I can't offer you either honours or wages; I offer you hunger, thirst, forced marches, battles and death. Anyone who loves his country follow me."[19]

But that all came later. The initial period of enlisting and organizing the unit was one of excitement and even fun. Most of the men eventually assigned to Company B initially gathered in Bangor, thinking they were destined for the Eighteenth Maine. The campground for the men was inside the city's racetrack and featured two on-site saloons. A few days after arriving, eighteen-year-old William Lamson wrote to his sister Jennie, "The musicians are 'going it' on all sides," creating an atmosphere of a county fair. Unsurprisingly, instilling discipline was difficult in such a setting. Using their Yankee ingenuity, men such as Lamson easily got around minor issues like chain of command. "I had a hard time getting out to see Anne Friday," he wrote. "Col Chaplin would not, and Lieut Lyford could not, give me a pass. So we formed a squad to go and drill and when we got past the guard I 'skedaddled,' that's the way the boys get out. An officer and eight men can pass the guard any time to drill, so one takes command and marches eight or more out and then we go back when we please." Such behaviors led former school principal Ellis Spear to huff, "All these assembled recruits and expectant officers presented when in camp the general appearance of a town meeting."[20]

Things were little better after the unit moved to Portland. On August 20, Lamson wrote, "We had a high time here last night with the sutler. He 'set up shop' yesterday forenoon and last night the boys 'drew rations' one corner of his shop and if the Maj had not come along and driven them off they would have 'drawn' everything to the ground. The sutler told the

Major that if he would guard it last night he would leave this morning and he'd better keep his promise." Given such gaiety, William T. Livermore wondered, "Who would not be a Soldier?"[21]

Then the colonel arrived.

Years later, Ellis Spear recounted the first meeting between the newly minted colonel and his charges:

> *The Colonel, a thoroughly trained soldier, saw things, to him new and strange, and perhaps with a prejudiced eye. It was his first experience with volunteers, and he found them in their most immature condition. The respectable citizen who seemed to be half loafing, half on guard at the Headquarters' tent did not salute, and, in fact, had nothing military to salute with, but cheerfully remarked "How do you do, Colonel." Him the Colonel regarded as a villain of the deepest dye and perhaps as a fool into the bargain.[22]*

Adelbert Ames (Maine State Archives)

The flabbergasted colonel, Adelbert Ames, had served for the first year of the war in the Fifth U.S. Artillery, rising to battery command with responsibility for six cannons and approximately seventy men, and just days earlier had been actively engaged in the Peninsula Campaign. The contrast between the seat of war and the "county fair" prevailing at the camps of his new recruits must have been jarring.

Ames was born in Rockland, Maine, in 1835. His father was a ship captain, and as a young man Adelbert sailed the world as a cabin boy. He had a different future in mind, however, and in 1856 secured an appointment to West Point. The West Point of the antebellum era is often derided as producing engineers rather than soldiers, and those making that argument point to the paucity of courses on military theory in the curriculum. Such a conclusion overlooks much. The year before Ames arrived, West Point adopted a five-year curriculum to address the deficiencies previous graduates had displayed in English, history, geography, modern languages, and military science. Under the revised curriculum, cadets had 120 hours more instruction in military science than previous classes. But even without this change, much of the military training at West Point took place *outside* of the classroom and is thus left out of any simple curriculum review. Each night, from 4:00 p.m. until sundown, the cadets drilled. Under the new curriculum, a five-year cadet had 695 hours of infantry drill, 252 hours of artillery drill, 268 hours of cavalry drill, and 216 hours of fencing. These drills covered everything from individual movements such as loading and firing weapons up to brigade maneuvers. The entering class served as privates, while the second-year students functioned as noncommissioned officers (corporals and sergeants) and the upperclassmen as lieutenants and captains. After 1,400 hours of drill at this level, it is safe to assume that most cadets understood the ins and outs of small-unit command and battle tactics. In fact, the revisions were so successful that former West Point faculty member James Morrison notes, "In 1856 the board of visitors complained that the prominence given to military training was seriously interfering with scientific instruction." The officers who came out of West Point may not have been prepared to lead a division, corps, or army, but they absolutely were ready to lead a regiment or battery, particularly if they had taken their studies seriously and finished near the top of their class. Ames fit that criteria, as he graduated fifth in the class of 1861. With this high rank, he was commissioned into the Fifth U.S. Artillery.[23]

Ames distinguished himself at First Bull Run. Battery commander Charles Griffin wrote, "Lieutenant Ames was wounded so as to be unable to ride a horse at almost the first fire; yet he sat by his command directing the fire, being helped on and off the caisson during the different changes of front or position, refusing to leave the field until he became too weak to sit up." Once he recovered, Ames was given command of the battery as a reward for his coolness.[24]

Ames was determined to show he was worthy of the position—and perhaps a higher one. He wrote home on December 4, 1861, "I have been laboring very, *very* hard. I am improving my battery greatly. A few months and it will be as good as any." Three weeks later, he wrote, "My battery is progressing finely. At Camp Hooker in Maryland my men were frequently under fire, and I hope when they meet the enemy they will not disgrace me. Heretofore they have displayed the proper spirit, and if I have influence they will hereafter." The following April, while participating in the Peninsula Campaign, Ames wrote of his junior officers, "They are good young men of the ordinary stamp, but not the best of officers. I am rather harsh and severe with them at times."[25]

A letter home to his parents in December 1861 illustrates Ames's commanding personality. They must have complained about his lack of correspondence, for Ames replied, "I received a letter from Father a day or two ago that really he ought to be ashamed of—and you, Mother—you appear to endorse it. No. You cannot persuade me from writing you by such a letter— I love you too much." But there was more than just one dimension to the man. A January 21, 1862, letter reveals Ames's sense of humor and playful side: "A large *rat* has taken possession of my tent—I ruling supreme during the day, and he during the night. He treats me very badly—wakes me up at night, runs through the mud and then drags his tail over my pillow, walks on my letter paper, makes his bed on me and pokes his nose into my private affairs, a course of conduct decidedly unkind, I think. I do not do so to him." But even in this passage Ames revealed his stern nature, for he concluded, "For his rudeness I am feeding him—bread and butter spiced with arsenic."[26]

Ames's strict standards paid off, however, as his battery performed well at Malvern Hill on July 1, 1862. The lieutenant was singled out by his commander, who felt Ames "deserves particular mention for gallantry and skill at the battles of Chickahominy and Malvern." The Mainer was subsequently breveted a lieutenant colonel in the regular army for his actions. Thus, when Governor

Washburn needed a colonel to take command of the Twentieth Maine, Adelbert Ames was an obvious choice. Ames accepted the position on August 13, 1862, and arrived in Portland to take charge of the unit a week later.[27]

Given Ames's nature, his standing as a professionally trained soldier, and the carnage he had witnessed on the Peninsula, it is no great surprise that he was less than pleased with his first impression of his new command and voiced his frustration with a "hell of a regiment." Ames was a man who had developed his own capabilities, leading to self-respect, and then had displayed those capabilities on more than one battlefield, earning the respect of others both for himself and for his men. Finally, as those actions had become more widely known within the army and back in Maine, he had developed a reputation even among those who did not know him. Now Ames would be starting all over.[28]

Ames quickly began to drill the regiment in an attempt—like his battery before—to get it up to speed on the basics and make it worthy of self-respect. He soon found that the men had much to learn. One night, while on parade, Ames grew enraged when the band either ignored or missed his signals to cease playing. Being a man of deeds, he took action, as Spear recorded, and "charged upon that musical body sword in hand. It was an unfair advantage, justifiable only on the ground of military necessity. The Colonel was armed and the drum corps had only drums and fifes, formidable for offence but not for defence."[29]

It was not just the enlisted men who lacked military experience but also the officers. As a West Pointer who had been on active duty since the beginning of the war, Ames was undoubtedly the most qualified of the five colonels appointed to lead Maine regiments in the summer of 1862. But on paper, he may have been saddled with the weakest initial grouping of officers of any unit. As Ellis Spear noted, "All of the officers, with few exceptions, were good men, but almost all of them were without military experience or training."[30]

Ames's second-in-command, Lieutenant Colonel Joshua Lawrence Chamberlain, was just such a man, a college professor with no military experience. Major Charles Gilmore had previously served in the Seventh Maine, so theoretically he was an asset, but, as Spear later chuffed, "I do not remember that [Gilmore] rendered any material aid in the organization or instruction of the regiment; but I do remember that he afterwards proved to be a most untrustworthy, worthless skulker." In 1864, Ames wrote to

Chamberlain lamenting that Gilmore had not been forced out and was nominally in charge of the unit, stating, "The Regt. is too good a one to have as its head a fancy-duty man." Of the ten company commanders, one had some experience from the Mexican War, "But he had forgotten much and proved to be too old to bear the hardships of active service." Another had served as a lieutenant in the Eighth Maine from September 1861 to April 1862. But that was the extent of the experience among the captains—two out of ten. Of the twenty lieutenants, just two had any experience.[31]

Ames had a serious job on his hands, and a tricky one too, for at twenty-six years old Ames was younger than both his lieutenant colonel and his major, eight of his ten company commanders, the majority of the lieutenants, and nearly half of the enlisted men. That may have been a barrier for other men, but Ames was not one to hold his tongue in the presence of his elders. In July 1864, he wrote to his father, "My last letter was somewhat sermon-like. Of course, good advice is always taken whatever may be its source. So I expect you will profit by mine."[32]

After just a few short days in Portland, the regiment was formally mustered into U.S. service on August 29, 1862, for a term of three years or the duration of the war. Four days later, they took a train to Boston and then boarded a ship and sailed for Virginia. For the enlisted men, the voyage contained an element of sightseeing, with many of the diarists commenting on the features of the Chesapeake Bay, the various ships and forts they passed, and even catching a glimpse of Mount Vernon. But for the officers it was a different story: "On the voyage Colonel Ames kept school for the officers. We studied Casey's Tactics, and so incessantly that there was no time for sea sickness."[33] After four days at sea, the unit landed in Alexandria, Virginia, on September 6.

They found a capital city in crisis, and Theodore Gerrish observed, "The demoralization of war was visible on every hand." After driving the Union army away from the gates of Richmond earlier in the summer, Robert E. Lee's Confederate Army of Northern Virginia had moved nearly one hundred miles north and attacked a newly formed Union army just thirty miles west of Washington at the Battle of Second Bull Run on August 28–30. An overwhelming Confederate victory, the battle cost the Union another fourteen thousand casualties. The disorganized and bloodied remnants of that army were now in Washington and visible to the new recruits. William T. Livermore wrote, "I am within 25 feet of a great Steamboat Hospital with 160 Wounded Soldiers from Bull run I can look in and See twenty five or So one died last night."[34] The high command was also in disarray, and the general who had led the Union troops in the battle—John Pope—was being exiled to the Midwest. George McClellan, who had been sidelined just weeks earlier, was once again placed in command and tasked with creating a coherent army from his units that had fought in the ill-fated Peninsula Campaign, Pope's regiments, recently arrived troops from the western part of Virginia, and an assemblage of newly formed units like the Twentieth Maine. To add to the crisis, on September 4–5, 1862, the Confederates crossed the Potomac River and headed north into Maryland, ultimately aiming for Pennsylvania. They could not be allowed to run free, potentially encouraging the border state of Maryland to join the Confederacy and discouraging Pennsylvanians from supporting the war effort. The anxiety in the capital must have been palpable.

After landing in Alexandria, the men of the Twentieth Maine moved into Washington on September 7 and drew weapons from the arsenal. Now fully equipped, they were ready to move to the front lines. On September 8, they were ordered out to Fort Craig on Arlington Heights. The march that ensued nearly broke the regiment and showed that Adelbert Ames had much to learn about leading men. Theodore Gerrish—in postwar years a reverend but in 1862 just a lowly private in Company H—huffed, "It was a most ludicrous march. We had never been drilled, and we felt that our reputation was at stake. An untrained drum corps furnished us with music; each musician kept different time, and each man in the regiment took a different step. Old soldiers sneered; the people laughed and cheered; we marched, ran, walked, galloped, and stood still, in our vain endeavor to keep step." James Rundlett, a corporal in Company G, wrote home, "We had not got more than 3 miles before they began to fall out side the roads and; when we got there there were more than 100 strewed along by the way. . . . Colonel Ames was a Capt. of the Artillery Com. and I suppose he is use to marching pretty fast on horses." Hezekiah Long of Company F noted that just seventeen men from his company made it to roll call that night. The thirty-seven-year-old was among the few who had held up. The problem was not just the soldiers' lack of experience with marching but also the weather. It was the hottest day of the entire month, and the temperature reached a scorching 88 degrees in the afternoon. Needless to say, these men from Maine were unaccustomed to such heat.[35]

James Rundlett (South Portland Historical Society)

James Rundlett noted that the colonel added insult to injury, say-ing, "Men, I have but this to say, if you cant march better than you have tonight, I would advise you to desert and go home." Rundlett added, "The soldiers were furious, and there was hardly a man but that could have shot him with a will." Ellis Spear explained why the insult landed so poorly: "The Colonel, annoyed by the straggling, upbraided the men and as those only heard the reproaches who had kept up, and therefor deserved praise instead of blame, the impression was not very favorable, and a very unfortunate prejudice arose against the commanding officer by an incident apparently trivial." Rundlett agreed with Spear's assessment and even went further: "[Ames] has killed himself for this regt. He has got the ill will of every private. I am sorry to write thus, but it is the truth and I am not ashamed of that. I am safe in saying that I have heard 20 men say that he will not come out of our first engagement alive."[36]

Maine adjutant general John Hodsdon had cautioned in 1861, "However skilled an officer may be in the school of the soldier, company and battalion, or however good his faculty for imparting his knowledge to those in his command, he is but poorly qualified for the discharge of his duties if he considers these all. Every thing conducive to the health, comfort and efficiency of his charge should engage his constant care and attention." Spear simply said that Ames was "without great experience in dealing with men and (like many of the West Pointers) understanding very little of the character of the volunteers."[37]

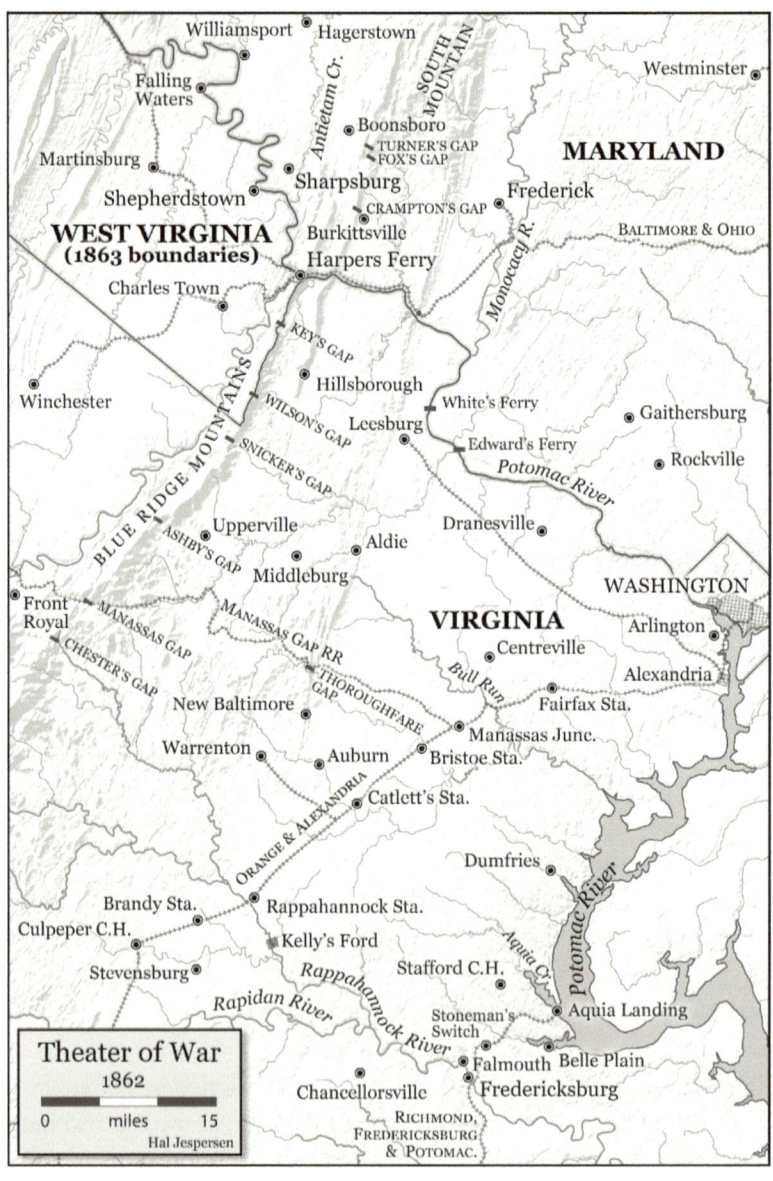

Robert E. Lee's men were still loose in Maryland, and the Twentieth was soon marching west toward the Rebels, giving the green soldiers their first taste of active campaigning. On September 10, Holman Melcher wrote home, "We have been three nights without tents, since we disembarked at Washington, but we have had our rubber blankets so it was not so bad." Samuel Keene wrote in his diary two days later, "Went to bed between two rows of potato hills. Slept finely."[38]

The marches west brought the Twentieth to the banks of Antietam Creek in time for the great battle on September 17, 1862, but fortunately the inexperienced regiment was part of the corps that General McClellan held in reserve. The Mainers did cross the Potomac River just a few days

Holman Melcher (Maine State Archives)

later and participated in a small fight known as the Battle of Shepherdstown, but this engagement offered the men just a glimpse of action. Harlan Bailey informed his sister, "Our Regt was nearly the first to cross the river The Rebels were keeping up a brisk fire which wounded several of our men. we had just crossed the river and I was empting the watter out of my boots when we were ordered to recross the river and away I went with one stocking on and one off."[39]

A primary reason why the Twentieth Maine was able to survive and become a highly effective regiment by the summer of 1863 was that it did not see any significant action during its first three months in service. With almost no training and green officers, any substantial involvement at Antietam could have inflicted catastrophic losses and a heavily damaged psyche on the unit. The Sixteenth Connecticut serves as an interesting counterexample. Mustered in just five days before the Twentieth Maine, the Nutmeggers went into action at Antietam on the extreme left flank of the Union army even though the unit's men had not yet mastered the steps of loading and firing their weapons. They were overwhelmed by a surprise attack from A. P. Hill's division and thus broke and fled in wild confusion, losing a quarter of their men. The dispirited men never recovered from this terrible start and deserted in large numbers in the battle's aftermath. In a blunt and accurate assessment, historian Lesley Gordon titled her recent book on the unit *A Broken Regiment*.[40] The inexperience of the men and the officers in the Twentieth Maine, along with the early feelings against Colonel Ames, ensured that the regiment got off to a rocky start. Missing out on Antietam, however, provided a lease on life by buying them time to prepare before their first major action.

In the aftermath of the Battle of Antietam, the Army of the Potomac remained in place for the next month. Commander George McClellan did not see a chance to chase Lee's weakened army and force another battle; instead, he saw an opportunity to rebuild and retrain his own organization. As historian Ethan Rafuse explains, "Once the Army of the Potomac was once again a well-ordered, adequately supplied, and properly trained and disciplined force, he would then undertake a truly decisive campaign against the rebels."[41] While at the strategic level that plan was too cautious and has been critiqued by observers then and now, it greatly benefited the

Twentieth Maine and the army's other green units who were not yet ready for a major battle.

After the whirlwind of marching during their first two weeks at the front, the men of the Twentieth Maine were now in a sedentary spot where they began to come to grips with army life. Their campground was less than ideal, Spear remembered, referring to its "low malarial ground" and concluding, "I do not know of any more unhealthy malarial location." Indeed, on September 24, 1862, William T. Livermore reported that three hundred men were on the sick list, and many more were suffering from dysentery. By November 1, the regiment officially stood at 931 men, but 335 were on the sick rolls. On Christmas Day, the morning report showed 479 sick out of 911 men—more than half of the regiment.[42]

What caused all the sickness? In addition to the rampant diseases passed from man to man, impure water and poor food caused (or at least made worse) many of the illnesses. On October 12, 1862, Private William Lamson wrote home to his sister, "I am getting along nicely although the climate or water makes me feel disagreeable. I guess it must be the water or the living for the climate has been a good deal like Maine for a few days." Ominous words, and less than a month later Lamson came down with a case of dysentery so severe that he was confined to an Alexandria hospital for three months before he recovered. The problem with the water was pretty straightforward: On the day of the Battle of Antietam, William T. Livermore wrote, "Turned out at 4 oclock and went a Mile to get a Canteen of water where more than 5 hundred had diped out of the Same Mud hole."[43]

Like the water, the food provided by the army was also less than ideal. In late October, twenty-one-year-old former teacher Holman Melcher wrote, "I have now got so that I can take what pleasure there is in camp life: strong and hearty, with appetite enough to eat my rations even if there is a little dirt with it." The lack of variety was a problem. "I do not know what to have for dinner," Hezekiah Long wrote home to his wife, "whether pork and hard bread or hard bread and pork as that is all I have to chose from. It bothers me often." Long's comment evinces a sense of humor, as well as a serious problem. The Civil War diet was—at least when the men were in camp—sufficient in terms of calories, fat, and carbohydrates but severely lacking in vitamins A, C, D, E, calcium, and folate. The lack of vitamins weakened the immune system, made recovering from wounds more difficult, and, in some cases, directly led to illnesses such as dysentery, chronic diarrhea, and night blindness.[44]

Thus, it was no surprise that disease ran rampant in the camps. There were six million cases of major disease among the nearly three million men who served in the Union army, meaning the average soldier was likely to suffer two incidents of disease during his three-year enlistment. By comparison, only around 110,000 Union men were killed in combat, and 250,000 more wounded. In other words, the average Yankee soldier was seventeen times more likely to suffer from disease than be hit by a bullet. The lack of vitamin C and folate helped bring on dysentery and diarrhea, and both killed more men than bullets, which is perhaps not surprising in light of Charles Francis Adams's comment that an army in camp was essentially "a city without sewage."[45] In pension applications the former soldiers made in the 1890s, many noted various war wounds before identifying their biggest problems as stemming from diseases they had picked up while serving in the army.

Compounding matters, the Twentieth Maine lacked a full complement of medical officers, a function of both their last-minute organization and the relatively low pay offered surgeons compared to what they could earn in private practice. Surgeon Nahum P. Monroe—or "Wormy," as the men called him—did not arrive until October 2. Had Monroe been a competent surgeon, this absence of five weeks would have been more troubling, but there is a strong argument that he was, at best, a neutral factor in the regiment's health and may have actually impeded it. Theodore Gerrish noted that the surgeon prescribed the same medication—either quinine or "blue mass"—for all conditions. However, "Fortunately for both the men and the government, the pills were never taken, and consequently many of them recovered." Quinine was an effective medication for those suffering from malaria but had a litany of side effects. "Blue mass" consisted mainly of mercury, leading those who took it over a long period to suffer from heavy metal poisoning. Samuel Keene was often sick and took a variety of medications, which may have given him as many problems as remedies. On December 16, 1862, he noted in his diary, "I am sick and weary. Took a dose of 3 blue pills." Three weeks later, he tried a different cure: "Not so sick but a good deal of fever about me—Took two doses of castor oil."[46]

Some men thrived, however. In early December, Hezekiah Long, the former prison guard, wrote to his wife, "My health is better than it was while at the Prison. . . . I can sleep amidst the roar of canon and the beat of drums as if there were no noise at all." In February 1863, James Rundlett noted that he weighed 155 pounds, "considerably more than I ever weighed before." Tom Chamberlain mused, "What makes it strange is that I should have gained 12 pounds living on worms."[47]

The five weeks along Antietam Creek were a breaking-in period. Theodore Gerrish later recollected, "The men were unused to the climate, the exposure, and the food, so that the whole experience was in direct contrast to their life at home." Some men became disabled and left the regiment for good: By May 1, 1863, the Twentieth was down to 714 men, a loss of around 250, despite only seven combat fatalities. The losses had been disproportionately among the older, married members of the unit, with the average age falling from 25.6 to 24.5 between enlistment and their arrival at Gettysburg and the odds of a man being married falling from 38 percent to

Thomas Chamberlain (Library of Congress)

29.5 percent. Those who were left were better physically prepared to meet the challenges of active campaigning and combat. As Lieutenant Colonel Chamberlain wrote in early November 1862, "Our Regt. is now reduced to about 550. But what there are left are of the right sort." Writing years later, former Quartermaster Sergeant Howard Prince asserted, "The weak, the weary, the fearful, the shirkers have been dropped; the chaff is sifted from the wheat; these men who are left can fight all day and march all night, and have been welded by discipline into a tempered weapon of steel that will never fail its master's hand in the time of need."[48]

On October 10, 1862, Colonel Ames wrote to his parents, "We have been doing picket duty and drilling. I do not imagine we shall have much fighting very soon. At least my regiment will be disciplined when we do."[49] While disease culled all but the heartiest members of the unit, Ames had a chance to teach both the officers and the men all of the formations and tactics they needed to master should they have any hope of standing up to Robert E. Lee's veterans in the Army of Northern Virginia.

In a letter home to his wife just after the turn of the year, Hezekiah Long described the soldiers' typical day: "We have to turn out at 6 in the morning and drill from 7 to 8, then there is guard mount from ½ past 8 to 9, then drill 9 ½ to 11, then Battalion drill from 1 ½ to 3, then dress parade, and then Roll Call at 7 in the evening." Long's captain, Samuel Keene, offered great insight into both the frequency and the variety of the drills that Long mentioned:

September 25: "Drilled the company an hour and half. Had officers drill before the Colonel one hour. Battalion drill in the afternoon. . . . Colonel very cross."

September 29: "Drilled in company drill till half past 9 drilled before the Colonel till 12 had battalion drill at ½ past 3 till 5. Acted as adjutant at dress parade."

October 9: "Drilled in forenoon. lounged till ½ past three and studied then had a hard battalion drill hot, dusty Colonel cross. Came in about sunset. Went on dress parade."

October 22, 1862—"Nothing but drill and drill."

December 2, 1862—"Drilled the company in the forenoon and afternoon mostly in the manual of arms."

December 3, 1862—"Drilled the company in forenoon and afternoon in skirmish drill."

December 4, 1862—"Spent the day on drill—company in forenoon, battalion in afternoon Recitation in evening."[50]

This training proved critical. In the words of historian Earl Hess, "The ultimate purpose of drill in the Civil War [was] to create an automatic response to orders from large masses of men who acted upon those orders as one." Author T. J. Stiles notes, "Every feature of his existence was standardized, homogenized—soldiers' clothes are called 'uniforms' for good reason." Throughout the fall of 1862, the men were drilled using Silas Casey's *Infantry Tactics* (1862), an updated version of earlier tactics books by William J. Hardee (1855) and Winfield Scott (1835). Casey covered tactics from the individual soldier up through an army corps. While the maneuvers could be intricate, the book was well written and made the evolutions reasonably understandable.[51]

First, the men had to learn all the possible ways to maneuver while getting to and around the battlefield, including dealing with any obstacles in their way. They did not want to emulate the example of Captain Abraham Lincoln in the Black Hawk War of 1832, who ran into a conundrum when his marching line of men approached a gate. "I could not for the life of me," he later reminisced, "remember the proper word of command for getting my company endwise so that it could get through the gate, so as we came near the gate I shouted: 'This company is dismissed for two minutes, when it will fall in again on the other side of the gate!'"[52]

Then they had to learn how to maneuver, possibly in the face of the enemy, from marching columns—four men abreast—into a double line that placed shorter men in front and taller men in back while keeping company coherence. Lastly, they had to learn the various maneuvers and formations they might need to use under fire to meet potential threats from the enemy and changes in their circumstances. At Gettysburg, the Twentieth would face a flanking maneuver from the Confederates and would need to lengthen or "refuse" their line by integrating their two lines into one and bending it back on itself at an acute angle. Once the regiment ran out of ammunition and was ordered to charge forward, it had to first "wheel" the line, with the left moving forward more rapidly than the right in order to straighten out the unit before moving down the slopes of Little Round Top. In Ken Burns's *The Civil War*, these actions are referred to as "obscure textbook maneuvers," implying that only a man of Chamberlain's intellect, learning, and memory could have thought to resort to them. But as Hess notes, "Changing front by refusing a flank, forming forward or backward on a subunit, moving by the flank, and wheeling were essential tools of the Civil War tactician." The key to combat efficiency was not creativity, Hess argues, but repetitive drill: "The units that did well in combat were those commanded by men who knew their Scott, Hardee, and Casey cover to cover and had the intelligence to quickly choose which maneuver they needed to meet each developing problem."[53]

Ames knew it was critical to ensure that the officers and men were proficient in the formations and maneuvers that might be required for orders to be instantly obeyed, so he drove them during the unit's long encampment. Spear remembered, "At Antietam Creek we worked hard. The line officers studied tactics & the manual of arms, & company & regimental drill, reciting to Ames, & were drilled by him, & then in turn drilled the men." Ames was putting into practice the methods he had learned as a cadet at West Point. James Morrison notes that, at the Academy, students were evaluated in all subjects on an almost daily basis and that the testing was "accomplished through an instructional device appropriately called the 'recitation.'" The key to passing was "the cadet's diligence in preparing his lessons and his ability to remember accurately what he had read in a text were tested orally, on paper, or at the blackboard."[54]

Many of the enlisted men did not yet see the value of the incessant drilling. "[We] could not understand how dress parades, guard mounting, reviews and grand rounds could ever crush the rebellion," Theodore Gerrish summarized, and thus, "They were all regarded in supreme contempt." In some cases, the contempt for the drill led to contempt for the man ordering the drill. As Gerrish mused:

One of the most difficult things in the world for a genuine Yankee to do, was to settle down, and become accustomed to the experiences of a soldier's life. He was naturally inquisitive, and wanted to know all the reasons why an order was given, before he could obey it. Accustomed to be independent, the words go and come grated harshly upon his ear. At home he had considered himself as good as any other person, and in the army he failed to understand why a couple of gilt straps upon the shoulders of one who at home was far beneath him, should there make him so much the superior.[55]

Historian Lorien Foote observes, "The most individualistic society on earth now demanded that its free men submit to the control of others," something that was not always easy for the men in the ranks. As evidenced by Samuel Keene's diary entries, the colonel was frequently "cross" and Hezekiah Long admitted that Ames "swears at them sometimes." Spear concurred, noting, "The terms he used were rather those of West Point than of a Sunday School. The criticisms, for which there was abundant occasion, were insistent and severe." Consequently, Keene was reporting as early as September 26, "Excitement against the Colonel high."[56]

"During all this time we were almost incessantly at work," Spear noted. "The Colonel drilled the officers part of the day and the officers drilled their Companies the remainder of the day, and studied tactics by night. It will not seem wonderful that some of the officers broke down." As Spear suggests, two simultaneous processes were ongoing at once: training the officers and training the men. The work was overwhelming for the officers, who had to take part in both elements, and Ames's demeanor rubbed many the wrong way. Consequently, seven of the ten company commanders resigned in the fall of 1862 and early spring of 1863. When Company B's Lieutenant James Lyford offered his resignation on November 26, 1862, Ames heartily endorsed the action, telling the brigade commander that the lieutenant had "failed to do his duty in a satisfactory manner." When asked "whether other and more competent men are ready to fill the place," Ames responded, "Of all the officers junior to Lt. Lyford, with one exception, none are, in my opinion, so incompetent as he." The death of Timothy Andrews in October 1862 meant that, of the original ten company commanders, only two were still with the unit at Gettysburg just ten months after their formation. By contrast, in the Sixteenth, Seventeenth, and Nineteenth Maine (the other Maine units raised in the late summer of 1862 and attached to the Army of the Potomac), only ten officers had resigned in total, with five dying and fifteen remaining with their units. But it turns out that these resignations were all part of Ames's plan to rid the unit of officers he deemed unfit, for he wrote home to his parents in January 1863, "Many of the officers I have been obliged to make resign." He later explained that the problem was that "merit was not considered in the original appointments." But with the deadwood now out of the way, Ames was able to promote from the lower ranks those who he had identified as promising leaders.[57]

The enlisted men—who did not have the officers' option of resigning before their three-year term of service was up—had varying opinions about who should shoulder the blame for the high turnover. Despite Ames's swearing at the men, Hezekiah Long noted, "As for me I like him very well." Holman Melcher felt the same: "Have been used first-rate by the Col. thus far, he is a very strict, stern man, but a noble officer, brave and decided." William Lamson of Company B suggested that the problem was with the officers who were leaving, not with Ames: "I never imagined that Lt Lyford or Capt Jefferds would leave their Co. and go home, as soon as this too, but we have got a good Capt. *now*." James Rundlett saw things differently: "There has been quite a no. of resignations lately. Co. B Capt. and First Lieut. start for Washington today. They have endured the Colonel's tiriny as long as possible. I have not said much about him for I suppose it is no use, but I will express myself once, he is a cruel, heartless rascall." William T. Livermore captured the divided opinions when he wrote on October 5, "Our Col is Acting Brigadier now I wish he would be Promoted or Resign although he is the Best."[58]

But things were improving. On October 28, 1862, Ames wrote to Governor Washburn, "I am happy to inform you that the 20th Regt. has made great progress in discipline and instruction." He continued, "It is true I had some opposition at first—it was thought I was too severe but now the officers know enough to appreciate my labors." Two days earlier, Lieutenant Colonel Joshua Chamberlain had suggested the completeness of the transformation of the regiment: "In the Army + by Regular officers we are already said to be a marked Regt," he wrote home to his wife, Fanny. "We have been applied for by three Generals out of our Brigade, + I believe that no other new Regt. will ever have the discipline we have now." Hezekiah Long of Company F concurred, writing home to his wife that many of the men who had previously despised Ames were beginning to come around.[59] A kinder, gentler colonel might not have driven his men so hard and likely would not have set off an impulse to prove him wrong about their capabilities. They may not have particularly liked their colonel, but the men were proud of the feeling of competence and confidence they were gaining as a unit and could not help but credit Ames for his role in their transformation.

This period represented a trying time for the men of the Twentieth Maine, and their connections—both to home and to one another—were essential in keeping their spirits up. As 1862 enlistees, most of these men were not marching off to war looking for adventure or itching to get away from home, as had some of the volunteers of 1861. Rather, they signed up during the low ebb of the war when they feared that not doing so might risk all that they so cherished at home. Thus, maintaining those bonds with the folks on the home front was crucial. Fortunately, the Maine men entering the army had a literacy rate of 97.4 percent, making contact with home possible for most men. The frequent receipt of mail was vital in keeping the soldiers' morale high, while too many days without missives from home could have the opposite effect. "Receiving the mail was always a season of joy and disappointment," Theodore Gerrish noted. A good letter from home could almost transport the soldiers back to Maine. "Yours of the 8th: was received with the greatest pleasure," Holman Melcher wrote his brother. "It was so free and natural, that I seemed to be present with you while reading it. You can't know yet, how much I appreciate such a letter; it makes me feel, on reading it, just as though I had been home visiting."[60]

Many of the men also received newspapers from Maine and kept abreast of all that was going on back in the Pine Tree State. William Lamson maintained a steady correspondence with his sister Jennie, and their letters were often in transit for just five or six days, allowing one another to stay up to date. Lamson also had pen pals other than his sister and was so in tune with the local community back in Sebec that he often passed along gossip about neighbors living just a few houses away that Jennie had not heard. On March 28, 1863, a single mail call brought William T. Livermore five letters from four different people, suggesting that these men remained a part of the communities they had temporarily left behind.[61]

Samuel Keene was an extreme example of connectedness. On January 5, 1863, he mailed his sixty-third letter to his wife Sarah and had just received the sixty-fourth of hers, meaning they averaged a letter every other day. Fanny Chamberlain, by contrast, rarely wrote to her husband, perhaps due to her frustration at his volunteering without consulting her. Chamberlain was distressed by their lack of correspondence throughout the war, bemoaning in early 1863, "I have not heard from my wife for six weeks at least."[62]

James Rundlett kept up the connections with folks back home, in part, by using local Maine landmarks that his pen pals understood to explain the location of the armies: "To give you an idea of the position of the forces would be to place the Union forces on Sprague Hill and all along that ridge by Dud Long's and so on, and the Southern over by Tyler's and along by Thompson's and Crockers . . . in the morn they were driven towards the Kennebec which is about the same distance from the fight that the Potomac was."[63]

The men were aware of what people and newspapers back in Maine thought of the war in general and of their unit in particular, and most were determined to earn an honorable reputation and return home with their heads held high. William T. Livermore measured everything he saw by his Maine standards, including the female inhabitants of Maryland: "Once in a great while I See a Woman But they are not like our Me girls When I get a Woman I Shall get her Just as near Katahdin as I can for the farther South I go the More Inferior the Inhabitants are." Ironically, Lee's Confederates agreed with the Mainer's assessment, with one soldier noting that Marylanders were "the ugliest women and men I ever saw. . . . They looked as if they had been smoked for half a century and then dried. They were chunky and nearly as long one way as the other. I saw but one family that presented at all a symmetrical appearance."[64] North and South were united in their evaluation of the unattractiveness of Marylanders, if nothing else.

As Colonel Ames transformed a bunch of civilians into a trained military unit, the men bonded with one another and created new friendships that sustained them until the end of their days. Whereas the other Maine units raised in the later summer of 1862 had been pulled from one of the four particular militia districts of the state and the soldiers throughout a company (and perhaps even an entire regiment) had preexisting bonds from their civilian days, the Twentieth was formed from stray and leftover clusters of men who hailed from all parts of the state. But as the fall wore on, those months spent together overcame intra-Maine differences and jelled the men into a coherent, committed group of comrades. James Rundlett found his new tentmates to be good friends: "J.P. West and young Macura from Jefferson tents with me. West is first rate, he is as good as an old woman."[65]

The physical stresses of hard marches, long days, and outbreaks of illness created a great need for the comradery of the soldiers if they were to survive, as well as the conditions for that comradery to grow. On September 11, 1862, Nathan Clark revealed the bonds that were already forming: "Our sick squad staid on Arlington Heights a number of days drilling and takeing care of each other. Osbert Rafford was one left sick with measles and I tended him."[66]

On September 14, 1862, Holman Melcher noted, "I stood the march much better than I expected, and I have warm friends in the camp and regt., those who are ready to assist me in time of need, even Lt. Col. Chamberlain took my blankets onto his horse this forenoon." In November, Theodore Gerrish fell ill from an attack of typhoid fever. Halfway delirious and disoriented, he was unable to care for himself, but his tentmates took over. The first night, they "exposed themselves to that fearful storm to protect me. With their bayonets they digged trenches around the tent, to prevent the water from pouring in; they piled their blankets and overcoats upon me to keep me warm and dry." The next day, the two men put Gerrish in an ambulance reserved for officers. When the surgeon threatened to throw him out, one of the tentmates replied, "If it is done, I will report it to every officer in the regiment, and will publish the facts in every newspaper in the state of Maine." The regiment and the ambulances became separated during the day, but that night Gerrish's comrades purchased some soft bread and sugar from a sutler and then walked over three miles to bring him the nourishment. A few days later, Gerrish was well enough to return to duty, but without the aid of his tentmates, his fate may have been very different.[67]

On May 6, 1863, Corporal William T. Livermore reflected on the value of his own friendships. After a hard day, he wrote, "We were wet all over but Spread down and Turned in at 11 oclock Soon after Lieut. Melcher came to the door and asked if I was there I asked him in he brought me a dish of hot Cayan tea as he Knew I was wet and could not heat ennything then he is All I could wish or expect of a Brother."[68]

Taking care of each other in sickness helped the men bond, as did playing together in better times. Gerrish recalled a failed midnight raid on a beehive in search of honey that drew the men closer. James Rundlett noted a similar action, this one a midnight raid on a nearby farm carried out with two comrades. Afterward, the men enjoyed their spoils of war over a shared meal. In February 1863, Samuel Keene recounted that his "boys had a jolly time snowballing," while in June Sergeant Livermore reported that "our Co. go out every night and play Ball one or two hours." The officer corps passed many a winter night playing whist and euchre, cementing their personal as well as professional bonds.[69]

The training and the bonding the men went through in September and October 1862 were invaluable and prepared them to survive and even thrive in the battles that loomed.

The six weeks that the army sat in camp following the Battle of Antietam may have been a great boon to training new units like the Twentieth Maine, but to the president, that time represented a missed opportunity. When George McClellan moaned that his horses were broken down, Lincoln famously retorted, "Will you pardon me for asking what the horses of your army have done since the battle of Antietam that fatigues anything?" Had the Army of the Potomac moved quickly, the president felt, it could have marched on Richmond or forced the Confederates into a battle. On October 26, McClellan finally began moving the army forward—but at such a deliberate pace that Lee easily countered his opponent's maneuvers. Fed up with the inactivity, on November 7, 1862, President Lincoln relieved McClellan of command. The new commander, Ambrose Burnside, passed up a direct but opposed line to Richmond and instead planned to head more east and cross the Rappahannock River at Fredericksburg before moving south toward the Confederate capital.[70]

The Twentieth Maine moved out on October 29, passing through Harpers Ferry the next day. A week later, they were outside Warrenton, around fifty miles due south. They stayed in that location for another week before moving to Stoneman's Switch, just north of the Rappahannock River, by the last week in November. Burnside was hoping to get across the Rappahannock quickly and continue his march on Richmond, but the pontoons he needed to bridge the river were delayed ten days. By the time they arrived, Lee had positioned his army on a strong, elevated position south of Fredericksburg and within sight of the river.[71]

Burnside faced a predicament, for while the prudent move would have been to continue to maneuver and not risk a river crossing in the face of the enemy, he had been put in charge of the army precisely because General McClellan had failed to fight. The Northern clamor of "On to Richmond!" made ending active campaigning for the season politically impossible. Thus, Burnside determined to send his army across the Rappahannock on pontoon bridges and seize the road to Richmond. The Confederates were shocked at the audacious—and foolhardy—plan, with artillerist Edward Porter Alexander commenting, "A chicken could not live on that field when we open on it." That evaluation was evident to men on both sides, with James Rundlett writing to his mother on December 8, "In spite of the energy and efforts of Burnside to advance and bring on a battle, it seems as though a Kind Providence has stayed his efforts and thereby prevented for a while, the destruction of human life which would necessarily follow." But not for long.[72]

On December 11, Union batteries shelled Fredericksburg in an attempt to drive out the few remaining Confederates and clear the way to build the pontoon bridges that would lead directly into the town. The artillery did not succeed in forcing William Barksdale's stubborn Mississippi Brigade out, but eventually men from the Seventh Michigan, Nineteenth Massachusetts, and Eighty-Ninth New York crossed the river in boats and expelled the Confederates, after which the engineers quickly completed the pontoon bridges. On December 12, approximately half of the Army of the Potomac's 120,000 men crossed the river, but the Twentieth remained on the east banks of the Rappahannock for one more day. Now the men had a clear view of the enemy's position, and, as Theodore Gerrish later remembered, "A vague suspicion filled our minds as we looked; and as we thought of the fearful carnage, the very air seemed tremulous with ominous signs."[73]

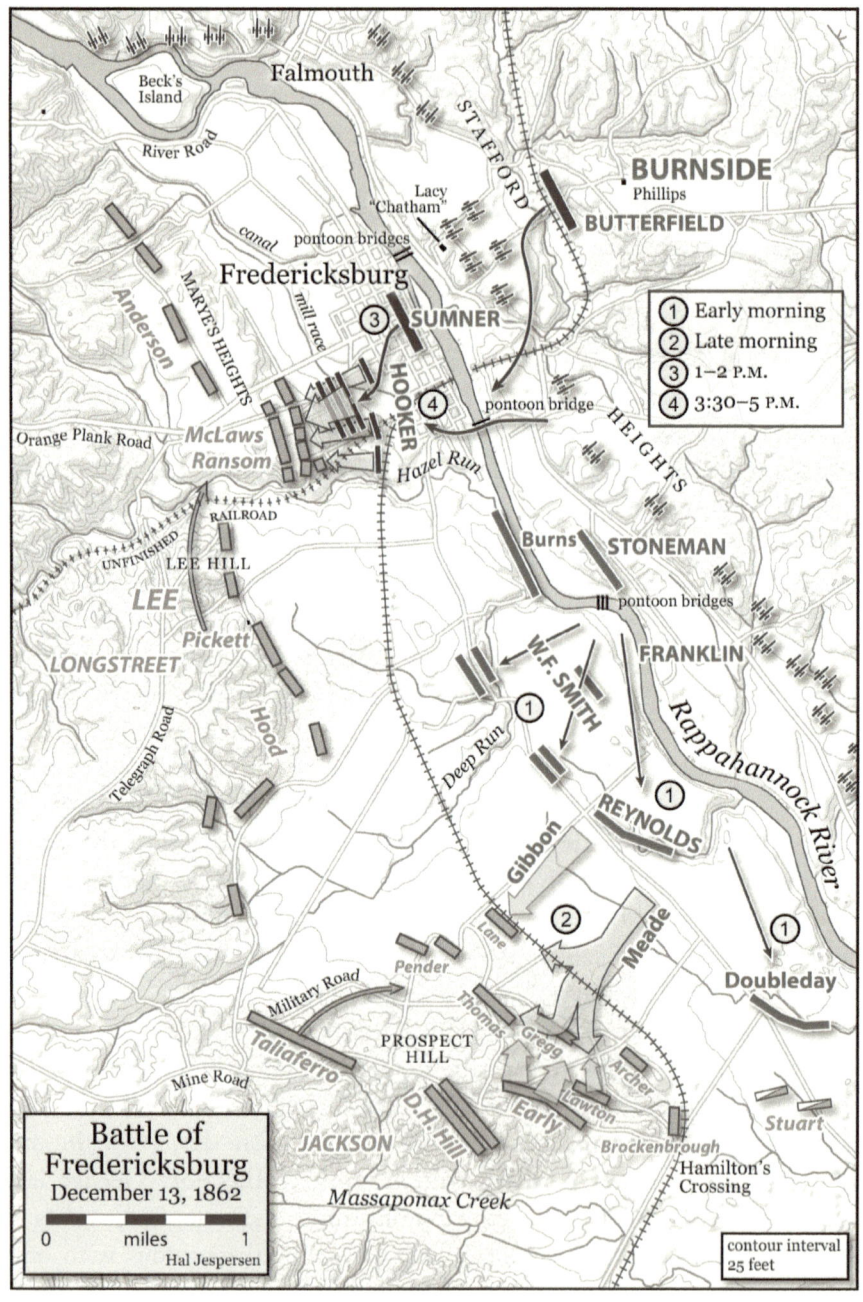

Battle of
Fredericksburg
December 13, 1862

0   miles   1

Hal Jespersen

On December 13, the Twentieth Maine was held on the east side of the river until the early afternoon, watching and yet unable to participate in the fight. Holman Melcher told his brother that, despite the slaughter unfolding before them, the men of the Twentieth "longed to assist them in their work." Burnside's plan was simple: His three "grand divisions," under William Franklin, Edwin Sumner, and Joseph Hooker, would each send their men forward to attack the entrenched Confederate positions and search for a breakthrough. The Confederate left, facing Hooker—and thus ultimately the Twentieth Maine—was the strongest part of the line. As Union attackers came out of Fredericksburg, they would have to cross an open plain, clamber through a millrace, and then traverse another five hundred yards of open field at an uphill grade to get at Confederate riflemen who were protected by a stout stone wall and artillery along Marye's Heights. The Confederate right was more vulnerable, as there was no stone wall and a swampy area meant the Confederates had left some sections devoid of defenders, but it was still a strong position overall.[74]

Union soldiers on the far left (Lee's right) had some early success, and a division under Pennsylvanian George Meade even managed to pierce the Confederate lines, but a lack of reinforcements meant the advantage could not be pressed or even held. On the Union right, Sumner's grand division was predictably unsuccessful in its early attacks against Marye's Heights. Burnside was convinced that this stronghold had to be taken, however, so in the early afternoon, he ordered Joseph Hooker to send his grand division forward to support Sumner's men. Hooker protested the order, arguing that the dwindling daylight meant an attack would accomplish little, but Burnside insisted that the men move forward.[75]

Thus, the Twentieth was ordered to advance in the mid-afternoon. Theodore Gerrish remembered, "We rushed across the pontoon bridges, and charged up through the city, until we reached its outskirts, where our brigade formed a line of battle about one-fourth of a mile from our most advanced position. For an hour we lay flat in the mud upon our faces, to escape the shells that were screaming and crashing over our heads."[76]

Division commander Charles Griffin decided to send his brigades in one at a time, and Stockton's Brigade—including the Twentieth Maine—would be the last to go forward. After an hour of lying in the mud, seeing one ineffective charge by their comrades after another, and with the sun already setting, the brigade bugler signaled for the men to move out. The situation quickly devolved, as the two regiments to the right of the Twentieth did not advance, leaving the Mainers with an exposed flank that was soon hit by a "double fire from the front, and also a battery at the right," Holman Melcher reported. It was a perilous moment that could have wrecked the regiment but for the unit's two top officers. Ames was leading from the front, the only regimental commander in the brigade to do so, and he now sent Chamberlain to stabilize the situation on the right. Melcher wrote, "By the prompt and efficient efforts of our brave Lieut. Col. Chamberlain, assisted by the Adjutant, the right wing advanced in good order. . . . It is useless to mention any one, for every officer and also the men seem determined to do their whole duty."[77]

The behavior of the unit caught the attention of others. Captain Robert Carter of the regular army recalled, "I saw the Twentieth Maine, which was in our division, coming across the field in line of battle, as upon parade, easily recognized by their new state colors, the great gaps plainly visible as the shot and shell tore through the now tremulous line. It was a grand sight, and a striking example of what discipline will do for *such* material in *such* a battle." Gerrish agreed, noting, "It was the first baptism of fire that our regiment ever received, but with the inspiration derived from such a man as Colonel Ames, it was a very easy thing to face danger and death."[78]

It was not merely the inspiration of Ames that was critical but also the training he had overseen. Ellis Spear noted, "My Company ran up against a board fence part of which we quickly pulled down, and I moved the Company by the right flank through the gap and then came forward into line."[79] Those who had previously questioned the laborious drilling Ames had overseen now understood that the veteran of the war's first year had not been trying to break them; rather, he had equipped them with the skills and discipline necessary to survive in battle. Crossing the pontoon bridge, moving through the town, crossing the millrace, and advancing on the enemy required mastery of multiple formations and maneuvers, something the men simply would not have been able to do three months earlier but now came as second nature.

"We pressed on until our most advanced line was passed," Gerrish noted, "and then halted under the cover of a little elevation of ground. Above us and almost within speaking distance was line after line of earthworks filled with rebels, while above them was the artillery vomiting fire and death incessantly. The utter impossibility of taking the rebel position was manifest to every man in the regiment, but we blazed away at the enemy, and they at us." Darkness brought a close to the fighting, but not the suffering. Trapped just yards away from the enemy, the men hunkered down for a frigid December night without their overcoats to keep them warm. It was an unnerving night for many reasons. "There was a singular conflict in our breasts," Theodore Gerrish admitted. "We were wishing the hours away, and yet dreaded to have the darkness disappear."[80]

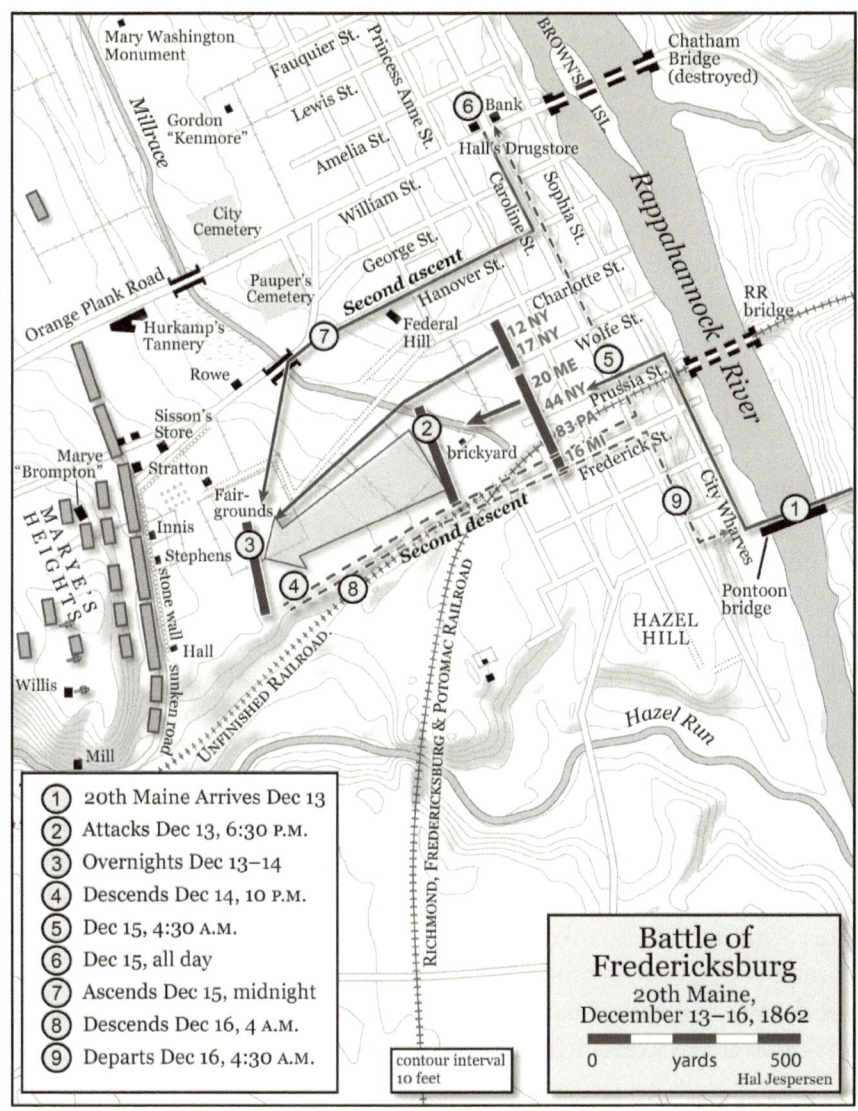

Battle of Fredericksburg
20th Maine,
December 13–16, 1862

1. 20th Maine Arrives Dec 13
2. Attacks Dec 13, 6:30 P.M.
3. Overnights Dec 13–14
4. Descends Dec 14, 10 P.M.
5. Dec 15, 4:30 A.M.
6. Dec 15, all day
7. Ascends Dec 15, midnight
8. Descends Dec 16, 4 A.M.
9. Departs Dec 16, 4:30 A.M.

contour interval 10 feet

0   yards   500

Hal Jespersen

The Twentieth spent Sunday, December 14, the Sabbath, pinned down in the same position. "No man could stand, without being shot down," Chamberlain wrote, and one man from Company B who insisted on rising to fire at the Confederates was shot in the head. The Mainers held their position for thirty-six hours, finally falling back late on Sunday evening and bivouacking in the streets of Fredericksburg for the evening. Unbeknownst to them, Burnside had intended to continue the assaults that day and even planned to lead one himself, but his subordinate generals made clear the futility of such obstinacy.[81]

The Mainers' work was not done. The following evening, Stockton's Brigade was pushed back toward the Confederates to shield the withdrawal of the rest of the army across the Rappahannock. As the night wore on, almost every other unit crossed back to the north side of the river, leaving the Twentieth and the other regiments of its brigade extremely exposed. Fortunately, no harm came their way before they were withdrawn the following morning.[82]

The battle proved a disaster for the Army of the Potomac and nearly for the nation as a whole, and in its aftermath President Lincoln mused, "We are now on the brink of destruction. It appears to me that the Almighty is against us." To a friend he remonstrated, "If there is a worse place than Hell, I am in it." But in their baptism of fire, the Twentieth did everything asked of them and could not have performed better. They had lost four men killed, three mortally wounded, and twenty-nine wounded. One of the wounded men had an arm amputated, and he, along with two others, was discharged a few months after the battle. John Haley of the Seventeenth Maine wrote, "The peculiar feature of war is that each expects *someone else* to fall." The modest casualties suffered by the Twentieth Maine allowed that fiction to persist for the men of the Twentieth Maine, increasing rather than wrecking their confidence. While these casualty numbers were modest, the experience the men gained in the battle was invaluable. Gerrish wrote, "Notwithstanding the grave situation of our army, as a regiment we were much elated. We had fought our first battle, had made a most brilliant charge with unbroken ranks, where veteran regiments had faltered in fear." Chamberlain agreed, writing, "Our men behaved gallantly, and we gained a good name both from our own companions and from the Rebels whom some of us afterwards conversed with."[83]

While the battle revealed the importance of training and thus changed the men's opinion of Ames, it also changed his opinion of them. Theodore Gerrish noted that after the unit had fallen back into Fredericksburg, "Colonel Ames passed among the men and complimented them for their gallant conduct; and we all appreciated such words of praise, coming from so brave and brilliant an officer." Ames called for Ellis Spear and praised him for the "handsome manner" in which the captain had handled his company, a particularly noteworthy moment as just a few weeks earlier Ames had ordered Spear placed under arrest for not keeping his men in proper formation during a march. James Rundlett, who had written so bitterly about the colonel earlier in the fall, noted, "It is plane to be seen, however, that the Colonel has a more favorable oppinion of the 20th since the battle, than formally."[84]

Fredericksburg was critical in showing the men what was required to be good soldiers and in showing their commander that they had great potential, a dual takeaway that Ames identified in a letter to his parents:

> I have greatly improved the condition of the Regiment. I like my Lieut. Col. very much. He is my best officer. My Adjutant has proved himself a good officer. At the battle of Fredericksburgh my Regt. did better than any other in the Brigade. . . . Up to the battle of Fredericksburgh I have been somewhat disliked by my men and officers, but at that battle the feelings in the Regt. changed completely. I was the only Colonel in the brigade who went in front of his Regt. and led his men into the fight. All of my men who were killed and wounded (thirty-six) were in rear of me when struck. My men now have confidence in me; and the battle taught them the necessity of discipline.[85]

Ames had worked hard over the previous three months to provide his men with the training that he knew they needed. At first Ames had not respected the capabilities of the men, which he made clear to them. But as they strove to prove him wrong and earn his respect, they developed into an excellent unit. Fredericksburg was a breakthrough moment, for in that battle the men demonstrated to Ames that they deserved his respect while simultaneously realizing that he, too, deserved their respect for the way he had prepared them for battle. Finally, their actions had not gone unnoticed by others. The following month, Ames wrote home, "My Regt. has an excellent reputation. I cannot ask for better success than what I have had."[86]

Ames was correct; his regiment did have an excellent reputation within the army. Twice that fall Ames was recommended for brigade command, showing how quickly his star was rising. But that opinion did not stretch back to Maine. Joshua Chamberlain bemoaned the dichotomy in a letter to his beloved wife: "I tell you Fanny the estimate of men + things is very different here from the popular one at home. Our Maine Regts. + our prominent officers, have quite a different name from the one they are given in the papers. . . . In the <u>Army</u> + by Regular officers we are already said to be a marked Regt." Why was the unit not given its proper due in Maine? The professor had a theory: "<u>We</u> employ no reporters—have no partizans at home—the papers do not load us with praise we do not deserve." Indeed, the fact that the Twentieth Maine came from all over the state meant that there was no hometown paper to sing their praises, no local politician to bang the drum for them and push promotions for their officers. Respected in the army, they were ignored or even dismissed by some back in Maine.[87]

Things reached a boiling point in February 1863. Newly inaugurated Governor Abner Coburn, seeing the high sick rate in the unit along with the large number of resignations, incorrectly believed the Twentieth to be a unit in disarray and refused to fill the vacancies in the officer corps until he could get a grasp on the situation. On February 6, 1863, the Twentieth's officers took matters into their own hands and penned a long letter to the governor.

> It has been unjustly represented that the Regiment has been subjected to harsh and unnecessarily severe discipline, & that the health of the men has been broken down through the fault of the commanding officer. In regard to the misrepresentations it is proper to state that the Regiment was brigaded a few days after its organization, that it has since performed no service of any kind that has not been performed by other Regiments of the Brigade. We have marched with the Army, and at no other times. All its drills have been those required by General orders from

Brigade or Division Head Quarters—the same for all Regiments. The occasion of so much complaint on the part of the men & officers who have left the Regiment, lies in the fact that the Regiment (notwithstanding the representations of the Col. that it was yet undisciplined) was called into the field before it had had a single Battalion drill. Thus, the men without experience & without being inured to the hardships of military life, were compelled to do the severest service at once; unacclimated they were encamped & did picket duty in unhealthy places along the Potomac. From all this, the men suffered more than older soldiers in the service in the same situations; but those evils were unavoidable, & certainly not through any fault of Col. Ames. To us he had been uniformly kind & courteous. He has spared no exertions in the instructing of officers & men. It is due to him that the Regiment is so well drilled & effective— that it has been able to face the fire of enemy with unwavering lines, & fully to sustain the honor & reputation of the State of Maine. It has been represented by officers who have left the Regiment, that the conduct of the Col. has been such that no men of spirit could serve under him.[88]

That disease had taken a toll on the regiment was undeniable, but the rate of sickness in the unit was not substantially higher than that in the other Maine regiments enlisted in August 1862. The adjutant general's report for 1862 showed a sickness rate of 36 percent among the men in the Twentieth Maine on November 1, 1862. The Sixteenth Maine reported an almost identical rate of 34 percent, while the Seventeenth was a bit better than its peers at 25 percent. The Nineteenth Maine did not provide its numbers.[89] The real issue, then, was less the disease rates than the high number of the original officers who had resigned and had complained to the governor about Ames's attempts to force them out.

Lieutenant Colonel Chamberlain was on furlough in Maine that month and called on Coburn. While their conversation was not recorded, the governor apparently spoke ill of the unit, for, on his return to the regiment, Chamberlain wrote to the governor that he was "hoping that by our continued good conduct your Excellency may have a better opinion of us than you were pleased to express to me, and believing that the good name we hold in the army will before long reach home in the state we honor."[90]

The enlisted men were also aware of a dichotomy in the unit's reputation, for Sergeant Hezekiah Long wrote home to his wife on March 1, 1863, "I understand that the Governor of Maine has a very poor opinion of some of the officers of the 20th Reg. especially the Col." The former prison guard disagreed with that assessment: "All I have to say is that I wish every Reg. had as good one as he is, I think they would be quite as efficient as they now are. There was quite a number of officers and men in the Reg. when we first came out that did not like him, but if it could be out to vote tonight I think 9 out of ten would hold up both hands for him to stay with us." The real problem, he suggested, was not with the men who remained but with those who had left. "It seems rather hard for me to stay here and try and do their duty while others who lack both pluck and ability and who never been [illegible word] at all if they had thought there would be any fighting for them to do, should go home and find people to credit their stories, but so it goes."[91]

The petition from the officers, Chamberlain's blunt missive to the governor, and Long's explanation from a man in the ranks all suggest how frustrated the men were with the gap between the deservedly excellent reputation they enjoyed within the army and the misguided views of those back in Maine. The only way to fix the perception problem, the men knew, was to prove their worth in battle.

Short of a battle, the men tried to impress in other ways. Holman Melcher wrote home in February 1863, "It is surprising to see what a change has come over [the regiment] since going into camp. When we first came out, say at Antietam, the men would let their hair and beard grow long. And clothes, face and hands dirty. Never think of blacking or oiling their shoes." But that had all changed. "Now, the men seem to take pride in having the brightest rifle, cleanest clothes, neatest equipment, blackest shoes, and best looking whiskers. . . . It is really interesting to see the rivalry among the boys about getting onto the post at Head Quarters. . . . They think themselves highly honored if they can only get the situation."[92]

They continued to drill every day, becoming increasingly familiar with different formations and maneuvers. Interestingly, they spent little time on marksmanship. On March 29, 1863, William Lamson wrote home, "I have not fired a gun since I left home. Oh yes I fired a little powder into the air once at Arlington Heights. Ain't that smart for a fellow that's been a 'soger' eight months and a half?" Lamson had been in the hospital in Alexandria from November 8 until February 21 and thus had missed Fredericksburg. Even so, for men whose primary tool was the rifled musket, this was a remarkable comment, though one that was consistent with the rest of the units in the Army of the Potomac. Earl Hess notes that most regiments did not spend time on target practice until 1864. Consequently, many units were not particularly accurate. In one Illinois regiment only four out of 160 men could hit a barrel at 180 yards, while in the Fifth Connecticut thirty-six out of forty men literally could not hit the side of a barn from one hundred yards away—a story almost too good to be true.[93]

Why were these guns so hard to aim? The Springfield and Enfield rifles fired a bullet through a parabolic arc, meaning a gun sighted for 300 yards would hit a man who was within 100 yards of the shooter, but then the bullet would be over the head of an oncoming attacker who was 100–225 yards away, dropping into the killing zone again between 225 and 350 yards. This meant that soldiers had to be highly proficient at estimating distances; otherwise, the new, supposedly superior rifled musket was no more effective than the smoothbores from the days of George Washington. The men in the Twentieth Maine were equipped with rifles that could be extremely accurate to three hundred yards, but with their lack of training, the actual distance at which they were effective on the battlefield was one hundred yards or less.[94]

If the men were not as comfortable with the guns as ideal, they had one other weapon at their disposal: the bayonet. The same week that Lamson wrote home about the unit's lack of familiarity with their rifles, William T. Livermore noted that his company had "Bayonet Exercise" in the after-noon.[95] That skill would come in handy sooner than any of the men could know.

As the spring mud dried up, the armies prepared for another campaigning season. To their consternation, the Twentieth was destined to miss out on the year's first major battle. In early April 1863, the Twentieth Maine was vaccinated against smallpox, a seemingly routine action. But soon three men were dead and eighty-one more were sick, with thirty-two gravely ill. The men had been infected rather than inoculated, and Hezekiah Long noted, "There is some tall swearing about it."

Nathan Clark was so furious that he saw darker forces at work: "By some treachery the rong material was used," he confided to his journal. Of great concern was the possibility that the sick men from the Twentieth could infect the rest of the army, and thus the entire regiment was isolated. This was "to our great disgust," Theodore Gerrish remembered. During this time the Army of the Potomac suffered a major defeat at the Battle of Chancellorsville. While the clash of arms was a decided setback for the Union, the Twentieth's absence once again deprived them of the opportunity to right the wrong impression folks back home had formed of them and made the men ever more desperate to get into action and *do something*. Hezekiah Long lamented, "We have to be contented to lay almost in sight of the enemy and suck our thumbs."[96]

Ames could not stand the disappointment, and James Rundlett noted that the colonel "has been as uneasy as a fish out of water lately." The colonel was furious with the regimental surgeon, Nahum Monroe, for suggesting the unit be quarantined. When it became clear that his protests were ineffective, Ames ensured that he would not miss the fight even if he had to leave his regiment behind. "Our Colonel has left as he couldn't bear for the Army to move without him," Hezekiah Long wrote home. "So Monday morning he went over to headquarters and got a chance on Gen Meade's staff for the present." It is curious that those at headquarters were not concerned about Ames potentially infecting them, but perhaps he had been inoculated earlier in life and thus had avoided the tainted batch given his men.[97]

Chamberlain also tried to get a temporary position but ultimately remained with the regiment and was able to perform a small service. He wrote to Governor Coburn at the end of the month, "I had a midnight order from Gen Butterfield to take possession of the signal wire from the Battle field to Head Qtrs. of the Army. This gave us enough to do, as the wire was tampered with & broken many times a night, & communication was of the utmost importance." This spin was trying to put a good face on the petty task given them, for Chamberlain surely felt as did Holman Melcher: "With our regiment in the condition it was before this broke out, and in the hands of Col. Ames and Lt. Col. Chamberlain, we would have made a 'mark' among the rebels."[98] But such was not to be the case.

One good thing did come in the aftermath of the Battle of Chancellorsville. Colonel Ames was promoted to brigade command in the Eleventh Corps in late May, a well-deserved recognition of his talents and future potential. Ames had taken the regiment as far as he could: Just four days before his promotion, Hezekiah Long wrote home, "Our Regt. was inspected a few days since. The Inspecting Officer says that it cannot be beat in the whole Army of the Potomac, which is quite a compliment to us." Ames and his men had gotten off to a rocky start, but by the time he left the unit, his former charges knew just how important he had been. On May 21, Holman Melcher wrote, "The Colonel to-day received his appointment as Brigadier General, and is to take command of a brigade in the 11th Corps. . . . I am very glad he has got his 'star,' for I think he is in every way worthy of it. He is as 'brave as a lion.'" A soldier from the ranks concurred: "Col. Ames has been appointed Brigadier General and takes a command in the Eleventh, Gen. Howard's Corps," Hezekiah Long wrote. "The soldiers are just beginning to find him out and like him, and the most of them are sorry to loose him." At an 1881 reunion, Samuel Miller asserted, "Without question much of the fame which the Twentieth Maine afterwards achieved was due to the sense of subordination and attention to duty, instilled by the teachings of its first commander." Addison Ames of Company D made his respect known eternally by naming his son (born in 1868) "Adelbert Ames."[99]

When looking at all the factors that contributed to the Twentieth Maine's metamorphosis from disorganized and untrained volunteers in the summer of 1862 into one of the crack regiments in the Army of the Potomac by the summer of 1863, the leadership of Adelbert Ames has to rank the highest. Ames held the officers and the enlisted men to lofty standards and demanded much hard work from them to achieve a level of mastery and competency that increased their self-respect as soldiers. Those still with the unit by the time it reached Gettysburg knew their tactics manuals inside and out, allowing the officers to order and the men to carry out the wide range of maneuvers needed on the battlefield. Further, Ames's exacting standards had rid the unit of many unfit officers and left it with only those who, while not perfect, had shown an admirable level of commitment and competence. While many officers resigned before Gettysburg, almost none of the officers present at the great battle resigned during the remainder of the war. In other words, Ames had ensured that the cream rose to the top. The men had been unsure of their commander at first, but by the time he left them, they had come around. In late 1863, the unit's battle flag—the one they carried at Gettysburg—had become tattered and was replaced. The men sent the old flag to Ames, a symbol of their respect for him and the role he had played in their formation.[100]

There were also other factors at play. The Twentieth was fortunate in not participating in a major battle until three and a half months after entering the service. Early involvement at Antietam, for example, might have wrecked the unit before it could be properly trained. Conversely, their strong performance at Fredericksburg—a result of the drilling they had undergone in the previous months—increased rather than decreased both their confidence and unit effectiveness. Lastly, the unit's relative lack of activity during the first ten months and the misperceptions that ran rampant in Maine as a result of the number of men who left the unit through disease or resignation meant that those who remained were desperate for a chance to prove themselves in battle and earn a reputation back in Maine that equaled the one they already possessed in the army.

Ames had formed one of the finest regiments in the army, and by late May 1863 they were mentally and physically prepared and emotionally desperate for a fight. But now command passed to Lieutenant Colonel Joshua Lawrence Chamberlain, a man who had been in the army for less than a year and had the mighty task of proving himself worthy of the men he led and the commander he succeeded.

2

The Professor's Education
Joshua Chamberlain's Rise to Leadership

On July 14, 1862, Joshua Chamberlain wrote to Maine governor Israel Washburn to "ask if your Excellency desires and will accept my service" in the army. "For seven years past I have been a Professor at Bowdoin College," he continued, but with the government's July 2 call for an additional three hundred thousand troops to put down the rebellion, he felt "every many ought to come forward and ask to be placed at his proper post." Though he had no military experience, "I know I can be of service to my Country in this hour of peril."[1]

Joshua Chamberlain (Courtesy of Pejepscot History Center)

A year later, on July 2, 1863, Colonel Joshua Chamberlain conducted one of the most effective small-unit actions in American military history, showing, per his Medal of Honor citation, "Daring heroism and great tenacity in holding his position on the Little Round Top against repeated assaults." Former commander Adelbert Ames wrote to Chamberlain on July 5, 1863, "I am very proud of the 20th and its present Colonel," offering particular praise for "the intelligence of your conduct yesterday."[2]

This chapter does for Chamberlain what the previous one did for the men of the Twentieth Maine. How did Chamberlain go from being a college professor on July 2, 1862, to performing acts that would make him one of our nation's most heralded citizen-soldiers just a year later? In other words, how did the professor gain his education?

Chamberlain's rise to leadership began not in the summer of 1862 but during his childhood. The man history knows as Joshua Lawrence Chamberlain was born on September 8, 1828, to Joshua Chamberlain Jr. and Sarah (Dupree) Chamberlain. Each of the three names—Joshua, Lawrence, and Chamberlain—is packed with significance.

Since their arrival in Maine in 1799, the Chamberlains had a distinguished history of military service. Joshua Chamberlain Sr., grandfather of our subject, served as a colonel during the War of 1812. At the Battle of Hampden in 1814, he was ordered to retreat but instead advanced, proclaiming, "There shall not a man leave the ground"—a phrase eerily similar to the one his grandson heard on Little Round Top a half century later. That Joshua Sr. was court-martialed for this action seems only to have raised his grandson's opinion of him. Joshua Lawrence Chamberlain wrote that his grandfather was "a stern man, with his own mind and speaking it; but gentle and loving to his own by blood or liking, patient towards the weak, forbearing to abuse advantage, scorning dishonor."[3]

Continuing the family tradition, Joshua Jr. served as a lieutenant colonel of militia in the Aroostook War, an 1830s dispute with British North America over Maine's northern border. The only blood shed during the Aroostook War was that of two British militiamen mauled by an angry bear who, presumably, harbored Maine sympathies. Though the "war" saw no combat, it was one more example of a Chamberlain answering the call to service.[4]

In both cases, the elder Chamberlains were not part of the permanent military; rather, they were citizen-soldiers who served their nation during a crisis and were elected by their peers to leadership positions. It should be noted that the historical record is sparse concerning the service of these two Chamberlain men, and much of what we know comes from the grandson. His father does not appear on the official list of men who served in the Aroostook War, and while his grandfather was definitely at the Battle of Hampden, he was a major at that time and there are no accounts that he refused to retreat when ordered. However, in terms of forming Chamberlain's mindset, the myths and legends that were either told to Chamberlain or imagined by him are more important than the verifiable historical record. In his 1904 memoir *Blessed Boyhood!*, Chamberlain explicitly drew links between his wartime actions and his formative years, indicating that he saw such stories and family legacies as crucial parts of his identity.[5]

If the last name hinted at a military past, the given name solidified that connection. At birth, our man was named "Lawrence Chamberlain," with the family Bible noting that he was "named for Commodore Lawrence of the American Navy." On June 1, 1813, James Lawrence led his ship, the USS *Chesapeake*, against HMS *Shannon* outside Boston Harbor. After exchanging broadsides, the two vessels came together, and the crews attempted to board one another. Within moments, Captain Lawrence was mortally wounded. As his men carried him from the deck, Lawrence uttered the immortal line, "Don't give up the ship! Fight her till she sinks." The British prevailed in the battle, and Lawrence died, but his final order became the battle cry of the navy and the nation. The boy in Maine, named after James Lawrence fifteen years after his death, heard this story throughout his childhood and took to heart its message of steely determination in the face of seemingly impossible odds.[6]

Chamberlain's parents bestowed on him no middle name at birth, but his mother rectified that years later with the addition of "Joshua" as the prefix, moving "Lawrence" to the middle slot. The biblical Joshua was a great military leader, and Chamberlain described him as one who "left nothing undone which the Lord had commanded." Differing from her husband, Sarah Chamberlain preferred a religious path rather than a military one for her oldest child, but in adding this third of a triumvirate of military-based names, she demonstrated that she was "loyal to her husband's house." Despite the addition, family members continued to refer to him as Lawrence throughout his life, and he would sign his letters to them "Lawrence."[7]

Lawrence was the first-born child, but four siblings followed: Horace in 1834, Sarah (or Sae) in 1836, John in 1838, and Thomas in 1841. At six years older than the next sibling, Horace, and a full thirteen years older than Tom, Lawrence noted that being the oldest brought leadership responsibilities: "He is the chief of staff to father and mother. . . . He can guard the younger to school, keep a watchful eye over them there, and 'lick' the big boys who torment the little ones."[8]

The Chamberlains attended First Congregational Church in Brewer, and on the rare occasion that the young man missed a service, such a transgression was "made up for by committing to memory one of the Psalms, an appointed portion of the 'Beatitudes,' or a hymn from 'Watts and Select.'" The skill of memorization came in handy throughout Chamberlain's life, both as a professor and as a budding military leader who pored over tactics manuals by candlelight in his tent.[9]

Chamberlain grew up, as did most Americans in the mid-1800s, on a one-hundred-acre family farm where he grew accustomed to physical labor. He wrote of much time toiling in the family fields and woodlots but also happy hours swimming in the summer, sledding in the winter, and "gunning" in the woods. He summited Mount Katahdin, Maine's tallest peak and one of the most difficult in the entire Appalachians. His father periodically worked as a surveyor, and the son accompanied him on long outdoor expeditions through the Maine and Canadian wilderness. Chamberlain became an academic, but he grew up an outdoorsman who was at ease being on his feet all day and sleeping in a tent or under the stars at night.[10]

As he entered his teenage years, "There were a few hints now on the double-decked paternal side of the house—quiet colloquies between the father and grandfather—as to West Point for a destination." If Chamberlain were to seek admittance to the military academy, he would need preparatory work first. His mother advocated for the seminary but that route also required preparation. Thus, at the age of fourteen, Chamberlain entered Charles Jarvis Whiting's military school in Ellsworth, around twenty-five miles from his home. If he was merely looking for education, Chamberlain might have matriculated at nearby Hampden Academy, while Bloomfield Academy in Skowhegan or Mattanawcook Academy in Lincoln were also possibilities. But Charles Whiting's school was the only one offering a military education.[11]

Charles Whiting was a West Point graduate whose story offered his young charges a personal example of determination and drive. Initially rejected by the Academy due to his small size, Whiting spent the next year hanging from tree limbs with bricks tied to his feet, gained a quarter inch, and was admitted upon his second try. After graduating fourth in the class of 1835, Whiting was commissioned into the artillery. He served just one year before resigning to take a job as a surveyor for a Florida railroad company. In 1839, Whiting returned to the land of his upbringing and opened the "Military and Classical Academy" in Ellsworth.[12]

Whiting's school was conducted entirely in French, so young Lawrence Chamberlain learned the first of the ten foreign languages he ultimately commanded. From Whiting, Chamberlain also learned "the drill, the heavy ordnance, seemingly old King's arms, relics of the grenadiers or the French and Indian wars; marching to church in columns of four." Perhaps, however, the most crucial part of Chamberlain's development was not strictly related to his studies: "In that school we got some notion how to take care of ourselves, and what we were good for—what we could dare and suffer, and do and be."[13]

Back in Brewer, Joshua Chamberlain Jr. made real estate speculations that did not pay off, and the family finances took a downturn. Lawrence did not return to Major Whiting's school the following year; instead, he cleared a six-acre woodlot to generate fast money and then, at the age of sixteen, began teaching school. Chamberlain's first teaching experience lasted just eight weeks before the school was closed because "he 'showed partiality' in the distribution of his calls among the families," and those he did not visit felt snubbed by the young man. He had learned an important lesson in human relations and gained insight into the behind-the-scenes politics that are often necessary for leaders to keep their positions.[14]

The following winter, a wiser Chamberlain took on a particularly tough job, showing something of his character. He reminisced, "The next winter the boy heard of a school 'up river' among the millmen, above Oldtown and 'above Sundays,' where they had broken up every school for three years, and had just pitched the master out of the window while he was at morning prayers, banged the Bible after him, bolted him out and turned the school into a pandemonium. This was the place." On the first day, when several of the older, larger boys refused to follow Chamberlain's instructions, he confronted the leader and knocked him out with a punch. The rest of the students dropped any dissent and were nearly silent for the remainder of the day. Chamberlain visited the boy and his family that night and continued to visit the young man daily until he was well enough to return to school. A sign of the complete transformation of the place and the young teacher's incredible impact came when Chamberlain started a choir to entertain the millmen. Chamberlain's refusal to budge on standards tempered with compassion for those he had to discipline, the combination of velvet glove and iron fist, would be critical in later years in nearly every leadership position he would hold.[15]

Chamberlain's determination comes to the fore through a particular story from this time. Out in the fields with his father, the wheel of their hay wagon became stuck between rocks. The older Chamberlain told his son to "Clear that wheel." When the boy inquired how he should go about the seemingly impossible task, his father replied, "Do it; that's how!" In a prodigious feat of strength, Chamberlain single-handedly lifted the wagon free of the obstacle. This incident did not quickly fade from memory but remained central in Chamberlain's mind and formed a key part of his life's outlook. You have the physical and mental capabilities, his father implied; as long as you have determination, you can accomplish anything. More than fifty years later, he wrote that his father's admonition—"Do it; that's how!"—became "the solution of a thousand problems."[16]

Finally, at age seventeen, Chamberlain had to decide whether to become a warrior or a minister, following the wishes of his father or his mother. He was not particularly taken with either option, feeling that they equally "offered but little scope and freedom. They bound a man by rules and precedents and petty despotisms, and swamped his personality." But he later recounted, "He was willing to please his mother and be a minister, if he could also be a missionary and go to some really heathen Country, like Africa or the Pacific Islands, where he could take part in civilizing a people and helping them to live right in this world anyway." To prepare for the ministry, Chamberlain would go to Bowdoin College.[17]

To gain admission to Bowdoin, Chamberlain had to demonstrate abilities in both Greek and Latin. They were abilities he did not yet possess. "Here was three years' work and one year to do it in," he later remembered. This was a seminal moment in the young man's development. To accomplish the task, Chamberlain ensconced himself in the family's unheated garret and taught himself the languages. When he became too mentally weary, or perhaps too cold, he took an axe and chopped wood previously tossed aside as too tough and knotty to be worth the effort. His mind and his body both grew stronger, and his commitment when fixed on something was in full evidence.[18]

By February 1848, Chamberlain had mastered Greek and Latin and joined Bowdoin's freshman class mid-term. Chamberlain later recollected that it had been a "green and pale-looking lad" who made the hundred-mile sleigh ride over the snow from Brewer to Brunswick, the home of Bowdoin College. Founded in 1794, Bowdoin had been Maine's first college and, in 1848, was one of just four in the state. Bowdoin's total enrollment was 191, including 65 medical students. Chamberlain was one of thirty-three students in the freshman class, thirty of whom were from Maine, one from New York, and two from New Hampshire, including Chamberlain's roommate, George Lafayette Hayes. The freshman class was more Maine-centric than the others: the sophomore and junior classes both had six out-of-staters, while the seniors had eight. Interestingly, there were two Mississippians, a Kentuckian, and two Tennesseans in the student body. None of those Southern men would fight for the Confederacy during the Civil War, but two of Chamberlain's Maine-born classmates did: John Merrill and William O. Otis. John Merrill, a doctor, moved to Missouri and then Mississippi in the mid-1850s and served as a Confederate surgeon during the war. William Otis moved to Texas a decade before the war and during the conflict served as a Confederate quartermaster.[19]

Chamberlain's grueling preparatory work made college seem relatively easy, and he wrote to his pastor at the end of his first year, "I am not obliged to study as hard as I did at home and the labor I there accomplished seems now almost impossible." Despite joining the class late, the young man passed all his first-year examinations at the end of the spring term.[20]

At Bowdoin, Chamberlain stood somewhat apart from his classmates, likely due in part to his late matriculation and in part to his religious devotion. He wrote to his pastor that, when he arrived at Bowdoin, he and one other student had been the only "pious persons in the class," but he suggested that the number had grown to six through his influence. Many of his classmates were fond of drinking, and "it was rather necessary for me to take a decided stand at the very commencement and resist the first temptation." Despite all this, Chamberlain was well liked by his classmates. When the president of Bowdoin demanded that Chamberlain identify boys who stole a tree while inebriated, he refused, to the point of expulsion, but his classmates rescued him by admitting to the crime. The ability to be on good terms with those around him while not being one of them was a valuable skill for Chamberlain both as he became a professor at the age of twenty-six and in his later capacity as a military officer.[21]

Chamberlain missed his third year of college due to a mysterious illness, a "fever [that] worked deep into the blood," leaving him exhausted and on death's door for many months before it finally eased and disappeared. After having been away from college for a full year, Chamberlain joined the class below him to finish his third and fourth years. He was glad he had not mistreated the younger students—as was common in those days—and learned a valuable lesson about not abusing your rank.[22]

The illness that kept Chamberlain back a year may have been serendipitous. A year older than his new classmates, Chamberlain breezed through his junior year and won the college's prizes in composition and oratory. He filled his free time by serving as the choir director and organist at First Parish Church, and it was there that he met Frances "Fanny" Adams, the adopted daughter of Reverend George Adams.[23]

Chamberlain likely was in the church on a fateful day in March 1851 when one of the other parishioners, Harriet Beecher Stowe, had a vision that profoundly impacted her life and national events. Stowe, whose husband, Calvin, was a professor at Bowdoin, came from a long line of reformers and had already written several temperance tracts. During that period, Stowe had turned her attention to slavery and had published three antislavery tracts in the preceding six years. The vision Stowe had while at First Parish Church brought forth another story, one that she titled *Uncle Tom's Cabin*.[24]

As Stowe began to put the story to paper, she shared it with "The Round Table," a literary group that met every two weeks to discuss their original works. Stowe headed the group and often hosted their meetings at her house. Joshua Chamberlain, a member of the select group, described their meetings thus: "On these occasions a chosen circle of friends, mostly young, were favored with the freedom of her house, the rallying point being, however, the reading before publication, of successive chapters of her *Uncle Tom's Cabin*, and the frank discussion of them." The story, which the *New Era* serialized between the summer of 1851 and the spring of 1852, was the most widely read and influential antislavery tract of all time. After appearing in the *New Era*, the story was published in book format. Within a year, it had sold 310,000 copies in America, a million in the United Kingdom, and more than two million worldwide with translations into more than a dozen languages.[25]

Chamberlain spoke little in the prewar years about the abolitionist cause, and one wonders what part he played in the "frank discussion" that followed many of Stowe's readings. The book was designed to elicit sympathy for the enslaved and was so effective that an Ohio paper noted, "He who can read this thrilling narrative without a heaving heart, a moistened eye, and a tear-bedewed cheek, can boast of sensibilities less susceptible than ours." Newspaperman Horace Greeley read the story on a train ride and was so moved that, on arriving at his destination, he had to retire to a private place to compose himself. In March 1852, just ten days before the final installment of *Uncle Tom's Cabin* was published in serialized form, Joshua Chamberlain wrote a senior paper titled "Despotisms of Europe." In that tract, Chamberlain noted, "It is a principle of despotism to crush every free expression, to obstruct every ray of light and truth. . . . We hold that every man who has not violated the laws of nature is fit to be free." Perhaps Stowe's words had taken hold. Chamberlain opposed the institution of slavery without believing in the equality of man—a stance echoed by most Northerners of that era.[26]

Despite Stowe's captivating story and the broad political and moral questions it raised, Chamberlain was somewhat distracted. Fanny Adams was also a part of the reading group, and as time wore on, romance blossomed. Fanny and Chamberlain's courtship was often challenging. In 1851, Fanny's stepfather, Reverend George Adams, married a woman only six months older than Fanny. Fanny found home life difficult after that point and, in late 1851, went to New York to study music with her new step-uncle. Ultimately, that only complicated matters, for after Fanny returned home, her father demanded reimbursement for the expenses Fanny had incurred. Thus, as Chamberlain and Fanny became engaged in 1852, their path was anything but straightforward. That fall Chamberlain enrolled at the Bangor Theological Seminary while Fanny accepted a position teaching music in Georgia. They would be twelve hundred miles apart for the next three years. The separation was trying—with Fanny writing infrequently and Chamberlain continually trying to prove himself. In October 1853, he lamented, "I hear so seldom from you, that there is not continuity enough for any great growth or progress in acquaintance or mutual influence." Her intermittent attention may also have driven his desire to do something notable and earn her respect. In January 1854, he wrote to her, "I must and will do something and be something."[27]

Fanny Adams (Courtesy of Pejepscot History Center)

Chamberlain longed to be near Fanny and even considered applying for a teaching job in Georgia during the fall of 1854. Instead, he remained in Maine, just a mile from the family home in Brewer, supporting himself by teaching German, playing the church organ, and overseeing the area schools. In the summer of 1854, he started a school for women "who have hitherto spent the Sabbath in <u>entertaining</u> their visitors," evidence of his comfort with people of all classes and walks of life.[28]

During a semester break in April 1853, Chamberlain accompanied his father on a trip to Canada, including visits to Montreal and Quebec. He wrote Fanny a lengthy description of his time in Quebec, and, as befitted a seminarian, he noted visits to the city's cathedral and various chapels. He devoted most of his letter, however, to describing the city's fortifications and the points associated with the battle that had occurred there a century earlier during the French and Indian War. A year into his seminary work, Chamberlain still harbored his military interest. The trip was also physically testing given the roughness of the roads. Chamberlain wrote Fanny, "I do not think I ever suffered such pain in my life. But I was determined not to complain and to keep up with the others. Father was very careful and kind to me, but there was no help and I resolved to 'grin and bear it' I've found meaning in that phrase I tell you particularly the grin."[29]

In 1855, Chamberlain finished his work at the seminary and returned to Bowdoin to deliver a master's thesis titled "Law and Liberty." The thesis presentation was a pivotal moment for Chamberlain, who sought to illustrate that "the whole Universe showed that freedom was a part of Law." His argument was convincing, and "the effect of this among those who heard it was an utter and overwhelming surprise to its author. The newspaper notices made him feel as if he had wakened in another world." So powerful were his words, as well as his overall academic record, that the faculty offered Chamberlain the post formerly occupied by Calvin Stowe. Chamberlain accepted the position of "Tutor in Greek, and Assistant Instructor in Rhetoric" over numerous other offers for both teaching and ministerial positions in Maine and New Hampshire. Fanny had also made plans to return to Maine but, much to Chamberlain's disappointment, delayed her return until October and missed both his thesis presentation and graduation. At long last, on December 7, 1855, the couple were married, concluding a four-year courtship and beginning a marriage that lasted nearly a half century until Fanny's death in 1905.[30]

After just one semester Chamberlain was promoted to "Provisional Instructor in Rhetoric and Oratory" and, by the fall of 1856, was the full-fledged "College Professor of Rhetoric and Oratory"—a quick rise. That particular posting, professor of rhetoric, also showed something of the man, for it had been that subject that had so troubled him previously due to a speech impediment. Chamberlain proved to be an innovative teacher, pioneering the idea of having his students take their corrected papers and rewrite and refine their arguments. He was also well liked, as evidenced by the small gift a dozen students bestowed on him at the end of his first term in recognition of "the kind and brotherly interest which you have ever shown in our temporal and eternal welfare."[31]

Despite these recognitions, Chamberlain's position at Bowdoin was less than idyllic. When Chamberlain accepted his job in 1855, he was just twenty-six years old, and most of the men who were now his colleagues had been his professors three short years earlier. Further, college politics weighed on the young man. Bowdoin was governed by a Board of Trustees that made most decisions for the college, as well as a Board of Overseers that had to sign off on those plans. In the 1850s, these two bodies were at odds, with the trustees wishing to introduce a more modern, liberal arts education, while the overseers wanted the school to remain true to its traditional roots in orthodox Congregationalism. In January 1860, Chamberlain wrote to his mother, "We have our usual amount of diplomacy this term—plotting + counter plotting. The game now is a professor of modern languages in which curious developments of human nature appear in full relief + how it will turn out I can't predict. My friend Prof. Upham still urges that professorship upon me, + argues the point with his customary shrewdness; but I believe I shall stay where I am; unless some greater inducement than I have seen yet, is offered for the change." Chamberlain was acceptable to both the overseers and the trustees and held a critical position as one who could bridge the divide. If he did not accept the position, the faculty worried that someone might be brought in from the outside. As this drama played out over the next several years, Chamberlain learned the vital skill of subtly positioning himself for higher office and not alienating any factions.[32]

Fanny and Chamberlain welcomed their first child on October 18, 1856. Showing their devotion, they named her Grace, though they called her Daisy. Potential parenthood had been a question of some discord during their engagement. In May 1852, Fanny wrote to her future husband, "You know full well how I hate little children," and five months later she followed up, "How we do agree about <u>almost</u> everything, don't we Lawrence?" But something changed, and Grace was the first of Fanny's five pregnancies. In November 1857, a baby boy was born three months premature and died shortly after. The loss of their child must have been overwhelming and was just one of many deaths Fanny and Joshua experienced during this period. Fanny's birth mother died in 1854, and her sister Charlotte in 1855. Another daughter—Emily—was born in 1860 and lived just four months. Later that year Fanny's brother, George, and her birth father, Asher, both passed away.[33]

Things were no rosier on the national stage than the personal one. The late 1850s saw the nation descend into conflict over the question of slavery, and any hope that the election of Abraham Lincoln would not lead to a national schism abruptly ended with South Carolina's secession on December 20, 1860. By February 1, six more states had joined South Carolina and formed a confederacy.

Chamberlain seems to have compartmentalized the impending crisis. On Lincoln's inauguration day, Joshua wrote to his brother Tom not of national events and what they might portend but of the simple joys of family life: "We have been having a great time with your sled this winter. I piled up a artificial hill against the barn, + make a long smooth track away out into the garden. Daise = Wyllys have enjoyed themselves greatly. They generally slide together—Daise behind. She can glide alone. There is not much need of <u>steering</u>. Once in a while the sled will go off the track, + plough them head forward into the snow but Daise says that is <u>all the fun of it</u>."[34]

Five weeks later, the Confederates attacked Fort Sumter in Charleston and the war began. Mainers rushed to enlist in response to Lincoln's call for seventy-five thousand men to put down the rebellion, but the professor from Bowdoin was not one of them. He had several good reasons for holding back. Many thought the war would be over in a matter of a few weeks—months at the most—and his father's experience of marching away from home in the 1830s and having the Aroostook War end without a single battle would have weighed on Chamberlain's mind. He also had two young children and was likely still grieving the death of young Emily the previous fall. April found him in the middle of the year's teaching commitments, and he undoubtedly would have met opposition from the faculty had he decided to quit at such a time and might even have lost his position at Bowdoin. Further, the two most significant personal influences on him—Fanny and his father—both opposed his joining the war effort. In 1861, those reasons proved enough to keep Chamberlain at home.

The professor did not ignore the war, however, and there were early signs that he was biding his time. In May and June 1861, Bowdoin students formed two militia companies to be prepared if the state called for additional volunteers. The first group, the Bowdoin Guards, hired a drill instructor named Charles Curtis, a Maine native who was then a senior at the military academy in Norwich, Vermont. The drill lasted only a short time, for when the school recessed in July, the instructor went to the front, but Curtis later recalled that Chamberlain "had shown considerable interest in the Bowdoin Battalion, frequently attending its drills, listening to commands and observing the responsive movements." One night the students made up cartridges and then used them to fire their guns and cause a general ruckus around campus. Curtis, Chamberlain, and Professor Woods investigated the situation. In Curtis's retelling:

> "Oh, Professor!" shouted an irreverent Sophomore from a window overhead. "First time under fire!—How do you like it?" The Professor looked amused and then turning to the President he said:
> "Doctor, I think Mr. Curtis is right, the boys will have to fire their last cartridge before they stop. We had better adjourn."[35]

While Chamberlain might have gained a bit of knowledge from watching these drills in the summer of 1861, his response to the students' revelry and their firing blank cartridges is more noteworthy. Chamberlain's sense of humor, perspective, and practical solution to the problem served him well the following year when he had his own exuberant soldiers to handle. When the government called for three hundred thousand more troops in the summer of 1862, Chamberlain decided it was time. Things on both the national and the personal front had changed.

The state of the Union cause in the summer of 1862—one of near-disaster that had prompted the call for more volunteers—was the most significant driving force behind Chamberlain's decision to volunteer at this particular time. Chamberlain wrote to the governor, "I fear, this war, so costly of blood and treasure, will not cease until the men of the North are willing to leave good positions, and sacrifice the dearest personal interests, to rescue our Country from Desolation . . . every man ought to come forward and ask to be placed at his proper post." In a later speech intended to convince his fellow Mainers to enlist, Chamberlain explained:

> *I feel that we are fighting for our country—for our flag—not as so many stars + stripes but as the emblem of a great + good + powerful nation— fighting to settle the question whether we <u>are</u> a nation, or only a <u>basket of drips</u> whether we shall leave to our children the <u>country</u> we have inherited—or leave them without a country—without a name. Without a citizenship among the great powers of the earth.*

The war raised the question of not just whether the country would be reduced by eleven states but whether it would persist at all. If eleven states were allowed to leave, many wondered, what other "drips" might follow?[36]

The timing was likely better for Chamberlain in 1862 as well. In April 1861, classes were in the middle of their session, and by May the state was no longer accepting volunteers. In 1862, the call for troops went out in July, with units forming into August, which coincided with the summer break. Further, Chamberlain had secured the elusive professorship of modern languages the previous fall, which carried with it both a two-year sabbatical and lifetime tenure. Chamberlain would not, in other words, lose his faculty position by volunteering.[37]

Lastly, a personal tragedy likely played into Chamberlain's decision. In December 1861, Chamberlain's brother Horace died, the result of a "cavity" in his lungs. Chamberlain took the death hard, writing to his sister the following February, "I feel bereaved as if something had gone from me—as if a support + stay rod suddenly taken away." In his autobiography Chamberlain wrote, "The friendship and sympathy between the brothers were of no common order, and the bereavement was a deep one." There was pressure on Chamberlain—from both faculty members and his family—not to join the war effort and be maimed or even killed. But Horace's death—following that of so many other relatives and two of his children over the past seven years—proved that staying home was no guarantee of safety.[38]

Thus, on July 14, 1862, ten days after Israel Washburn had announced that Maine would raise four new regiments, Chamberlain wrote to "ask if your Excellency desires and will accept my service." The professor had made up his mind to join the war, forgoing the two-year sabbatical that he was otherwise about to begin. Chamberlain did not know the governor, so he provided biographical information as well as his views on the current conflict. He identified himself as "a son of Joshua Chamberlain of Brewer." Washburn had served as a U.S. congressman from 1851 to 1861, representing the district that included Brewer and "knew the father and grandfather of his candidate." The letter continued, "For seven years past I have been Professor in Bowdoin College." That line was quite significant, for in 1862 there were just over two hundred institutions of higher learning in the United States, and barely over 1 percent of the nation's men graduated from college. Holding not only an undergraduate but also a graduate degree and occupying a position as a professor, Chamberlain was one of the educated elite. He alluded to that in his following sentence: "I have always been interested in military matters, and what I do not know in that line I know how to learn." That final line was undoubtedly true and is the key to understanding Chamberlain's near-seamless integration into the military. He *had* always been interested in the military, and he had learned much along the way from Major Whiting's school, his tour of French and Indian War fortifications a decade earlier, and his more recent observations of the student drills. Further, he certainly did "know how to learn." Chamberlain's core ability to quickly learn and become proficient in a particular area, as evidenced by his conquering of Greek and Latin in a matter of months, was invaluable as he would go through a crash course in military tactics and command in the fall of 1862.[39]

Israel Washburn (Library of Congress)

A particular line in Washburn's call for volunteers had caught Chamberlain's attention. The governor asked Mainers to "unite in the work that is before them, each laboring in his own sphere, doing what he can by his example, influence and sympathy—proffering his treasure, his time, his strength, his heart and his highest hopes to the cause of this country!" Chamberlain embraced that sentiment, echoing, "Your Excellency presides over the Educational as well as the military affairs of our State, and, I am well aware, appreciates the importance of sustaining our Institutions of Learning. You will therefore be able to decide where my influence is most needed."[40]

The governor responded quickly, asking on July 16 whether Chamberlain could meet with him two days later. On July 17, Chamberlain made his position clear: "I only wish to be where I can best serve you. I do not wish to stand in the way of others—especially of our gallant men on the Potomac." By the time Chamberlain met with the governor, Washburn had already made appointments at ranks of colonel, lieutenant colonel, and major in each of the four regiments that Maine was raising. The incredible turnout of volunteers, however, had led the governor to consider adding a fifth regiment, and he offered Chamberlain the hope "of my having it."[41]

Excited by the possibility of a field command, Chamberlain threw himself into recruiting. He had told the governor, "Nearly a hundred of those who have been my pupils, are now officers in our army; but there are many more all over our State, who, I believe, would respond with enthusiasm, if summoned by me, and who would bring forward men enough to fill up a Regiment at once." On July 20, Chamberlain joined the convalescing General Oliver Otis Howard for a speech at the Brunswick train depot. Two undated speeches among Chamberlain's papers were evidently given at this time as a part of his recruiting effort and may have even featured at the train depot. In one he noted:

> *I believe, fellow citizens, friends, that we are all agreed in this that we must show our strength now whatever may be our theory of the war—the origin or conduct of it—whatever we may think of the administration or of the commander in chief (+ for me I have confidence in both) we cannot <u>shut our eyes to the facts now before us</u>—we must strike a blow. This war can only be quelled by a swift + strong hand. Gentlemen may cry peace, peace, but there is no peace. We cant have peace till we take the chief city of the rebels. They will have no respect for us unless we whip them.*

In both speeches, Chamberlain echoed the language he used in his initial letter to the governor, which revealed his motivation for supporting and ultimately joining the Union war effort.[42]

Chamberlain's speech and his presence next to Howard must have made quite an impression, for the following day an article appeared in the local paper:

COLONEL OF THE 20TH REGIMENT. Lawrence Chamberlain, Professor of Modern Languages at Bowdoin College, has accepted the Colonelcy of the Maine 20th Regiment. Prof. Chamberlain is the son of Col. Joshua Chamberlain, of Brewer. This is a most significant and gratifying index to the state of public feeling in the present crisis. When such men relinquish high positions of comparative ease and safety to enter the service of their country, it is evidence that the danger is pressing, and that the patriotism of the men of '76 still burns brightly in the hearts of their descendants. Now, as ever, the centres of learning are also the nurseries of freedom.

On July 21, the *Portland Daily Press* ran two short pieces noting that Chamberlain had accepted the colonelcy of the Twentieth Maine. That revelation shocked some in Brunswick, including the subject himself. A much-chagrined Chamberlain wrote to the governor on July 22, "I beg your Excellency will understand that these mortifying reports in regard to my appointment, did not come from me in any way that I can imagine."[43]

Josiah Drummond, the state's attorney general, also took note of the article. At the end of a long letter to the governor about various war matters, including some potentially disloyal officers, Drummond added a final "Private" section. "Have you appointed Chamberlain Col. of the 20th?" Drummond inquired. "His old classmates etc. here say you have been deceived: that C. is nothing at all. That is the universal impression of those who knew him." The letter sounds damning, but there was a backstory that Drummond missed. Chamberlain had not deceived the governor as to his capabilities; instead, the attorney general's informants had pulled the wool over *his* eyes. In his postwar autobiography, Chamberlain noted that Bowdoin's faculty had started the whisper campaign against him, an action he referred to as "a strange exhibition of affection." Their purpose was clear: "The young Professor held for them a strong position. This chair was much sought for; and those competent to fill it were for the most part, not of the strict orthodox persuasion. In case this chair should become vacant, as the experiences and prospects of war rendered highly probably, the chances were that it would be filled by one of the adverse party." Professor William Smyth became so infuriated with his colleague's decision that he warned Chamberlain he may "return 'shattered' + 'good-for-nothing,'" an argument that only hardened Chamberlain's resolve to leave Bowdoin behind and join the army.[44]

On August 8, Chamberlain wrote to the governor, "I find I have to encounter an unexpected degree of opposition in the Faculty of the College. They are unwilling to give me any sort of countenance. But I feel that I must go, & I trust that the representations that they propose to make to induce you to withhold my commission, will have no more weight with you than with me here." Fortunately, the governor "had no thought of letting his own judgment be superseded," and had already decided to offer Chamberlain the position of lieutenant colonel of the Twentieth Maine. Chamberlain later stated that he had previously told the governor to "give the colonelcy of the regiment to some regular officer now in the field. I will take a subordinate position, and learn and earn my way to the command," but in his July 22 letter to the governor, he noted, "Though it was scarcely probable that a new Regt. would be raised, yet in case it should be, I had received the impression that you thought favorably of my having it." But rather than be disappointed in receiving the secondary position, Chamberlain wrote, "I should prefer the office you tender to any other." The ambitious Chamberlain was likely putting a good face on the disappointment he must have felt at not receiving a regimental command.[45]

The Bowdoin faculty were not alone in their opposition to Chamberlain's new position. His father was a Democrat who may have had Southern sympathies—he did, after all, name his third son John Calhoun Chamberlain. The older Joshua Chamberlain pleaded with his son to "distinguish yourself and be out of it." But, since the son *had* volunteered, he admonished, "Come home with honor, as I know you will if that lucky star of yours will serve you in *this war*." Fanny, too, opposed his going, writing bitterly in November that he "ought to be at your own home." Chamberlain's inner need to earn the respect of Fanny and those around him, evident since the days of their courtship, lingered, and seven years into his academic career it was obvious that his current life offered no such opportunities. Maybe military service would be different.[46]

In writing to the governor, Chamberlain implied that men would follow him into the army, and he was correct. Most notably, his youngest brother, twenty-one-year-old Thomas Davee Chamberlain, enlisted as soon as he heard that his brother had volunteered and would be appointed to the Twentieth Maine. Their father wrote to Joshua Chamberlain imploring him to look after Tom and secure him a noncombatant position if possible.[47]

Over the ensuing ten days, Chamberlain put his affairs in order while simultaneously recruiting more men for the regiment and attending to the unit's needs. He reported to the Twentieth Maine's rendezvous point at Camp Mason in Portland on August 18 and took charge of the regiment until Colonel Adelbert Ames arrived near the end of the month. The men who were joining the Twentieth were excited about their lieutenant colonel. Ellis Spear later recollected, "(Chamberlain) was fresh from a Professorship in Bowdoin College where I had known him when I was a student there. He was (and is) a gentleman and a scholar and although he was without military knowledge or experience he was a man of such intelligence and urbanity and kindliness of feeling that he exerted a useful influence even in the organization of the regiment."[48]

On August 29, 1862, the Twentieth Maine was mustered into federal service, and the men prepared to transfer to the front. On September 1, prominent townspeople of Brunswick gave Chamberlain a splendid horse. The formal presentation, with a speech from those gifting the horse and one from Chamberlain in reply, was in stark contrast to the lack of pageantry surrounding the Twentieth Maine's departure for the front lines the following morning.[49]

Joshua Chamberlain, 1862 (Courtesy of Pejepscot History Center)

On September 4, 1862, halfway through the four-day voyage that brought the Twentieth Maine to the front lines, Chamberlain wrote to Fanny. First, he alluded to her vexation at his leaving and tried to charm her: "I feel too the force of your noble self sacrifice, your heroism greater than mine, inspiring my soul." To cushion the blow of his departure, he implored her, "First of all have everything you want. Do not deny yourself anything you may desire. You have given up enough. I have made arrangements to have a hundred dollars a month paid into the Bank to your credit, and I want you to use for your comfort and the children's." As a lieutenant colonel, Chamberlain was paid $198 per month, allowing Fanny to live comfortably in his absence. In a final attempt to convince her that volunteering had been for the best, Chamberlain wrote, "I am glad I am here, and so are you, and so will all my real friends be." Unfortunately, Fanny was far from convinced, and her displeasure with his decision became a significant theme in their relationship ever after.[50]

Colonel Ames used the four days on the transport ship to begin tutoring the officers on the drills and tactics they needed to master. Though some of the original officers did not take to Ames's instruction and the hard work required to become competent officers, Chamberlain was an eager pupil and quick learner. Ames quickly developed confidence in Chamberlain's abilities and left him in charge of disembarking the Twentieth from the *Merrimack* on September 6. That night, the unit was assigned to the Fifth Corps. Chamberlain later wrote of that unit, "Most of its commanding officers in the superior grades were West Pointers, and experienced officers of the old army, and prided themselves on strict observance of Army Regulations and military habitudes."[51]

Two days later, on Chamberlain's birthday, the Twentieth was ordered to march to Fort Craig, six miles west of the city and just beyond the estate that had been the home of Confederate commander Robert E. Lee and would later become Arlington National Cemetery. One of the nearly seventy forts that protected the city, Fort Craig was a modest-sized outpost boasting just a dozen cannons. The march out to the fort was arduous for the new soldiers, and Chamberlain estimated that thirty or forty men fell out along the way. The unit was warned they might be attacked that night, but Ames trusted his subordinate enough to leave Chamberlain in charge while he returned to Washington. Ames's trust was well placed, for Chamberlain and Major Charles Gilmore posted sentinels, provisioned the men with sufficient ammunition, developed contingency plans if the Confederates attacked, and went to bed with arms in hand and their horses saddled and ready. This was a good showing from the lieutenant colonel, especially on his first night in the field. However, the next morning revealed that he still had much to learn: "We discovered that we were on the wrong side of the fence, and were <u>outside</u> of our own lines. We were not long in changing from <u>that</u> position I assure you." Despite the blunder, Chamberlain was enjoying himself. He offered Fanny a jocular summary: "Well Fan, fancy that for a first night's experience."[52]

This incident likely made Chamberlain realize how much he had to learn before being competent to take men into battle. He wrote, "I am working hard to make myself equal to my position and able to handle the men in case the Colonel is absent. We all 'get along,' as the miserable phrase is, finely. The Colonel and Major are very kind and considerate towards me." And then he revealed to Fanny, in part, his motivation: "You will never be ashamed to read my record to my children if they have no other legacy will have that of honor."[53]

After three days at Fort Craig, the Twentieth Maine marched west on September 12. With the Confederates on the loose in Maryland, the Army of the Potomac sought to bring them to battle and force them back across the Potomac River. Over the ensuing three days, the Twentieth marched more than fifty miles, a challenging undertaking for these new soldiers who were accustomed to physical labor but not to walking such great distances. In contrast to Colonel Ames's upbraiding of his men following their march on September 8 was Chamberlain's quiet concern, as evidenced by his carrying of Holman Melcher's blankets (as previously detailed).[54]

The Melcher incident is the first of many recorded by enlisted men in the regiment that reveals something about Chamberlain's leadership style. Not afraid to discipline those who needed it, Chamberlain was also empathetic to the trials and tribulations of those around him and ready to help in whatever way he could. Small acts like carrying Corporal Melcher's blankets soon became known throughout the regiment, with the consequence that while the men were quite skeptical of their colonel's concern for their well-being, they had no such doubts as to their lieutenant colonel. When John Chamberlain visited with the Twentieth Maine in June 1863, the men told him that their affection for his brother stemmed from the fact that he "don't say go boys but come."[55]

Chamberlain's first experience under enemy fire came on September 20 during the Battle of Shepherdstown. Union general Fitz John Porter sent four of his Fifth Corps brigades across the Potomac River to pursue Lee's retreating army, only to almost immediately order a retreat when they ran into a large body of Confederates under Stonewall Jackson. The majority of the casualties on the Union side—269 of 366—were from the 118th Pennsylvania. The battle ended up being of little consequence, a footnote to the twenty-three thousand casualties suffered at Antietam three days earlier, but provided the Twentieth Maine with their first experience under hostile fire. Chamberlain wrote to Fanny, "I was ordered to stand in the middle of the river & urge on the men who halted for fear of the fire. The balls splashed all around me during the whole time & just as I reached the shore two struck just over my head in a tree. Some times our own shells would explode right over our heads & scare the men dreadful. No sooner had we got over in line then we were ordered to recross." He reported that four men were wounded, though none seriously. Furthermore, the horse he rode that day was shot from under him, the first of six times that Rebel bullets would hit his mounts.[56]

A week later, Chamberlain elaborated on this first experience under fire: "Our crossing of the ford of the Potomac the other day (which I wrote you something of, but I fear you did not get the letter) was quite a nice little affair; though the newspapers said nothing of us and greatly praised another Regiment [118th Pennsylvania] that was with us and because it was poorly disciplined lost a number of men, we did not accomplish much it is true, neither did they, but we kept our men in line of battle and brought them off in good order." Chamberlain was proud of the unit's behavior and of his own: "I have been under fire two or three times, and more than once have been a mark for sharp shooters, and though that is no great thing, still it makes a man a better thinker I believe, and a better judge of things, including himself." These passages reveal Chamberlain's pride in both his personal and his unit's behavior and actions as well as his frustration that others were being lauded while the Twentieth was overlooked, even though they were performing to the same or even a better standard.[57]

Regardless, the men of the Twentieth were impressed by what they saw of the former professor. On October 5, 1862, William T. Livermore of Company B wrote, "Our Lieut Col is one of the finest men that ever lived." An anonymous letter published in a Maine newspaper a few weeks later noted, "Lieut. Colonel Chamberlain is almost idolized by the whole regiment. . . . Of course, I do not have much to do with him, yet, if I wanted any favors, I should apply to him at once, knowing that I should get them, if it were in his power to confer them." A letter to Fanny in October about his philosophy of child-rearing is indicative of Chamberlain's general approach to discipline: "Be sure and have a pleasant time and give the children a few extra indulgences—only <u>obedience, always, instant, and entire.</u> Those are my orders! That is the way to save children. But give them every comfort in the way of <u>clothing</u> and of <u>toys</u>." This simple statement captures Chamberlain's leadership philosophy: Leaders must ensure that they and those under them maintain the organization's standards, but do so while treating subordinates well and showing them kindness whenever possible.[58]

Chamberlain found his new leadership position enthralling: "Every third day I am detailed as Field officer of the Day for the Brigade + I have charge of all the outposts + advanced guards for miles around. That gives me a fine chance to ride over the country. . . . Often I am 12 or 15 hours a day in the saddle." He could not help but make comparisons between his new and old lives. He wrote to Fanny on October 10, "I have my care + vexations too; but let me say no danger no hardship ever makes me wish to get back to that college life again. I cant breathe when I think of those last two years. Why I would spend my whole life in campaigning it, rather than endure that again. . . . My experience here + the habit of command will make me less complaisant, will break upon the notion that certain persons are the natural authorities over me." Chamberlain elaborated on that comment two weeks later, writing, "The '<u>glory</u>' Prof. Smyth so <u>honestly</u> pictured for me I do not much dread. If I do return 'shattered' + 'good-for-nothing', I think there <u>are</u> those who will hold me in some degree of favor better than that which he predicted." These extreme attempts by some Bowdoin faculty members to keep Chamberlain from volunteering turned out to have the opposite effect. Army life had its physical dangers, but it seems the petty monotonies of academia had become just as hazardous to Chamberlain's spirit.[59]

Chamberlain was fortunate to avoid the illnesses that infected many and greatly reduced the regiment's strength during their time in camp after Antietam, instead using the time to get up to speed on military affairs. On October 26, 1862, he wrote to Fanny, "<u>I study</u>, I tell you every military work I can find. And it is no small labor to master the evolutions of a

Battalion + Brigade. I am bound to understand <u>every</u> thing. And I want you to send my 'Jomini, Art of War' in a package Lt. Nichols is to have sent soon. The Col. + I are going to read it. He to instruct me, as he is kindly doing in every thing now."[60]

Baron Antoine Henri de Jomini was a Swiss general who served in both the French and the Russian armies during the Napoleonic Wars and at one point served on Napoleon's headquarters staff. Napoleon never produced a clear treatise on his theories of warfare, leaving Jomini's 1830 *Summary of the Art of War* as the book that came closest to revealing the great general's methods. The manuals that Chamberlain had already studied—Silas Casey's 1862 *Infantry Tactics* and possibly a predecessor volume on the same topic by William Hardee—offered an extensive overview of drill and small-unit tactics but were narrow in scope. Jomini—while often writing in obtuse language that made his points difficult to grasp—included much more on the operational and strategic level with extensive discussions on strategy as well as logistics and sea power. Colonel Ames had learned about Jomini at West Point but now was anxious to dive in deeper with a study partner. Jomini is often credited with greatly impacting Civil War tactics, but as historian Carol Reardon points out, "Jomini accounts for only three citations in the index to the original 128-volume *War of the Rebellion: A Compilation of the Official Records of the Union and Confederate Armies*," suggesting that his teachings were not top of mind for most regimental commanders.[61]

Regardless of the impact of Jomini, the effect of all this work is evidenced in Chamberlain's letters home. Through October, his notes focused on his efforts to learn all that would allow him to become an effective officer. Beginning in early November, his language shifted. On the fourth day of the month he wrote home, "Give my regards to all my friends, + tell them I am beginning to understand my business, + shall probably be enabled to look them in the face again if I get home." On November 27, he asserted, "I like the <u>field</u> and <u>the command of men</u>."[62]

By November, he was entirely accustomed to army life. In the early part of the month, he wrote that John Marshall Brown, the Twentieth's adjutant, "says I am the most careless + improvident fellow he ever saw—take no care of myself at all—sleep on the ground when I have the whole Regt. at my command to make house for me. But I hate to see a man always on the spring to get the best of every thing for himself. I prefer to take things as they came, + I am as well + comfortable as any body, + no one is the worse for it." The consequence of such rough sleeping was playing out in his appearance:

Picture to yourself a stout looking fellow—face covered with beard—with a pair of cavalry pants on—sky blue—big enough for Goliath, + coarse as a sheep's back—said fellow having worn + torn + ridden his original suit quite out of the question—enveloped in a large cavalry overcoat (when it is cold) of the same color + texture as the pants; + when wearing the identical flannel blouse worn at Portland—cap with an immense rent in it caused by a Picket raid when we were after Stuart's cavalry. . . . This figure seated on a magnificent horse gives the peculiar point + quality of incongruity which constitutes the ludicrous.

On November 22, he wrote, "We have been sitting all of us—the Col., Major, Adjutant, Doctor and I around our tent fire which we have tonight in the middle of our big tent, telling ghost stories and other marvelous tales and have enjoyed ourselves very much." But in more somber passages, Chamberlain acknowledged the possible consequences of his position: "Bless the dear children. I don't dare to think of them too much. It makes me rather sad, & then I do not forget that I am here in the face of death every day. You must not let them dwell too much on me, & keep me too vividly in their affections. If I return they will soon relearn to love me, & if not, so much is spared them."[63]

As it was for the men of the Twentieth Maine writ large, the two months the unit camped along Antietam Creek were invaluable, as this time allowed Chamberlain to develop his capabilities before facing his first major action. Chamberlain had long desired a reputation that stretched beyond his immediate orbit, and when he had entered the army, he knew that he had much to learn before he had the skills to perform in battle in a way that would earn the esteem of others. In the first few months of army service, Chamberlain's letters carry a cautious tone that emphasized the work he was putting in to build those skills, but by late October, his confidence in his military capabilities solidified. By the time the army began to move toward the Confederates in late October, the men in the Twentieth Maine were eager for a battle, Chamberlain not least of all. They would get that chance at Fredericksburg, Virginia.

The Twentieth Maine arrived at Stoneman's Switch on the east side of the Rappahannock River in late November. While most of the unit was too far rearward to witness the artillery barrage that began the Battle of Fredericksburg on December 11, Chamberlain and Adjutant John Marshall Brown rode to an overlook to observe the firing. Chamberlain wrote, "the scene (let the word include sounds as well as sights) was grand beyond anything I ever witnessed or expect to witness." His observation was not a mere matter of curiosity but one of professional interest, evincing his continued drive to understand warfare and all its components.[64]

Half the Union army crossed the Rappahannock the following day and attacked the Confederate positions west of Fredericksburg. The Fifth Corps, including the Twentieth Maine, was held back on December 12. Even during the early part of the battle on December 13, the Maine men remained across the Rappahannock River, watching their comrades without being able to help. Chamberlain wrote home four days later, "I see tears in the eyes of many a brave man looking on that sorrowful sight, yet all of us are eager to dash to the rescue."[65]

Ames and Chamberlain had confidence in their men, and both were desperate to demonstrate the high standard to which they had trained the unit and begun to secure for it, and for themselves, a worthy reputation. Finally, in the late afternoon, they were ordered forward across the pontoon bridges, through Fredericksburg, and toward the infamous stone wall on Marye's Heights. When their brigade was ordered to advance, the two regiments to the right of the Mainers did not move, creating a potentially disastrous situation. Colonel Ames dispatched his second-in-command to oversee the threatened right flank, demonstrating his trust in the professor despite this being his first major battle. Chamberlain performed well, with Corporal Holman Melcher noting, "By the prompt and efficient efforts of our brave Lieut. Col. Chamberlain, assisted by the Adjutant, the right wing advanced in good order." Part of those "prompt and efficient efforts" likely included Chamberlain's leadership when some of the men hesitated in taking down a fence line that was impeding their advance. The lieutenant colonel dismounted his horse and moved to undertake the work himself, asking the men, "Do you want me to do it?" They responded immediately, ripping the fence apart and resuming their advance. That Chamberlain handled the right wing on his own competently was to be expected of a lieutenant colonel, but it was also a testament to how far he had come and how much he had learned over the past three months. The hours of study with Colonel Ames showed.[66]

The unit advanced until it became apparent there was no chance of taking the stone wall, at which point the Twentieth Maine hunkered down behind a tiny rise mere yards from the enemy position. In an article written on the fiftieth anniversary of the battle for *Cosmopolitan*, Chamberlain painted a vivid image of his night's repose: "For myself it seemed best to bestow my body between two dead men among the many left there by earlier assaults, and to draw another crosswise for a pillow out of the trampled, blood-soaked sod, pulling the flap of his coat over my face to fend off the chilling winds, and, still more chilling, the deep, many-voiced moan that overspread the field." In the night, Chamberlain was disturbed by a man who lifted the coat flap over his face, peering to see whether the lieutenant colonel was still among the living. Waking in the middle of the night, Chamberlain rose to see what he could do for the regiment's wounded—ultimately finding and bringing water to a number of them. It was during those long hours on the night of December 13, perhaps even more so than during the earlier advance, that Chamberlain exhibited both his mettle and his leadership.[67]

The Twentieth Maine held their line throughout the following day, and what a miserable day it must have been. Chamberlain wrote, "We laid up a breastwork of dead bodies, to cover that exposed flank. . . . We lay there all the long day, hearing the dismal 'thud' of the bullets into the dead flesh of our life-saving bulwarks." They fell back on the night of December 14 but were called into action again the following day and sent to shield the army's withdrawal across the Rappahannock River.[68]

Eventually, the Twentieth Maine escaped across the river without further casualties. Still, Chamberlain was incensed by the poor leadership in the upper levels of the army and what it had cost the Union both in lifeblood and in opportunities lost. As the unit moved to the rear, General Joseph Hooker appeared. In his *Cosmopolitan* article, Chamberlain said that Hooker greeted him by saying, "You've had a hard chance, Colonel; I am glad to see you out of it." Chamberlain was in no mood for pleasantries and responded, "It was chance, General, not much intelligent design there!" Hooker huffed tersely, "God knows I did not put you in!" Chamberlain replied, "That was the trouble, General. You should have put us in. We were handled in piecemeal, on tasking-forks." Hooker, to his credit, did not rebuke this "plain talk" from a man who was three rungs lower on the military hierarchy than he was. Parts of Chamberlain's article on Fredericksburg were sensationalized by the magazine's editors, and it is possible this exchange was fabricated or at least exaggerated. However, in 1864 Chamberlain did question orders from commanding general George Meade that he thought were foolhardy, evincing his unwillingness to blindly send his men into harm's way for no good reason and making the above exchange with Hooker at least possible. If true, such displays must have cemented the bond with any of his men who were within earshot.[69]

A bullet grazed Chamberlain's ear at Fredericksburg, but he suffered no more than that and gained much from the experience. Just days after the battle, Colonel Ames wrote to his parents, "I like my Lieut. Col. very much. He is my best officer." The men felt the same, and in mid-January, Sergeant James Rundlett wrote to his mother, "Lieut. Col. Chamberlain is a fine man and will without doubt be Colonel." The reputation he had so desired was now well established, at least within the regiment.[70]

Rather than resting on his laurels, Chamberlain sought new ways to improve his understanding of military life and the tactics and maneuvers he might need in the future. The Fifth Corps contained many West Point graduates, and in the winter of 1862–1863, Chamberlain convinced a number of them to hold study sessions for officers like himself who lacked formal military background. They covered "all the points pertaining to active duties in the field," and Chamberlain no doubt emerged with an even firmer grasp of his responsibilities.[71]

It was fortunate Chamberlain had his studies, for his relationship with Fanny was under strain. He wrote to a colleague on January 6, "I have not heard from my wife for six weeks at least." He, meanwhile, had written her several letters detailing the Battle of Fredericksburg and the role he played. Having been lauded by his commander and his men for his conduct, he no doubt assumed, or at least hoped, that his wife would be proud. Instead, he heard nothing and wondered "whether you have forgotten me." He signed his letter to her on January 5, "Your Stupid L." He finally received a letter from her on January 11 and claimed, "I ought to be willing to wait seven weeks for a letter such as that." He learned that she had published his letter detailing the Battle of Fredericksburg in the newspaper, a validation of his achievements that was quite meaningful to him. But still, the lack of correspondence was difficult to take and hints at the emotional distance that she felt when they were not in physical proximity.[72]

Chamberlain's belief that he was underappreciated extended from his home life to his professional life. He later wrote, "There was a manifest prejudice against the Fifth Corps at Government Headquarters,—particularly at Stanton's,—on account of the supposed attachment for McClellan and Porter among its members." Things were no better in Maine. In February, Chamberlain secured leave and returned home to visit Fanny and the children. He also met with the new governor, Abner Coburn, but rather than buoying his spirits, that visit did the opposite. On returning to camp, Chamberlain wrote to Maine's highest official recommending promotions for the eleven vacancies that the Twentieth Maine had in the officer corps. He closed, "Hoping that by our continued good conduct your Excellency may have a better opinion of us than you were pleased to express to me, and believing that the good name we hold in the army will before long reach home in the state we honor." The problem was not regarding what the Twentieth Maine or its leaders had done but what they had *not* done. The lack of battle action, combined with the still high death rate due to disease, led some to question the worth of this particular regiment.[73]

Chamberlain, Ames, and the rest of the Twentieth Maine were desperate to prove themselves once the spring campaign season began. Thus, the smallpox outbreak was almost too much to bear. When Ames secured a place on General Meade's staff, Chamberlain was given temporary command of the regiment, but the unit was quarantined and sidelined for the upcoming fight. The former professor was so desperate that, when the battle began, he rode to headquarters and asked to be placed anywhere along the battle line, pleading with his superiors, "If we couldn't do anything else we could give the rebels the small pox." Ultimately, the Twentieth was assigned to guard the telegraph and signal lines, an essential but disappointing posting.[74]

Chamberlain was so downhearted over the lack of action and chances to prove himself that his frustrations nearly boiled over in the aftermath of the Battle of Chancellorsville. He wrote to Fanny, "What would you think, Fanny, of my obtaining the colonelcy of one of the new Regiments to be raised in Maine under the recent Law—the 'conscript' or 'drafted' Regts. Would you leave the <u>old 20th</u>? I declare it makes my heart heavy to think of it." Ames, who had been considered for brigade command six months earlier, had not had the chance to further prove himself—like his regiment—and was still just a colonel. He was frustrated and told Chamberlain that if he did not receive a promotion soon, thereby opening the colonelcy for the professor, Chamberlain should seek command of another unit. But, Chamberlain decided, "I'll see it through one more battle, anyway." Just two weeks later, Colonel Ames's promotion paved the way for Chamberlain's ascent to colonel and command of the Twentieth Maine.[75]

By the time Joshua Chamberlain assumed command of the Twentieth Maine, he was well prepared for his new responsibilities. That preparation did not begin with Chamberlain's enlistment in August 1862; instead, it stretched back nearly to the beginning of his life. August 1862 did not mark a break in Chamberlain's life but an evolution. As Chamberlain would say in 1889, "No man becomes suddenly different than his habit and cherished thought." From his earliest years, Chamberlain had been interested in and a student of military affairs. That interest was partially due to his nature and also likely influenced by his family's past. Chamberlain's dedication to learning and his ability to quickly master novel and complex topics was a mindset and skill that served him in a variety of capacities, from student to professor to military man to, in postwar years, politician, writer, and public figure. Perhaps most important, Chamberlain's basic humanity—including his ability to get along with others, draw them to him, and ultimately convince them to follow him—is the greatest skill any leader can possess. By the time the Civil War began, Chamberlain knew who he was. His title had been professor, but he was a leader of men.

Chamberlian had excelled in every professional endeavor he had undertaken previously, winning competitions and academic promotions at a remarkable pace. He was a man who always held a strong reputation, and he sought the same in the army. But in the army, the greatest factor in building a reputation was performance in combat, and for the Twentieth Maine and Lieutenant Colonel Chamberlain there simply were no major battles in which either could earn laurels. By the spring of 1863, Chamberlain was increasingly desperate for a moment that would allow him to prove his worth and earn a reputation.[76]

That moment would come at Gettysburg, but first Chamberlain faced one of the greatest crises of his life, one that tested all the leadership skills he had amassed thus far and would determine the fate of his regiment.

3

"So clumsily done"

The Second Maine Mutineers

On May 22, 1863, Joshua Chamberlain wrote to his brother John, "We receive the three years men of the 2d Maine tomorrow morning, & that will make us by all odds the best Regt. from Maine."[1] Having been mustered into service for two years on May 28, 1861, the Second Maine was being disbanded, and all original members were sent home to be discharged. Recruits who had joined the regiment after May 28, 1861, however, had signed three-year enlistment contracts and were to be transferred to the Twentieth to fulfill their obligations.

The next morning, Tom Chamberlain noted in the Twentieth Maine's Consolidated Morning Report that "Private Ariel Layton transferred from the 2nd Maine Regt. to Company H." Three days later, the unit "gained by transfer 69 privates from the 2nd Maine." While the numbers were promising and were further bolstered over the following two weeks, it soon became apparent that integrating these men into the Twentieth Maine would not be a simple matter of adding their names to the rolls. On May 27, the day after his transfer, Henry Moore made his feelings known. As Captain Joseph Fitch called for the Second Maine men who had been assigned to his Company D to fall in for duty, Moore began shouting, "Stand out boys! I had as lief [happily] die here as anywhere. Don't do a thing. I will be shot before I'll do another damned thing, if the whole government goes to hell." On the last day in May, Adjutant Chamberlain noted, "31 privates from 2nd Maine under guard for mutiny." In command of the Twentieth Maine for less than two weeks, Chamberlain faced a major crisis that could make or break his unit.[2]

Ultimately, Chamberlain convinced all but a handful of mutineers to drop their protest and join the Twentieth Maine, adding seventy-two battle-hardened men to his unit—men who very well may have made the difference on Little Round Top a month later. The mutiny has been too narrowly understood previously. Its full story—including its causes, Chamberlain's intervention strategies, and the later military service of these men—offers a fascinating window into the volunteers' views of their rights and responsibilities as soldiers, the ways they responded when they felt they were disrespected, and the dynamics of effective small-unit leadership.

Word of the Confederate attack on Fort Sumter on April 12, 1861, and the garrison's surrender the next day, reached Maine on Sunday, April 14. That Monday, President Abraham Lincoln called for troops to support the Union and suppress the rebellion. The president's legal authority to do so came from the Militia Act of 1795, which stated, "Whenever the laws of the United States shall be opposed, or the execution thereof obstructed, in any state, by combinations too powerful to be suppressed by the ordinary course of judicial proceedings . . . it shall be lawful for the President of the United States, to call forth the militia of such state, or of any other state or states, as may be necessary to suppress such combinations." The act did not give Lincoln unlimited power, for it noted that the president could not compel any volunteer to serve for more than three months of a year. A further restriction in 1799 set the maximum size of the provisional army at seventy-five thousand men. Thus, in his proclamation of April 15, 1861, Lincoln was limited to calling for seventy-five thousand men to serve for three months to put down the rebellion. The president asked for one regiment from Maine.[3]

The members of the Maine State Legislature worried that such a call was insufficient given the size of the task at hand—the Confederates, after all, had already called up one hundred thousand men to serve for a year—so a week later they authorized raising ten regiments to serve for a two-year term. Companies then mustering in the Portland area were designed the First Maine, while those near Bangor became the Second Maine. In these early days of crisis, few volunteers were concerned about the exact terms of their contracts. As John Gould of the First Maine later explained, "Our constant fear was that we should never get away from Maine till after the N.Y. and Mass. Militia had suppressed the rebellion. And for this reason no man cared what kind of a roll he signed or what old law he conformed to." Despite some having previously signed rolls enlisting for three months, the men joining the First and Second Maine now signed preprinted "State of Maine" contracts, which noted that they had "Voluntarily Enlisted to serve as a Soldier for the period of two years, unless sooner discharged by proper authority, as a member of the Volunteer Militia of Maine, raised under a requisition from the President of the United States of America."[4]

The Portland companies were slightly ahead of those from the Bangor area and were fully enrolled by April 25. They were officially mustered into federal service on May 3, but at that time the federal government was still operating under Abraham Lincoln's original call for troops, so the First Maine was "accepted by the United States for 'three months from the date.'" The assertion of the Maine State Legislature and Governor Israel Washburn that far more than seventy-five thousand men were needed, and for a longer term than three months, was echoed by many of the North's loyal governors. Thus, on May 3, 1861, President Lincoln called for another eighty-two thousand troops and lengthened the term of service to three years, a measure that could not be made official until Congress convened on July 4 but which he encouraged "all good citizens" to follow immediately. Behind the scenes, Secretary of War Simon Cameron asked that units then forming should change their term of service to reflect the president's new requirement of three-year terms. On May 24, Maine adjutant general John Hodsdon ordered any men from the Third, Fourth, Fifth, or Sixth Maine who did not agree to the new terms to be paid and discharged. The First Maine had already mustered into federal service for three months, so they were left undisturbed.[5]

The Second Maine was already out of the state and on the way to Washington by May 24. Ten days earlier, crowds had gathered in Bangor to send the men off to war in sixteen train cars pulled by three locomotives. In Augusta, Governor Washburn addressed the men before they continued on to Portland. After spending the night in the port town, the train carried them on to Boston on May 15. The steamer *State of Maine* took them from Boston to New York City, where they arrived on May 16. After a parade through the city, the men spent the night on another steamer, awaiting their departure for Washington the next morning. Early on the morning of May 17, doctors discovered that the regiment had an outbreak of measles and ordered the unit quarantined at Willetts Point in Queens to wait for the disease to run its course before proceeding to Washington.[6]

Ultimately, the Second Maine was camped at Willetts Point from May 17 until May 30. The adjutant general's report makes the simple observation that, during this time, "It was mustered into the United States service at Willett's Point May twenty-eighth." In fact, the situation was far more complex than this single sentence indicates. Horace F. Hanson, a private in Company G, later explained, "While in quarantine at Willett's Point a United States officer came to muster us in—May 28th 1861,—but declared he had no authority to muster in men for a less term than three years. Thereupon a large part signed new papers for three years, but a considerable number refused. All started, however, for Washington." It was quite a hodgepodge of enlistments and a situation filled with such opaqueness that future confusion and conflict were almost inevitable.[7]

In the rush to get soldiers where they were needed most, enlistment terms were just one of the many things not yet standardized. Unit size was another area where there was a difference between state and federal standards, and thus the Second Maine left the Pine Tree State with fewer than eight hundred men—far short of the federal standard of roughly one thousand men per regiment. Even before the men arrived in Washington in early June, reinforcements were on the way. On June 3, 1861, seven men were mustered in to join the Second Maine: James Anderson, John Carr, John Driscoll, Samuel Morrison, James Smith, Thomas Townsend, and John Wallace. An additional three men followed later that month and then 107 during July.[8]

Those additional men were desperately needed. Between their mustering in on May 28 and their first battle action on July 21, the unit was further shrunk by twenty-six men who were discharged for disability. One man was discharged after just twenty-eight days in federal service and described as "worthless" in the adjutant general's report—a judgment equally damning on both the individual and the doctor who signed off on his medical examination. The current estimate that perhaps 750 women disguised their identities to serve in the ranks during the Civil War suggests the cursory nature of most medical exams.[9]

What had been a mild need for additional manpower turned into a full-blown crisis after the Battle of Bull Run (or Stone Bridge, as many men called it at the time) on July 21, 1861. The Union had thirty-five thousand soldiers at the battle, with half of them actively participating and twenty-seven hundred becoming casualties. The Second Maine was one of the hardest-hit regiments. With 13 men killed, 24 wounded, and 118 captured, the total casualties of 155 meant the unit suffered the seventh most losses of the thirty Union units actively engaged during the battle. Though the Second Maine fought in another dozen battles over the ensuing twenty-two months, never again did they lose so many men in a single fight. At least one of the recent recruits was not only present at the battle but also taken prisoner by the Confederates. Henry Scribner had joined Company G on July 3 and was not even with the unit three weeks before his capture. He was first sent to Richmond and then transported to Georgia. Scribner was eventually exchanged and later transferred to the Twentieth Maine. At the time of the Battle of Gettysburg, he was on detached duty with the First Ohio Light Artillery. Having served his three years, Scribner was mustered out on July 3, 1864.[10]

In the aftermath of Bull Run, both the Union writ large and the Second Maine in particular were in rough shape. In a letter to Governor Washburn on August 15, 1861, Lieutenant Colonel Charles Roberts bluntly noted, "Since the late disastrous battle at Stone Bridge we have been shamefully treated," and the unit was presently "encamped upon a miserable and unhealthy spot which during a rain is hardly fordable." The previous day, a petition signed by nearly all the regiment's officers laid bare the extent of the problem: "Since the engagement at Stone Bridge, we have been unable to procure Shoes or clothing of any description, while other regiments and those lately organized have been amply supplied."[11]

The allusion in this final passage that the men of the Second felt unfairly treated, compared to the other Maine regiments in the field, was their main frustration. On July 31, 1861, the First Maine left their post in Virginia, marched to the train station in Washington, and began the journey home. They reached Portland on August 3 and were mustered out of federal service just three months after enlisting. Technically these men still owed twenty-one months of military service either within the borders of the state or in another unit, but, as the regimental historian noted, "The State did not, however, press its claims," and less than two hundred men from the unit would join its successor regiment, the Tenth Maine. The chronicler noted they had "to contend with nothing more serious than the measles" during their service.[12]

Both the First and the Second Maine had signed three-month enlistment papers under Lincoln's April 15 call for seventy-five thousand volunteers before agreeing to serve two years at the behest of Governor Washburn. The difference was that the First Maine had been mustered into federal service before leaving Maine at a time when the federal government was still accepting men for only three months, while by the time the Second Maine mustered in at the end of May, the government was now looking for longer commitments and accepted the unit for two—or perhaps three—years. The men of the Second Maine were fuming at this inequity. Officially designated the "Second" Regiment of Maine Volunteers, the men from Bangor had left the state before the lot from Portland—and had played a significant role in the war's first major land battle while the First Maine had remained safely behind in the capital's defenses.[13]

Regimental commander Colonel Charles Jameson had performed heroically at Bull Run, advancing at the head of a group of men to recover the regimental flag when the color bearer fell near Rebel lines. He then led a group of six volunteers through a gauntlet of cannon fire to recover and bring off the field six of the regiment's wounded men and, finally, provided the cover needed for the entire division to safely retreat in the face of Confederate cavalry. It was a shock, therefore, when Jameson announced on the night of August 13 that he was handing in his commission and returning home to attend to personal financial matters.[14]

Jameson's resignation was the final blow. Lieutenant Colonel Charles Roberts reported that, on the morning of August 14, "Much to my Surprise & Sorrow nearly four entire companies together with liberal detachments from others refused longer to do duty. the reason for so doing was that their time of service had expired."[15] The men argued that if the First Maine was being sent home, then they should be as well. At that very moment, the Seventy-Ninth New York was engaged in a similar protest. Brigade officers—including William T. Sherman—threatened execution if the men continued their mutiny, and the majority of the men—but not all—backed down.[16]

A letter written later that day and signed by nearly every officer in the Second Maine asked authorities to send the unit home. The petitioners explained, "In consequence of a misconstruction long existing in the regiment in regards to their term of service, fifty eight privates, and four non-commissioned officers, have this day refused duty, and in consequence of said disobedience, have by order of General Scott Commander in-chief, been sent to the 'Dry Tortugas' in the Gulf of Mexico, on 'detached service' there to serve until the Government deems it expedient to transfer them Northwards." These mutineers were taken to Fortress Monroe in Virginia to await transport to Fort Jefferson on Dry Tortugas—a remote island less than a quarter square mile in size located more than fifty miles west of Key West, where the Union army sent its worst prisoners. Ultimately, the men were not sent to Tortugas but, in early October, were transferred to the Second New York Infantry, a garrison regiment stationed at Fortress Monroe. The men served with that unit until August 1862, when the survivors were transferred back to the Second Maine.[17]

The men who had dropped their mutiny slowly found the situation improving. George McClellan had taken command of the army after the debacle at Bull Run, and he quickly brought structure to the army's training regime and supply system, ensuring that the men were well fed and clothed. On August 26, Samuel Hoskins wrote Governor Washburn, "Men are better contented—everything looks better."[18]

There had now been two dustups—one turned full-on mutiny—over the service terms for these men in the Second Maine. The worst was yet to come.

Second Maine, Christmas 1861 (Photo by Matthew Brady; National Archives)

On January 30, 1863, Quartermaster Sergeant Samuel Nash wrote to Maine adjutant general John Hodsdon asking for "a duplicate of my enlistment form." Private Harrison Gould of Company A made the same request ten days later. Both men had been original members of the unit mustered into state service on May 2 and had then been a part of the group that signed three-year papers on Willetts Point ahead of their muster into federal service on May 28, 1861. Clearly, they were anxious over their situation. Two months later, Gould still had not received any information and took time while home on furlough in Bangor to renew his request. It does not appear that he ever received an answer to his queries.[19]

By mid-March, the regiment was wild with rumors. Leonard Carver of Company D wrote, "We hear the government intends to keep our Regt. another year: Many of the men are regularly enlisted but for Two years and any attempt to keep them longer will cause trouble. I am enlisted but for Two years; yet I intend to stay until the war is ended. Many of the men are anxious to get home this spring, and there is continual uproar about it." In fact, Carver was enlisted for three years, whether or not he was fully aware of it at the time. The enterprising corporal sought a promotion to the officer ranks and a position in a U.S. Colored Troops unit, noting, "I am tired of fighting in a political army, for this or that political General. I want to get from politics to principles. Then I can fight with a whole heart." Ultimately, Carver was denied a promotion, mustered out with the unit on June 9, 1863, and did not reenlist. Perhaps the mishandling of the situation soured him on further service, or perhaps he had sought a promotion only to gain officers' status so he could freely resign and not be subject to a particular enlistment term.[20]

More letters from the unit followed, and on April 1, 1863, Colonel George Varney wrote to Hodsdon inquiring whether state officials had decided how to handle the regiment's term of service. He noted, "There seems to be an impression among the officers + men that the whole regiment will be mustered out of service at the expiration of two years." Varney warned, "The time is so near at hand that it is quite important that the matter should be settled. I have not forgotten the affair at Fort Corcoran in August 1861, and do not wish it repeated."[21]

Toward the end of the month, another layer of complexity emerged. In addition to the confusion over whether the original members of the unit would all be allowed to go home the following month or would all be held to another year of service, or whether those who had refused to sign three-year enlistments on Willetts Point be allowed to return home while those who did sign the papers had to remain for an additional year, there now arose the question regarding the fate of the unit's later recruits. On April 22, Lieutenant George Brown, commander of Company B, wrote to Governor Abner Coburn:

I respectfully refer to you for information concerning Sergt. Kennedy Steward, and Privates Samuel Morrison, James Anderson, and Thomas Townsend of my Co. who claim to be enlisted for two years only. They were enlisted at Houlton June 3rd by one Capt. Freese, and joined co. I of this Regt. as recruits and were transferred to my Co. Dec. 23rd 1861 Their Description lists were lost in Co. I consequently they have nothing to show. Their names were entered in the Muster Rolls as enlisted for 3 years as it was supposed that no men were enlisted at that date for a shorter period. They claim to have been enlisted for the 7th Maine but were not accepted as they were enlisted for 3 years then they volunteered to come into this Regt. If you can furnish a true statement of their case it will enable me to do the right thing by them, for they are excellent soldiers and only ask that justice may be done them.[22]

Abner Coburn (Maine State Archives)

The governor did not respond in written fashion, but he did visit the regiment in the field just a few days later. Watching from afar, Sergeant James Rundlett of the Twentieth Maine observed on April 26, "[Governor Abner Coburn] visited the 2d Me today, three of their Co. stacked arms yesterday, and refused duty because their time was out. The Gen told them to be good boys and he would let them off as soon as he could get transportation. This set things all right." It was exactly two years earlier, on April 25, 1861, when the unit had been mustered into state service for two years, leading many men to feel their commitments expired on the very day the governor visited. Rundlett likely overestimated the calming effect of the words Coburn offered the Second Maine men, for the next day William T. Livermore of the Twentieth Maine recorded that "they looked rather Sober." The lack of clarity must have been galling, particularly as they watched the Thirteenth New York of their brigade depart their camps on April 28 and begin the journey home.[23]

As the Thirteenth New York headed home, the Second Maine tramped toward another battle. On April 27, the entire Fifth Corps (including the Second and Twentieth Maine) moved out on a march that culminated in the Battle of Chancellorsville. Years later, one member of the unit, James Bacon, remembered, "As it was rumored that there was to be a general advance on the enemy, rather than to refuse duty on the eve of battle, every man that was able to march went into the fight." The men of the Second Maine must have feared becoming casualties in their unit's last significant action, but ultimately they were not heavily engaged in Robert E. Lee's signature victory. Stonewall Jackson's famous flank march that sealed the victory came on May 2, two years to the day after the regiment was mustered into state service. Some of the men, their nerves no doubt on edge after the battle that turned sixteen thousand of their comrades into casualties, felt that May 2 should have marked the end of their service.[24]

On May 8, Company A commander Lieutenant James Dean noticed that his company was short at morning muster. Soon came the intelligence that an entire tentful of men was refusing duty: James Bacon, Nehemiah Doe, Stephen Fowler, William Fowler, Charles H. Plummer, and Lewis Snow. Going to the men, Dean inquired, "Boys why don't you fall in are you not able to march[?]" Consciously or not, Dean had

Lieutenant James Dean and five men of the Second Maine who mutinied in early May 1863 (Collections of the Bangor Historical Society)

offered the men an easy out—the chance to claim that physical infirmity prevented them from doing their duty. But the men were fed up and had the courage to speak the truth, saying, "We consider our time out." Dean later alleged that Stephen Fowler added, "We shant do any more duty." Dean conferred with Colonel Varney and then returned, took the names of the six men, and placed them under arrest.[25]

In drafting court-martial charges against the men, Colonel Varney noted that they "did on the morning of May 8 1863 join in a mutiny to resist the orders of the War Department and to disobey the lawful commands of [their] commd'g officer." Specifically, each man "resist[ed] and refuse[d] to fall into the ranks of his company when ordered to do so by his commanding officer Lieut. James Dean, his Regt and company then being under orders to march toward the enemy." Varney reported that each man claimed "he had done all the duty he should do in the Regt."[26]

During his court-martial proceedings ten days later, James Bacon pleaded not guilty to all charges and offered a spirited defense of his actions centering on the intricacies of the differing dates when he had enlisted, had been mustered into state service, and finally had been accepted for federal service. After hearing the charges against him and Lieutenant Dean's description of what had happened on the morning of May 8, Bacon opened his defense by asking, "What time does the term of my enlistment expire?" Dean responded, "All I know about it is the decision of the War Dept which is that it expires on the 28t of May the enlistment was on April 25t and the muster on May 28t 1861 for two years." Bacon followed up with a perceptive question that got to the heart of the matter: "Was the muster on the 28t of May 1861 for two years or three years and was it a legal muster." Dean responded, "The original muster was for two and three years—as to its legality I cannot answer." Even at this late date, just two days before the original members of the unit began the journey home, the regiment's officers were still unable to provide their men with clarity over the enlistment term.[27]

In his formal statement, Bacon noted, "I enlisted on the 25t of April 1861 for two years. The last company was assigned and mustered into the state service on the 2d day of May 1861. The orders of the War Dept that were read to us stated that the term of service of the Regt expired on the date that the last company was mustered in being the 2d day of May and what I claim is that if the muster on the 28t of May was a legal muster it was for two years instead of three that being the time stated in the muster."[28]

In his trial, William Fowler also pleaded not guilty to all charges. Fowler was a minor when he volunteered in 1861 and thus had required his father's approval to enlist. At his court-martial, "The accused also shared to the court an affidavit from his father stating that he had consented that his son who is a minor might serve the Government for two years from the 25 day of April 1861 and no longer." Fowler likewise claimed that an order had been read to the regiment noting that May 2 marked the expiration of their term of service but that he had not raised his objections on that day because his regiment was in line of battle at Chancellorsville and he had been willing to do his part. Having first made the legal argument for his position, Fowler also looked to add another line of defense, asking Lieutenant Dean, "Did I not give as a reason for not marching that I was unable to march." Dean replied, "Not before [you] were under arrest that I remember."[29]

In their defenses, Nehemiah Doe, Stephen Fowler, Charles H. Plummer, and Lewis Snow all claimed that when Lieutenant Dean asked for their names, they thought he was putting them on a list of men physically unable to do duty that day rather than being categorized as refusing to do duty. At the time of the incident, Dean testified, Fowler had said he was refusing duty because his term of service had expired, but eleven days later he had changed his story.[30] Caught up in the moment, Nehemiah Doe, the Fowler brothers, and Lewis Snow had all refused to do duty on May 8 but backed off—in some cases within a matter of minutes—and claimed that physical disability was at the root of their absence that morning. James Bacon, however, made the ideological argument from beginning to end.[31]

Despite these differing defenses, all six men faced the same punishment: guilty on nearly all the charges, with the punishment being to forfeit either six months' pay or all pay due plus any allowances and to be dishonorably discharged. The one charge thrown out—likely because there was confusion and contradiction over who may have uttered it—was the attribution of the specific statement, "He had done all the duty he should in the Regt."[32]

This second mutiny in the Second Maine, following the one at Fort Corcoran in August 1861, had only muddied the waters further. James Bacon's question of Lieutenant Dean and the court-martial board had hit the nail on the head and, in doing so, had surfaced the lingering anxiety men in the Second Maine faced: "Was the muster on the 28t of May 1861 for two years or three years and was it a legal muster."[33]

A week before the court-martials, William Owen of the Twentieth Maine wrote home to his sister Abbie, "I suppose the 2nd Maine will go home this month. . . . There was a Reg't went down to the cars today on their way home. They felt pretty well I can tell you. They will be going home every day for some time. Four or five have already gone. What we are to do after they are gone is more than I can tell. But I presume we can do as well as we have done yet." Will Owen was not the only one worried about the impact the expiring enlistments would have on those who remained in the field: Army commander Major General Joseph Hooker was at that very moment grappling with the broader implications of the question.[34]

In May and June 1863, the army faced the challenge of losing nearly sixteen thousand men who had enlisted in 1861 for two-year terms or had joined the previous fall for a shortened period of just nine months. From the division the Second and Twentieth Maine belonged to, the 122nd Pennsylvania, Twelfth New York, Fourteenth New York, and Seventeenth New York would all see their terms expire and those units disbanded. Those losses were substantial and presented a real threat to the army's manpower just as the spring campaigning season was getting underway. Desperate to keep hold of any men they could, the government decided that any later recruits to these units who still had time to run on their enlistments would be transferred to other regiments to serve those obligations. In the Twentieth Maine's brigade, the Twelfth and Seventeenth New York were disbanded between mid-May and early June, with the three-year men transferred elsewhere to finish their terms.[35]

Not that it would have eased their frustrations, but the men of the Second Maine were not unique in their predicament. On May 16, William T. Livermore noted in his diary, "The 25 NY were glad to take Arms after being under Guard one week with little or nothing to eat." Facing a situation analogous to that of the Second Maine, that unit had been organized in New York on May 10, 1861, but not mustered into federal service until June 28, 1861, for a term of two years. It appears many of the men—similar to the six from the Second Maine who had refused duty on May 8—felt they should not have to serve past that early May date.[36]

The army's final decision for the Second Maine was that any man mustered into federal service on May 28, 1861, at Willetts Point was allowed to return home regardless of whether he had stuck to his initial two-year enlistment or had signed three-year papers. Recruits who had joined the regiment after that date, however, owed the entire three years. The seven men who enlisted on June 3, 1861, missed six days of service and, consequently, would give up another year of their life serving in the army. Some of these "later" recruits had joined the regiment early enough to participate in the First Battle of Bull Run, just like the "original" members of the unit. From the perspective of the three-year recruits, had all those who headed for Maine on May 20 been two-year enlistees, that might have been one thing, but the fact that many of those men were also known to have signed three-year enlistments made it all feel arbitrary and disrespectful of the service they had already done.

On May 18, Livermore noted that he and some of his comrades from Company B went to the camp of the Second Maine to visit. "Had a fine time," he wrote, further observing, "The 2 years Men feel well but the recruits feel bad." Livermore and many men in the Twentieth returned the following night "to See the Boys for the last time in VA found them in good Spirits Staid with them until 10 ½ in the eve then returned to camp and turned in." Nathan Clark, William Lamson, William Owen, Holman Melcher, and William T. Livermore all commented on the Second Maine's departure the following morning. Livermore offered the fullest description of the scene: "At 6 oclock we heard the beating of drums and on looking out Saw the 2nd Escorted by the 18 + 22 Mass Marching past us towards Stonemans Switch unexpectedly our Bugle Sounded to fall in and our Regt fell in before eating breakfast and Marched to the Switch where we Stacked Arms and went and Shook hands with the Boys feeling glad for themb that they are on there way home But Still feel Sad to part with themb We cheered themb and received hearty cheers and Tigers in return til they left." Melcher noted, "Yesterday the old 2nd Maine went, all but a handful of them. The 2nd are noble men, men that have fought for their country's rights in every battle from the 1st Bull Run till the 2nd Fredericksburg."[37]

Melcher must have had large hands, for the "handful" of men left behind numbered more than one hundred and made up nearly one-third of the total size of the Second Maine that morning. What exactly was to become of them was as yet unclear. When the Twelfth, Fourteenth, and Seventeenth New York had been disbanded, their recruits were transferred to the other New York unit in the division, the Forty-Fourth. It was as good a guess as any that the men from the Second Maine would be transferred to the only other Maine regiment in the division, the Twentieth, but nothing was official yet.

By May 22, the Second Maine recruits still had no idea of their ultimate fate. Frank L. Grindle, who had enlisted in October 1861 alongside two family members to join four others already in the unit, appealed directly to leaders back in Maine who he hoped had the governor's ear:

Camp Varney May 22d '63

Mr. Wilson. Dear Sir. Knowing you as one who takes some interest in soldiers affairs I will let you know just how we are situated and as we have no chance to speak for ourselves perhaps you will see that a fair statement of the case is given to Governor Coburn. as you enlisted me of course you will wonder why I wish to be discharged before my 3 years term is expired. simply because I enlisted to serve in the 2nd Me. and as there is no such Regt. in the field, I have reasons for thinking myself entitled to a discharge. The officers in our Regt. appeared to be doing all they could before they left for our good but since circumstances have come to light that show a concerted scheme to keep us in the service if possible. orders were rec at regimental headquarters and not read to us because they ordered that when a reg was mustered out the entire Reg was included. another very poor mean trick was the way in which they left us. the old members were ordered into line and marched away and no officer gave a parting word to us. we number 118 most of which have been in all the reg has seen except the 1st Bull Run. we were left without arms, guard, officers, or rations, and have had none appointed since. of our own number we have appointed one to take charge, and we have set a guard.

Gen. Barnes has sent word to us that he shall transfer 70 into the 3d Mass Battery and if we don't mind what he says and be good he will have us all court martialed and sent to the 20th Me. The men have been very quiet so far but we consider all this as humbug and are anxious to have our case represented in the right light, and to the proper authorities. if you will use what means appear to you the most efficient you will have our thanks and I am authorized to say that any expense you may incur will be paid by the members of Co. B.

F. L. Grindle[38]

There is much to draw from this letter. First, the change in governors complicated everything. Abner Coburn was new to the seat and unaware of any promises or deals his predecessor, Israel Washburn, might have authorized recruiters to make on his behalf. Second, the men's frustrations with their officers went far beyond the enlistment contracts. If anything, General James Barnes, their brigade commander, had added to those feelings. Initially holding out the carrot of a potential transfer to the Third Massachusetts Battery—a less dangerous branch than the infantry—he ultimately made them feel as though a transfer to another Maine infantry unit was a punishment. Finally, despite all this, the men were reasonably petitioning the governor, asking for redress. There was no sign of a mutiny, but what happened next would be critical to the ultimate resolution of this situation.[39]

J. B. Wilson passed the letter on to Governor Coburn, but by the time he did so, ten days had elapsed, and it does not appear that the governor took any action on behalf of the mutineers. For better or worse, the army had finally decided what to do with these men, for on May 22, Joshua Chamberlain wrote home, "We receive the three years men of the 2d Maine tomorrow morning, & that will make us by all odds the best Regt. from Maine." Things would not be nearly so smooth. When notified that they were to be transferred to the Twentieth Maine—signaling that no time would be allowed for them to hear from their governor—the men of the Second Maine refused to go. If the governor had shown the men the respect of a return letter, they might have acceded peacefully; however, the lack of a response was galling, and they refused to be treated so poorly. In military terms, the refusal to follow a superior officer's orders is classified as a "mutiny," making this the third mutiny for the Second Maine in the two years of its existence.[40]

Pennsylvanian George Gordon Meade was the commander of the Fifth Corps and not a man to accept a challenge to his own authority. The 118th Pennsylvania was ordered to load their weapons, fix bayonets, and forcibly move the mutineers to the Twentieth Maine's campsite. On May 23, William T. Livermore observed, "The recruits from the 2nd Maine Came in to day A few volunteered But nearly all were marched under a Strong Guard of the 118 Penn with loaded Rifles." Samuel Keene noted that the men were "rather mutinous." Along with the mutineers came orders from General Meade instructing Chamberlain "to draw up my Regt and fire on them if they refused to do duty."[41]

In charge of the unit for just three days, Chamberlain must have known that his future as the leader of this unit hinged on this very moment. Too much leeway with the mutineers was unlikely to get them to recommit to the organization and—perhaps of even more consequence—might upset the men of the Twentieth Maine if they perceived a double standard was in play. However, threatening mass execution might have the same effect. In an attempt to untie his hands, Chamberlain "immediately rode to Genl Meade + got permission to manage the men in my own way." The corps commander was willing to offer latitude on the methodology Chamberlain employed as long as the result was an end to the mutiny.[42]

As he later recollected, Chamberlain "called [the mutineers] together and pointed out to them the situation: that they could not be entertained as civilian guests by me; that they were by authority of the United States on my rolls as soldiers, and I should treat them as soldiers should be treated; that they should lose no rights by obeying orders, and I would see what could be done for their claim." Having treated the men with respect and promised them soldierly treatment, Chamberlain immediately followed through. "I then took off all guard, supplied them with food, which had not been issued to them for three days—assigned them to companies without giving them any specific orders whatever expecting them to be treated + to behave, like other soldiers." By assigning the mutineers to various companies, Chamberlain's intent was "to break up the 'esprit de corps' of banded mutineers"—a sound tactic.[43]

On May 25, Colonel Chamberlain wrote directly to Governor Coburn about their status:

There is another matter, Governor, about which I wish to have a word with you. The transfer of the "three years men" of the 2d Maine has been so clumsily done, that the men were allowed to grow quite mutinous—left uncared for in their old camp after the 2d had gone for several days + having time + provocation to work themselves up to such a pitch of mutiny that Gen. Barnes had to send them to me as prisoners, liable to severe penalties for disobedience to his orders. You are aware, Governor, that promises were made to induce these men to enlist, which are not now kept, + I must say that I sympathize with them in their view of the case. Assured as they were that they would be mustered out with the 2d, they cannot but feel that they are falsely dealt with in being retained + sent to duty in other Reg'ts. They need to be managed with

great care + skill; but I fear that some of them will get into trouble for
disobedience of orders or mutiny. My orders are to take them + put them
on duty which they have already refused to Gen. Barnes + others. I shall
carry out any orders whatever may be the consequence; but I sincerely
wish these men were fairly dealt with by those who made their promises.
All their papers say they are enlisted for three years just as the men of this
regiment are, + for us in the field there is no other way but to hold them
to it. What you may be able to do for them I do not know.

Several things about this letter are striking. First and foremost, Chamberlain's empathy—a phrase that did not officially enter army doctrine until 2011—put him in a good position to solve this dilemma. Second, the section on the mutineers appears halfway down the second page of the letter and takes up a total of one and a half pages of the four-page letter. Chamberlain's first topic, and therefore presumably his bigger priority, was finding a replacement for the recently resigned regimental surgeon Nahum Monroe. The final page mostly concerns the regiment's actions during the Battle of Chancellorsville. The relative placement of Chamberlain's missive on the mutineers is a reminder that he had many other things to deal with as a newly minted regimental commander and that the 707 men of the unit—of whom 516 were present—who were there before the mutineers arrived demanded as much or more of his attention than these new additions. Lastly, despite this letter and another one on May 27, the governor offered Chamberlain no guidance. It was up to him to find a solution.[44]

The next day, May 26, was a sliding-doors moment. Nearly seven hundred miles to the north, the original members of the Second Maine were now, via steamship, reaching their home. At 4:00 a.m., they arrived in Bucksport, Maine, a dozen miles downriver from Bangor, where they were met by their former colonel carrying the unit's original flags. After the ship coaled, it continued to Bangor, arriving around 10:00 a.m. at the steamboat wharf, where "cannon announced their arrival and people rushed in crowds" to welcome the soldiers home. "The regiment disembarked, and escorted by militia and engine companies with bands of music, marched to Broadway where an immense throng had assembled, filling the entire square. . . . All along the line the buildings were decorated, flags flying, and the shipping had put on its best suite." After a bountiful meal, a half dozen prominent men made speeches, including Adjutant General John Hodsdon, former governor Israel Washburn, and U.S. Vice President Hannibal Hamlin. It was a fitting celebration to mark the end of the Second Maine, but the controversy was not over, even for those lucky enough to be in Maine rather than Virginia on this particular day. While the men who had only ever signed two-year enlistments were all mustered out on June 4, 1863, the authorities were initially unsure what to do with those who had signed three-year papers at Willetts Point. Eventually, after an additional wait of five days, they, too, were mustered out.[45]

To the men in Virginia, a delay of five days would have been a welcome alternative to their fate. On May 26, the same day that the original members of the Second Maine were feted with food and speeches in Bangor, Adjutant Tom Chamberlain noted that the Twentieth "gained by transfer 69 privates from the 2nd Maine." With the men officially on the regimental rolls, it was time to get them integrated into the unit. That night, Joshua Chamberlain drafted the following circular to be distributed to each of his company commanders:

> *Hd. Qrs. 20th Maine*
> *May 26, 1863*
> *Circular*
> *The men transferred from the 2nd Maine for whose equipment has been provided will be required by the commanders to whom they have been assigned to appear on company drill tomorrow morning. Company commanders will take care to have their orders legal + military in all cases. If refusal or disobedience, to have full + proper evidence of the same, they may use their own discretion as to the manner in which they enforce their authority.*
> *No man who disobeys must go unpunished. At <u>the very least</u> every such man will be arrested + confined + charges made out against him without delay. Should any violence occur care will be to injure none but the guilty.*
> *By order of Col. Chamberlain*

This short order offers significant insights into Chamberlain's leadership style and the reasons why he was so effective. The first critical piece is that Chamberlain set guardrails in terms of his expectations of what needed to happen but then let his subordinates determine how exactly "they enforce their authority." Rather than micromanage his company commanders, Chamberlain gave them the same latitude to find solutions that he had requested from General Meade. Second, having already extended the velvet glove to these mutineers, Chamberlain also held up the iron fist. The Twentieth Maine, the Army of the Potomac, and the United States Army writ large all had standards to which the men had to adhere. If they could not be persuaded to do so, they would have to be compelled.[46]

That next morning, around two-thirds of the men relented and picked up their weapons, but not all. One private assigned to Company C, Henry Moore, was so incensed by affairs that, on seeing Captain Joseph Fitch of Company D "endeavoring to bring to duty certain privates recently assigned to his company from the 2d Maine Volunteers," he stalked over to the group and shouted, "Stand out boys! I had as lief [happily] die here as anywhere. Don't do a thing. I will be shot before I'll do another damned thing, if the whole Government goes to hell."[47]

Remarkably, Moore was not immediately arrested and confined following this outburst, for the next morning, May 28, he failed to report for morning roll call and then rebuffed a request by his company commander, Charles Billings, to take up his weapon and go on duty. Not content with a subdued protest, Moore "did absolutely refuse to obey, muttering and murmuring and using violent language against the authority of his commanding officers; and did, by his example and influence, excite other members of his company to disobedience, saying, 'I'll never take a gun in the United States service again; I will be shot first; my term of service is out.'" Moore continued, "The United States treats their soldiers worse than the rebels, and I would rather serve under the laws of the rebels; if I was clear of the service, I would not stay under the protection of the flag six weeks." When another private assigned to Company C, George Mills, consented to return to duty, Moore spat that he was a "damned fool."[48]

Henry Moore had joined the Second Maine in September 1861 due to the recruiting efforts of Lieutenant James Dean. The recruit had been born in Canaan, Maine, on November 11, 1836. Sometime in the 1850s, the Moore family—comprising father Joseph, mother Phebe, and six additional siblings—made the roughly fifty-mile move to Bangor.

The 1860 census listed Henry Moore as literate, living at home with his parents, and working as a lumberman. The family was not wealthy, with Joseph's real estate holdings assessed at $1,000 and his personal property at $100. His military records variously list Henry as a lumberman and a cooper, the latter being the profession of his father and oldest brother, so he may have alternated between working in the woods and in the family business.[49]

Moore indicated some receptiveness to enlisting but told Dean that he could not enlist for the standard three-year term because he had a sick mother and brother at home and could not be gone for that long. Dean "assured me that if I would enlist for the 2d Maine, that my time of service would expire when that of said Regiment did + that I should then be mustered out," Moore recollected. Dean assured Moore that he was authorized to make such a promise by the highest authority in that state: "Lieutenant Dean also said that he had authority from Gov. Washburn to say to men who he enlisted that they would be held no longer than the Regiment remained in service." Though that seemed like a firm promise, Moore sought counsel from two other community leaders: "I also talked with Genl. Samuel P. Strickland and with William Boyd of the Custom House, and both urged me to enlist and assured me that my term of service would expire with the regiment." With those caveats in place, Moore enlisted on September 9 and was mustered into federal service a month later for three years, though of course he did not anticipate serving that long. He was never absent from the Second Maine, but his files reveal a series of medical incidents during his service.[50]

Just a month after he was mustered in, Moore "was taken with Black Measles at Halls Hill, Va. In Nov 1861. I had some come in my ears as soon afterwards I commenced to do duty and was troubled with dizziness and have been so bad that I would fall down from the dizzy spells while in the army." In August 1862, he contracted diarrhea and piles (hemorrhoids) while near Harrison's Landing in the aftermath of the Peninsula Campaign. Then, at the Battle of Fredericksburg, Moore was wounded by cannon fire:

I was wounded by an exploding shell in the side or back near the heart. The pieces of shell did not enter my breast but bruised my side very much and I bled some from the wound at the time and the injured parts became very much swollen. They puffed up the size of my double fists. The shell knocked me down and I was taken from the field. I was carried off the field at the time. I was treated by Dr. Samuel B. Morrison our regimental surgeon for this wound. He dressed the wound several times. He treated me in the regimental hospital and in my quarters for this wound. I was sick and excused from duty by the Regimental doctor from the effects of this wound all the rest of that winter and as such did but little duty until after we were transferred to the 20th ME vols in May 1863. The effects of the wound were then and have been ever since a sort of heart trouble which affects my breathing.

He later noted a second wound during his service with the Second Maine, but it must have been slight, as it is not in his official military records.[51]

It is not hard to see why Moore felt betrayed. Having suffered through severe illness and battle wounds, Moore had likely long looked forward to his assumed return to Maine in May 1863, only to be told at the last minute that he owed another year and a half of service. If anyone knew what trials and tribulations could come in that amount of time, it was Henry Moore. It is no wonder that he refused to accept his situation quietly.

Moore's experiences with disease and sickness were not unprecedented among these mutineers. Of the men transferred to the Twentieth Maine, thirty-two had already been wounded—some multiple times. Another eleven had been captured and made prisoners of war, a particularly harrowing experience. Additionally, 139 men in the Second Maine had died (of disease or battle injury) during the previous two years, nearly 11 percent of the total number of men in the unit. These men had already suffered a great deal and would have anticipated more of the same during the additional service time now required of them. As it turned out, they would pay a far higher cost than their previous service foreshadowed. Of those transferred to the Twentieth Maine, at least twenty-seven would be wounded, eight captured by the Confederates, and eighteen would not survive the war. Eight of the wounded were hit by a bullet a second time, with that second injury proving fatal in two cases.

Moore was not alone in expressing his discontent. Benjamin Coombs had also been in Company D of the Second Maine, like Moore, and was also in Company C of the Twentieth Maine. When Company C commander Charles Billings told Coombs to get his gun and equipment and fall in for duty, Coombs replied, "I will never carry a gun again in the service of the United States." In describing the incident, Adjutant Tom Chamberlain noted that "there being at that time a combination to resist lawful authority," Coombs was "thus joining in a mutiny."[52]

Between May 27 and May 29, there were several incidents, such as those instigated by Moore and Coombs, that Chamberlain handled at the regimental level without referring them to a court-martial board. On May 27, Chamberlain wrote to Governor Coburn again, noting, "The men of the '2d' are quite unhappy; still feeling that great injustice has been done them in holding them to service longer. I have taken a liberal course with them because they are nearly all good + true men, but I shall be obliged to carry a firm hand. They are now ordered on duty, + their orders must be carried out." Likely referencing Frank Grindle's earlier letter, Chamberlain continued, "They are expecting to hear from you in reply to a communication of theirs + their expectation of this keeps them in an undecided state of mind as to doing duty." In clearly explaining his way forward, Chamberlain said, "I sympathize with the men, but while under my orders, they will be strictly held to obedience."[53]

On May 30, things came to a head. For the third time in four days, Henry Moore interfered with the attempts of the Twentieth's officers to get other mutineers to rejoin the ranks. This time, it was Company A, and Moore "did, by his actions and language, encourage and excite the said privates of company A to resist the efforts and authority of Lieutenant Besse." Over in Company E, Thomas Townsend bluntly told Captain Clark, "I won't do duty," and "by his example and influence did join in and encourage a mutiny." Chamberlain ordered the arrest of anyone who had refused duty, with Adjutant Tom Chamberlain noting on the day's report, "26 privates transferred from 2nd Maine under arrest." Those arrested included six men in Company A, four in Company C, five in Company D, three in Company E, five in Company F, and three in Company I. Henry Moore's case was the most extreme, and the commander drew up court-martial charges against him the following day.[54]

In a remarkable letter home to his father on May 31, Captain Charles Billings of Company C offered an overview of the mutiny and unique insights into Henry Moore—a man, it turns out, he had known before the war.

> *We received last Monday about 90 men from the 2nd Me who have been transferred to the Regt., most of them are opposed to serving any longer as they were promised that they should go home with the Regt. about half of them came under guard and 30 or more are now under arrest for refusing to do duty. They will be courtmartialed or a part at least soon as an example to the balance. eleven were assigned to my co. 1 sargt. 2 corps. & 8 privates the three first were willing to do duty, three of the others have gone on since though unwilling at first and 4 are under arrest one absent without leave, but I understand he is about here. I believe they ought to go home if as they say they were promised so. many have been here nearly two years and do not feeling like coming into any other regt. one of the worst ones is a grandson of Miller Moor of Canaan. His name is Henry M. Moore and he has been a rover most of his days from Hudson Bay & red river of the north three years with the Chepewa Indians run rafts on the Mississippi etc. etc. cares for nothing, he will be tried among the first as he has used his power to keep others from doing duty, it will go hard with him.*[55]

Billings was correct that Moore would be the first—and, it turned out, the only—mutineer to be tried. On June 3, William T. Livermore noted, "Moore one of the 2nd Maine Recruits that was assigned to Co. C + the ringleader of those that Stood out was Courtmartialed to day he was marched 10 miles to the C.M.L. By C. C. Durgin and one Private with Rifles loaded and Caped and orders to Shoot him if he Attempted to escape." Due to his various outbursts, Moore faced three charges:

Charge I: "Violation of the 7th Article of War."
Charge II: "Disobedience of orders."
Charge III: "Insubordination; conduct to the prejudices of good order and military discipline."

The seventh Article of War stated, "Any officer or soldier who shall begin, excite, cause or join in, any mutiny or sedition in any troop or company in the service of the United States, or in any party, post, detachment, or guard shall suffer death, or such other punishment as by a court martial shall be inflicted."[56]

Under each charge were two or three "specifications" detailing the particular incidents giving rise to the accusation. Moore pleaded not guilty to all aspects of the first charge accusing him of trying to incite others to refuse to do their duty. For the second charge of disobedience of orders, Moore denied that he had refused a request by his sergeant to fall in for morning roll call on May 28 but admitted that he had not followed Captain Billings's orders to pick up his weapon and join the ranks. To the overall charge, he pleaded not guilty. Finally, to the third charge of "insubordination; conduct to the prejudice of good order and military discipline," Moore admitted to personally voicing opposition to further service but denied the charge that he had encouraged others to do so. He pleaded guilty to the overall charge.[57]

Of the seven examples of poor conduct outlined in the court-martial charges, Moore admitted to nearly all the incidents of personal statements or actions of dissent but uniformly denied that he had tried to incite others to disobedience or munity. This was undoubtedly a wise course, as the explicit punishment for such actions was death. The men previously tried for refusing duty on May 8 had all been accused of personal action, not of trying to encourage others to join them, and thus had escaped with relatively light punishments. Moore was not so lucky.[58]

Though finding Moore not guilty of the specification that he had refused his sergeant's order to report for morning roll call on May 28, the board found him guilty of all three charges. Their hands tied given the finding that Moore had violated the seventh Article of War and incited others to mutiny, the board sentenced Moore "To be shot to death by musketry, at such time and place as the General commanding the Army shall order and direct; two-thirds of the members concurring therein."[59]

After his conviction, Moore was returned to his unit to await execution. No doubt within a few hours the whole unit knew his fate, and it seems to have had the desired impact of discouraging such actions, for June 3 marked the peak of the mutiny with thirty-two men under arrest. By the time the next morning report was taken four days later, the number of men under arrest had dropped precipitously from thirty-two to fifteen and decreased to eleven by June 13. Some of that decrease may have simply been the passage of time and the subsequent cooling off during the week since most of these men had initially been placed under arrest. Some may have also been due to their treatment at the hands of Chamberlain, the company commanders, and the mutineers' new comrades in arms in the Twentieth Maine. John O'Connell, a former Second Maine man who had also been assigned to Company C with Henry Moore and Benjamin Coombs, later noted, "Though not liking the Regt at first we got around all right owing to the Disposition of Col. Chamberlain and the officers of the Regt. to treat us well." Edwin Witherell was more effusive in his praise of his new commander:

I was transferred to his regiment from the 2d Maine the last of May 1863 under circumstances which made it hard for those who were put in a strange regiment and it was there that those men transferred came to learn the sterling qualities of this man. He seemed to feel with us the unpleasant features that were ours as we were placed in different companies among new faces, and he—from what I have since learned—urged upon the officers and men of his command to show us that we were to be received with all consideration and shown all due courtesy, which soon won from us the devotion and love which increased with the months and years that we were under him.

In a word, Chamberlain treated these new men with respect and demanded that those around him do so as well. In addition to Chamberlain's impact, the preexisting relationships between the men of these two units undoubtedly played a role the longer the disgruntled men were around their old acquaintances and friends from the Twentieth Maine. Samuel Veazie had known Tom Chamberlain before the war, and they kept up their friendship by visiting back and forth when their two units were encamped nearby. Thus, when Veazie was transferred to the Twentieth, he requested to be assigned to Tom's Company G so that he would be near a friend.

Their bond remained such that Veazie submitted a letter in support of Tom Chamberlain's pension application in 1890.[60]

Either way, there had been cracks in the mutiny, and it is telling that the last time daily diarist William T. Livermore mentioned the affair was on June 4. Hezekiah Long perhaps best summed it up in a letter to his wife on June 13: "We had about 100 from the 2nd Maine. They undertook to not do duty when they were transferred but the most of them have come to it."[61]

It was nearly two weeks before another morning report was completed on June 25, and by then only nine men were still under arrest, with two from Company C, two from Company D, and five from Company E. Three more men joined the ranks during the few days before the Battle of Gettysburg, leaving just John Lynes Jr. of Company D plus Charles Brown, John Conway, Thomas Townsend, and William Wentworth of Company E still under arrest and facing court-martial charges, along with the still-present Henry Moore. As it turns out, Moore was in limbo partly because of the intervention of no less a personage than Abraham Lincoln himself.[62]

On June 8, Major General Joseph Hooker, commander of the Army of the Potomac, forwarded the record of Henry Moore's charges, trial, and conviction with the notation, "The proceedings in the case of Private Moore are approved but in consideration of all the circumstances of the case the record is respectfully forwarded with recommendation that the sentence be commuted to confinement at hard labor at such point as the President may designate during the period of the war." On June 26, Abraham Lincoln commuted Moore's sentence to imprisonment at hard labor during the remainder of the war. Moore's commutation was not surprising: Of 2,764 men charged with mutiny during the war, only five white soldiers and four-teen African Americans were executed for the offense. Moore was finally transferred to Fort Delaware in October to serve his sentence.[63]

The beginnings of the Gettysburg Campaign and the army's subsequent marches over the next two weeks put a pause on any further court-martials. On June 12, Chamberlain made out charges against Thomas Townsend, but he was never brought to trial. By June 13, the Twentieth Maine was in pursuit of Lee's army and would have no time for such proceedings until the campaign was over, and by then Townsend had picked up his weapon. On July 1, the Twentieth Maine crossed the Mason-Dixon line into Pennsylvania, now just miles away from Robert E. Lee's Confederate army. Though the mutiny had largely died out by this time, with just six men under arrest, there were still some disgruntled soldiers in the ranks. As soon as they hit Northern soil that day, five of the former Second Maine men who had been assigned to Company D deserted, taking their guns and a full set of equipment with them. They were James Kelley, Samuel Morrison, Edward Spaulding, James Wallace, and Benjamin West. In the days before electronic records, Samuel Morrison emerged three years later and enlisted in the Seventh United States Infantry, but the rest were never heard from again and were still listed as deserters at war's end. Having deserted when marching toward the enemy, they would have been harshly dealt with if caught by the Provost Guard. It seems likely that these men had waited until they were in the North, where they more easily could find a way to journey either home or to a new place. Benjamin Coombs took the same route, deserting on July 4 and disappearing from the historical record.[64]

On July 1, 1863, the Twentieth's color bearer, Charles Proctor, got drunk on duty and was relieved of his position. The man who carried the national flag into battle occupied a position of great honor and one of great danger. Some regiments at Gettysburg suffered a half dozen or more men shot down while carrying the flag. In choosing who should take Proctor's place, Chamberlain further showed his respect for the Second Maine men and cemented their integration into the Twentieth by selecting one of their own, a twenty-five-year-old former mariner from Plymouth named Andrew Jackson Tozier.[65]

With this symbolic act, the mutiny was over. Of the roughly 125 men who had transferred to the Twentieth Maine, all but seven had dropped their dissent or would do so by the middle of the month. Andrew Tozier was among the seventy-two former Second Maine men who stood on Little Round Top as members of the Twentieth Maine, adding invaluable strength and experience to their new unit.

For his part, Chamberlain had handled the potential crisis masterfully. His mindset from the start, even before the men were transferred to him, of seeing the mutineers as potential assets and treating them with respect was key to everything that followed. There is no record of what latitude he requested from General Meade, but his actions suggest that what he sought

Charles Knapp, a former Second Maine man who served with the Twentieth at Gettysburg (Maine State Archives)

was time. Over the following days, Chamberlain's empathy was on full display as he immediately set about feeding the men and listening to their frustrations. For some, this sign of respect alone was enough. For those who were more recalcitrant, each passing day moved them further away from their old grievances and allowed time for them to start building relationships with their new comrades in the Twentieth Maine. By not forcing the men to do duty or be court-martialed immediately, Chamberlain

Ezra Marden, a former Second Maine man who served with the Twentieth at Gettysburg (Maine State Archives)

provided space to let their frustrations crest and then fade away, content to let them occupy a middle ground for a week or two before they came out the other side and were ready to commit to their new organization. At the same time, Chamberlain upheld the standards of the organization, and when Henry Moore, Benjamin Coombs, and Thomas Townsend violated those standards, he held them accountable. It was a varied approach rather than a one-size-fits-all mentality. Close to a decade later, Chamberlain explained how he dealt with the students at Bowdoin College when he took over as president of that institution: "In establishing my relations with the students I made them see and understand that I should deal with them as gentleman, that I should hold a man's word of honor as better than foreign testimony, that I should allow neither spy nor suspicion to hold any place between me and them, and that I should not abandon my confidence in them until they were false to themselves. But where a man dealt untruthfully, I regarded him as rotten at heart and good for nothing." That methodology was precisely what he applied with the Second Maine men, and it was remarkably successful.[66]

For their part, it is a testament to the character of these men labeled "mutineers" that, despite the injustice done to them, they committed to their new organization and were at the forefront of the battles to come. The length of their service had never really been the issue for most; it was the sense of injustice at their arbitrary treatment compounded by the disrespectful nature in which authorities handled their reassignment that led most to refuse duty. But the quiet words of Chamberlain and the goodwill extended by the unit's officers and enlisted men dampened the crisis. While most of the attention and credit that accrues to Chamberlain and the Twentieth Maine focuses on the climactic moment on Little Round Top, part of the groundwork for that day was laid not during a moment of fire and fury but during mundane days in late May when Chamberlain quelled a mutiny and the men of the Twentieth Maine welcomed their new comrades into the regiment.

No one could have known in May 1863 the importance of integrating these mutineers into the Twentieth Maine and what the costs would be for those men. Three were dead by the time the Battle of Gettysburg was over, with two more to follow shortly thereafter, but the entire Twentieth Maine might have been lost had those seventy-two veterans not stood by them on the rocky hill. Forevermore the Second Maine "mutineers," Twentieth Maine, and Joshua Chamberlain would be inextricably linked.

4

"With fixed bayonets and a yell"
Gettysburg

ON OCTOBER 3, 1889, THIRTY-TWO VETERANS OF THE TWENTIETH MAINE gathered on Little Round Top to dedicate their monument. Unit historian Howard Prince transported the men back to July 2, 1863, with a detailed account of the day's battle. When Prince finished, Joshua Chamberlain stepped forward. "We were young then," he acknowledged. "We do not count ourselves old yet; and these things were done more than twenty-six years ago. We believe we could do them now; but wonder how we could have done them then." Of the result and its importance there could be no doubt. "You were making history," evidenced by the fact that "the world recorded more for you than you have written," he asserted. "There is no need that I should recount to the friends who stand around us here, what would have happened had this little line—this thin, keen edge of Damascus steel—been broken down from its guard . . . Round Top lost—the day lost—Gettysburg lost—who can tell or dream what for loss thence would follow."[1]

This chapter is the story of the Twentieth Maine in the Gettysburg Campaign and its battle on Little Round Top on July 2, 1863, one of the best-documented small-unit fights in the Civil War. The narrative of the unit's actions during the four weeks of the Gettysburg Campaign leading up to the battle reveals the soldiers' experience and their daily tribulations during the campaigning season when they were constantly ill informed, overmarched, and underfed before being rushed into a battle that they would only come to fully understand years later. The dozens of accounts the men penned, accounts that Chamberlain admitted were "not consistent with each other" and "yet all of them true in their time and place, and so far as each actor is concerned," reveal exactly what happened during one of the war's most famous firefights and offer a window into how the common soldier experienced combat. Finally, while some modern critics suggest that a failure by the Twentieth Maine—the breaking of the "thin, keen edge of Damascus steel"—would have been inconsequential, the testimony offered by Union and Confederate leaders in 1863 makes clear both the importance of Little Round Top and the contribution these Maine men made to holding that position, a moment that finally secured the reputation they had long sought.[2]

After the flurry of activity around the Battle of Chancellorsville and then the transfer of the former Second Maine men into their ranks, the soldiers of the Twentieth Maine were back to a state of normalcy by late May 1863. On May 28, they abandoned Stoneman's Switch, the area just a few miles north of Fredericksburg they had called "home" since the previous November, and moved ten miles west to take up a position guarding the Rappahannock River crossing known as United States Ford (or simply U.S. Ford). The Mainers constructed rifle pits in case the nearby Confederates should make a move toward the ford, but for the moment, it was quiet enough that some men of the Twentieth swam out into the middle of the river, where they shook hands with Confederates who were doing the same. Soon the men devised an "exchange" system for these mid-river meetups. Sergeant James Rundlett of Company G confided to his mother that men "put what they wish to swap into their caps and swim to the middle of the River.—shake hands and go at the trading, Coffee stands high with them." Rundlett had procured a "Secesh bill which I will send you."[3]

Little was required from the men at this time other than to "go on parade two nights for a week." The few hostilities that existed were directed not at the Rebels but at one of their own. On June 3, Livermore confided in his diary, "Our Sutler was Shot up this morning for celling his goods at different Prices." But even that incident did not make much of an impression upon the more acerbic, for Captain Spear simply noted, "All quiet in camp."[4]

Mere yards away, on the south bank of the Rappahannock River, all was not so quiet. On June 3, Robert E. Lee inaugurated his second intended invasion of the North by pulling many of his troops back from their advanced positions along the Rappahannock and Rapidan Rivers and starting them west and then north through the Shenandoah Valley. Lee had tried a similar invasion the previous fall but had been checked in Maryland at the Battle of Antietam and never reached Pennsylvania. Despite that setback, Lee remained committed to moving into the North in 1863. In February, Stonewall Jackson had ordered cartographer Jedediah Hotchkiss to "prepare a map of the Valley of Va. extended to Harrisburg, Pa., and then on to Philadelphia."[5] Then, just a week after Chancellorsville, Lee went to Richmond to confer with President Jefferson Davis about Confederate strategy. Davis, a Mississippian, was fearful of Ulysses S. Grant's campaign against Vicksburg in his home state and wanted to send part of Lee's army west. Not surprisingly, Robert E. Lee did not want to see his army diminished and, over the course of four days, laid out a compelling argument for keeping his army intact and embarking on a northern invasion. It took a second trip to Richmond at the end of the month, but Davis eventually gave Lee his blessing and the Gettysburg Campaign became a matter of when, not if.[6]

Thus, the Twentieth Maine's days of lazy guard duty came to an abrupt halt. While the Union army high command was unsure of the exact intent or even direction of the Confederate movement, it was clear that something was afoot. On June 4–5, the Twentieth Maine marched ten miles farther west and took over guarding Ellis Ford but was ordered to be prepared to march at a moment's notice. William T. Livermore was skeptical enough of such a possibility that he "worked all this afternoon [June 5] and got our tent done." James Rundlett speculated, "We are as liable to move from here in 3 hours as we are to stop for 3 days, and as likely to stay here 3 weeks as any thing."[7]

Rundlett was confused by the Confederate movements, noting, "It is plain to be seen that they are making a demonstration to cross, but all the while I think they are sending reinforcements to whip Grant." Lieutenant Melcher shared Rundlett's sentiments, admitting to his brother, "The movements of both armies are very perplexing now. I suppose Gen. Hooker knows what he is about and where all the army is going, but all I know about is what our Regt. is doing. All matters of rumors reach our ears—a telegraph announces the fall of Vicksburg, another that we are falling back upon Alexandria via the Alexandria and Orange R.R., and another that we are to advance on Richmond via Culpepper-Gordonsville etc."[8]

Melcher would have been concerned to find out that, in fact, General Hooker did *not* know what exactly was going on and where the Rebel army was heading, for he admitted to President Lincoln in a telegram on June

5 that it was "conjecture" whether Lee had retreated toward Richmond or was embarking on offensive maneuvers. There was undeniably a concentration of Confederate cavalry to the northwest, but whether they were about to inaugurate a raid, intended to screen a movement of the Rebel infantry, or just meant to confuse and distract the Union army was unclear. Hooker needed information, so he sent his cavalry to the northwest to scout while he ordered the Sixth Corps to cross the Rappahannock River south of Fredericksburg and make a reconnaissance.[9]

The soldiers in the Twentieth Maine could clearly hear the Sixth Corps reconnaissance despite being approximately twenty-five miles to the west. All the diarists and anyone writing a letter that day noted the cannonading and their suspicion that they would soon be under marching orders. The Sixth Corps reconnaissance revealed that most Confederates had pulled out of their lines. Hooker proposed taking advantage of the now-open road to Richmond to launch an attack on the Confederate capital, but President Lincoln and General Henry Halleck feared that such a move would leave Washington open to the Confederates and argued that Lee's army should be Hooker's true objective. Reluctantly Hooker acquiesced and began shifting more of his troops to the north and west to try to discern Lee's intent.[10]

While there was a flurry of activity at army headquarters, there was little in the Twentieth's camp at Ellis Ford. On June 9, the men heard "cannonading on the right and firing all day," Captain Sam Keene noted, a product of the war's largest cavalry battle that was fought that day twenty miles to the northwest at Brandy Station. Seeking to cripple the Confederate cavaliers and discern their broader movements, around eleven thousand Union cavalrymen launched a surprise attack on ten thousand of Jeb Stuart's troopers and their infantry support. Despite a good showing from the newly reorganized Union horsemen, neither objective was fully accomplished, and General Hooker remained in the dark about the Army of Northern Virginia's exact center of gravity and Lee's intent.[11]

The Twentieth Maine remained in place on June 10. The taciturn Ellis Spear took time to enter a single word in his diary: "Warm." Sam Keene noted, "All quiet, very dull in camp." Albert Fernald reported that despite the lack of military activity there was some commotion in camp: "Lieut. Nichols officer of the day—Got drunk and was put under arrest by the Col." Livermore added that Nichols had his sash and belt taken away from him—a symbolic loss of rank and privilege during his time under arrest. The men were in limbo again. Lieutenant Melcher opined on June 12, "Our duty here is very light, but it is rather dull, as we have no drills, no dress parades, no drum, no bugles, no 'nothing hardly' that is military anymore."[12]

Melcher spoke of dullness too soon. That very night Adjutant Tom Chamberlain awoke from his slumber with a start, a reaction to the sound of "100 shots fired." The younger Chamberlain ran to Captain Atherton Clark's tent, and "they turned the Co. out and the Adj. ran to the guard house and asked why they did not give the alarm." The men in the guard house were confused, as they had heard nothing concerning. Further investigation revealed that the "100 shots fired" was "nothing but poor mule Lya," who was "kicking a bread box which was in too close proximity to his heels." Hezekiah Long—the grizzled old prison guard turned sergeant—wrote amusedly, "Some of the officers were scared about out of their wits" by the not-so-domesticated animal.[13]

June 13 marked the end of such idleness. Early that morning General Hooker definitively determined that Lee was moving toward Pennsylvania, and further reports around midday indicated that the Confederate First and Second Corps had passed through Culpeper and Sperryville fifty miles northwest of Fredericksburg and were clearly heading for the Shenandoah Valley. The valley's tilt from southwest to northeast made it a perfect invasion funnel for Lee's army, offering him protection as he moved toward south-central Pennsylvania and the politically significant cities of Harrisburg, Baltimore, and even Washington. With this new information, Hooker ordered the troops remaining along the Rappahannock River to move north.[14]

Late on June 13, "as the red in the west was fading away," the Twentieth Maine formed up to march. Just hours earlier Hooker had learned that the Union garrison at Winchester, Virginia, had been attacked by Richard Ewell's corps, giving clear indication of both the Confederates' northerly line of march and just how far their leading elements had advanced. The men of the Twentieth Maine plodded ahead on dark roads for eight miles, halting around 11:00 p.m. at Morrisville. Sergeant Albert Fernald confided in his diary, "Morrisville consists of one chimney minus the house." The next morning, the foot soldiers waited while everything with wheels—artillery, ambulances, and supply trains—moved out first. The roads must have been choked with dust by the time they got underway at noon. After marching fifteen miles, they reached Catlett's Station at 8:00 p.m. They were retracing the same route they had followed the previous fall, but now in reverse, an unescapable symbol of the war's unfavorable trajectory. William T. Livermore and Albert Fernald, tough soldiers both, commented that it had been a hard march. It would only get worse the next day.[15]

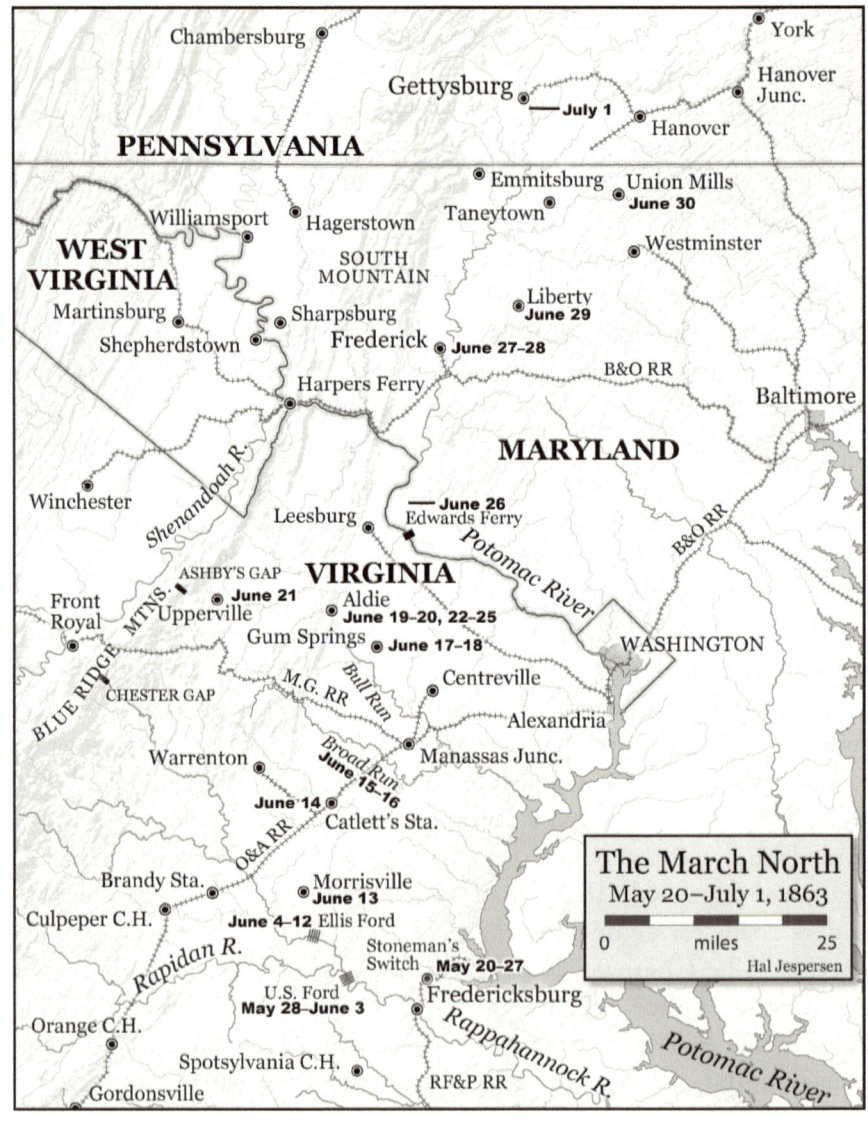

The March North
May 20–July 1, 1863

0   miles   25

Hal Jespersen

On June 15, reveille sounded at 4:00 a.m., and the men were moving an hour later. The sun rose while the men were underway, and soon the laconic Ellis Spear noted it was "exceedingly hot." Sam Keene wrote that it was "very hot—no air," and James Rundlett called it "sultry and oppressive." By 7:00 a.m., after just two hours of marching, "The men began to throw away blankets, shirts, tent flies, etc., and generally to lighten their loads." No one was spared from the general offloading, and "every Man threw away some Knapsacks Blankets Tent pieces Coats Caps," William Livermore noted. "But for all this," Rundlett observed, "9 o'clock found them falling out by the way." The mercury continued to rise, and by 2:00 p.m. an observer in Georgetown recorded the temperature as 92 degrees. Since leaving Ellis Ford, the men had not found a spring from which to get fresh water, leaving them to make do with the "poorest kind" of "stagnant water." Despite halting at noon at Manassas Junction before the day's hottest hours, many men had already fallen out with sunstroke. Albert Fernald called it the "hardest march I have ever had." James Rundlett withstood the march but noted, "When we arrived at Broad Run the men were as badly used up as I ever saw them." Sergeant Rundlett reported that two men in Company G, George Preble and David Bailey, had become "senceless and partially sun struck; one of them was speechless for some 5 hours but they are better now and have been sent by rail to Washington." Will Livermore was the only one of the four-man color guard to keep up with the march. Sam Keene barely made it and "was very nearly exhausted." When the men reached Broad Run, just shy of the old Manassas battlefields, they immediately threw themselves into the water and sought relief. The water had been turned "thick as cream" by the horses who had already been through, but it was a literal lifesaver for many. The long months of training had prepared them for battle, but there was little they could do to combat the weather and suffered almost as badly as they had the previous September when the temperature had last reached the same heights. By nightfall the temperature had dropped to 80 degrees, and the men had recovered enough that they went on the picket line about two miles from their camp.[16]

What the men saw as they moved around that afternoon and evening was a stark reminder that sunstroke-inducing marches were not the biggest threat to their health. Will Livermore observed scads of musket balls on the ground, remnants of the great battle of Second Bull Run that had been fought nearly ten months earlier. More ominous were the graves. Albert Fernald counted 198 burials, while Livermore estimated the trench to be 250 feet long.[17]

The next morning the men were relieved from their picket duties and returned to their camp, where they rested for the remainder of June 16. It is a sign of their exhaustion that both Nathan Clark and Ellis Spear misdated their diary entries, with Spear describing the actions of June 17 under his entry for the 16th and Clark writing about the horrendous march of June 15 as though it had occurred on the 16th.[18]

Throughout the day on June 17, the men heard firing to their front coming from a cavalry battle near Aldie that cost the Union 305 casualties. Jeb Stuart's Confederate troopers were trying to keep the prying eyes of Union cavalrymen east of the Blue Ridge Mountains so they could not observe the steady stream of Confederate soldiers moving north. Union cavalry chief Alfred Pleasonton surmised, "Lee is playing his old game of covering the gaps and moving his forces up the Shenandoah Valley," but until Lee's army could be observed by Union officers with the ability to interpret what they were seeing, Lee's ultimate objective would remain a mystery. Later that night the men of the Twentieth Maine learned that Colonel Calvin Douty of the First Maine Cavalry was one of fifty Union soldiers killed during the day's actions.[19]

Back among the infantry, "It was a hot day and a severe march, the roads were thronged with stragglers." The heat soared to 94 degrees, and the men marched 25 miles before halting at 6:00 p.m. at Gum Springs. Despite being from the coldest climate of any regiment in their brigade and the least used to such extreme temperatures, James Rundlett boasted "the Me. Boys stood it the best of any." *Best* was a relative term, for in Rundlett's own company thirteen men had fallen out. Perhaps of greatest concern, Rundlett noted, "Col. Chamberlain was taken very sick at night." The men knew Lieutenant Colonel Shepard Gleason of the Twenty-Fifth New York had died that day from the heat and were worried about their commander. An ambulance took Chamberlain to a nearby house for rest and recuperation, and his return was uncertain.[20]

On June 19, the Twentieth moved four miles west and encamped at Aldie, the scene of the cavalry fight two days earlier. Confederate cavalry remained just a few short miles to the west guarding the mountain passes, and the entire First Division went into camp in line of battle in case they were needed. A nighttime rainstorm cooled the air and brought fresh water but also soaked the men. They were past the worst of the heat.[21]

Saturday, June 20, saw more rain and clouds, with Sam Keene dubbing it a "blue lonesome day." Chamberlain's health no doubt played into the atmosphere, for while he rejoined the unit, Ellis Spear noted that he was "no better, rather worse." Rumors from the cavalry battles indicated that the First Maine Cavalry had been dreadfully cut up and lost five officers, and while that proved to overstate the toll, they had lost a captain and four enlisted men as well as their beloved colonel. Mounds of cavalry carbines and sabers picked off the battlefields at Aldie and Middleburg (June 19) portended what was to come. It was one ominous sign too many for Major Charles Gilmore, who reported as sick and left the regiment. Gilmore had avoided most of the previous fighting through such ruses and was despised by many.[22]

The major took his leave just in time. On June 20, General Pleasonton requested permission to attack Stuart's cavalry that was east of the mountains. General Hooker approved the plan and promised infantry support from General Meade's Fifth Corps. Meade selected James Barnes's First Division to fulfill this task. One of the three brigades of that division was commanded by Strong Vincent and included the Twentieth Maine. After months of inaction, the Mainers were about to test themselves against the legendary cavalrymen who had so often embarrassed their Union foes.[23]

The soldiers in the Twentieth Maine woke to reveille at 1:00 a.m. with orders to be ready to march by 3:00 a.m. They were to leave their tents and knapsacks behind but bring three days' rations and blankets. There was but one problem for the Twentieth, as summed up by Nathan Clark: "Our colonel is off duty and we dread to go into action without him." Chamberlain still suffered from heatstroke, and while he remained with the regiment, he was in no condition to lead it into battle. In the absence of an officer above the company level, Strong Vincent ordered Lieutenant Colonel Freeman Connor of the Forty-Fourth New York to lead the Mainers on this day.[24]

Vincent's brigade left camp at the appointed hour and marched five miles along the Ashby Gap Turnpike (modern Route 50), reaching Middleburg around 5:00 a.m. Two miles farther west, the Confederates occupied a defensive line along a ridge overlooking Kirk's Branch, an offshoot of Goose Creek that bisected the turnpike. The previous evening General Pleasonton had outlined his battle plan: "The infantry had best pass to the left of Middleburg, and operate by the left, occupying the stone fences and woods. General Hooker recommends an attack in front with a small force, and turn the enemy's position with your main body. I shall, therefore, send [John Buford's cavalry division] to the right, let the infantry take the left, and [David Gregg's cavalry division] the center."[25]

Strong Vincent (Library of Congress)

Vincent's brigade was selected to assist the cavalry, with the rest of Barnes's division remaining in Middleburg. The brigade moved to the left, taking up a position on the south of the turnpike and facing west. Vincent noted, "The dismounted men of the enemy were in a position on the south side of this road, behind a series of stone walls running at right angles with it, the cavalry in the fields, and a battery of six guns placed near the road on the left." Judson Kilpatrick's cavalry brigade began moving against the Confederates along the turnpike around 9:00 a.m. but made little headway. On Pleasonton's orders, Vincent advanced the Sixteenth Michigan to clear away the Confederate "carbineers" or sharpshooters from the Jeff Davis Legion, and the First North Carolina deployed behind a line of stonewalls just beyond Middleburg. The terrain, with abundant stonewalls, streams, and elevation, gave many advantages to the defenders, and an impatient Pleasonton soon ordered Vincent to commit more troops and force a breakthrough. The Forty-Fourth New York and Twentieth Maine went forward "with instructions to press the enemy hard and to pick off the gunners from his battery."[26]

William T. Livermore described the part taken by the Twentieth Maine: "At 8 ½ Our Batteries opened on themb But received no reply Our Brigade then formed in line of Battle the 20th on the left And advanced to the edge of the field where we met the Rebbel Pickets dismounted Cavalry Co. E were deploid as skirmishers in our front." Fortunately, Holman Melcher noted, "Most of the shelling went too high and burst in our rear, as we advanced so rapidly that they could not get the precise range." It was now about 10:00 a.m., and while three regiments from the brigade made the frontal assault on the Confederate skirmish line, Colonel Vincent "directed Captain Woodward, commanding Eighty-third Pennsylvania, to move rapidly through the woods to our left, keeping his forces concealed, and, the instant he had passed the stone walls, to emerge and take the enemy in the flank and rear."[27]

Vincent had shown his tactical nous, and within an hour "the movement was quite successful." Will Livermore was more to the point, noting that they "drove themb back." The Confederates fell back in "confusion, and the Sixteenth Michigan, under the lead of Lieutenant-Colonel Welch, advanced on the double-quick on the right, and gallantly compelled them to abandon one piece of their battery, a fine Blakely gun." From there the brigade engaged in a running fight. The Confederates made a series of stands behind the ubiquitous stone walls, but Vincent's brigade kept moving forward, "Dislodging them at each attack." Melcher noted that the Confederates "would not remain long enough to allow us to get near them to open upon them with rifles," but the effectiveness of the Union skirmishers meant that as they advanced, "here would be a private stretched dead upon the field or severely wounded, and there would be an officer suffering the penalty of fighting against a good government." After falling back for a mile to where Cromwells Run bisected the turnpike, the Confederates "made a sharp resistance, and opened an artillery fire, from which we suffered," Colonel Vincent reported. Vincent sent his skirmishers splashing across the run, flanked the Confederates, and soon "had them on the run." Will Livermore painted a vivid summary of the afternoon's running fight: "Our Brigade then charged across the field which was fenced with high Stonewalls. . . . But on we went climbing Stonewalls And did not halt til we came to Goos Crick" nearly two miles farther west.[28]

The battle's signature moment was nigh. Goose Creek was a more substantial body of water than Kirk's Branch or Cromwells Run, and the Ashby Gap Turnpike was carried over it by a half-century-old, two-hundred-foot-long stone bridge. The three remaining guns of Hart's Battery, plus a fresh

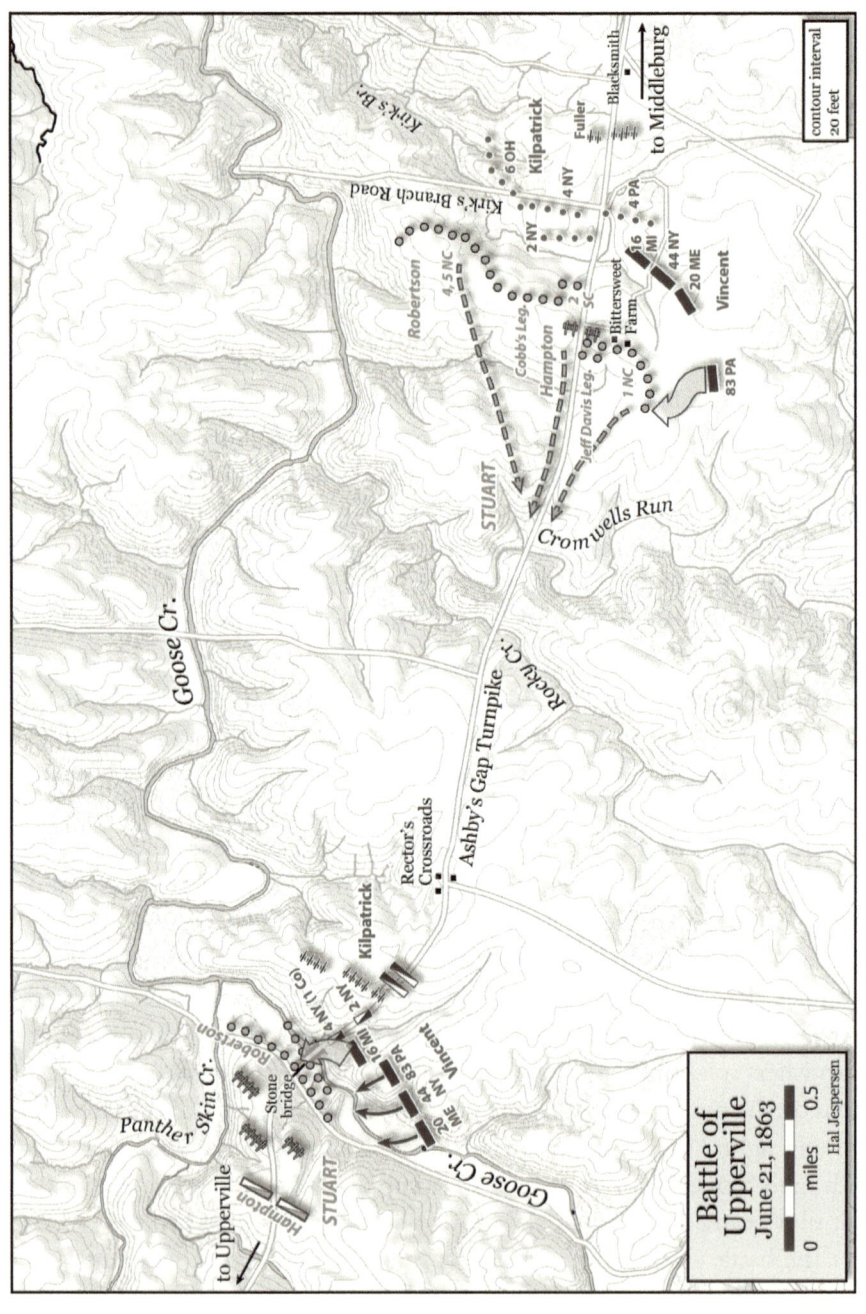

Battle of
Upperville
June 21, 1863

0 miles 0.5

Hal Jespersen

contour interval
20 feet

battery under Captain M. N. Moorman, protected the bridge, and as the Twentieth Maine advanced, Sam Keene noted that the unit "got a severe shelling." The men were ordered to lay down behind a substantial stone wall that largely protected them. One man, however, was not so fortunate. Ellis Spear wrote, "A solid shot or unexploded shell struck one of my men John P. West, a non-commissioned officer, and tore his leg from his body. I was near him but nothing could be done for him, for although he seemed to be breathing faintly he was not conscious and the leg was torn off close to the body, & appeared to be connected only by a single tendon on one side." West's death—the regiment's first combat fatality since Fredericksburg six months earlier—made an impression, with all the regiment's chroniclers noting it in their diaries or letters home. Spear, West's commander, felt the death particularly hard and covered it extensively in both his diary and two postwar recollections. Both men were from Wiscasset and had likely known each other before the war. Spear may well have known West's widow, Martha, and their two children, seven-year-old Martha and three-year-old Ida. Spear had also recruited West and might have felt some responsibility for West's presence in the unit and his untimely death. James Rundlett had been West's tentmate, his closest companion in the unit. In a letter home to his mother three days later, he relayed, "We have had a skirmish on Sunday in which Corp West was struck with a shell, it stove in his hip to pieces and he died in a few minutes. I will write particulars soon." But he never did, perhaps finding it too painful to describe his friend's death.[29]

A second Union cavalry division led by John Buford was operating on the right, or north of the Ashby Gap Turnpike, seeking to find the left flank of the Confederate line and force them to abandon their defenses of the mountain passes. General Kilpatrick worried that if the Confederates could hold the Goose Creek Bridge with a small force, they would be free to send the bulk of their troops after a now-badly outnumbered General Buford. Kilpatrick considered ordering a cavalry charge across the bridge to forestall that possibility but wisely opted to deploy the infantry instead, telling Vincent to "clear the position." While skirmishers from the entire brigade splashed into the stream to threaten the Rebel flanks, "The Sixteenth Michigan, led by Captain Fuller, gallantly rushed over the bridge and up to the stone wall under a severe fire, dislodging the enemy and capturing a number of prisoners." This action decided the battle, and "the enemy fled in confusion, followed by our cavalry, who drove them repeatedly from one position to another from this point into and beyond Upperville."[30]

At this point, the Confederates were pulling back, seeking to reunite all their forces and get through the critical juncture in Upperville before either the combined Vincent/Kilpatrick column along the Ashby Gap Turnpike or John Buford's men a mile and a half to the north could cut them off. The infantrymen now became nearly spectators, and Colonel Vincent was mesmerized: "The charges of the cavalry, a sight I had never before witnessed, were truly inspiring, and the triumphant strains of the bands, as squadron after squadron hurled the enemy in his flight up the hills and toward the gap, gave us a feeling of regret that we, to[o], were not mounted and could not join the chase." Following the cavalry at some distance, the infantrymen proceeded another three or four miles to Upperville, where they moved into line defending their batteries against possible counterattacks. At 6:00 p.m., they were relieved by the First Brigade of their division, whereupon they moved a few miles to the rear and encamped for the evening.[31]

Sometime during the latter part of the day, Company B's Captain Walter Morrill had a surprising encounter. As some of the captured filed past, Morrill recognized a Confederate lieutenant—possibly Louis or Lewis B. Sutton of the Fourth North Carolina Cavalry—with whom he had worked on the Penobscot River in Maine in the prewar years. The two men shared a moment of conversation before Morrill returned to the business at hand.[32]

The men of the Twentieth Maine had been up for fifteen hours and engaged with the enemy for nearly ten by the time they were relieved. They had forced the famous Confederate cavalry to retreat seven miles and, at least three times, had maneuvered them into abandoning strong defensive lines behind stone walls and streams. William Livermore reveled that they had made the Confederates "Skedaddle." Two captured cannons were tangible evidence of their accomplishments. "We lay down weary," Livermore noted, "but feeling finally we had Seen the Rebs run for the first time and gone over there ground." For the men of the Twentieth Maine, this battle, small as it may have been, marked the first time they could claim to have been part of the victorious side during their service, and it must have built their confidence as a unit.[33]

Despite the overwhelming success of Vincent's men, there were costs. The brigade had lost 2 men killed and 19 wounded, to go along with 10 deaths, 111 wounded, and 67 captured in the two cavalry divisions. On June 22, Captain Spear took a few men and buried John West "near the stream above the stone bridge on Goose Creek." In 1896, he reflected, "Whether his remains still lie there or not I do not know." Seven other men were wounded, with Albert Robinson, also of Spear's Company G, succumbing to his wounds at the end of July. Tragically, Robinson's wife passed away just two weeks before he did, which he likely did not know at the time of his own death. Their three-year-old daughter was orphaned. Of the other six men wounded on June 21, half were with the regiment at Gettysburg, while three others were wounded seriously enough to miss that battle but not to be discharged from the service. Holman Melcher narrowly avoided serious injury: "A piece of shell struck me on the leg above the knee, but was not permitted to wound me for its force was taken away so that it did not cut through my pants, although it bruised my leg quite badly. I thought at the time that my leg was broken, but I soon was able to go ahead. Had it been with a little more force I should have lost my leg." The Twentieth's tactical victory had come at a cost, yet another sign of things to come.[34]

Having returned to Aldie on June 22, the men remained in the vicinity of that village for the next few days. The unit was joined that day by twenty-five-year-old John Chamberlain, meaning all three living Chamberlain brothers were now with the Twentieth Maine. John had left Maine on June 1, 1863, at his brothers' request for a visit. In Boston, he visited with Charles Demond of the Christian Commission—an organization that brought relief, supplies, and religious support to the troops in the field. At Demond's urging, John continued his journey to the regiment as an agent of the Commission. On June 6, he arrived just north of Fredericksburg, but by then the Twentieth Maine had moved on. John spent time in the hospitals visiting the Twentieth's wounded and heard many glowing reports about his two brothers. When John caught up to the regiment on June 22, however, he found his older brother "looking poorly, had a dangerous sunstroke."[35]

The men remained in their camp for the next three days, enjoying a much-needed rest. Sam Keene spent June 23 "feasting upon cherries, sleeping," while the next day he "slept, ate, and did nothing in particular." On June 25, he visited the estate of former president James Monroe, then owned by Confederate major John Fairfax. It was not just the Twentieth Maine; there was little movement in the whole Army of the Potomac from June 22 to June 25. On June 22, Fifth Corps commander George Meade grumbled to fellow corps commander Oliver Otis Howard, "I don't know what we are going to do. I have had no communication from headquarters for three days." The sense of being in the dark trickled down to the Twentieth, with Holman Melcher lamenting, "Nothing but rumor lets us know that the world is yet alive." By June 24, General Hooker knew that Richard Ewell's Second Corps was north of the Potomac River while the other two Confederate corps remained south of that dividing line. Hooker feared that Washington or Baltimore might still be the Confederate target, and until he knew more, his troops were in a strong covering position allowing him to protect those two cities.[36]

As more reports came in over the next two days that suggested the Confederates continued to move into Pennsylvania, Hooker pushed his army farther north. The Twentieth Maine resumed the march on June 26, moving through Leesburg and crossing the Potomac at Edward's Ferry before encamping three miles farther north, covering more than twenty miles through rain and mud. Crossing the river—an acknowledgment that the war was going badly enough that the men were now going to have to fight in the north—was "Shameful!" in Holman Melcher's estimation. "As to the present state of affairs," he wrote to his brother, "I will not write my feelings, for you can imagine the disgust at the bungling blunders that have transferred the seat of war to our borders, that is now destroying the property of good citizens and that have caused these tedious marches that kill more men than the battle-field of the Rappahannock." Sam Keene echoed his lieutenant's feelings, bemoaning the "long tiresome blue march" and rhetorically wondering "Who's fault is it? The fault of government. Poor management, imbecility, etc. etc." Perhaps worst of all, "No mail" from his dear Sarah. As he so often did, Hezekiah Long cut right to the heart of the matter: "We are now in about the same place that we were in the middle of last September." The men were furious with the state of the war and desperate to repel the Rebels. Approximately fifty miles to the north there was a skirmish just west of Gettysburg, Pennsylvania, that day as six hundred emergency militia troops who had been civilians just ten days earlier unsuccessfully tried to block 150 Confederate cavalrymen from moving into the town in search of supplies.[37]

Back in Maryland, on June 27 the Twentieth Maine marched from 6:00 a.m. until 6:00 p.m., from the north side of the Potomac River near Leesburg to the outskirts of Frederick, Maryland. On reaching the

Monocacy River, the men found the water to be "up to our middle" and "very rapid," and the entire division was ordered to disrobe and cross at once. Melcher wrote his brother a letter, lamenting the continued sickness of their leader. "Our beloved Col. Chamberlain is not able to command us owing to sickness, but he is on the recovery and we all hail the day he is able to resume his command of the regiment." Chamberlain had refused to leave the unit. His brother John "tried in vain to persuade the Col. to take an ambulance for it was raining. He would ride like a man he said." Despite this show of bravado, Chamberlain was far from over his recent bout with sunstroke and the lingering effects of a case of malaria he had picked up that spring.[38]

On June 28, the men remained in camp near Frederick, where they had an inspection at noon and their first mail call in more than two weeks to break up the day. Albert Fernald reported the receipt of seven letters, which must have been like Christmas for a soldier in the field. The mail also brought the official commissions for Joshua Chamberlain as colonel and Charles Gilmore as lieutenant colonel, posts they had both been filling since Ames's promotion to brigade command a month earlier. The irony of Gilmore's promotion arriving after he had fled the front lines with a battle imminent was not lost on the men.[39]

Those were not the only promotions of note. Abraham Lincoln and General-in-Chief Henry Halleck had grown frustrated with army commander Joseph Hooker, and in the predawn hours on June 28, James Hardie, the chief of staff to Secretary of War Edwin Stanton, was dispatched to the Army of the Potomac with orders that promoted George Meade of the Fifth Corps to army command while removing Hooker from his position. Several men in the Twentieth Maine noted this command change but with little comment. Meade represented the fourth commanding general the Mainers had seen since joining the army less than ten months earlier, a churn that was both a factor in and a product of their lack of victories.[40]

By the time Meade took command, there was no doubt that the Rebel army was in Pennsylvania, at least two days march north of his present position. On June 29, the Twentieth Maine marched close to twenty miles, turning northeast after passing through Frederick and continuing for another fifteen miles before camping about two miles beyond Liberty (now Libertytown). This movement took the Fifth Corps away from the Confederates but was part of the plan to keep the Army of the Potomac positioned to block any roads leading to either Washington or Baltimore while they moved to contact with Lee's army. As the men marched through Frederick, many were impressed by their reception. William T. Livermore observed that "the Stars and Stripes were flying from most every windo there was hundreds displaid," while Sam Keene noted "smiles, words of encouragement, etc. etc." The reception in Liberty was even more positive. "Some Ladies waved there handkerchiefs," Livermore reported, while "others wishing more to benefit the Soldiers than to look pretty Stood at the gates with water for us as we passed." It was, he concluded, "Quite a town." Some of Maryland's finest may have offered the men more than just water, for Sergeant Charles Proctor, the bearer of the regiment's United States flag, procured liquor and then began abusing the regiment's officers. Elisha Coan of the color guard had a front-row seat to the debacle: "A stronger enemy than rebels got the better of Color Sergeant Proctor, as brave a soldier as we had in the 20th by the way—the day we marched through Frederick City Md. on our way to Gettysburg, King Alcohol, and thereby the Colors of the 20th were 'trailed in the <u>dust</u>' for the first and only time that day." The regiment's officers took the flag away, and Proctor fell out of the ranks. For his indiscretion, Proctor was stripped of both his rank and the position of honor as the regimental color bearer.[41]

Joshua Chamberlain now faced the monumental decision of who to assign to guard the regimental flag, the Twentieth Maine's most important symbol and manifestation of their identity and a key communications system during battle when extreme noise made visual cues critical. He selected Andrew Tozier, a Second Maine man who had just recently joined the unit.

If one man represented the very best of what the Second Maine men brought to their new unit, Andrew Jackson Tozier might have been that person. Born on February 11, 1838, Andrew was the fifth of the seven children of John and Theresa Tozier. The Toziers struggled financially, with the 1850 census showing just $200 worth of property next to John's name, while in 1860 he was listed as a pauper. The 1850 census listed oldest son Augustus as a sailor, and the following year young Andrew followed the same path. A half century later, Andrew's wife Lizzie (Bolden) explained,

"He went to sea at the age of thirteen years and followed the life of a sailor continuously [for a decade] accept short visits to his parents until he enlisted." Tozier's embrace of maritime culture included the acquisition of two tattoos, later described by an examining physician as "Female on ant. aspect [inside of] right arm" and "five pointed star in first interosseous space of right hand." The second tattoo was likely a nautical star symbolically guiding sailors to their destinations and eventually back home.[42]

When the Civil War began, Andrew returned home and enlisted in the Second Maine as a recruit on July 15, 1861, around six weeks after the unit's formal mustering-in. Not surprisingly, given his worldly experience, Tozier stood out, and despite being a later addition, he was promoted to corporal in early 1862. June of that year was a watershed in Tozier's life, as he suffered the trifecta of disease, battle wound, and capture. Fellow soldier William Jones later testified that Tozier "did become disabled by having contracted Disease of heart, brought on by heavy lifting in building bridges and curdoroy roads and exposure to miasma in the Chickahominy swamp . . . being affected by it in such a manner as to become faint and unconscious frequently." Jones's recollection was supported by that of William Foss, also of the Second Maine, who wrote, "Being in the mud and water and hard work he was taken with Heart trouble. He did not go away to the Hospital but staid with the Co. He had fainting spells and would have to be helped to the Doctors tent."[43]

On June 25, 1862, Robert E. Lee launched the offensive known as the Seven Days Battles. On the third day, Lee sent his largest-ever attack, fifty-eight thousand men, against the Union lines at Gaines's Mill. The entire Confederate assault was arrayed against the men of the Fifth Corps, and the Second Maine suffered ninety casualties. Tozier wrote, "After Fighting from 10 oclock till after five in the afternoon on June the 27th 1862 at the Battle of Gaines Mill I was wounded through the left Hand & just after was shot on the inside of my left ankle & was taken prisoner the Ball did not go through but lodged & was taken out by a Southern Doctor the next day." The second wound limited Tozier's mobility, leading to his capture along with fifty other men from the unit. Tozier's hand wound was severe, with his middle finger requiring amputation at the first joint and his ring finger damaged and later so stiff as to be practically useless. In the postwar years, Tozier's left arm measured three-quarters of an inch smaller than his right, evincing its limited usefulness.[44]

His Confederate captors moved Tozier to Richmond, confining him first in Libby Prison before transferring him to Belle Isle. Fortunately, Tozier was not a prisoner for very long. Union general John Dix and Confederate D. H. Hill standardized a prisoner exchange agreement on July 22, and within days the exchange system went into effect. On August 3, 1862, Andrew Tozier was one of three thousand Union prisoners on Belle Isle traded for a similar number of Confederates. Due to his wounds and ongoing sickness, Tozier was sent to a hospital outside Philadelphia and remained there until he was fit to rejoin his unit in late October.[45]

On returning to the Second Maine, Tozier was immediately promoted to sergeant and then to first sergeant on January 1, 1863. When transferred to the Twentieth on May 26, Tozier immediately caught his new commander's eye as "an example of all that was excellent as a soldier." Chamberlain's selection of Tozier as color sergeant was likely in part a recognition of the man's record, in part due to a belief that he would perform the duty well, and in part a continuation of his efforts to fully integrate the Second Maine men into their new unit. No matter what the motivation, it would prove to be an inspired decision.[46]

At 4:00 a.m. on June 30, the men continued their march north, covering twenty-five miles over the next thirteen hours before halting in Union Mills, Maryland. Just as had been the case nine days earlier at Upperville, they were on the heels of Jeb Stuart's cavalrymen. As it became increasingly evident that battle was imminent, it must have been a comfort to see Colonel Chamberlain shake off his illness and return to duty.[47]

The next morning, the Battle of Gettysburg began when John Buford's cavalry division fired on Confederate infantry advancing east on the Chambersburg Pike toward Gettysburg. Midmorning ten thousand men of the Union First Corps joined the battle and were augmented as the day wore on by the Eleventh Corps. Initially the men of the Twentieth Maine were unaware of the action just fifteen miles to their northwest, and their leisurely morning evinces the extent to which Gettysburg was a "meeting engagement"—a battle that begins when enemies collide unexpectedly. The Twentieth did not leave their overnight camp in Union Mills until 10:00 a.m., hours after the battle began, and then moved due north ten miles to Hanover, where they halted for two hours. At this point, it was still not apparent that both armies would fully concentrate at Gettysburg, and the Fifth Corps remained under orders to screen against a potential eastern thrust by the Confederates. Finally, the Fifth Corps was ordered to Gettysburg, and the Twentieth took up the march again, covering another ten miles before camping a few miles east of Gettysburg near midnight. Wild rumors floated through the ranks about the battle fought that day and even that the soldiers' old favorite, George McClellan, was back in charge of the army. For thirty of the Mainers, it was their last night among the living.[48]

For nearly three weeks, the Twentieth Maine had moved north along a vast road network. In their two-hundred-mile journey from the outskirts of Fredericksburg across the Mason-Dixon line into Pennsylvania, they had traversed dirt roads that grew dusty in the heat and muddy when it rained and were always a challenge for wagons, as well as the improved or macadamized all-weather "pikes" that featured crushed rock roadbeds, peaked centers, and culverts that facilitated drainage and considerably eased an army's logistical challenges. While soldiers on foot could traverse open fields, both artillery and supply wagons needed roads and lots of them. With all their support and supply wagons, every one thousand men in an army occupied one mile of roadway, necessitating the use of multiple parallel or somewhat parallel roads to keep an army concentrated and moving in the same direction. In 1863, Gettysburg was the junction of ten roads plus a railroad line from the east, and it was that road network that ultimately determined where the battle was fought and how the particular action played out. When John Buford moved into Gettysburg on June 30, his objective was to continue gathering intelligence on the location of the Confederate forces and to deprive them of the use of the Chambersburg-York Pike (modern Route 30), the only macadamized east-west road for thirty miles in either direction.

At the end of the fighting at Gettysburg on July 1, the Union troops were forced back from their position astride the Chambersburg Pike, retreating a mile or so to high ground south of Gettysburg that formed an arc around the Taneytown Road and Baltimore Pike. Over the next few days, these two roads would be critical in bringing soldiers and supplies to the battlefield and providing a retreat route should that become necessary. The Baltimore Pike was particularly important, with its all-weather surface giving the supply wagons a direct link to the railhead at Westminster,

Gettysburg Battlefield
July 1–3, 1863

0   miles   1

Hal Jespersen

Maryland, around twenty-five miles away. If the Chambersburg-York Pike had been the critical road feature on July 1, the Baltimore Pike would be that—at least from the Union perspective—on July 2–3.

On the south edge of Gettysburg is Cemetery Hill, a relatively flat and open prominence that rises approximately eighty feet above the town and in 1863 was covered in nearly equal parts by the Evergreen Cemetery, cornfields, and an orchard. Both the Taneytown Road and Baltimore Pike leave Gettysburg and pass over this hill on their way south. Slightly to the east of Cemetery Hill is Culp's Hill, which is of a similar height to Cemetery Hill but almost entirely wooded. Union soldiers positioned astride these two hills could keep Confederates coming from the north and northwest away from the two crucial roads. Running due south from Cemetery Hill for approximately two miles is Cemetery Ridge, a rise of about thirty feet that faces west and the Confederate attacks that could come from that direction, providing the dual advantage of the elevated terrain and masking Union movements along the Taneytown Road and Baltimore Pike in its shadow. At the terminus of Cemetery Ridge are two hills now known as Little and Big Round Top, though they were then called by various other names. Little Round Top rises approximately 150 feet above the surrounding area, while Big Round Top is twice that tall. The western-facing slope of Little Round Top was largely denuded of trees, giving it a wide-open view to potential Confederate advances and allowing the placement of Union cannon on its crest. From the Union perspective, this position was almost textbook perfect: substantial hills on either end to anchor their line, an elevated ridge in the middle with clear fields in front, and two roads behind this protected arc to supply the army.

When the Union First and Eleventh Corps retreated from the first day's battlefield, they took positions on Cemetery and Culp's Hill. When the Twelfth Corps arrived, it was added to the defenses on Culp's Hill, while the Second and then Third Corps extended down Cemetery Ridge to the base of Little Round Top. The late-arriving Fifth Corps—including the Twentieth Maine—was to act as a reserve, with hopes that the army's final corps, the Sixth, would show up in time to take part in whatever fighting might occur on July 2. Thus, the Twentieth Maine awoke early on July 2 and moved from their position east of Gettysburg to one along the Baltimore Pike from which they could quickly deploy wherever they may be needed. The men were not sure exactly when or where that would be. At 3:00 p.m., William Lamson continued a letter to his father that he had started the previous night, writing, "We've now been resting about three hours about a mile from Gettysburg." Their rest would not last much longer.[49]

Miles to the west, the men of the Fifteenth and Forty-Seventh Alabama (who would eventually face off against the Twentieth Maine later that afternoon) tramped along the Chambersburg Pike toward Gettysburg. Along with the Fourth, Forty-Fourth, and Forty-Eighth Alabama, they belonged to Law's brigade of Hood's division of James Longstreet's First Confederate Corps. At 3:00 a.m. that morning, as his men slumbered in their bivouac in New Guilford, Pennsylvania, brigade commander Evander Law received orders to get his men up and march the twenty-four miles to Gettysburg as quickly as possible. The Alabamians covered the distance in just eight and a half hours, a stunning rate that led corps commander James Longstreet to label their exertions "the best marching done in either army to reach the field of Gettysburg."[50]

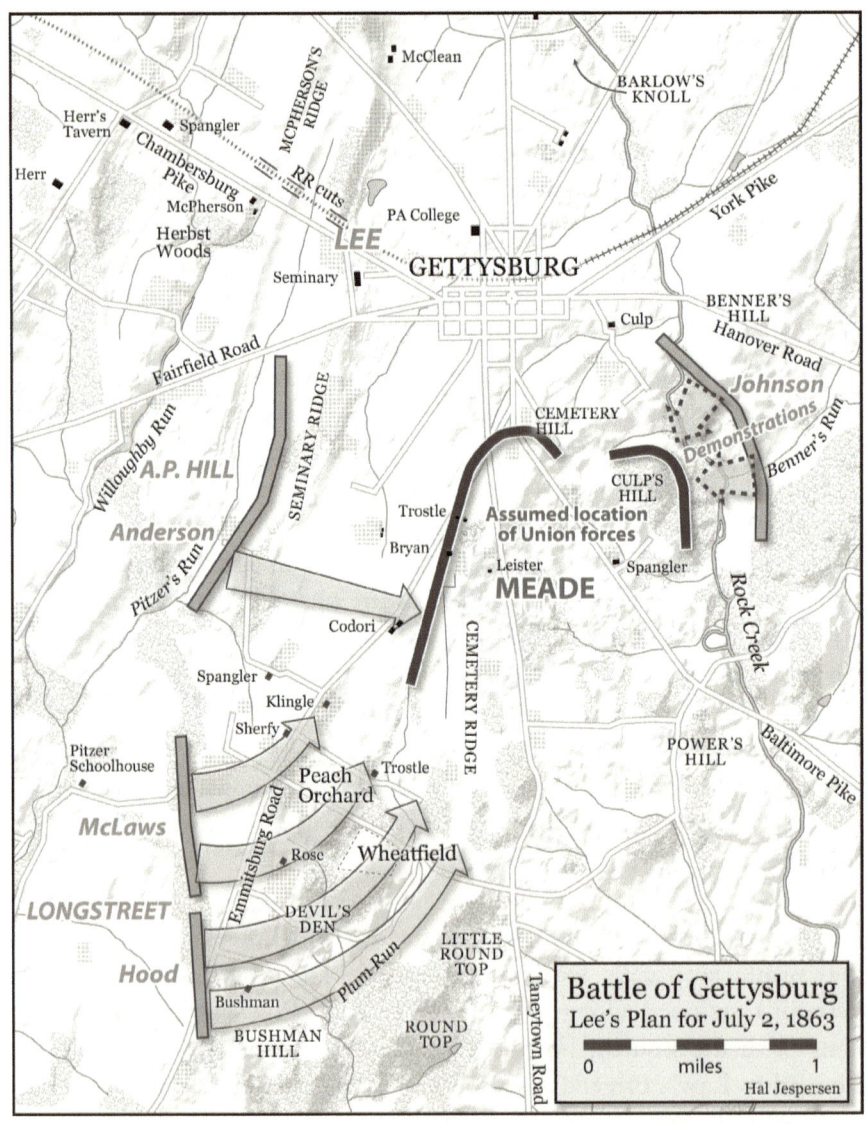

Battle of Gettysburg
Lee's Plan for July 2, 1863

0   miles   1

Hal Jespersen

While Law's men marched in from the west, Robert E. Lee made his battle plan. At the south end of both lines, "The enemy held a position from which, if he could be driven, it was thought our artillery could be best used to advantage in assailing the more elevated ground beyond. [Longstreet] was directed to endeavor to carry this position, while General Ewell attacked directly the high ground on the enemy's right, which had already been partially fortified." Lee's plan called for an attack on the south end of the Union line, with Hood's division on the far right, Lafayette McLaws division to their left, and Richard Anderson's division farther left/north.[51]

Longstreet was concerned about his manpower, so he asked for and received permission to wait until Law's brigade arrived, which they did close to noon. As Longstreet's corps moved to their attack position, "engineers, sent out by the commanding general and myself," Longstreet reported, "guided us by a road which would have completely disclosed the move. Some delay ensued in seeking a more concealed route." The clock ticked, ticked, ticked. In the pre–daylight savings era, sunset on July 2, 1863, was at 7:40 p.m.[52]

Back along Union lines, Third Corps commander Daniel Sickles was about to make one of the great blunders of the war, without which people today may have never heard of the Twentieth Maine or Joshua Chamberlain. Ordered to occupy a position on Cemetery Ridge running from the left flank of the Second Corps (near the modern Pennsylvania Monument) to the base of Little Round Top, Sickles observed that some points of his line were lower than the terrain in his front along the Emmitsburg Road. Remembering all too well what had happened at Chancellorsville when Confederates had gained the high ground of Hazel Grove, with disastrous consequences, Sickles spent much of the morning trying to convince George Meade to allow him to move his corps forward to the higher ground. Meade, who was busy with other matters and generally despised Sickles, largely ignored his subordinate until he received reports that all ten thousand men of the Third Corps had moved a half mile in front of their assigned position and formed into a salient along the Emmitsburg Road. Meade hastily rode out to Sickles's line to give the general a piece of his mind. Meade no doubt pointed out the obvious, that Sickles's forward maneuver had broken the Union's coherent line of defense, creating three flanks where previously there had been just one, that he had uncovered Little Round Top, and that the supposed high ground he now occupied was, in fact, no-man's-land. Before the two men could discuss "the propriety of his withdrawing," George Meade wrote, "The enemy opened on him with several batteries in his front and on his flank, and immediately brought forward columns of infantry and made a most vigorous assault." All hell was about to break loose.[53]

After a thirty-minute artillery barrage, the Confederate attack moved forward. General Hood had placed Law's brigade on the far right, and they aimed at the end of the Union line between the Wheatfield and Devil's Den, a slightly elevated, rocky outcropping. The Fifteenth Alabama was in the middle of the brigade's five regiments, with the Forty-Fourth and Forty-Eighth Alabama to their right and the Forty-Seventh and Fourth Alabama to their left. As the brigade moved toward the Union left, it came under fire from men of the Second United States Sharpshooters posted along the base of Big Round Top, losing Lieutenant Colonel Isaac Feagin to one of their bullets. At the same time, the two rightmost regiments, the Forty-Fourth and Forty-Eighth Alabama, were ordered to move to the left to fill a gap that was opening between the brigades of Law and Jerome Robertson. Colonel William Oates of the Fifteenth Alabama took charge in this moment of potential crisis, ordering his regiment and the Forty-Seventh Alabama next to him to face more easterly where they could attack the sharpshooters. The Confederate line rolled forward, the attack poised to do all its planners envisioned.[54]

As the Confederates hit the Union line, George Meade started sending reinforcements from both the Second and the Fifth Corps to the besieged areas. Barnes's division was sent to the Wheatfield, with Vincent's brigade and the Twentieth Maine among the critical reinforcements that Meade hoped would salvage the Union's defensive line. Nathan Clark remarked that the Twentieth "marched like horses untill we reached the left of our line of battle." On Little Round Top, the Army of the Potomac's chief topographical engineer, Gouverneur Warren, could see the Confederate attack unfold below and foresaw the inevitable near-term moment when Hood's men seized the now-vacant Little Round Top. Warren dispatched

Little Round Top (Photo taken by Matthew Brady's team, mid-July 1863; Library of Congress)

Lieutenant Ranald Mackenzie of his staff to find General Sickles and secure a brigade to occupy the hill.[55]

Sickles could spare no man; however, elements of Barnes's division of the Fifth Corps were now arriving, and Lieutenant Mackenzie thought perhaps they could provide the necessary manpower. Corps commander George Sykes agreed to direct a brigade to the hill and sent a staff officer to find Barnes and give the order. Barnes was still completing the scouting and coordination necessary before placing his men and thus was not with the division when Sykes's aide approached. In the words of Oliver Norton, the Third Brigade bugler, "Vincent was sitting on his horse at the head of the column, waiting orders. Seeing Sykes' aide approaching, he rode forward to meet him. . . . 'What are your orders? Give me your orders.' The captain answered, 'General Sykes told me to direct General Barnes to send one of his brigades to occupy that hill yonder,' pointing to Little Round Top. Vincent said, 'I will take the responsibility of bringing my brigade there.'"[56]

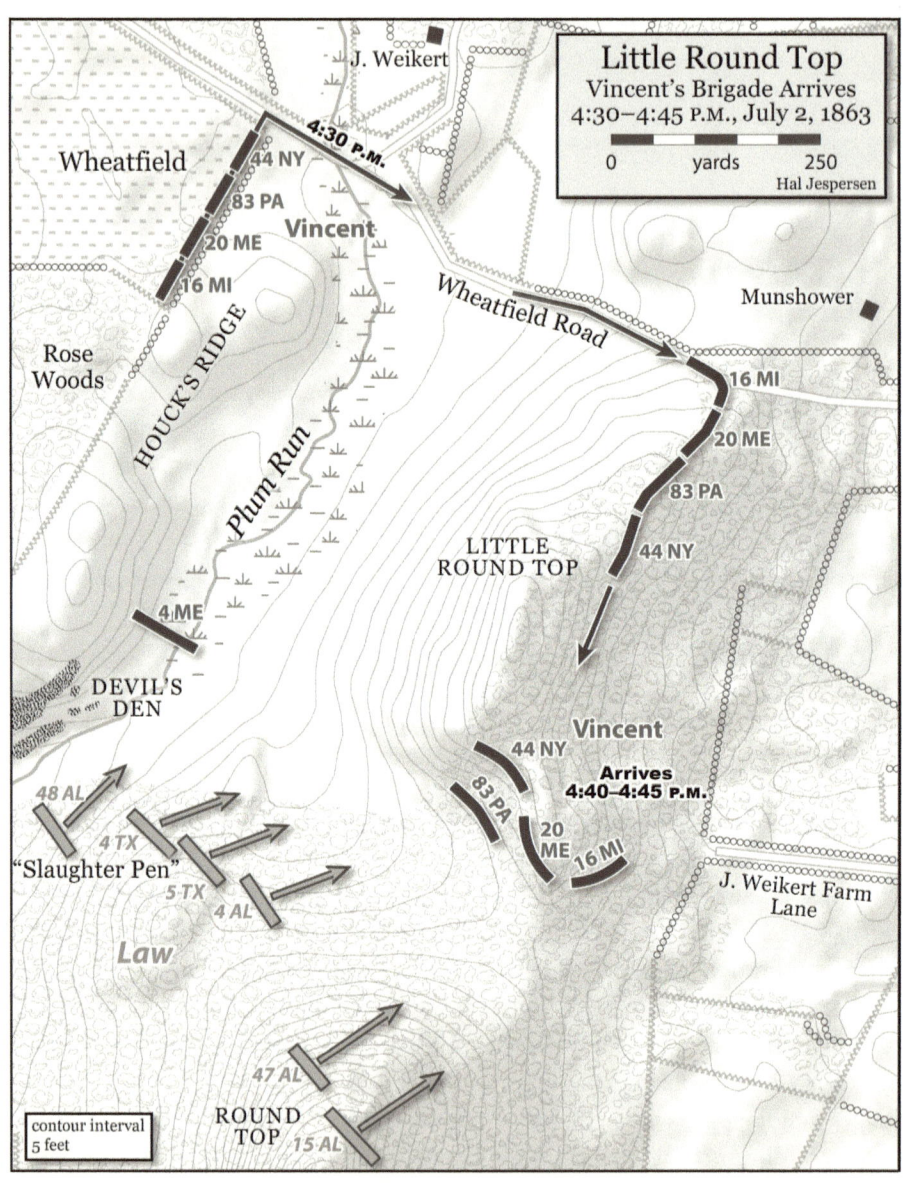

Little Round Top
Vincent's Brigade Arrives
4:30–4:45 P.M., July 2, 1863

0   yards   250

Hal Jespersen

Rather than going into the Wheatfield, Vincent's brigade now headed for Little Round Top. With the Forty-Fourth New York in the lead, followed by the Sixteenth Michigan, Eighty-Third Pennsylvania, and Twentieth Maine, the brigade followed the Millersville Road (modern

Wheatfield Road) onto the northern shoulder of Little Round Top and then passed through the woods behind the crest of the hill to a position along the south slope in the saddle or spur between Little and Big Round Top. "The position chosen by Vincent for his brigade was the best possible for preventing the Confederates from turning or capturing the hill," Norton wrote. "Had he placed his men on the crest of the ridge the enemy could have turned his flank and attacked from the rear."[57]

Senior regimental commander James Rice asked that his Forty-Fourth New York and Eighty-Third Pennsylvania be placed next to one another, a request Vincent accommodated. Vincent initially placed the Sixteenth Michigan on the extreme left flank, with the Twentieth Maine, Eighty-Third Pennsylvania, and Forty-Fourth New York stretching to their right. Soon, however, Confederate action near Devil's Den convinced Vincent he needed more support in that direction so he moved the Sixteenth Michigan from the brigade's far left to its far right, leaving the Twentieth Maine to hold the left flank. Vincent must have been at least passingly uneasy with the prospect of placing his greenest unit and newest commander on the extreme left flank of the entire Union army, for he took the time to impress on Chamberlain the gravity of his situation. "Colonel Vincent indicated to me the ground my regiment was to occupy," Chamberlain wrote years later, "informing me that this was the extreme left of our general line, and that a desperate attack was expected in order to turn that position, concluding by telling me I was to 'hold that ground at all hazards.'" But why, exactly, was that position so critical?[58]

In his testimony before the Joint Committee on the Conduct of the War the following March, General Meade identified Little Round Top as "the key-point of my whole position," noting, "If they had succeeded in occupying that, it would have prevented me from holding any of the ground which I subsequently held to the last."[59] Recent works by Peter Vermilyea on George Meade's Pipe Creek Circular, Kent Masterson Brown on George Meade, and Troy Harmon on the impact of road, rail, and water on the battle all highlight Meade's extreme concern with the security of the two main roads that ran behind his lines, the Taneytown Road and Baltimore Pike. While he remained in Gettysburg, those roads supplied Meade's army. Should the battle turn against him, they would be his retreat route. Discussions about the importance of Little Round Top often center on the

notion that a successful Confederate assault would have enabled the placement of Rebel artillery on the hill, which could have made the Union position untenable. But the reality is far simpler than that. Confederate soldiers
on Little Round Top would find themselves less than three hundred yards
from the Taneytown Road—within rifle range.[60] Even without taking Little
Round Top, ordnance trains on the Taneytown Road were so close that
Colonel Oates of the Fifteenth Alabama could not resist the temptation
to detach Company A of his unit and send them after the bounty. Union
officers were well aware of the threat. James Rice of the Forty-Fourth New
York wrote that Confederate capture of Little Round Top would have
"opened to him a vast field for successful operations in the rear of our entire
army." Confederate brigade commander Evander Law wrote that "our true
point d'appui was Round Top, from which the Confederate right wing could
be extended towards the Taneytown and Baltimore roads, on the Federal
left and rear." Even the presence of just a few Confederate regiments astride
the Taneytown Road and interposed between the bulk of the Union army
and their supply and retreat route would have posed an existential threat
to the Army of the Potomac and, unless an immediate counterattack could
have dislodged the interlopers, very likely would have led George Meade
to withdraw and seek a safer place from which to resume battle. While
Cemetery Hill was the Union's most advantageous position, Little Round
Top was "the key-point of my whole position," as Meade himself testified.[61]

From his earliest days, Chamberlain had heard the stories of the War of
1812 when his grandfather had ordered his troops at the Battle of Hampden,
"There shall not a man leave the ground," and his namesake, James Lawrence,
had exhorted, "Don't give up the ship! Fight her till she sinks." Vincent's
order to "hold this ground at all hazards" tapped into Chamberlain's very
identity and ensured that there would be no retreat from this position.

Which company commander was the Twentieth's best was debatable,
but the most experienced was Walter Morrill, who had served with the
Sixth Maine for a year before being promoted to lieutenant and joining
Company B in October 1862. His company also hailed mainly from the
deeply wooded forests of Piscataquis County and thus may have found
themselves most at home in their current environment. "In compliance
with orders from you to take my Co. 'B' and cover your front and left
flank at the time your regiment went into position," Morrill conveyed to

Walter Morrill (Maine State Archives)

Chamberlain in his after-battle report, "I immediately deployed my men as skirmishers and moved to the front and left."[62]

As Morrill moved out, Chamberlain oversaw the placement of his remaining nine companies. Years later, unit historian Howard Prince described the moment:

Let us glance down the line from the right. "Pap" Clark is acting as field officer, and E is commanded by Sidelinger, then comes Fogler, always cheerful, with his sturdy men of the coast, then the irrepressible Jim Nichols, who always had trouble to make "K" wheel, but not the least in keeping himself and "K" up to the front in a fight, then the two companies at the bloody angle, under the beloved Keene and quiet Lewis, the farmer boys of A and F., half of who are soon to fall in death and wounds. Next Aroostook's hardy sons, giant in form and stout of heart, and behind them Joe Land, who won't stop cracking his jokes till the Johnnies strike his front. Here come the

"Oxford Bears," with Billings, calm, modest, but true as steel, his moments of life already numbered, and D with jolly Fitch, and last old reliable G, over which Spear, never wanting in the hour of need, still keeps a fatherly eye.[63]

Among the company commanders, both Jim Nichols and Addison Lewis had something extra at stake. Nichols had been arrested earlier in June after appearing drunk on duty, a recurrent problem that had prevented his promotion, but Chamberlain acknowledged to Governor Abner Coburn, "Mr. Nichols is a brave & energetic officer, & these good qualities have made us more lenient with him than we should otherwise have been." Addison Lewis had also been under arrest during the march north for overstaying a leave of absence, and Chamberlain noted that the young man "would have been dismissed the service without doubt, had not the battle of Gettysburg cut the proceedings short." With the battle imminent, Colonel Vincent ordered the men back to their posts. For both, the next few hours offered the possibility of redemption.[64]

Redemption was the theme of the hour—for the regiment that had yet to see a major fight, for the officers under arrest, and for the mutineers of the Second Maine. Sixty-six of the former mutineers were among the companies now arraying themselves for combat on the rocky slopes, while six remained under arrest but with the unit. With the battle nigh, John Lynes Jr. and John Conway dropped their dissent, picked up rifles, and joined in the defense of Little Round Top. The already-court-martialed Henry Moore continued to refuse, as did Charles Brown, Thomas Townsend, and William H. Wentworth. In the coming battle, the men formerly of the Second Maine stood out, and their veteran presence no doubt comforted their new comrades.[65]

"We had not been in posision more than fifteen minutes," Nathan Clark recalled, "when the skirmishers on our right was forced back into the ranks and the enemy advanced close after them." With a deadly portend, Will Livermore remembered, "We heard terrible musketry on our right which rolled along, coming nearer and nearer." The Fourth Alabama, Fourth Texas, and Fifth Texas were attacking the rightmost regiments of Vincent's brigade. "Soon scattering bullets came singing through the trees," Livermore observed. And then "I saw a rebel and fired at him. The same instant a sheet of fire and smoke belched forth from our line." Clark relayed, "When the enemy's line hove in sight they wer at short range and we opened fire on them and they replied with grate fury." These men were seven companies of the

Forty-Seventh Alabama, around 150 men in total, and Ellis Spear thought he knew the reason for their anger. In a humorous letter written to his grand-daughter nearly fifty years after the battle, Spear explained, "They saw that they had not gotten behind us, but that we were there looking right in their faces, as much as to say—the trick didn't work. They were so mad they began firing at once; and, of course, we fired right back, as was right since they began it." Now aware of the presence of the Mainers, "The enemy, or many of them, crept forward & took shelter behind boulders, and fired on us from some par-tial covering." "Their manners," Spear chided, "were bad from first to last."[66]

The men of the Forty-Seventh Alabama were not the only ones surprised at that moment. Company B was to the left front of the Twentieth, just begin-ning to advance up Big Round Top, and Captain Morrill "was somewhat surprised to hear heavy volleys of musketry in our rear, where we had just left the regiment." The trees made visibility difficult for all involved. Morrill was now worried, as it appeared he had a much larger force interposed between his forty-four men and the rest of the regiment. Not daring a direct return to the unit, Morrill found a stone wall around two hundred yards to the Twentieth's left that ran perpendicular to the regiment's present position, allowing Morrill to "guard against a flank movement on the left." In addition to the stone wall, "I found some twelve or fifteen U.S. Sharpshooters under the com-mand of a non-commissioned officer," Morrill reported, "and he asked leave to remain under my command during the battle." The noncommissioned officer was Sergeant Grove Scribner of Company H, Second United States Sharpshooters, and this squad had been among those who had fired on Law's brigade earlier as it advanced toward the Round Tops, leading to the redirec-tion of the Forty-Seventh and Fifteenth Alabama. Carrying Sharps rifles that were accurate to twice the distance of the Mainers' weapons and could be fired three times as fast, these men added substantially to Company B's firepower.[67]

Writing in *Maine at Gettysburg*, Chamberlain noted, "The most for-midable assailants of the Twentieth did not, however, advance by way of the valley. They came over the summit of Big Round Top." The Fifteenth Alabama had arrived.[68]

On paper, the Fifteenth Alabama was just about everything the Twentieth Maine was not. Organized at the beginning of the war, its men had been in the army for two years versus the ten months for the Twentieth. Mere time does not tell the whole story, however, for those two years had been full of action, including seven major battles. They fought under Stonewall Jackson during the Shenandoah Valley Campaign of 1862, losing nine dead and thirty-three wounded during their first major engagement at Cross Keys. Marching east, the men joined Robert E. Lee for the Seven Days. At Gaines' Mill, the unit helped break the stubborn Union defenses, but at a cost of another 34 killed and 110 wounded—a full third of the regiment's 412 members. It is possible they encountered the Second Maine that day, including some of the seventy-two men now on Little Round Top. As the fighting shifted north, they fought at both Second Manassas and in the Maryland Campaign, suffering another 30 men killed and 166 wounded.[69] Both the Fifteenth Alabama and the Twentieth Maine fought at the Battle of Fredericksburg in December 1862, but whereas it was the first significant action for the Mainers, the Fifteenth Alabama could claim to be a battle-hardened, crack unit that had already suffered hundreds of casualties and forced Union troops to run from more than one battlefield.[70]

Casualties among the officer corps and a major who avoided battle at all costs—like the Twentieth's Charles Gilmore—meant that Captain William C. Oates of Company G had commanded the unit since late September 1862. Like Chamberlain, Oates was a civilian before the war, had no formal military training, had just recently been promoted to colonel, and also had a younger brother who served under him. He was even fond of quoting Shakespeare and, after the war, served a term as governor of his state. Gettysburg became the defining moment of his life, too—despite being wounded six times in other battles. But in other ways Oates's background was far different from Chamberlain's. Five years younger than Chamberlain, Oates had grown up rough. He had struck a man in the head with a hoe during a brawl when he was just seventeen and, fearing he had committed murder, fled his home state. The man lived, but an arrest warrant was made out against Oates for the assault. In Shreveport, Louisiana, Oates attacked an employer who refused to pay up, striking the man in the face repeatedly while simultaneously choking him. Fleeing another arrest warrant, Oates headed for Texas. Eventually he returned to Alabama, though to another county where he was not liable to be arrested, and became a lawyer and a newspaperman in the late 1850s. Throughout the first two years of the war, Oates became an excellent commander beloved by his men, a leader from their own ranks.[71]

William C. Oates (From his book *The War Between the Union and the Confederacy and Its Lost Opportunities*)

The Fifteenth Alabama had been in the vicinity of Chambersburg from June 27 until the early morning hours of July 2 before completing their twenty-four-mile march to Gettysburg. Along the way there was little water, most of it already having been used up by the preceding elements of Lee's army, and Oates's men arrived on the battlefield parched. After marching another four miles to their attack position on Warfield Ridge, near the present-day Texas Monument, Oates sent twenty-two men—two each from his eleven companies—to fill up the unit's canteens from a well roughly one hundred yards to their rear at the Alexander Currens house. The attack order came quickly, before the canteen-laden men had returned, and Oates was forced to advance, hoping they might catch up. They never did. As they tried to find their way back to their attacking comrades, the detail was captured by men from the Second United States Sharpshooters, depriving Oates of roughly 5 percent of his strength and the critical water. Not only was water needed to rejuvenate the parched men, but it was also essential in the rifle-cleaning process that each weapon needed after every fifteen or twenty shots. In a fight determined by the finest of margins, this was a blow that Oates believed "contributed largely to our failure to take Little Round Top."[72]

The Fifteenth's fight against the sharpshooters during the initial phase of their attack was costly, with Lieutenant Colonel Feagin just one of several casualties. Oates's shift to the east in pursuit of those sharpshooters brought him directly up Big Round Top. The temperature reached 81 degrees, and the punishing climb up the hill, with no water, left some men fainting from heat and exhaustion and must have decreased the fighting capabilities of the entire unit. With his right flank on the summit of Big Round Top and his left trailing off to the west down the slope, Oates and his men rested for a few moments. In the interlude, Oates tried to convince one of General Law's staff officers that Big Round Top was a better position than Little Round Top, a potential "Gibraltar" that after thirty minutes of work "I could hold against ten times the number of men I had." Grasping that Oates's job was an offensive rather than defensive one, the staff officer relayed that General Law was anxious for Oates to "drive everything before me as far as possible" and urged him to continue the attack.[73]

Oates reluctantly began moving forward again, descending the north slope of Big Round Top unopposed. Reaching the saddle between the two hills, he spotted a Union ordnance train parked along the Taneytown Road three hundred yards to his east. Oates detached his Company A, approximately forty men, and sent them after the prize. The ordnance train was a distraction that further bled Oates's manpower, for the forty men did not return in time to participate in the fight on Little Round Top. Oates had now lost more than sixty-five men since he had lined up on Warfield Ridge—what he would have given for those additional riflemen in the ensuing hours. Sending men to get water had been a wise move with an unlucky outcome, and the casualties caused by the sharpshooters were beyond his control, but detaching Company A was a self-inflicted wound, a critical weakening of his manpower that might have made all the difference.[74]

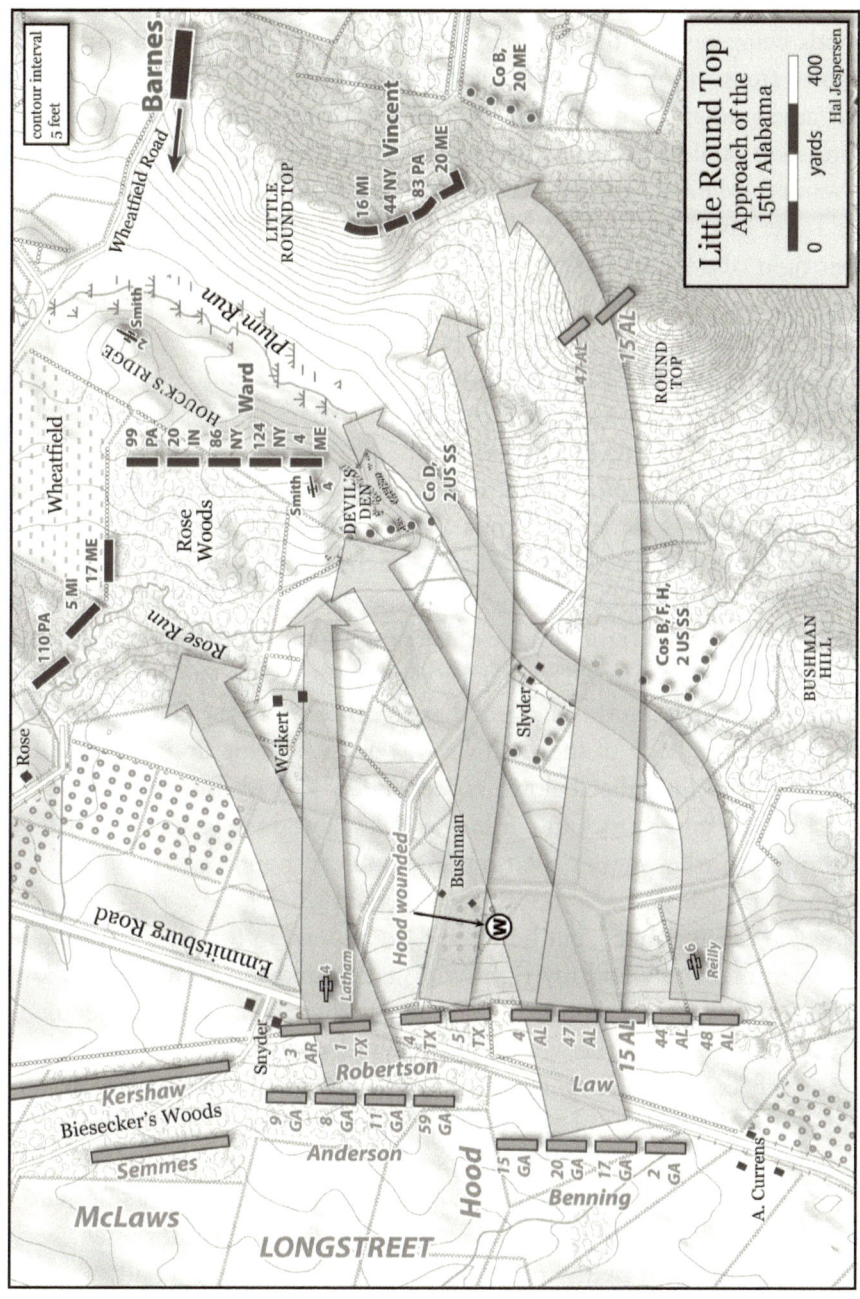

contour interval
5 feet

Little Round Top
Approach of the
15th Alabama

0   yards   400

Hal Jespersen

Barnes

Wheatfield Road

Co B,
20 ME

LITTLE
ROUND TOP

16 MI
44 NY Vincent
83 PA
20 ME

47 AL

15 AL

ROUND
TOP

Smith

Plum Run

HOUCK'S RIDGE

Ward

99 20 86 124 4
PA IN NY NY ME

Smith
4

BUSHMAN
HILL

Wheatfield

DEVIL'S
DEN

Co D,
2 US SS

Cos B, F, H,
2 US SS

17 ME

5 MI

Rose
Woods

Rose Run

110 PA

Slyder

Rose

Weikert

Bushman

Hood wounded

W

6
Reilly

Emmitsburg Road

Latham

Snyder

3
AR

1
TX

4
TX

5
TX

4
AL

47
AL

15 AL

44
AL

48
AL

Robertson

Law

A. Currens

Kershaw

Biesecker's Woods

9
GA

8
GA

11
GA

59
GA

Anderson

Semmes

15
GA

20
GA

17
GA

2
GA

Benning

McLaws

Hood

LONGSTREET

157

"Advancing rapidly," Oates wrote, "without any skirmishers in front, the woods being open without undergrowth, I saw no enemy until within forty or fifty steps of an irregular ledge of rocks." Oates and his two regiments had advanced into an area in front of the Eighty-Third Pennsylvania and were soon taking fire from that unit and the Forty-Fourth New York and Twentieth Maine to either side. The Alabamian called it "the most destructive fire I ever saw," and, after a short time, he moved the Fifteenth Alabama to their right (the Union left) in search of both the flank and fewer opponents.[75]

Men and officers all along the Twentieth's line spotted the movement and sent warnings to their commander. In the postwar years, Jim Nichols of Company K and Ellis Spear commanding the unit's left wing each claimed to have brought the concerning movement to Chamberlain's attention. Speaking at the dedication of the regiment's monuments in 1889, Chamberlain explained, "I take note also of the surprise of several officers to hear that it was some other than a single one of them who came to me in the course of the fight with information of the enemy's extended movements to envelop our left. Now, as might well be believed of such gentlemen and soldiers, they are all right; no one of them is wrong." Offering further details, Chamberlain continued, "It was quite early in the action, and while as yet only our right wing was hotly engaged, that an officer from the center reported to me that a large body of the enemy could be seen in his front, moving along the bottom of the valley below us, deliberately towards our extreme left and rear. I sprang upon a rock in our line, which allowed me to see over the heads of those with who we were then engaged, and the movement and intent of the enemy was plain to be seen." If Chamberlain let the move pass unchecked, he would be outflanked, but how could he respond to this new challenge?[76]

"I immediately had my right wing take intervals by the left flank at 3 to 5 paces," Chamberlain explained to his division commander four days later, "Thus covering the whole front then engaged; & moved my left wing to the left & rear making nearly a right angle at the color." Chamberlain had "refused" his line—bent it back on itself at roughly a 90-degree angle so that he could face multiple fronts and protect his own rear. To do that, his men first had gone from two ranks to one—making their line twice as long but half as strong—and then slid to the left. "This movement was so admirably executed by my men, that our fire was not materially slackened in front while the left wing was taking its new position."[77]

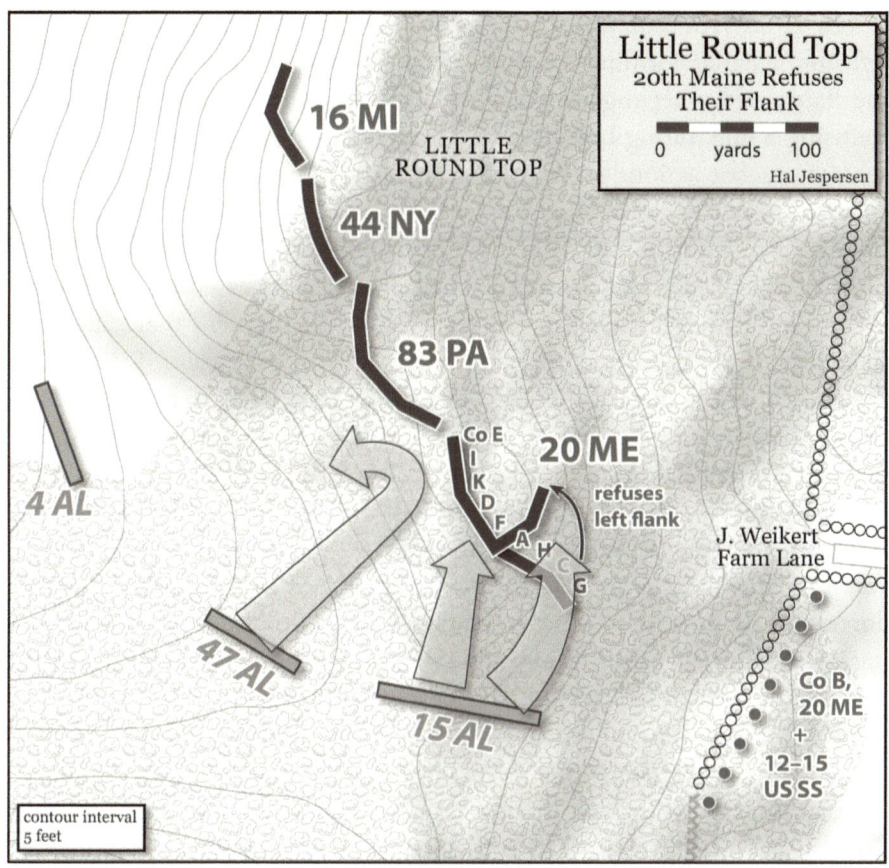

In his landmark book on the Twentieth Maine, John Pullen called the orders "completely fantastic, considering the fact that the regiment was already under fire." He describes the movement of the 506 men with bewilderment as "that of a single, living organism responding to a sense of imminent danger. Or—it was almost as though every man had been party to a quiet conference, where everything had been diagrammed and perfectly understood." It was, Pullen suggests, almost a miracle. Ken Burns's documentary *The Civil War* refers to Chamberlain's invocation of "obscure textbook maneuvers," with the implication being that only someone of Chamberlain's intellect and proficiency for deep study could have conceived of such a thing in the moment. Nothing could be further from the truth.[78]

In *Civil War Infantry Tactics*, Earl Hess notes, "Changing front by refusing a flank, forming forward or backward on a subunit, moving by the flank, and wheeling were essential tools of the Civil War tactician." Refusing a line during battle was far from obscure and featured in 28 percent of combat actions Hess studied. Effective Civil War officers did not get creative in the moment and order their men to do things they had never tried before. Instead, they fell back on their thousands of hours of mutual training and all the maneuvers they had practiced repeatedly on the training ground to select the appropriate tactic for the moment that they knew their men could execute with just a few words of instruction. John Pullen is correct that the men of the Twentieth "had been party to a quiet conference, where everything had been diagrammed and perfectly understood," but that conference did not take place on July 2 at Gettysburg; it had taken place dozens of times throughout the fall of 1862 and spring of 1863 as the men had gone through drill after drill to prepare themselves for this very moment. The great martial arts expert Bruce Lee once said, "Under duress, we do not rise to our expectations, but fall to the level of our training." Chamberlain asked of his men the routine, the well practiced, not the obscure, not that which would have perplexed them.[79]

With the Twentieth now in their adapted position, "Not more than two minutes elapsed before the enemy came up in column of Regiments with an impetuosity which betrayed their anticipation of an easy triumph. Their astonishment was great as they emerged from their cover, & found instead of an unprotected rear, a solid front." With maneuver and flanking options exhausted, the only thing left for both sides was to fight it out and see who gave up first.[80]

William T. Livermore, stationed in the center of the line with the color guard, wrote, "They came to within four or six rods [22–33 yards] covering themselves behind big rocks and trees, and kept up a murderous fire, which was returned by us." Three weeks after the battle, Ellis Spear described the scene: "Bullets hissed all about; splinters flew from the trees and the men were dropping every second. There was no shelter; the trees were small and the ground smooth, and the men faced the storm of bullets." At such close range, the danger and opportunity were two sides of a coin. "Every one who dared raise his head," Livermore wrote, "was sure of his man, but many lost their brains in the attempt." On the other side, Colonel Oates observed that "the fire was so destructive that my line wavered like a man trying to walk against a strong wind."[81]

Between the vegetation and needing to take what cover was available, the soldiers were effectively blind. Today's readers have maps of the battlefield and timelines of the action to provide a big picture of what was happening on other parts of the hill and battlefield, but fighting in this wooded spur, the men on both sides could see perhaps one hundred yards, not even rifle distance, and knew little of what was happening beyond their immediate vicinity. Earl Hess contends that "the blindness that many soldiers endured on the battlefield heightened their fears" and that "battle was an experience of the senses." Ellis Spear wrote, "I remember that there was noises so loud that the shouted orders could scarcely be heard."[82]

A few hundred yards away—and a world apart, in battlefield terms—the fighting was just as heavy. Two regiments of Texans attacked the rightmost regiment of Vincent's brigade, the Sixteenth Michigan, and part of the unit fell back while others desperately held their ground. The Texans sensed an opportunity and poured forward, only to be checked by the timely arrival of the 140th New York. The Empire State men lunged over the crest of Little Round Top and into their Confederate foes with bayonets only, stabilizing the Union line but suffering 40 percent casualties, including their beloved commander, Patrick O'Rourke. Two guns of Charles Hazlett's battery now fired from the heights, but the rifled weapons were ineffective at short ranges and were of little benefit to the infantrymen around them.

Back on the extreme left, the firefight that the Twentieth was now engaged in was fierce and yet relatively common for the Civil War. While the rifle musket had increased a soldier's theoretical effective range to three hundred yards or more, most combat took place at much shorter distances. Recent studies suggest soldiers were typically only 75–130 yards apart as they fired at one another. Thus, the combat on Little Round Top was certainly at close range, but not abnormally so. Despite the number of bullets in the air, relatively few men were actually hit. Each of the 506 men in the Twentieth Maine was issued sixty rounds of ammunition on the morning of July 2, and by the end of their firefight, all or nearly all of those bullets had been used, bringing the total expenditure to thirty thousand rounds. The Fifteenth Alabama had approximately fifty men killed and one hundred wounded, meaning only one out of every two hundred bullets fired by a Mainer found its mark, with only one out of every six hundred killing a Rebel soldier. At a distance of just twenty to thirty yards, those ratios seem preposterous if taken on their own. Quartermaster records reveal, however, that there were nine million bullets fired at the Battle of Gettysburg, resulting in ten thousand deaths and thirty thousand wounds. Thus, for the battle writ large, only 1 in 225 bullets fired hit someone, and just 1 in 900 led to death. The Twentieth Maine and the Fifteenth Alabama were right at those averages. Paddy Griffith's studies into Napoleonic and Civil War combat came to a similar conclusion, noting that two regiments in exposed positions firing at one another from thirty yards typically hit just one or two men per minute, and "casualties mounted because the contest went on so long and there were so many combatants, not because the fire was particularly deadly." Not just a nineteenth-century phenomenon, this severely ineffective fire also continued to Vietnam, where fifty thousand bullets were fired for every enemy soldier killed. How could it be that so few bullets hit a human target?[83]

During World War II, U.S. Army historian S. L. A. Marshall studied the combat experience of soldiers and concluded that the repulsion of killing another person was so great that not more than 15–20 percent of American riflemen fired their weapons in combat. These non-firers were not cowards or shirkers—they were on the front lines in dangerous positions getting ammunition, running messages, and putting themselves in just as much danger as those who were firing—they simply refused to take another's life. Some have attacked Marshall's methods and conclusions since their publication in 1947, but at least one piece of data from Gettysburg offers circumstantial support. When the battle ended, nearly 90 percent of the 27,574 rifles recovered from the battlefield were loaded. Twelve thousand contained multiple loads, and six thousand had three or more bullets rammed down the barrel. One had twenty-three balls lined up! Given the lengthy loading process and the instant it took to fire a shot, one would expect perhaps 10 percent of the recovered guns to be loaded, not 90 percent, which suggests men might have resisted firing. The firearms found with multiple loads could be indicative of battle stress leading to improper loading procedures but could also indicate soldiers who avoided shooting at other humans.[84]

In another World War II study, authors Roy Swank and Walter Marchand concluded that just 2 percent of combat soldiers were free of the mental resistance to killing that typified their comrades and would fire at enemy soldiers without experiencing "the resultant psychiatric casualties associated with extended periods of combat." If that 2 percent number applied to the Twentieth Maine and Fifteenth Alabama, perhaps just ten men on either side were actively trying to kill or maim their opponents. Those ten men, firing six hundred rounds between them, may well have accounted for the 130–150 killed and wounded suffered by each side.[85]

In all the known accounts of the fighting on Little Round Top, only two men from the Twentieth Maine wrote about killing anyone, and both were in private letters or journals. In his army journal, compiled well after the war, Nathan Clark wrote that, during the bayonet charge, "I took two prisoners from behind a rock where I had been selecting my targets for some time and others lay thare lifeless." More pointedly, at the end of a lengthy letter to his brother on July 12, included almost as an afterthought, Eugene Kelleran of Company I wrote, "I did think of sending home for a hat but I have one now in the fight there was a reb behind a rock trying to shoot me but I was to quick for him my ball took him in the mouth & passed through his head so I took his hat it is a hard saying but I cant help it do not noise it about it was the only one that I know of hitting for sertain." No other man in the Twentieth directly acknowledged wounding or killing an enemy soldier.[86]

As the fight raged on, the Alabamians made continual attacks against the Twentieth's line. "They advanced however within ten paces of my line," Chamberlain wrote, "making what they call a 'charge'—that is, advancing & firing rapidly. Our volleys were so steady & telling that the enemy were checked here, & broken. Their second line then advanced, with the same ardor & the same fate, & so too a third & fourth." As the Fifteenth Alabama made their third attack, Chamberlain "saw with consternation that our centre was nearly shot away, and the color guarded only by a little group, who seemed to be checking the enemy by their heroic bearing and not by numbers." He sent his brother Tom, the regiment's adjutant, to implore Captain Keene and Company F to hold on, but "so little expecta- tion had I that the adjutant could live to reach the spot, I pressed into my service a trusted sergeant and dispatch him with the same message." Long- ago promises made to his parents to keep his twenty-two-year-old brother in a safe position—and not now kept—must have rung in Chamberlain's head as he sent Tom into the thickest of the fighting.[87]

Colonel Oates reported, "We drove the Federals from their strong defensive position; five times they rallied and charged us, twice coming so near that some of my men had to use the bayonet." In an 1897 letter, Oates claimed that he had pushed the Mainers back 120 steps and categorized all of the following action as an attempt by the Twentieth to regain their original position. Chamberlain described a much more contained ebb and flow: "This struggle of an hour & a half, was desperate in the extreme: four times did we lose & win that space of ten yards between the contending lines, which was strewn with dying & dead." The truth is likely somewhere in the middle. The men of the Twentieth Maine do not describe falling back any great distance or multiple attempts to retake their original posi- tion, and William Jordan of the Fifteenth Alabama later wrote that Colonel Oates "was endeavoring to swing around and turn the enemy's left, but it was impossible."[88]

One of those dying was a young man named George Buck of Company H. Six months earlier, Buck had been a sergeant who "took great pride in discharging every duty in a soldierly manner." While on the sick roll and excused by the surgeon from any duty in early January 1863, Buck had been ordered by Quartermaster Alden Litchfield to cut some wood. When Buck refused on account of his illness, Litchfield attacked him with his fists and feet. Without a hearing, Buck was stripped of his sergeant's stripes and reduced to the ranks. Now Buck was among the first wounded in the fighting, and it was evident that the wound was mortal. During a lull, his comrades gathered around and heard him mutter, "They reduced me to the ranks, but I will show them I am not afraid to die." As Colonel Chamberlain came over, Buck whispered, "I was disgraced." In a further display of the compassion and fairness he had shown the men since their enlistment ten months earlier, Chamberlain knelt by Buck and promised, "You are now exonerated, and promoted to a sergeancy."[89]

Not including Morrill's Company B, nearly a third of the Twentieth's men had been hit by a bullet during their fight with the Alabamians. Among the officers, Charles Billings of Company C was mortally wounded in the knee while James Stanwood was wounded in the leg, Joseph Fitch of Company D was wounded in the thigh, a ball hit Samuel Keene of Company F in the abdomen—his life saved by his sword belt—and Warren Kendall of Company G was shot in the throat and would die three days later. Chamberlain had been hit twice: once in the foot by rock shards that sliced open his boot and skin, and once in the sword by a spent round. Even many of those whose flesh was not pierced and thus were not official casualties felt the wrath of the enemy's .577 Enfield rounds. In reporting his wounded two weeks after the battle, Colonel Chamberlain acknowledged, "Some who were very slightly struck, are not reported here. Hardly any one in the Regt. escaped without some mark in his clothing, at least." Elisha Coan noted, "A bullet went through my cap half an inch from the 'scalp,'" his nearest brush during the war, while Albert Fernald "got a bullet shot through my blanket."[90]

Not surprisingly, the casualties were unevenly dispersed along the line. After the Fifteenth Alabama had slid around looking for the Twentieth's left flank, there had been little action on the Twentieth's far right. The two companies posted there, E and I, suffered just two men killed and six wounded out of ninety-four engaged. The three companies on the left flank, H, C, and G, had a combined strength of 107 men and lost 15 killed and 28 wounded. It was in the center that the fighting was the fiercest, with the ninety-three men in the three center companies (D, F, and A) plus the color guard suffering nearly 50 percent casualties, with sixteen men killed or mortally wounded and thirty wounded. Elisha Coan noted that the loss of the men meant, "Instead of being too crowded as at first, *there is room enough now*." When Chamberlain refused the line, he created a salient that nearly begged to be attacked, and the Confederates happily obliged. Howard Prince later wrote, "The two companies at the colors, receiving a fire from three sides, are swept like trees by a whirlwind." Eli Brown of Company F suffered a head wound but escaped with his life. "He is a very short man," Hezekiah Long explained to his wife. "The ball just struck the top of his head enough to break his skull. If he had been half an inch taller, it would have been

John Reed, Company A, Twentieth Maine; killed at Gettysburg (Maine State Archives)

all day with him, so you see what he gained by being very short." Brown stood just 5'4" tall.[91]

As the Confederates continued their attacks, the Union line swayed and at times was pushed far enough that the Alabamians' wayward rounds hit the men of the Eighty-Third Pennsylvania in their flank. Things were so desperate that Captain O. O. Woodward of that unit pulled his men back slightly, fearing that the Twentieth had been flanked and that Confederates would soon be in his rear. In the early 1900s, Colonel Oates sought permission to put up a monument marking both the point of his unit's further penetration into Union lines and the spot where his younger brother, John, fell with multiple bullets in his body. The boulder that Oates identified as that very spot is well within the Twentieth's lines, indicating just how fluid the lines of attack and defense had become.[92]

Amid this surreal scene of Union and Confederate bodies mixing with one another and lines in flux, the Twentieth Maine's colors never wavered and stood as the metaphorical and literal anchor point for every man along the line. Andrew Tozier held the flag aloft and was protected by four men who had been hand selected to form the "color guard." On Tozier's right stood Charles Reed, and behind him William T. Livermore. On the left was Melville Day, with Elisha Coan behind him. During the fighting, Melville Day fell dead with five bullets in him, while Charles Reed was shot in the wrist. Years later Reed recounted, "Sergt. Tozier said Reed you take the colors and let me shoot and we exchanged and I was wounded." Tozier fired several shots from Reed's musket, William T. Livermore later recollected. Years later Ellis Spear wrote, "What I most distinctly remember there . . . was the Color Sergeant Tozier, who had picked up a musket dropped by one of the killed or wounded, and with his left arm about the colors, stood loading and firing, and chewing a bit of cartridge paper." The scene, the color sergeant holding the flag while firing a rifle, became one of the fight's iconic images. Tozier's calmness under fire and the example he set for others were recognized with a Congressional Medal of Honor in 1898.[93]

Tozier was not the only one of the Second Maine men making a difference. In their post-battle reports, Lieutenant James Stanwood of Company C noted that Andrew Deering "came under my especial notice," while Henry Sidelinger of Company E reported that John Sherwood and Charles Haynes "behaved with unusual courage and great bravery." In his first major public speech on the battle in 1865, Chamberlain offered similar praise: "We had in our regiment several mutineers from the 2d Me., and among the number was one James R. Martin, who was tried and found not wanting. Generosity on the part of the Government had reacted on himself. He was seen fighting in the foremost ranks, and one hour after, a ghastly wound in the head laid him low. 'My mother will not know,' said he, 'Tell her I do not die a coward.'" Illustrating the incredible cost of holding those Second Maine men to the extra year (or more) of service, three lay dead on the slopes of Little Round Top, six more were wounded, and of the injured, Company B's George Leach was captured and died in a Confederate prison.[94]

Without those men formerly of the Second Maine, it is doubtful the Twentieth could have held out to this point, but even with them the hour of crisis had arrived. "Half my left wing lay on the ground," Chamberlain observed, leaving him with "a mere skirmish line" in that sector. An hour or more into this firefight, those still standing were scraping the bottom of their cartridge boxes, their sixty rounds exhausted or nearly so. Chamberlain's requests for more ammunition had brought no results, likely a consequence of the death of so many of the superior officers on Little Round Top and the broken chains of command and logistics that resulted from the piecemeal way in which Union units had fed into the battle to shore up Sickles's Third Corps line. During a break in the assaults, Chamberlain implored his men "to gather the contents of every cartridge box of the dead & dying, friend & foe, & with these we met the enemy on their last & most desperate assault." Oates had sensed, "It was now our time to deal death and destruction to a gallant foe," and he led the sixth charge forward. The two lines merged into one, and the Twentieth "was driven back from this ledge, but not father than to the next ledge on the mountain side," Oates asserted. The Fifteenth Alabama's color bearer was next to his colonel when "A Maine man reached to grasp the staff of the colors when Ensign Archibald stepped back and Sergeant Pat O'Connor stove his bayonet through the head of the Yankee, who fell dead." The Twentieth Maine shoved the attackers back a few yards, but now an even bigger problem surfaced. Chamberlain summarized simply, "Our ammunition utterly failed." The ever-practical Will Livermore knew exactly what this meant: "We stood until our centre had lost half our men, and we knew we could not stand longer."[95]

There is a harsh but simple way to summarize what came next. Both Colonel Chamberlain of the Twentieth Maine and Colonel Oates of the Fifteenth Alabama knew their men were out of ammunition, had suffered roughly 30 percent casualties, and were utterly exhausted. Oates had been ordered to take Little Round Top, Chamberlain to hold it at all hazards. In the moment of crisis, Oates ordered his men to retreat, while Chamberlain ordered his to fix bayonets and charge.

Two things happened nearly simultaneously within the Mainers' line: Chamberlain determined on the charge and sent word to his left to prepare to move forward. At the same time, Lieutenant Holman Melcher of Company F requested permission to advance his company to recover the wounded. Chamberlain replied that he was about to order the *entire* regiment forward and sent Melcher back to his company. "As a last, desperate resort," Chamberlain wrote four days later, "I ordered a charge. The word 'fix bayonets' flew from man to man. The click of the steel seemed to give new zeal to all. The men dashed forward with a shout."[96]

In the postwar years, a debate arose that lasts to this day as to whether Chamberlain ordered his men to "charge" or merely directed them to fix their bayonets. The men writing in July 1863 do not uniformly describe the language Chamberlain used in that critical moment, but they leave no doubt that they understood his intent. In his diary that night, William T. Livermore wrote, "We were ordered to charge them when there were two to our one. With fixed bayonets and a yell we rushed on them." Writing a letter for the *Portland Daily Press* published three weeks later, Ellis Spear noted, "When it was perhaps uncertain whether we should hold the place assigned us or be driven back, the Colonel ordered a charge! Nothing could have been more opportune."[97]

Writing in 1885, Holman Melcher (the man who some later credited as the leader of the charge) described the order and the scene: "The time had come when it must be decided whether we should fall back and give up this key to whole field of Gettysburg, or charge and try to throw off this foe, that were rapidly drawing the life-blood of our regiment by their deadly fire. It must not be the former; how can it be the latter? Col. Chamberlain decides it can be only the latter and gives the order to 'fix bayonets,' and almost before he can say 'Charge'! the regiment, with a shout of desperation, leaps down the hill and close in with the foe, which we find behind every rock and tree." Oates had already told the Fifteenth Alabama they were about to retreat. Seeing the Maine men surge forward, he gave the signal and "we ran like a herd of wild cattle."[98]

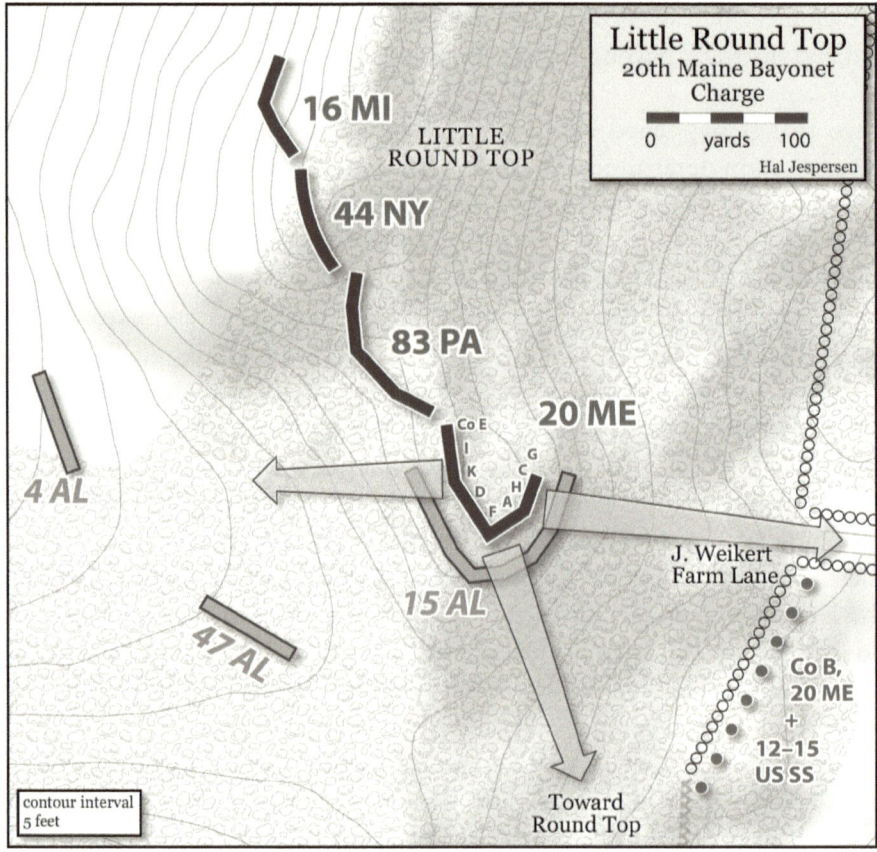

Though the Twentieth Maine had practiced with the bayonet during their long hours of drill over the previous ten months, Chamberlain's order to use the weapon at this moment likely surprised his own men as much as the Alabamians. Bayonets featured in only 12 percent of the small-unit actions Earl Hess studied and half the time did not result in hand-to-hand combat. If the charge was a good idea, the enemy tended to run away, while if it was a bad idea, those under attack would simply shoot those who had brought knives to a gunfight. It is not clear that the Mainers ultimately bayoneted *any* Confederates, which would not be surprising when considering the low rate of wounds inflicted by edged weapons during the Civil War. There is no evidence of a single bayonet wound during the hand-to-hand fighting that occurred during the repulse of Pickett's

Charge the following day. From May 1 to July 31, 1864, the period of the war's heaviest fighting and including the Wilderness, Spotsylvania, Cold Harbor, and the beginnings of the siege at Petersburg, surgeons for the Army of the Potomac treated just thirty-seven bayonet wounds. During the war's final actions from February to April 1865, they treated just three such wounds. Most compellingly, in a postwar account of the 1864 Battle of the Wilderness, Holman Melcher noted, "This was the first, and I am glad to say, the last time that I saw the bayonet used in its most terrible and effective manner." This statement by a man who was at the forefront of the charge is strong evidence that no Confederates were bayoneted on Little Round Top. Amos Judson of the Eighty-Third Pennsylvania supported that notion, asserting that "the first time the bayonet was ever *used* in all the battles of the Army of the Potomac" came in May 1864. Judson continued, "When I say used, I mean used by a charging column, in actual conflict: for in ninety-nine hundredths of all the bayonet charges that are ever made, either the attacking columns are checked, or the party attacked give way before coming into close encounter."[99] Such was precisely what happened on Little Round Top.

"Col Chamberlain gave the order fix bayonets, Charge bayonets Charge and of we went with a wild yell that surprised the enemy," Nathan Clark wrote, "they at that time being not over four rods from us. They had but little time to choose between surrender or cold steel, so the most of their front line droped their rifles and steped to our rear for safety. I took two prisoners from behind a rock." Just to Clark's left, William Livermore had a similar experience: "With fixed bayonets and a yell we rushed on them, which so frightened them, that not another shot was fired on us. Some threw down their arms and ran, but many rose up, begging to be spared. We did not stop but told them to go to the rear, and on we went after the whipped and frightened rebels." Chamberlain offered nearly identical words four days after the battle: "In this charge the bayonet only was used on our part, & the rebels seemed so petrified with astonishment that their front line scarcely offered to run or to fire—they threw down their arms & begged 'not to be killed', & we captured them by whole companies."[100]

Nearly every man was capturing Confederates. Chamberlain was at the front of the charge and took his own prisoner: "At the first dash the commanding officer I happened to confront, coming on fiercely, sword in one hand and big navy revolver in the other, fires one barrel almost in my face; but seeing the quick saber-point at his throat, reverses arms, gives sword and pistol into my hands and yields himself prisoner."[101] Two weeks later, Chamberlain wrote to Fanny and downplayed the danger he had faced, saying, "I took several officers in the fight prisoners + one of them insisted on presenting me a fine pistol as a reward of merit I suppose."[102] Ellis Spear had been sick to his stomach on the march to Gettysburg and thus had left his belt and pistol on his horse, not wanting the pressure on his midsection. Armed with only his sword, he still managed to capture enemy combatants. "There were two behind one rock on which I leaped," Spear recollected, and they "rose up . . . surrendering at once."[103]

There was a simple reason why so many Confederates surrendered. "The final formation of the regiment was such," Lieutenant Melcher wrote, "that when the charge was made it was in a direction directly to the rear from the rest of the regiments of the brigade were facing and fighting; and the enemy, or the most of them, were driven in their flight, at first, directly to the rear to the line of battle of our army, and accounts in part for so few of them escaping."[104] The Twentieth's charge had forced the Rebels to flee not in the direction from which they had come but farther to the east. "Then we discovered Morrill and Co. B," Captain Spear wrote. "They had been behind a stone wall in rear of the enemy, and had been paying their respects to him in true backwoods fashion. They were all sharpshooters, Captain and all, and loved a gun."[105]

Hidden thus far, these men must have been anxiously awaiting their opportunity to take a more substantial part in the fighting for more than an hour at this point. Just in the last few minutes they had been spotted by Colonel Oates, who mistook them for two regiments of sharpshooters— a misidentification that had played into his decision to order a retreat. "About that time your regiment charged them," Walter Morrill wrote to Chamberlain six days later, "at which time we opened fire on them, at the same time giving loud commands to charge, in order to have them think I had a large body of troops there." Reinforced by the sharpshooters, Morill's fresh troops with full cartridge boxes had an outsized impact. Already believing there were two regiments of sharpshooters in his rear, Colonel Oates claimed to have run into dismounted cavalry during his retreat—possibly mistaking the sound of the sharpshooters' carbines as those of cavalrymen. The Alabamians were completely confused, fleeing for their lives and unsure where to go. Ellis Spear cheekily told his granddaughter, "They all seemed to remember something they had left at home, or had forgotten to do, and they ran like mad, intending, I have no doubt, to go in the direction of home and their mothers."[106]

Watching from his position to the right, Amos Judson of the Eighty-Third Pennsylvania described the scene unfolding below with amazement: "The Twentieth continued the pursuit, their line swing around upon a moving pivot, like a great gate upon a post, until its left had swept down through the valley and up the sides of Big Round Top."[107]

A farm lane lined by a worm fence ran down the back or east side of Little Round Top, connecting with the Taneytown Road after just a few hundred yards. When hit with the unexpected fire from Company B, "A great many, two or three hundred, ran into a worm fence lane," Spear wrote. "They did try to get out, some of them, and these got upon the fence, and, painful as the necessity was, we were obliged to shoot them." Referring to the same moment, William T. Livermore wrote, "On we went after the whipped and frightened rebels, taking them by scores and giving those too far away to be captured deadly shots in the back." Men were surrendering in whole squads now, and William Lamson of Company B wrote home, "When one held up a white flag 15 came in and surrendered."[108]

In one of the most remarkable battle accounts ever penned, Elisha Coan of the color guard shared with comrade Samuel Miller his experience during the charge and pursuit:

> For a short time after the charge was made while we were busily engaged collecting the prisoners, a man at my right belonging to Co. F. pointed to an open field a few rods from us and to the left of our position and said "See those Rebs running across that field, let's have a shot at them," I was loading my rifle as he spoke, and he with another man from Co. F (I dont remember their names) and I, started for the edge of the woods to give them a "parting kiss!" As we reached the place one of the men fired at a squad of them that were running for "dear life" and one of the men fell whereupon the others had stopped, turned and saw us and raising their handkerchiefs, or something else, in token of surrender.

Elisha Coan (Bowdoin College Library)

There were several other squads a little further on and I raised my rifle (which I had now loaded and at the same <u>time</u> four other men turned and seeing the man surrounded and some chance that they might get hit called loudly for us not to fire.[109]

Corporal Livermore recollected in 1899, "No man in the Regt. had more interest in the flag than E. S. Coan and no man was among the prisoners sooner than he. He took five to the rear and I believe it was the first squad started in that direction." Perhaps the first, but certainly not the last.[110]

The total number of prisoners the Twentieth Maine captured is still debated. On July 6, Chamberlain told division commander James Barnes that the Twentieth had captured 393 prisoners and 300 rifles. He later revised down to 308 men and 275 stands of arms—a substantial number that nearly equaled his strength. Nathan Clark of Company H wrote that they captured two hundred prisoners, while Adney Boothby estimated the number as "about 250." Oates claimed to have lost only eighty-four previously unwounded prisoners, plus the wounded left in his front. But those wounded were substantial: He reported that 277 fewer men answered the evening roll call on July 2 than had been present that morning, though some turned up later. Considering that the Twentieth captured men from the Forty-Seventh Alabama and some from the other units of Law's brigade, both commanders may be accurate in their accounting.[111]

Writing to Fanny two days later, Chamberlain boasted, "My Regt was the extreme left & was attacked by a <u>whole Brigade</u>." Some modern critics cite this statement as an intentional exaggeration by Chamberlain to claim greater glory, but most of the men in the Twentieth Maine held this belief after the battle. Albert Fernald jotted in his diary that night, "Our Regt. fought a brigade," while Adney Boothby wrote home a fortnight later, "Our Regt. alone fought a whole brigade and drove them." Nathan Clark reported, "The prisoners say they had a whole brigade massed on our regt." These men were mistaken in their belief that they had bested an entire brigade, but it was an honestly held view at the moment, a function of their having fought against two different forces during the battle and taking prisoners from as many as five regiments during their charge. Such overestimates were not confined to the Twentieth Maine: In various places William Oates argued that his Fifteenth Alabama fought against the Forty-Fourth New York, Eighty-Third Pennsylvania, Twentieth Maine, two regiments of sharpshooters, and a unit of dismounted cavalry—a total of six regiments.[112]

Though there were still Confederates in the vicinity, and the battle raged to the north, the Twentieth's charge had cleared the immediate threat to the left flank. Elisha Coan was "forty or fifty rods away" from the regiment when he stopped moving forward and taking prisoners. Realizing that he was closer to enemy lines than comfort allowed, "I then hastened back to the Regt and found them resting in line."[113]

With the firefight over and the situation stabilized, the men began to care for the dead and wounded. Chamberlain noted that at least fifty dead Confederates were in their front, plus one hundred wounded. Both numbers generally square with the estimates provided by Oates if we also include the casualties of the Forty-Seventh Alabama. The Twentieth's own losses were similar. On July 13, Chamberlain reported total casualties of thirty-two killed, ninety-seven wounded, and two missing, a total casualty rate of 25 percent, slightly above the average for the Union regiments engaged at Gettysburg. The wounded were sent to the rear, and, further subtracting those detached to guard the prisoners, the number of men available for duty was reduced to just 198.[114]

If the Mainers believed their work was done, they were mistaken. James Rice, now commanding the brigade due to Strong Vincent's mortal wounding, had been ordered to occupy Big Round Top. Corps commander George Sykes feared that, if the Confederates took the taller hill, they could use it to launch further attacks on Little Round Top. A brigade of Pennsylvania Reserves had arrived on Little Round Top to bolster its defense, and Rice asked their commander to send troops up to Big Round Top. As Chamberlain explained years later, Colonel Joseph Fisher of the Reserves "emphatically declined, & I remember his saying that his men were armed with some inefficient rifle—'smooth bores' it seems to me he said, & especially that the ground was difficult & unknown to his men. He & his men were also much agitated." A disgusted James Rice asked Chamberlain to undertake the duty. But with his men "worn out, and heated and thirsty almost beyond endurance," Chamberlain could scarcely imagine ordering them to hike up the "high steep hill" covered with boulders and ravines. So instead he asked for volunteers. Writing that night from their new position on Big Round Top, Will Livermore described the scene: "Col. Chamberlain says: 'Boys, I am asked if I can carry that hill in front.' We all say, 'Yes.' Our little regiment fell in (only 8 in Company A.) and marched over rocks and through brush to the top of the hill, without meeting any foe." Asking rather than ordering his men to secure Big Round Top was yet another demonstration of Chamberlain's leadership qualities, with the unanimous response a sign of the respect and affection the men held for him.[115]

Before the Twentieth moved out, Colonel Rice secured three thousand rounds of ammunition for them so that they were no longer reliant solely on the bayonet. That was fortunate, for it soon became apparent that the Confederates were closer than anticipated. Will Lamson wrote, "After dark we went onto a mountain on picket and took 25 prisoners that came to our line thinking it was theirs and we soon found ourselves within a few rods of the same brigade we fought in the P.M." The prisoners belonged to the Fourth Texas, part of Robertson's brigade that had attacked the Sixteenth Michigan and Forty-Fourth New York during the fight earlier that evening.[116]

Throughout the night, the Confederates took potshots at the Union lines, and some came too close for comfort. "While we were resting," Lamson recounted, "I was lying 'with my back to the field and my feet to the foe' one of them sent a bullet so near my face that I felt it pass, but 'A miss is as good as a mile' sometimes." Not all were as fortunate. Corporal Livermore lamented that, during an exchange between the Twentieth's pickets and a Confederate sharpshooter, "Lieut. Linscott took one of the boy's muskets and went in advance of our pickets to get a shot at them, but received a severe if not mortal wound in the thigh." After lingering in a field hospital for nearly a month, Linscott died on July 27.[117]

On July 3, the Twentieth was relieved of its duties on Big Round Top and ordered to a reserve position in the army's center. On the way, "We marched back over the ground where we fought the night before seeing the dead rebels just where we lay them," Livermore noted. "Our boys had been buried and nothing but the blood was to be seen." The Twentieth Maine heard the awful cannonading that afternoon but played no role in repulsing Pickett's Charge. Their work had been done the day before.[118]

There was no resumption of the battle on Independence Day. Robert E. Lee began retreating that night, conceding defeat and now hoping to make it back across the Potomac to the safety of Virginia. "It seems quiet to-day," Will Livermore wrote, "I think they are withdrawing." The one activity that occupied the unit's time was gathering up Springfield rifles from the battlefield, exchanging them for the Enfields the unit had carried into the fight. Nearly identical in every way that mattered in battle, the Springfields were easier to clean, and allowing his men to switch out the guns was one more example of Chamberlain looking after the little things that made a difference to his soldiers.[119]

The Duke of Wellington said that next to a battle lost, the saddest thing is a battle won. On July 5, the Twentieth Maine advanced through the Peach Orchard over the ground so heavily contested three days earlier. The scene was simply horrific. "In one place 17 horses lay almost touching each other," Will Lamson wrote. "In a burned barn were the remains of 5 wounded rebels nearly all burned up. The smell was awful." Writing only to himself in his diary, William T. Livermore painted an even more graphic and horrific picture: "Men killed the 2nd lying in the burning sun present an awful spectacle. Swollen to double their natural size they cannot be moved but are buried as well as possible where they fell. Men cannot be recognized. The stench is sickening. I never saw anything like this."[120]

Writing to his brother Charles the next day, Livermore revealed how different it was to be on the winning side for a change, the side that held the field after a victory: "We were told to go over the field and get the guns while the Pioneers & detailed men by the hundreds were burying the dead I started immediately for the Rebel line of Battle where they formed behind a fence and there was where the Rebels left their things I followed it about half a mile and it was a solid row of Blankets knapsacks haversacks cartloads of bread some that they had stolen There was cartloads of everything that soldiers carry left & I got what things I wanted." That night, the Twentieth was ordered to pursue the retreating Rebels, and they began racing to the Potomac River.[121]

In addition to the thirty-two men who perished on Little Round Top, another six died of their wounds over the ensuing days and weeks, bringing the total of killed and mortally wounded to thirty-eight. One of the mortally wounded was Isaac Estes. Both his wife and his daughter had died before he enlisted in the summer of 1862, and now Isaac followed them on July 10, 1863. Eugene Sweeny, Jotham Tibbets, and George Leach were all captured, with the latter two dying in Confederate prison camps before the year was out. There were ninety-one wounded, many of whom were left behind. They had been moved from the initial aid station behind the Twentieth's line to the Trostle Farm on the night of July 2 and morning of July 3. J. B. Wescott was detailed to that location on the morning of July 3 and later wrote down what he had witnessed. The Trostle Farm "consisted of a very small house and a very large barn," Wescott remembered, which was typical of battlefield hospitals. The barn was "filled to its utmost capacity." The caretakers did all they could for the wounded, and "beds of hay were arranged on both sides of the floor, also in the bays. Here many of the severely wounded were made as comfortable as circumstances would admit." In these initial days, the surgeons were hard at work. Four men lost a limb to amputation and were subsequently discharged. Three lost a finger or two and were transferred to the Veteran Reserve Corps for light duty. Ben Clifford lost an eye. Adding insult to injury, "It was several days before supplies for so large a number could be furnished by the hospital department and we were obliged to skirmish around the country to get something for the wounded to eat," Wescott remembered. For those still hospitalized, slowly things improved, at first with the arrival of relief workers from the Christian and Sanitary Commissions who brought supplies, then with the establishment of a cleaner tented hospital, and finally with the transfer of those still needing care to Camp Letterman, the massive temporary hospital established on the east side of Gettysburg. Most of the wounded eventually returned to duty, and at least thirty would be wounded again—or killed—before the war was over.[122]

By July 9, the Twentieth Maine was just a few miles away from the Antietam battlefield in Maryland. "We have had some hard marching," Will Livermore admitted, but "we are still in the best of spirits over our victories. . . . I hope we shall have another big Battle on this side of the river for we had better fight them here than in Va."[123]

The following day, July 10, 1863, the Twentieth Maine skirmished along the Sharpsburg Pike, their third and final engagement during the Gettysburg Campaign. Two men were killed or mortally wounded: Sergeant Gardner Schwartz and Private Thomas Townsend. Six more were taken prisoner: Lowell Brock, John Conway, Alvin Cutler, William L. Davis, Lewis Flanders, and John Lenfest. All eight casualties came from Company E, which suggests it may have been the lone company engaged. Lowell Brock was never heard from again and is presumed to have died in a Confederate prison. The other five captured men are confirmed to have died in Confederate prisons, with Cutler, Davis, and Flanders perishing in the infamous facility at Andersonville, Georgia, while Conway and Lenfest died in Richmond. Conway and Townsend had been holdout mutineers from the Second Maine, with Conway picking up a rifle only when the fight on Little Round Top was imminent. "Thomas Townsend, who was also awaiting trial took his gun & his place in the ranks, & was killed in a fight on the Sharpsburg Pike," Chamberlain wrote in expunging his record just a few weeks later. The Second Maine men had paid heavily for their continued service.[124]

Despite the hopes of many in the Twentieth for a chance to fight again on Northern soil and defeat the rebellion, such was not to be the case. On the morning of July 14, 1863, the last elements of Robert E. Lee's army slipped back across the Potomac River, bringing the Gettysburg Campaign to a close.

If the men were frustrated at not having a chance to land another blow against the Rebels, they could at least take solace in the part they had played in the war's first great Union victory in the East and in establishing their regiment's reputation. Even before the battle ended, they began receiving accolades. Despite being positioned on the opposite end of the Union line and reeling from his new brigade's immense losses on July 1, former commander Adelbert Ames knew of the Twentieth's actions and found them so noteworthy that he wrote to his former subordinate on July 3, "I was very proud of the 20th and its present Colonel. I did want to be with you and see your splendid conduct in the field. God bless you and the dear old Regiment. . . . The pleasure I felt at the intelligence of your conduct yesterday is some recompense for all that I have suffered. My love to the officers and men. Ames." In their official reports, both brigade commander James Rice and division commander James Barnes singled out Chamberlain for special mention.[125]

Later that summer Rice noted, "For the brilliant success of the conflict upon the second day of the struggle, History will give credit to the bravery and unflinching fortitude of the 20th Maine volunteers, more than to any other equal body of men upon the field." Division commander Barnes wrote to Chamberlain, "Your skillful management of your command, your gallant charge upon the enemy—the evidence of which is found in the prisoners and arms taken by you—entitle you to my special commendation as commanding the Division and to the most favorable notice of the Government." On July 4, Chamberlain wrote to Fanny, "The 20th has immortalized itself." He also wanted his wife to know, "I am receiving all sorts of praise, but bear it meekly." To those who have recently suggested that the reputation of both the Twentieth Maine and its colonel was a postwar, even late twentieth-century creation, these contemporary affidavits show otherwise.[126]

The men in the ranks knew what they had been through and accomplished, and after long months with little to brag about, they were anxious to write home with both word of their safety and of all the unit had achieved. On July 4, Adney Boothby wrote to "Folks at home," saying, "Our Regt. took about 250 prisoners alone and our Regt. alone fought a whole brigade and drove them, it was the old Stonewall Brigade and they say that they never was whipped so before." John Lenfest told his wife five days later, "They fought like devils but they found their match this time. They weren't in Virginia this time." That same day Sylvester Baker bragged they had "fought old Jacksons Brigade and licked them," taking two hundred prisoners. As was so often the case, William T. Livermore perhaps described it best: "The Regiment we fought and captured was the 15th Alabama. They fought like demons and said they were never whipped before and never wanted to meet the 20th Maine again."[127]

Chamberlain wrote to Governor Coburn on July 21, "Our services have been officially acknowledged, though no partial friend has published our praises in the state whose name we are proud to bear, & which, we believe, we have not dishonored." Such an oversight was both puzzling and frustrating, for on July 9 the *New York Times* had put the Twentieth Maine on page 1, with correspondent L. L. Crounse telling readers about the Twentieth and Colonel Chamberlain "gallantly" securing Big Round Top and taking twenty-five prisoners in the process and assuring them that regimental commanders (including Chamberlain) would "nobly sustain" the brigade's "old fighting reputation."[128] Ellis Spear sought to rectify the lack of coverage of the Twentieth Maine with a public letter on the battle that was published in the *Portland Daily Press* on July 24, as did Elisha Coan with an account that appeared in the *Ellsworth American* the same day. The unit had won a reputation within the army, but without a hometown newspaper singing their praise or a particular region viewing the Twentieth Maine as its own, it would be up to the men to tell their own story and secure their hard-won reputation.[129]

For the first ten months of their army career, the men of the Twentieth Maine had prepared for combat, but except for a small role at the Battle of Fredericksburg, they had largely been left to "suck our thumbs," as Hezekiah Long had once written. "For the men of the 20th," Howard

Prince reflected, "this was the first real stand up fight." Now, in what turned out to be the war's deadliest battle, and arguably the one with the most at stake, they had been thrust into a critical position where failure could have meant disaster for themselves, their army, and perhaps even their nation. Facing off against a larger, more experienced unit, they emerged victorious. In *The Leadership Moment*, author Michael Useem says, "Leadership is a product of today's actions and yesterday's groundwork." The Twentieth's performance on Little Round Top was not a miracle; rather, it was a result of the groundwork they had undertaken since August 1862. The intense training and the bonding they had been through; the leadership journey of their now-commander, Joshua Chamberlain; and the incorporation of the former mutineers of the Second Maine—each a subject of this book's preceding chapters—were the elements that prepared the Twentieth Maine for success on Little Round Top. Without any one of these three elements, it seems unlikely they could have held that critical position.[130]

The Twentieth Maine was heavily engaged in combat throughout 1864, taking severe losses at the Wilderness, Spotsylvania, and Peebles' Farm, but Gettysburg was their first sustained experience in combat. Before the battle, the men—and likely modern readers—had a skewed sense of what Civil War combat was like, but the combination of the firsthand accounts from our subjects and modern studies offers a more accurate view of the soldier experience during battle. The Twentieth's ability to refuse their line under fire, then make continual movements to straighten their front, and finally wheel and charge the enemy with bayonets all reveal the high standard to which the unit had been trained and their ability to understand complex tactical maneuvers conveyed by just a few words. Despite their high effectiveness in maneuverability, however, they were stunningly ineffective with their weapons. Even though the Mainers had been armed with rifles that could hit the enemy at three hundred yards, most Civil War combat took place at much closer distances; on Little Round Top, the accounts are unanimous that the men were typically just twenty to fifty yards apart, a distance at which they almost could not miss one another. Yet they did. Despite the expenditure of perhaps fifty thousand rounds between the Twentieth Maine and the Fifteenth Alabama, the combined number of killed and wounded was under three hundred. Most men, it seems, were more willing to be shot than to shoot another.

Controversy has plagued the Twentieth Maine in recent years—the inevitable backlash against the post-*Gettysburg* interest in their actions and, specifically, Colonel Chamberlain. Such controversies are not new. As early as the 1880s, some questioned where the charge originated and whether it was Chamberlain's idea or that of another officer. More recently, some have contended that the Twentieth Maine's actions were considered of little note in the immediate aftermath of the battle and only grew to prominence later due to skilled writers—first Chamberlain and then Michael Shaara. Lastly, many have questioned just how critical it would have been if the Twentieth had not held their position. The answers to all three of these questions are contained within the 1863 accounts. Man after man in the Twentieth Maine noted that Chamberlain ordered the charge—even the one, Ellis Spear, who later changed his story due to a late-in-life falling-out with his former commander. As to how critical these actions were, multiple reports from higher up the chain of command highlighted the importance of the Twentieth Maine in holding Little Round Top, with now–brigade commander James Rice noting, "History will give credit to the bravery and unflinching fortitude of the 20th Maine volunteers, more than to any other equal body of men upon the field."[131] Finally, in response to those who dispute the importance of Little Round Top, and thus the Twentieth Maine's actions in holding that height, commanding general George Meade himself called Little Round Top "the key-point of my whole position," saying that if it had fallen into enemy hands, "it would have prevented me from holding any of the ground which I subsequently held to the last."[132] The mistake many modern writers make is that, when they conceive of Little Round Top and the danger it posed if in Confederate hands, they metaphorically stand on the crest of the hill, next to Rebel artillery, and look north along the Union line. They need to look east. The biggest danger in losing Little Round Top was never that the Confederates would use it as an artillery platform (for which the hill was ill suited); it was that Confederates would place themselves across the Taneytown Road just three hundred yards to the east. In his 1913 article for *Hearst's Magazine*, Chamberlain wrote, "There entered and met in the town two great thoroughfares, the Baltimore Pike and Taneytown Road, perfectly commanded by Little Round Top. The latter road opened the direct way to Washington, and in the aspect of affairs was our only practicable line of retreat in case of disaster."[133] Had

Oates and the Fifteenth Alabama forced the Twentieth Maine from its position, there is every chance that George Meade, seeing the threat to his retreat route and supply line, would have retreated from Gettysburg.

The great Civil War historian Harry Pfanz once said that July 2, 1863, was a day that needed a lot of saving. The Second United States Sharpshooters saved the day by delaying Hood's division as they advanced on Little Round Top. Strong Vincent saved the day by seizing the initiative and leading his brigade onto the hill. The Sixteenth Michigan, Forty-Fourth New York, and Eighty-Third Pennsylvania, along with the 140th New York, saved the day through their stubborn defenses of the exposed crest of the hill. Units on the north of the line held critical positions on Culp's Hill and Cemetery Hill against great odds. And so, too, did the Twentieth Maine save the day with their stubborn defense and shocking bayonet charge.[134]

The Twentieth Maine served for nearly two more years, fighting in many more battles and seeing horrific combat across Virginia in 1864 and 1865. But in the postwar years, it was to Gettysburg they would always return: with their reunions, with their monuments, in their reminiscences, on their tombstones, and in their obituaries. This was the moment that defined their lives.

5

"Almost worn out"

From War to Peace

IN THE SPRING OF 1870, GOVERNOR JOSHUA CHAMBERLAIN, IN THE midst of his fourth and final term, reviewed the recommendation for a pardon that his executive council had placed in his hand. Staring at him was the name "Andrew Jackson Tozier," his former color sergeant at Gettysburg and a man Chamberlain later declared "all that was excellent as a soldier." Falling on hard financial times after the war, Tozier had gone on a multi-year crime spree that included robbing a clothing store and cattle rustling. The contrasting fortunes of these two heroes of Little Round Top—the two men later awarded the Medal of Honor for their actions during that firefight—could not be starker: Chamberlain occupied the state's highest elected office and had a personal net worth he estimated at $21,000, while Tozier was penniless and now serving a five-year prison sentence.[1]

Most books on the Civil War end with the conflict's conclusion in 1865. John Pullen's landmark *The Twentieth Maine* (1957) closes with the regiment's formal muster-out in Virginia on June 4, 1865, and does not follow the men home or hint at the trajectories of their postwar lives. The other exemplary unit history of that era, Alan Nolan's *The Iron Brigade* (1961), ends with the Grand Review in Washington on May 23, 1865. But in the post-Vietnam era, historians have increasingly explored what impact military service has on veterans and how they adjust to returning home, an inquiry that has taken on more immediacy and spawned greater interest and insights following the wars in Iraq and Afghanistan.

While the wartime experiences of the men who fought on Little Round Top were, in most cases, both shared and somewhat similar, their postwar lives diverged in myriad ways while also containing common strands. Chamberlain and Tozier may have ended up with wildly different "professions" and bank account balances, but their experiences during the war and the crippling wounds both had suffered impacted nearly everything they did in the postwar years and all that they became.

After briefly following the unit to the end of the war, this chapter examines how the men adjusted to returning home, the impact of their wartime service on their postwar lives, and what they made of themselves in the nation they had just helped save.

On July 17, 1863, the Army of the Potomac crossed their namesake river heading south in pursuit of the Army of Northern Virginia. Hezekiah Long ruefully noted, "We shall now have a race for Richmond with the Rebs," but that did not transpire. Over the next ten days, the men moved south another fifty miles, but then they set up camp and remained for a couple weeks. The respite was needed after six weeks of perpetual motion punctuated by one major and two minor engagements with the enemy. Lieutenant Holman Melcher wrote to his brother, "I am afraid that the army is almost worn out, and I know we all need a rest."[2]

There was no better example of this exhaustion than the unit's commander. On July 28, Joshua Chamberlain requested—and received—a twenty-day furlough "for the benefit of my health." He had contracted malaria in the spring of 1863 and then suffered sunstroke on the march to Gettysburg and was still struggling. "I had a severe attack of illness during the recent campaign," he wrote, "but unwilling to leave the command of my Regiment while in the face of the enemy, I went on duty before I was able without detriment to do so." It was not yet apparent, but Chamberlain would never be well again.[3]

Though most men could not go home, the period of rest improved their health and outlook. They were fortunate to be surrounded by blackberries, and men of all ranks enjoyed eating their fill. The pause in active operations, combined with the anniversary of their muster-in on August 29, 1863, gave the men time to reflect on their service thus far. Hezekiah Long wrote to his wife Sarah, "I have seen considerable in this year, but do not regret that I entered the service when I did."[4]

At the end of August, Colonel Chamberlain returned after having recovered some of his health, but rather than take command of the Twentieth Maine, he was assigned to a higher position. Sharing this update with Maine governor Abner Coburn, Chamberlain wrote, "I have been assigned by Gen. Griffin to command of the 3d Brigade of the Division . . . I regret being thus obliged to leave even temporarily, the noble Regiment with which I have shared so many hardships & perils, & not a few honors too." He did not know it at the time, but between his temporary assignment, furloughs due to sickness, extended court-martial duty, and finally permanent promotion to lead a brigade, Chamberlain would only command the Twentieth Maine again for a few days. With Lieutenant Colonel Charles Gilmore perpetually "sick" or on one detached duty or another, Ellis Spear was the unit's de facto commander for most of the rest of the war, though at times temporary command passed to various other men, including Atherton Clark and Walter Morrill, among others. The unit performed well in the battles that followed, but without Chamberlain at its head, and with the loss of so many who had earned the regiment's reputation on Little Round Top, the crack unit that had fought so magnificently at Gettysburg was never quite to be seen again over the ensuing two years of war.[5]

The ten months that followed Gettysburg were much like the ten that had preceded the great battle; the Twentieth Maine had a few false alarms and minor skirmishes but engaged in only one battle, and even that was on a purely voluntary basis. In early November, the armies faced off across the Rappahannock River again, with the Rebels holding a bridgehead behind heavy entrenchments at Rappahannock Station. That bridgehead on the north side of the river was problematic for the Union, as it provided the Confederates with a toehold from which they could launch an attack in any direction. General George Meade ordered a column to cross the river to the east at Kelly's Ford early on November 7 and then for elements of the Sixth Corps to assault the entrenchments close to dark.

The Union assault force consisted of just two thousand men, including the Sixth Maine. The Twentieth Maine was to play no part in the fight, but on hearing that his old comrades in the Sixth Maine were heading into combat, Company B's Walter Morrill determined to lend a hand. No man was compelled to go, but it spoke to the men's affection for Morrill and their general *esprit de corps* that, when he asked for volunteers, more than eighty men raised their hands. Telling readers back home of their exploits via a letter to the *Portland Press*, Holman Melcher reported, "The 20th furnished three officers [Walter Morrill, Weston Keene, and Hiram Morse] and eighty men . . . and when the 6th Maine charged the enemies' works the skirmishers of the 20th charged also, and shared with them the dangers and glory of that brilliant achievement." The achievement was substantial, with the Union forces capturing the Confederate position and sixteen hundred Southern troops. Hezekiah Long wrote, "It was a brilliant little affair to us." The Sixth Maine suffered nearly 140 casualties, including 56 dead. One of the volunteers from the Twentieth was killed, one was severely wounded, and six suffered slight wounds. The one man killed at Rappahannock Station, Frederick Kinsel, had not been with the Twentieth at Gettysburg, though the severely wounded Seth McGuire had been on Little Round Top.[6]

The affair at Rappahannock Station marked the regiment's only death caused by enemy fire from the end of the Gettysburg Campaign until the Battle of the Wilderness the following May. In fact, excluding men who succumbed to their Gettysburg wounds and those who had been captured during the campaign and died in Rebel prisons, only three veterans of Little Round Top passed during the ten months following that battle. James Erskine and Lewis Fenderson died of disease, while William Pennell was accidentally shot and killed on the last day of February 1864. Compared to the immense death toll from disease the previous fall and winter, these were healthy times.

In addition to their good health, other things made the winter of 1863–1864 pleasant, or at least more agreeable than the previous year had been. Furloughs of fifteen days were available, and many applied for the chance to visit home even briefly. On December 20, 1863, Will Livermore reported that seven men started for home on a furlough. For some, the furlough proved to be too expensive—Albert Fernald estimated it cost $75 to return home—and thus it tended to be officers more than enlisted men who availed themselves of that opportunity, just one of the many ways in which rank had its privileges.[7]

As the new year dawned, many former Second Maine soldiers were among the 136,000 men in the Union army with less than a year to serve. Fearing the loss of these veteran soldiers, the authorities went to great lengths to keep them in the army. The federal government offered a reenlistment bounty of $402 to any man with less than a year to serve who committed to a new three-year term, plus a thirty-five-day furlough with travel expenses covered. The state of Maine topped up that bounty with a further $300, making for an astounding total of $702. Roughly one hundred thousand men reenlisted under these terms, four thousand of them from Maine, with many of the former Second Maine men finally receiving some recompense for all they had been through.[8]

The thirty-five-day furlough must have been a dream for many men, but not all. Hezekiah Long reported, "There was a man went home from this Regt. this winter that had been absent over two years. His wife had a young one about a week old when he got home." Presumably, this was one of the Second Maine men, but which one is unclear.[9]

William Ward was one of those Second Maine men who reenlisted, secured the thirty-five-day furlough, and returned home. Despite feeling he had been the victim of "ambitious treachery" by those who had held him past May 1863, he had, Ellis Spear later noted, "Bore good character while with the regiment." Ward departed for Maine on January 5, and after a month at home, he began making his way back to the unit. He soon ran into trouble. "I left Boston for my Regt. the 10th of Feby, five days before my furlough expired," Ward later testified. "[I] went to Worcester Mass, got drunk and when I came to myself to know what I was about I was fifteen days over my time, then I went to work in Worcester. I did not intend to desert should have gone back but was afraid to." He was eventually arrested near Orono on January 3, 1865. At a court-martial, he was sentenced to six months of hard labor and saw his term of service extended by almost a year to make up for his lost time.[10]

Ward was one of the twenty-two former Second Maine men who reenlisted that winter. Fourteen others decided to serve out their term and return home. One of those who chose not to reenlist was Andrew Tozier. Perhaps his physical condition had deteriorated—his assignment to the ambulance corps in late 1863 is suggestive of that possibility. At some point previously he may also have learned of the death of his younger brother Ezra in a Confederate prison camp—a sad fate compounded by the fact that Ezra had initially been wrongly suspected of deserting to and serving in the Rebel army. Given the debacle with the extra year of service, the treatment of Ezra, and his deteriorating condition, Tozier may have desired to get out of the army as soon as possible.[11]

While many soldiers went home to visit their families, their families also came to the front. In February, Sergeant Long reported that there were nine women in camp, all wives of officers, and they are present in a photograph of the officers taken that winter. In addition to the regular social calls and card games, the soldiers also occupied themselves with skating on an ice-covered Rappahannock River using a pair of blades James Rundlett had procured.[12]

The decidedly different tone in the Twentieth's camp in the winter of 1863–1864 as compared to 1862–1863 was largely due to their performance at Gettysburg. A year earlier they were still a junior partner among the Army of the Potomac's regiments, a largely untried unit with no reputation that was still working desperately to prepare for their first major engagement. But at Gettysburg they had proved themselves to all, and the anxiety of the previous winter gave way to pride by late 1863. When Joshua Chamberlain visited Maine in early 1863, he was peppered with questions about the unit's losses to disease and resignations. Now every man could tell stories of the great Battle of Gettysburg and their part in securing Confederate defeat.

As spring dawned, however, the men's attention turned back to warfare. Hezekiah Long told his wife the "government is going to let us wast a little ammunition in the way of target practice." For a month beginning in late March, the men practiced three times per week. William Livermore reported that "we were exercised in estimating distances, and target shooting." Whether the men improved their accuracy is unknown. Livermore hit five of ten targets during a session on April 4, 1864, and one hopes that the month of estimating distances and seeing where their shots hit—or did not—would have made a positive difference in their combat effectiveness. The battles in 1864 were some of the war's bloodiest, if that is any evidence.[13]

On April 22, 1864, the officers' wives were ordered out of camp—a sure sign that battle was imminent. The men knew it, too, as William Lamson wrote home on May 3, "We'll soon be in business." There was good reason for optimism. As the spring campaign began, the Army of the Potomac consisted of 127,000 men and 316 pieces of artillery, the largest army the Union ever assembled in the Civil War. General Ulysses S. Grant, elevated to the rank of lieutenant general and put in charge of all Lincoln's armies in March 1864, had decided to make his headquarters with the Army of the Potomac, evincing the resources and brainpower that was being put into effect to finally crush Robert E. Lee's Army of Northern Virginia and end the war. Grant's plan called for the Army of the Potomac plus the independent Ninth Corps under General Ambrose Burnside to move south, advancing on Richmond, while separate commands under Benjamin Butler moved on Richmond and Petersburg from the southeast and other forces under Franz Sigel tried to secure the Shenandoah Valley.[14]

On May 4, 1864, the Army of the Potomac got underway, crossing the Rapidan River around twenty miles west of Fredericksburg and east of the main Confederate defensive line along Mine Run. Just below the Rapidan is a densely wooded area of approximately seventy square miles known as the Wilderness. Grant and Meade hoped to move through this area quickly and did not expect significant opposition from Lee, assuming that he would remain behind his defensive line. Instead, Lee sent his troops streaming east along the Orange Turnpike and Orange Plank Road to confront the Union army in the Wilderness. The result was a three-day battle that saw more than seventeen thousand Union and eleven thousand Confederate casualties, becoming the Union's second-bloodiest battle behind only Gettysburg.[15]

The Twentieth crossed the Rapidan at Germanna Ford on the night of May 3–4, camping a mile west of Wilderness Tavern and spending May 4 building entrenchments. On May 5, they awoke to the news that the Confederates were just two miles to the west and bearing toward them on the Orange Turnpike. When an attack had not come by noon, the men moved

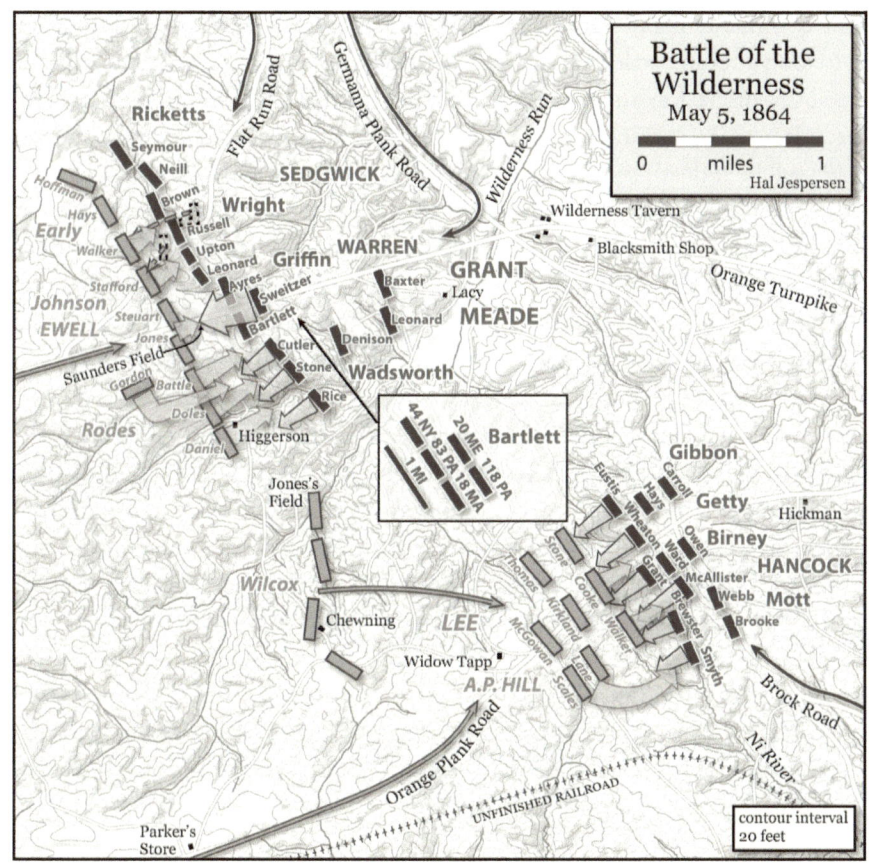

forward into the opening known as Saunders Field. Along with the other units of their brigade and division, the Twentieth charged across the field and into a hail of bullets belching forth from Confederate rifles. Saunders Field was but a small opening surrounded by thick forest, and consequently "it was a disorganized battle," Theodore Gerrish later remembered. "Every man fought for himself and by himself, but all faced the enemy." At the point of their farthest advance, the unit came under flanking fire from their right and rear, leading Lieutenant Colonel Spear to order the men to fall back to their morning position. Captain Morrill led a delaying action until he was shot in the face, leaving a gruesome wound but one from which he recovered.[16]

In a sign of the Wilderness's confusion, on the far left flank Company F commander Holman Melcher and seventeen men never heard the order to retreat, and instead they continued to advance. Soon they were nearly encircled. Two days earlier, Melcher had written to his brother that he had been "assigned to the command of a Company numbering 38 men, whose wants and interests I am to look after in battle. While it is my duty to urge them on to great deeds, yet I must use discretion and protect them from enemies fire in any possible way. I need wisdom." Knowing that capture meant time in a Confederate prison and could well be a death sentence, Melcher determined to fight his way out or die trying. The isolated soldiers stealthily advanced up to a Confederate line and then attacked with bullets and bayonets, capturing thirty-two men and then running a gauntlet to return to their lines. Two of the men with Melcher were killed during their running fight, but one man who refused to get to his feet and join them was indeed captured and died as a prisoner at Andersonville.[17]

The Twentieth had taken eighty-five casualties—eleven killed, fifty-eight wounded, and sixteen captured. Over the ensuing two days they advanced again, and though they were in a supporting role, an additional six men were killed and twenty-one wounded. Four of those who were initially listed as wounded succumbed to those wounds, bringing the total number of killed and mortally wounded to twenty-one. That number was roughly half of what they had sustained at Gettysburg but more than any other battle. Of the twenty-one who lost their lives at the Wilderness, two-thirds had been at Gettysburg ten months earlier. Some of the unit's best soldiers, including Captain Morrill, William T. Livermore, and Will Owen, also had been wounded. It was three and a half months before Will Livermore recovered from his wound and rejoined his company.[18]

Three straight days of combat leaving multiple men dead and wounded each day was unprecedented for the Twentieth, and they no doubt anticipated a break before facing another battle. Such was not to be the way of the war under Ulysses S. Grant, however. As Union soldiers began marching on the night of May 7, they did not turn north to retreat but instead turned south, and the Wilderness's record as the Union's second deadliest battle of the war would last just a single day.

Leading the way south, on May 8 the Fifth Corps tried to seize the crossroads at Spotsylvania Court House a dozen miles below the Wilderness but was checked by the Army of Northern Virginia's First Corps. The Twentieth arrived after the fighting had begun and did not go into action until approximately 6:00 p.m. They were ordered to charge up Laurel Hill at the same time the enemy charged down the hill, leading to "a struggle at close quarters, a hand-to-hand conflict, resembling a mob in its character," as one soldier remembered. The Twentieth held the position, forced the Confederates back, and took prisoners, but also suffered heavily again, with another dozen men killed or mortally wounded, including Captain William Morrell and Charles Knapp. One of the Second Maine men, Charles Knapp was a twenty-two-year-old farmer who had risen to the rank of sergeant. He had been wounded at Gaines' Mill and then again at Gettysburg before his third and final wound at Spotsylvania. Also among the injured were both Howard Prince and Holman Melcher. The battle lasted another dozen days before the armies moved south again to the North Anna River (two men killed) and then Cold Harbor (five men killed) before settling into what turned out to be a nine-month siege of Petersburg, Virginia.[19]

In 1863, there were four battles and five total days when the Twentieth engaged in combat that led to the death of a member of the unit. In 1864, they engaged in seven such battles, and there were at least thirteen days on which men were killed or mortally wounded. Combat had shifted from intermittent to continuous and from confined to all consuming. The death of Captain Samuel Keene on June 22 was emblematic of that shift, as he was shot dead by a skirmisher or perhaps a sharpshooter while within his own lines and at a time when there was not a substantial fight underway. Ellis Spear wrote that Keene "fell into my arms, exclaiming as he fell, 'Write to my wife. It is all well. I die for my country.'" Samuel and Sarah Keene had been married for only three months before he enlisted in the Twentieth Maine. Sarah was six months pregnant when Samuel was killed.[20]

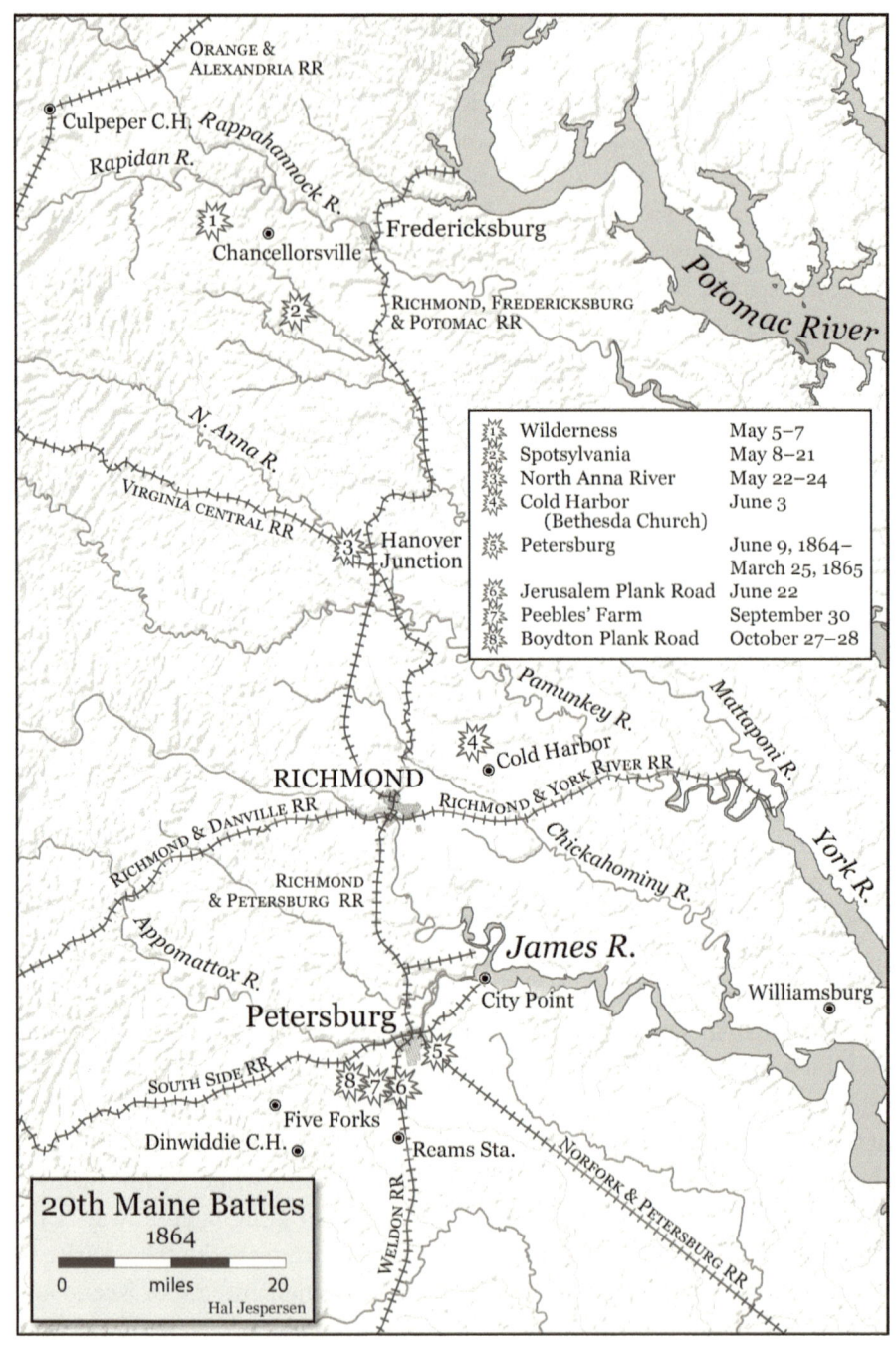

ORANGE &
ALEXANDRIA RR

Culpeper C.H.

Rappahannock R.

Rapidan R.

1

Chancellorsville

2

Fredericksburg

RICHMOND, FREDERICKSBURG
& POTOMAC RR

Potomac River

N. Anna R.

VIRGINIA CENTRAL RR

3 Hanover
Junction

	Wilderness	May 5–7
1		
2	Spotsylvania	May 8–21
3	North Anna River	May 22–24
4	Cold Harbor	June 3
	(Bethesda Church)	
5	Petersburg	June 9, 1864–
		March 25, 1865
6	Jerusalem Plank Road	June 22
7	Peebles' Farm	September 30
8	Boydton Plank Road	October 27–28

Pamunkey R.

Mattaponi R.

4 Cold Harbor

RICHMOND & YORK RIVER RR

York R.

RICHMOND

RICHMOND & DANVILLE RR

Chickahominy R.

RICHMOND
& PETERSBURG RR

James R.

Appomattox R.

City Point

Williamsburg

Petersburg

SOUTH SIDE RR

5

8 7 6

Five Forks

Dinwiddie C.H.

Reams Sta.

WELDON RR

NORFORK & PETERSBURG RR

20th Maine Battles
1864

0   miles   20

Hal Jespersen

Four days earlier, Joshua Chamberlain had also been shot. Hurrying back to the army from court-martial duty in Washington, Chamberlain arrived during the lengthy Battle of Spotsylvania Court House. He filled in as temporary commander for a couple of brigades and then led the Twentieth for a few days in early June before receiving permanent command of the First Brigade of Griffin's division. On June 18, 1864, Chamberlain's brigade faced an entrenched Confederate position at Rives' Salient along the Petersburg lines. When division commander Charles Griffin ordered an attack on an artillery position reinforced with a line of infantry dug into a railroad embankment, Chamberlain ruminated on the premonition of death he had the previous evening, when "a shadow seemed to brood over me, dark wings folding as it were and wrapping me in their embrace," he later remembered. "Something said, 'You will not be here again.'" He was convinced he would not live another day.[21]

Griffin gave Chamberlain the latitude to develop a plan that could succeed with minimal casualties. Before he could carry it out, however, a courier arrived with a verbal message from higher up the chain of command ordering an immediate frontal assault on the works. Chamberlain dashed off a note explaining the futility of such an attack, but he was ordered to proceed. At 3:00 p.m., Chamberlian had his bugler sound "charge," and the units moved forward. Chamberlain was on foot, his horse having been shot earlier, and was down several staff officers already. Soon the color bearer also fell, and Chamberlain picked up the standard. Moments later, "I felt a sharp hot flush that seemed to cut the spinal marrow out of my back-bone," Chamberlain remembered. He drove his sword point and flagstaff into the ground in order to keep standing. "I felt in my sword hand a gush of hot blood. I looked down then for the first time. I saw blood spurting out of my right hip-side, and saw that it had already filled my long cavalry boots to overflowing, and also my baggy reinforced trousers, and was running out at both pocket wells." Ironically, seeing his pockets full of blood cheered Chamberlain, as he realized the wound was in his side and not his back as he had initially feared.[22]

Artilleryman John Bigelow saw his brigade commander go down and dispatched men to bring him off the field, which they did despite Chamberlain's protests that they were wasting time and resources. At the field hospital three miles in the rear, the first surgeons who saw

Chamberlain evaluated that the wound to his lower abdomen left him with no more than a 10 percent survivability rate and set him aside to prioritize others. Chamberlain wrote one final letter to Fanny, sending his love to his family and assuring them that "my mind & heart are at peace." But by then word of Chamberlain's wound had reached the Twentieth Maine, and Tom Chamberlain and Ellis Spear informed surgeons Abner Shaw of the Twentieth and Morris Townsend of the Forty-Fourth New York of the situation, and all headed out looking for their wounded comrade. They eventually found him and determined to do what they could via open surgery.[23]

They soon found that a bullet had entered Chamberlain's body just below his right hip, passing through his bladder and urethra and lodging behind the socket in his left hip bone. In short, he had been shot nearly through and through. The hole was so large that the doctors cast aside the standard surgical probe and instead used a rifle ramrod to trace the bullet's route. Painstakingly, they reconnected urinary organs and removed the round. At one point, the two doctors stopped the surgery, fearing the pain they were inflicting was to no end. But Chamberlain asked them to continue their work, so they pressed on. Even after finishing the surgery, all knew there was little hope. On hearing of the colonel's fate, his superior officers, starting with Fifth Corps commander General Gouverneur Warren and continuing through generals Meade and Grant, recommended a battlefield and supposedly deathbed promotion to brigadier general, a promotion that was swiftly made. But, it turns out, Chamberlain had other ideas. He slowly recovered, and by the end of July, it was clear that, while he remained extremely fragile, he was no longer in mortal danger. The wound, however, had life-altering consequences for Chamberlain and was a constant challenge for the remainder of his pain-filled life.[24]

While his comrades fought across Virginia, Calvin Bates was shuttled from one Confederate prison to another. Captured at the Battle of the Wilderness, Bates was first taken to Danville, Virginia, and then to the infamous prison named Camp Sumter in Andersonville, Georgia, arriving on May 23, 1864. The sight he confronted must have been a shock. The prison was just 16.5 acres and designed to hold ten thousand men, but by June 1864 there were twenty-six thousand within its walls. A later expansion enlarged the prison by ten acres and brought a peak population of thirty-three thousand. Bates was held at the prison for close to four months, a timeframe that saw at least eight men from the Twentieth Maine at Andersonville. If the Twentieth Maine men had clustered together, Bates would have seen Luther Borneman, David Courson, Alvin Cutler, and Thomas Welch all succumb to a combination of wound, disease, and malnutrition between late June and early September. They were just a few of the thirteen thousand soldiers who died at Andersonville during the prison's fourteen months in operation. Bates remained at Andersonville until September 12, when he was transferred to another prison in Florence, South Carolina.[25]

As summer turned to fall, the men in the Twentieth Maine carefully watched both the political situation in Maine and the military one in Virginia. On September 12, 1864, Maine voted for its governor and rep-resentatives to the United States Congress. William Livermore confided in his diary, "As to day is the day for our State election we would like to help overpower the copperheads which we are confident will be done." Union candidate Samuel Cony was elected with more than 60 percent of the vote, while the entire congressional delegation consisted of Republicans or Unionists. Crucially, the state's voters also decided almost unanimously to amend the state constitution to allow soldiers in the field to vote in the upcoming presidential election.[26]

Before election day, however, the unit fought in its last major conflict of the year, Peebles' Farm. As with most engagements around Petersburg, the Confederates were behind a line of earthworks with four artillery pieces inside a small fort. With the rest of their brigade, the Twentieth "was formed for a charge." As they advanced through both musketry and canis-ter, "many of our men fell and our flag was riddled with bullets," Theodore Gerrish wrote, "but with wild cheers our men rushed on." They took the fort and captured one artillery piece the Confederates could not haul away. Officially the regiment suffered another seven men killed and forty wounded, but those totals are too low, for at least ten men who had been on Little Round Top were killed or mortally wounded that day, includ-ing Sergeant Vincent Pinhorn. A twenty-eight-year-old mariner from Orrington, Pinhorn had been previously wounded at Second Manassas while a member of the Second Maine and then again at Gettysburg. He left no wife or children behind, but a widowed mother reliant on the $10 a month he sent home later filed a pension claim seeking support. Hezekiah Long aptly summarized the day: "We had a hard fight on Friday but accomplished nil that we undertook."[27]

On other fronts, political and military, things were more positive. In the presidential election, the unit cast 137 votes for Abraham Lincoln and just 13 for his opponent, their old commander, George McClellan. The men were committed to seeing the war to its successful conclusion, and only a vote for Lincoln ensured that the job would be finished. Word from other theaters of war was also encouraging, as first came news of the defeat of Confederates under General John Bell Hood at Nashville, followed by news of General William T. Sherman's progress as he moved to and then through South Carolina. Finally, it seemed as though the war's end was within reach.[28]

As 1864 turned into 1865 and the men prepared for what they hoped and assumed was the final season of war, William T. Livermore counted down the days until he could return home to his beloved Maine. On January 29, 1865, he marked in his diary "(7 Months)," the time remaining before his enlistment expired. The Confederates also knew it was nearly over, and Lee's army melted away that winter. In addition to the Confederates who struck for home, deserters came into the Twentieth's lines in large numbers in late February and March 1865.[29]

When the men packed up their winter clothes that spring, they had them shipped home rather than held in nearby storage for the following winter. The knowledge that little time was left also made some of them cautious. Holman Melcher, who had been at the front of the charge at Gettysburg, wrote to his brother on March 2, "I would not expose myself again for half of this Nation." Melcher was not disillusioned with the cause—far from it. On February 3, he rejoiced at the passage of the Thirteenth Amendment: "We are at last a Free Nation with the approval of the States. Thank God!" But with the war so close to being over, he did not want to become one of its last casualties. "It was not strange that these soldiers were a little anxious about the future," Theodore Gerrish explained, "and wondered if they had been spared through all the past, to fall in that last campaign of the war."[30]

The Twentieth was engaged in several actions in early 1865, though they suffered few casualties until the Army of the Potomac's final campaign. On March 29, the unit, now under the command of Walter Morrill, broke camp. They skirmished that day and then were sent (with the rest of the brigade) to relieve Chamberlain's brigade, which had been heavily involved throughout the day. On March 31, they advanced again and struck the Confederate lines. The fiercest fighting came on April 1 as a part of the Battle of Five Forks. Fighting back and forth over Confederate entrenchments, the Twentieth finally carried the position and forced the fleeing Confederates into the hands of Union cavalry. The musketry was so intense that Will Livermore later counted four bullet holes in his pants. Some men may have been loath to risk their lives in one of the war's final fights, but certainly not all. Captain Albert Fernald "dashed among the enemy and captured a flag," an act for which he was soon awarded the Medal of Honor. There were both unit and personal accolades for their actions that day, but another thirteen men lay dead in the Virginia dirt, killed less than two weeks before the fighting ended for good.[31]

Albert Fernald (Maine State Archives)

With the loss at Five Forks, it was nearly all over for the Confederate Army of Northern Virginia. The following day, the Confederate lines around Petersburg broke, leading to the evacuation of Richmond and Lee's desperate flight to the west, hoping to link up with the forces under Joseph Johnston and together continue the fight. But as the Confederates headed west, even more of their army melted away. On April 2, Holman Mecher recorded, "We have been capturing prisoners all day." After a week-long running pursuit that brought the two armies nearly one hundred miles toward central Virginia, it all ended abruptly. On April 9, 1865, Will Livermore wrote, "We were closing in on Lee with heavy force and within sight of their trains When a flag of truce came in." Melcher wrote to his brother, "Stern officers who have never failed on the bloody field of battle, wept like children, for joy, and grasp each others hands in silence and tears, unable to speak from emotions of joy. . . . After almost superhuman efforts, we at last succeeded in surrounding Lee's army today and were about to crush him between our forces, when he sent a flag of truce." After negotiations at Appomattox Court House, Robert E. Lee agreed to surrender his army. The formal surrender occurred three days later, four years exactly after the war had begun at Fort Sumter.[32]

On that fateful day, Will Livermore recorded, "Our Brigade has been drawn up in line from 6AM til 1PM to receive the arms of Gen Longstreet and Gordans ~~divi~~ corps. They marched from there camp and stacked arms and left there colors in our front and marched back to camp." Livermore did not mention that the Twentieth was reunited with Joshua Chamberlain, the man selected to oversee the Confederate surrender. Chamberlain longed to share the day with his old command and received permission to temporarily take charge of the Third Brigade and the Twentieth Maine once again. Seeking to bring, in his eyes, a fitting close to the combat between the two armies, Chamberlain ordered his men to show respect to their now-former foes. "Instructions had been given," he wrote nearly fifty years later in the third person, "and when the head of each division column comes opposite our group our bugle sounds the signal and instantly our whole line from right to left, regiment by regiment in succession, gives the soldier's salutation, from the 'order arms' to the hold 'carry'—the marching salute." Chamberlain well knew the value of respect, had worked and fought during the first year of his service to secure it for both himself and the Twentieth Maine, and now was showing it to the soldiers they had vanquished.[33]

Lee had surrendered, but more than two months passed before most men in the Twentieth were mustered out of the army and returned to civilian life. Joseph Johnston's army was still on the loose in the Carolinas, and the Army of the Potomac could not disband until that Rebel force had also surrendered. That eventuality finally came to pass two weeks later, on April 26, 1865.

In early May, the unit began heading north through Petersburg, Richmond, Fredericksburg, and finally to the outskirts of Washington, where it would participate in the Grand Review of the Armies on May 23 and 24. On May 6, they marched through Richmond, the city that had been their objective for nearly three years. "Of course we flaunted our banners and the men-stepped-like-conquerors," Holman Melcher admitted to his brother. "We passed down Carey Street on which are 'Castle Thunder' & 'Libby Prison,' were labeled with large letters, so that all the soldiers would recognize these noted places." Libby had claimed the lives of some of their comrades, while others in their very column had survived imprisonment in the notorious prison.[34]

As the men continued north, their march took on the shape of a walk down memory lane. In some cases, those memories were nightmares. On May 8, they passed the battlefield at Spotsylvania Court House precisely one year after fighting there. Holman Melcher was one of the many men wounded that day, and he did not care to revisit the battlefield. The following evening they camped at Falmouth, across the Rappahannock from Fredericksburg, and were reminded of the great battle in that town, their winter camp of 1862–1863, and the hospitals where many of them had recovered after wounds during the various battles in 1864.[35]

One final fatality came on May 11 when George Wood was accidentally shot by a sergeant in the Thirty-Second Massachusetts. "The ball went through his left hand and into his abdomen inflicting a severe if not mortal wound," Will Livermore lamented. Wood succumbed to the wound two weeks later. Of the 1,621 men who served in the Twentieth Maine during the war, Wood became the 293rd to die during the conflict. Those who died as a consequence of battle (146) virtually equaled the lives lost to disease, accidents, and confinement in Confederate prisons (147), a much higher percentage than the average and one that evinces how hard fought a unit the Twentieth Maine had become despite their slow start.[36]

Wood's death must have made the men more desperate to get home. As the other units around them began to head home, they chafed to have the same privilege. Finally, on June 4, 1865, the men who had not reenlisted in 1864 and whose term of service was up by October 1865 were mustered out. The rest of the men—the new recruits, the transferred men from the Second Maine who had reenlisted, and later leftover elements of a few other Maine units—remained outside Washington for another six weeks before also returning home.[37]

This moment of transition was a complex one for many of the men. Some were simply desperate to get home. Others—particularly those who had excelled during the war—were unsure which way to turn. Should they remain in the army, return to their former profession, take up a new one, or move to a different state with more opportunity? Holman Melcher had risen from the rank of corporal to major, but now he wondered, "What is to be my life business? Why am I not decided on some occupation? These are questions I am constantly thinking about." As an officer, Melcher did well financially during the war, investing his pay—up to $300 at a time—in government bonds earning 7.3 percent. He considered remaining in the peacetime army but was not selected to do so and returned home with the second batch of men in mid-July.[38]

The initial group moved through Philadelphia to New York, where they met up with the Sixteenth Maine, Seventeenth Maine, Nineteenth Maine, and Seventh Maine Battery before proceeding to Boston. They arrived in Portland on June 8. The city celebrated their arrival—particularly that of the hometown Seventeenth Maine—with a parade and a "sumptuous repast the ladies had provided." They went to bed sure they would be paid and then released to civilian life the following day.[39]

Instead, "When we awoke in the morning, we were surrounded by reminders of war. The encampment was inclosed by a fence . . . [and] we were informed that no one could pass out without obtaining passes from the officer who was in charge of the camp." No passes would be issued, the major commanding the compound noted, and then he added insult to injury by sending the soldiers worse rations than they had received in the field: coffee with no sugar and a two-thirds ration of moldy hardtack. This was a step too far, and the veterans "caught up the contents of the hard-bread box, and opened a brisk fire upon the portly form of the officer." It was, the men thought, likely that man's first time "under fire." This was but the opening salvo. "We held a council of war," Theodore Gerrish recalled, "and it was unanimously decided that the safety of the country demanded the destruction of the gates." As the men undertook to obtain their freedom, the major commanding the post ordered members of the Invalid Corps to load their guns and shoot any soldiers leaving the post. The Twentieth took a calculated gamble that these men, veterans themselves, would not open fire and rushed out. "The gates were broken into pieces, and heaped upon the parade ground, thus making excellent material for the bonfire we built as a signal of our victory."[40]

The incident had consequences, however, and the men's discharge was delayed. By June 14, William T. Livermore, now in Maine for nearly a week but still under the thumb of the government, wrote, "We all feel ugly." The following day, the private soldiers were paid and allowed to depart, but the noncommissioned officers and officers were still held. "We are mad," Livermore fumed, showing as much emotion as he had at any point during the prior three years. Finally, on June 22, two weeks after returning to Maine, the rest of the men were paid and allowed to go home.[41]

Of the 506 men who had fought on Little Round Top, 116 were dead by the war's end. Of the deceased, eighty-seven were killed or mortally wounded in battle, thirteen died as prisoners of war, eleven died of disease, three in accidents, and two of unrecorded causes. There were 390 still alive, though not all were with the Twentieth. Five men had joined the Signal Corps in the fall of 1863, while ten men joined the navy in early May 1864. Two—James Rundlett and Lewis Merriam Jr.—took officer's commissions in the United States Colored Troops. Fifteen of the former Second Maine men went home on the expiration of their three-year term, though some later joined other units.

And then there were those who were pretty well shot up or laid low by disease. By war's end, forty-one had transferred to the Veteran Reserve Corps—a unit for men no longer fit for active campaigning but capable of garrison or other light duty. Several of those men had lost fingers in battle. Another thirty-six men were discharged for disability or wounds before the war ended. Beyond those, thirty-one more were discharged by General Order No. 77, a cost-saving measure issued two weeks after Lee's surrender that directed the immediate muster-out of any men currently in hospitals who did not need ongoing care.

Regardless of where they were at war's end, of those 390 survivors, 160 had been wounded at least once, twenty-nine had been wounded two times or more, and at least four men had been wounded three or more times. Joshua Chamberlain had been hit by enemy bullets six times, while Charles Avery suffered wounds at Gettysburg and Fredericksburg before a third wound at the Wilderness led to his capture. He survived his time in a Rebel prison but made it only six years beyond the end of the war before dying at the age of thirty-six. Henry Sanders was wounded in the hand at Gettysburg, then again at the Wilderness, and finally on April 1, 1865, when he lost an eye. The other man to suffer three wounds was John O'Connell, one of the Second Maine men. Wounds resulted in leg amputations for nine men, while another five lost an arm, at least three underwent surgery to amputate one or more fingers, and three were missing an eye. William Whitney was paralyzed on his left side by a wound at Peebles' Farm and died in 1886 at the age of thirty-eight. He had enlisted at the age of fifteen and suffered his life-changing wound at seventeen.[42]

In addition to the thirteen who died as prisoners of war, twenty-two survived imprisonment at some point during their term of service. Half of those men had been captured at the Battle of the Wilderness. The time in prison does not seem to have negatively impacted their life expectancy compared to their peers who avoided capture and came home in 1865. The average (mean) life span of the twenty former POWs for whom there is a death date available was just over forty-two years beyond the end of the war, while 1910 marked the median point at which half had passed away and half remained alive—two years later than it was for the rest of the unit. George Bowman was captured in August 1864 and held for six months before exchange. In his pension, he noted lingering health effects from his confinement, but he lived until 1900, dying at the age of fifty-eight. Oscar Thomas was captured at the Wilderness and held for nearly eleven months before his release on March 25, 1865, and yet he lived another sixty-eight years before passing away in 1935. Their longevity is remarkable, but the fact that they had survived a Confederate prison suggests they were pretty robust individuals from the outset.[43]

Some men fit more than one of the previous categories. Lewis Carter was wounded at Cold Harbor on June 3, 1864, later transferred to the

Veteran Reserve Corps, and then discharged by General Order No. 77. Charles H. Haynes, one of the former Second Maine men who reenlisted in early 1864, was wounded and captured at the Battle of the Wilderness, had his left leg amputated, and was discharged for disability on April 10, 1865. One statistic cuts through all the potential overlap: Of the 506 men who had stood on Little Round Top, just 166 returned home without having suffered a wound, captivity in a Confederate prison, or a debilitating disease leading to a discharge before the war's end.

While detailed information about the wartime fate of soldiers in other units is not always readily available, the basic rates of wounding and death exist and can be compared to the Twentieth Maine. In his 1889 work *Regimental Losses in the American Civil War*, William Fox noted that 293 of the 1,621 men who served in the Twentieth Maine throughout the war perished—a mortality rate of 18.1 percent. That number was higher than the average of all Union volunteer troops during the war, which was 15.2 percent, but slightly lower than the average for all Maine troops, which stood at 18.9 percent. The other three Maine units raised in the summer of 1862 that had similar wartime postings as the Twentieth—the Sixteenth, Seventeenth, and Nineteenth Maine—each suffered more total deaths (440, 370, and 376) than the Twentieth, with a combined mortality rate of 25 percent. The final unit raised in the summer of 1862 was the Eighteenth Maine, which was redesignated the First Maine Heavy Artillery in 1863. On June 18, 1864, this unit of 900 men made a charge at Petersburg that resulted in 632 casualties. In total, the unit suffered 423 men killed in battle—the most of any Union unit—and another 260 deaths to other causes for a total of 683 dead out of 2,202 enrolled—a mortality rate of 31 percent.[44]

In other words, the picture painted here of the war's incredible impact on the lives and bodies of the men in the Twentieth Maine does not mean they were uniquely impacted by combat. If anything, the opposite is the case. While the circumstances and impact of every man's wound, captivity, or debilitating disease were unique, their experiences overall were quite common among their fellow veterans.

The families at home had also suffered severely in many cases. Daniel Keene of Bremen, Maine, married Harriet Hardy in 1831, and they had five children together. Harriet died the day after Fort Sumter surrendered in 1861. The two younger boys, Weston (born 1838) and Daniel (born 1844), enlisted in the Twentieth Maine in 1862 and were present at Gettysburg. The oldest daughter, Lydia, died on August 29, 1864, and then Weston was killed at Peebles' Farm a month and a day later. Daniel transferred to the United States Colored Troops at the end of the war but contracted typhoid fever in South Carolina and died before he could return home. It is hard to imagine the grief the few remaining family members must have felt.

In other cases, the death of a servicemember meant the breakup of the family. Though the circumstances are unclear, Andrew Deering died sometime in 1864. He left behind two daughters, eight-year-old Ellen and eleven-year-old Eva. It appears his wife Martha could not care for them on her own, and the two girls were separated and sent to two of Andrew's brothers so that they could be raised with their families.[45]

In 1887, the *Lincoln County News* carried the following story:

Turns up after many years.

Waterville, Sept. 3

A young man in Waterville, who supposed his parents were both dead, was somewhat surprised not long ago by the appearance of his father, who had been in California for the past 20 years. When the war broke out the father enlisted in the 20th Maine regiment, and was, according to report, killed in the service, but after this long time he turns up all safe and sound and ready to claim his child. The son, who is over 20 years of age, has spent most of his life in knocking about from one point to another living here, and there, and everywhere.

Unfortunately, the identity of the son or the soldier is lost to time.[46]

While most of the volunteers returned to Maine, some decided to stay in the peacetime army. Mattson Sanborn had enlisted in the First Maine Light Artillery in December 1861 as a seventeen-year-old and served with that unit until he accepted a lieutenancy with the Twentieth Maine in November 1862. He received a brevet (or honorary) promotion for bravery for his actions at Bethesda Church in July 1864 and then a permanent promotion to first lieutenant later that month. Sanborn went home at the end of the war, but three months later he enlisted in the regular army. In March 1867, he received two brevet promotions, raising him to the honorary rank of captain. Serving with the Seventh U.S. Infantry, Sanborn was posted to Fort Shaw, Montana, in 1872. In early 1873, he was granted a leave of absence and went to Helena to visit friends. The local paper explained his demise: "Saturday night last he was engaged for several hours in rolling ten-pins, and this violent exercise, to which he was not accustomed, is attributed the cause of his sudden taking off." Around midnight, Sanborn fell into a fit of apoplexy, and despite the work of two doctors, he passed away five hours later. He had survived three years of warfare and six charges on Little Round Top only to overexert himself bowling.[47]

John O'Connell was born in Waterford, Ireland, in 1840, but by the outbreak of the Civil War, he was living in Portland and working as a laborer. He enlisted in the Second Maine on July 5, 1861, and thus was required to serve three years rather than two. Wounded three times during the war, O'Connell left the service on the expiration of his term on July 5, 1864. He reenlisted in late 1864 and was placed in the Eleventh Maine, where he remained until that unit was mustered out on February 2, 1866. Twice during the war he was promoted to corporal and then later reduced to the ranks, and in June 1865, he forfeited one month's pay due to a field court-martial. The likely cause of his reductions in rank and field court-martial becomes clear when viewing his postwar record. O'Connell enlisted in the U.S. Army Engineers Battalion in April 1866 for a three-year term and then reenlisted for a series of five-year terms before retiring in 1891. At the end of his second and third terms, O'Connell was held to fifteen and ten extra days to make up for time he had been absent without leave. From 1869 until 1879, he was hospitalized and treated for "alcoholism" or "inebriation" on thirteen occasions, typically for three days at a time. His last two treatments, however, lasted for ten and eight days, respectively. In 1879, O'Connell transferred to a different unit within the Engineer Battalion, and all mentions of his drunkenness ceased. Whether the drinking stopped or a different commander chose to look the other way is not in evidence. What is clear is that the army did not view O'Connell's transgressions as disqualifying him from further enlistments. Finally retiring from the army in 1891, O'Connell lived another fifteen years before passing away in New York.[48]

Lewis Merriam transferred to the Sixty-First United States Colored Troops toward the war's end and was a lieutenant until mustered out in late 1865. He rejoined the Sixty-Fifth United States Colored Troops as an officer in early 1866 and served another sixteen months. He returned to Maine in 1867 and, in 1870, married Olive Pray of Houlton. The marriage lasted just five years and ended in divorce in 1875, with both spouses remarrying shortly thereafter. In 1872, Merriam had reentered the army, joining the Fourth U.S. Infantry. Whether he enlisted to escape a failing marriage or his enlistment caused the marriage to fail is not apparent. He remained in the service until 1893, rising to the rank of captain in the regular army.[49]

Perhaps most interesting of those who served in the regular army after the war's end was Albert Titus, a seventeen-year-old farmer from Waldoboro when he enlisted in 1862. The ninth of fifteen children born to Weston and Sarah Titus between 1833 and 1856, Albert had already experienced the death of five siblings. Father Weston "had been disqualified for labor for more than ten years on account of long continued and excessive intemperance," while neighbors reported that he "neglected to provide for his wife and family." Service in the Civil War may have been a way for Albert to escape an unpleasant home life and provide economic support for his mother and younger siblings.[50]

Albert thrived in the army, with promotions to corporal on January 1, 1863; sergeant on July 1, 1864; first sergeant on October 22, 1864; and second lieutenant on April 26, 1865. He managed to avoid wounding, capture, or major disease and returned home in June 1865. He started farming again, and it seems he was living with his parents, but then on January 7, 1867, Titus enlisted as a private in Company C of the Twentieth United States Infantry. Perhaps he was returning to a place where he had previously excelled, or maybe he was escaping from a rocky return home.[51]

Titus was posted to east Texas, where many of the army's efforts supported the operations of the Freedman's Bureau, an organization created to help African Americans in the aftermath of slavery's end and oversee fair labor contracts between freedmen and the landholders—most of them the former owners of the freedmen. In June 1867, Freedman's Bureau agent William Kirkman learned of the killing of an African American by a notorious gang leader named Cullen Baker. This was just one of many times that Baker and his gang killed African Americans, agents of the Freedman's Bureau, or those who employed the formerly enslaved. Though romanticized by some as the inventor of the fast draw, Baker was little more than a ruthless murderer who most often killed unsuspecting enemies with a shotgun.[52]

Kirkman gathered soldiers to look for Baker but could not find him. Baker sent a note to Kirkman demanding the surrender of the entire garrison and then waited for their return while "refresh[ing] himself with a couple of cans of oysters and a few drinks of whiskey at a grocery hard by." Titus's commanding officer reported that he was "one of a party of soldiers sent to arrest a desperado named Baker at Boston Texas." As the soldiers entered the town, Baker opened fire with a shotgun and pistol. In the ensuing fight, the soldiers made thirty bullet holes in the building where Baker was hiding, but Baker got a clear shot at Albert Titus and fired a shotgun round into the Mainer's heart, killing him instantly. Freedman's Bureau agent Kirkman wounded Baker, but the wound did not prove fatal, and Baker terrorized the region for another eighteen months before meeting his end in January 1869. An excellent soldier who had made it through nearly three years of the Civil War, Titus deserved a better end than death at the hands of such a man.[53]

If his health had been better, Andrew Tozier might have followed the same path as those who remained in the army or at least might have reenlisted in 1864 to gain the large bounties on offer. But Tozier's health was so poor that he did not think his body could stand up to another enlistment, so he declined the financial inducements to reenlist and looked forward to the release from his three-year term of service in July 1864. Before he could return home, however, Tozier was wounded yet again. On May 26, 1864, at the North Anna River, Tozier "recd a wound from a ball which struck the left side of head 7 inches behind & above the left eye, & part of the ball escaped & part remained in the wound." This wound, along with heart troubles, became his most significant health concern in the postwar years.[54]

Seven weeks after receiving his final wound, Tozier mustered out on July 15, 1864, receiving $100 in bounty money due to him from 1861 plus $30.43 from his unused clothing allowance. He likely returned home via train, arriving in Maine in late July. In May 1863, the original members of the Second Maine had returned home to a parade in Bangor, and in June 1865, the Twentieth Maine would have the same treatment in Portland. But Tozier had no such closure, nor any idea of what to do next. He made his living through physical labor before the war, but now he had a crippled hand and ankle, heart trouble, and a bullet fragment lodged in his skull.[55]

On the interpersonal front, at least, there was promise, for on February 28, 1865, Andrew married eighteen-year-old Lizzie Bolden, his third cousin. Sometime during that winter, Tozier had the lead fragment removed from his head, but rather than making things better, it brought on intermittent headaches. On May 24, 1865, Tozier applied for a pension, claiming total disability resulting from his heart troubles, crippled hand and ankle, and head wound. For a man who had been independent since he was thirteen to admit that he could not support himself in his current condition must have been a blow. Lizzie became pregnant sometime around July 4. The couple might have known this by August 18 when the Pension Bureau declared that the thrice-wounded Tozier was "very slightly" disabled and deserved only one-third of a pension, amounting to $2.67 a month. This appears to have been the final straw.[56]

The *Portland Daily Press* of September 1 reported, "HEAVY ROBBERY OF CLOTHING.—The store of Mr. Larkin, at Livermore Falls, was broken into Tuesday night, and clothing of the value of $2000 was stolen. A reward of $200 is offered for the recovery of it." Ultimately, it emerged that, on the night of August 29, two men broke into Michael Larkin's store in Livermore Falls and used a stolen cart to carry away 154 coats valued at $1,920. Though it did not come to light for another four years, the robbery was committed by Andrew Tozier and his half brother, Lewis Cushman.[57]

Having gotten away with the merchandise, Tozier must have realized he would have difficulty turning the coats into cash without arousing suspicion, so he hid them at his brother-in-law's in East Dixmont. Meanwhile, on December 15, 1865, Joshua Chamberlain gave his first public address on the fight on Little Round Top. Reprinted five days later in the *Eastern Argus*, Chamberlain's speech brought the name of Andrew Tozier before readers across the state just as the man was desperate to keep a low profile.[58]

Seeking an increase to his paltry pension, Andrew presented himself again in January 1866, with the examiner noting in the application, "Gen. Chamberlain recommends him highly." The Toziers welcomed a baby boy named Andrew Jr. on April 4, 1866, and three months later saw a slight pension increase, bringing the monthly amount to $4. Tozier struggled physically and mentally during this period, for his doctor observed, "There is evidently considerable cerebral disability," while another noted that, during a recent examination, Tozier was "so bewildered" that he had to sit down abruptly. By February 1867, the pension was increased to $6 a month, a still tiny sum to support a family of three.[59]

Desperate, Tozier again turned to crime and, with Cushman and Charles Shorey, stole six oxen valued at $850 in Cherryfield on October 9, 1868. The men drove the cattle a hundred miles to be slaughtered in Augusta, but Tozier stopped short of the capital. While the other two men were disposing of the cattle, they were caught and arrested. The ensuing trial took place in Kennebec County. Both Shorey and Cushman pleaded guilty and implicated Tozier in the crime. As Tozier did not enter Kennebec County while engaged in the crime, however, he was dismissed for lack of jurisdiction. This was but a small victory, as he was immediately arrested by authorities from Washington County, the locale from which the cattle had been purloined.[60]

The April 1869 trial in Washington County was an absolute spectacle. Tozier pleaded not guilty. Accomplice Charles Shorey served as the principal witness for the prosecution—an act for which the state paid him $33.90 for his time and distance traveled—and a dozen others who had seen the three men with the cattle verified Shorey's testimony. Tozier's attorney, George Brown, hoped to create reasonable doubt through misidentification, so he placed Andrew's older brother and near doppelganger George in the courtroom's front row, closer to the witness stand than Andrew, and asked one of the younger witnesses to identify the cattle thief. The trick backfired when the youngster passed over George and pointed to Andrew. Frustrated and perhaps embarrassed that his shenanigans had not worked, Brown spewed that he "did not care if Tozier was found guilty—Gov. Chamberlain would pardon him." Indeed, most of Brown's "defense" of Tozier was a recounting of Andrew's war record rather than a rebuttal to the overwhelming evidence of his crime.[61]

Attorney Brown had calculated well, for the jury found Tozier not guilty. Three of the twelve jurors had served in the Civil War, and foreman Luther Hanscom had a son who served in the First Maine Cavalry. A fifth juror, Harris Plummer, was the same age as Tozier, was also a seaman, had meager real estate totaling just $150 in value, and had two young children at home. In short, if Tozier and Brown had hand-picked a jury, they could have done little better.[62]

Tozier had mere seconds to celebrate his victory before he was arrested by officials from Androscoggin County and charged with robbing Larkin's store four years earlier. During his imprisonment and guilty plea, Lewis Cushman had admitted to the theft at Larkin's and identified Tozier as his partner. On May 14, 1869, Tozier was arraigned in Livermore Falls and released on a $1,000 bond to await trial at the next session in September.[63]

Cushman told the court officials about the coats, which were found in their original hiding place. Tozier claimed he had purchased the goods from Charles Shorey, offering a somewhat plausible story that a jury might have bought, but in the end, it all came down to a small thing: the stolen cart. During the Washington County trial, a spectator recognized Tozier as the man who had sold a cart to his neighbor in 1865 using the false name of "Day." As the details of the clothing store robbery emerged, that man realized the cart was likely the one Tozier had stolen that night and used to transport the coats. Authorities recovered a wheel from the cart and positively identified it as the one stolen on August 29, 1865, whereupon Tozier finally pleaded guilty.[64]

The Maine Statutes determined that larceny—a crime committed without the use of violence and without danger to people—exceeding $100 would be punished by at least one but no more than five years in prison. Tozier's five-year sentence was "punishment by confinement to hard labor," which was both the standard of the day and a ridiculous irony given that it was Tozier's inability to labor that led him to crime in the first place.[65]

Tozier was incarcerated at the state prison on February 17, 1870, one of fifty-three men sent to that facility in 1870. Lewis Cushman was already serving a four-year sentence—likely reduced due to his testimony against Tozier. While incarcerated, Tozier worked manufacturing carriages, boots, or shoes, with the sale of those items making the prison economically self-sustaining.[66]

Tozier had served just three months and six days when the governor's executive council recommended that Joshua Chamberlain pardon his former color sergeant. Interestingly, Chamberlain might not have even been the person most familiar with Tozier sitting in the governor's chambers that day. When transferred to the Twentieth Maine in 1863, Tozier was assigned to Captain Prentiss Fogler's Company I. In 1870, Fogler served as Chamberlain's secretary and messenger, and one suspects that he eagerly awaited Chamberlain's decision.

Prentiss Fogler (Maine State Archives)

Throughout his four years as governor, Chamberlain pardoned fifty-nine men, a rate in line with his predecessor and successor. In 1870, Chamberlain pardoned eleven, and Andrew Jackson Tozier was one of those, fulfilling lawyer Brown's boast during the second trial that a guilty verdict would lead to the governor interceding.[67]

While on the surface the governor and his former color sergeant were worlds apart, they actually shared much in common. For all of his public success, Chamberlain had also been privately suffering ever since the end of the war. The professor had taken to warfare and commanding soldiers like a duck to water and would have been content to make a life in the armed forces had his health permitted and a continued conflict demanded combat operations. But neither was the case. In late June 1865, Chamberlain wrote to a confidant, "I shall return very soon to my private life. Soldiering in time of peace is almost as much against my grain as being a peace man in time of war. My wounds too, I find, now that I am called on no longer to bear up against them, are very troublesome, and I need to be fitted at home a while." Ten days later, he wrote to the army's adjutant general requesting a posting in either Maine or Washington while waiting for surgery. He explained, "The state of my wounds is such as to require care and attention. I shall be obliged to undergo a severe surgical operation as soon as the heat of summer is past." Despite the operation that ensued, a doctor who examined Chamberlain in 1869 for a possible pension rated him as "totally incapacitated for obtaining his subsistence by manual labor" due to his Petersburg wound. Chamberlain himself noted that he had "received a gunshot wound through both thighs near the privates, and through the neck of the bladder on the 18th of June 1864 in the assault on Petersburg Va. This was followed by a urethral fistula from which he still suffers, as well as from the effects of the original wound." The doctor added, "Bladder very painful + irritable—whole of lower part of abdomen tender + sensitive. Large urinal fistula at base of penis in front of scrotum, which is exceedingly troublesome. Suffers constant pain in both hips from wound." He concluded, "It will materially abridge his life." The Pension Bureau agreed, awarding Chamberlain a pension of $30 a month backdated to his discharge in early 1866.[68]

Despite the inner wounds, Chamberlain outwardly appeared the dashing military hero destined for any number of leadership positions within the state. He resumed his former post at Bowdoin but was clearly marking time. He quickly became an in-demand speaker on the Civil War, and much of his correspondence was aimed at gathering information for lectures he delivered on Gettysburg, the final surrender, or the war writ large. He intended to write a history of the Fifth Corps and began procuring material to do so in the fall of 1865. His obsession with the war and its memory is perhaps best demonstrated by the bracelet he designed for Fanny to mark their tenth wedding anniversary in December 1865. The bracelet featured a Maltese Cross—the symbol of his beloved Fifth Corps—and contained the names of the two dozen battles in which he had risked his life. Fanny's reaction to the gift is not recorded.[69]

In the 1860s, Maine elected its governors to single-year terms, and it is no great surprise that the Republican party leaders encouraged Chamberlain to become the candidate for the "Union" Party throughout 1866. Having grown beyond a professorship at a small college, Chamberlain accepted the nomination and won the general election that fall, polling what was then the largest margin in the state's history. Chamberlain served four terms before declining to run for a fifth, holding office from 1867 until 1871. Only two prior governors—of thirty-one—had served as many terms as the war hero when he stepped down to return to civilian life. While in office, Chamberlain supported the ideals of Radical Reconstruction rather than the more lenient terms favored by President Andrew Johnson, but in Maine the major issues were more basic: He advocated utilizing the state's natural resources, improving transportation, and attracting out-of-state investment and businesses. Two areas of controversy arose—the state's ban on alcohol and its continued use of capital punishment. Chamberlain's decisions to pardon some condemned inmates while allowing the sentences of others to be carried out—particularly in the case of former slave and convicted murderer Clifton Harris—brought the first real opposition to Chamberlain's leadership and suggest that the man who had fought to restore the Union and end slavery was unwilling to extend equal treatment and rights to African Americans.[70]

Despite Chamberlain holding the state's highest office, there were continued struggles beneath the surface for the family. In 1865, the Chamberlains' youngest child, Gertrude, passed away. Conceived in the spring of 1864 (perhaps during her parents' trip to view the battlefield at Gettysburg), Gertrude was the last child the Chamberlains were able to have due to the general's horrific Petersburg wound. Two years later, Chamberlain's brother John died from tuberculosis, a disease the family thought he likely contracted during his wartime service with the Christian Commission. Whether it was a result of Gertrude's death, Chamberlain's continued pain from his Petersburg wound, difficulty by one or both spouses adjusting to the end of the war and the resumption of cohabitation, or some other reason, Fanny and Joshua Chamberlain were at odds by 1868.[71]

On November 20, 1868, Joshua wrote an explosive letter to Fanny about the status of their marriage. In the recent past, both her friends and his had reported that she was "complaining to everyone who came into the house of my conduct & treatment of you," but after a clear-the-air conversation, Chamberlain had believed she received his words with "kindness," and he was "satisfied," even "nearly happy" with the result. But now a confidant told him that a Brunswick schoolteacher was spreading the word that Fanny claimed "I abused you beyond endurance—pulling your hair, striking, beating & otherwise personally maltreating you, & that you were gathering up everything you could find against me to sue for a divorce." From a century and a half in the distance, the third-hand allegations of abuse are impossible to investigate further. However, the distance that had grown between them is evident from Chamberlain's admonition, "If it is true (as Mr. Johnson seems to think there is a chance of its being) that you are preparing for an action against me, you need not give yourself all this trouble." Stating that they could mutually work out a separation without the involvement of other "low people," Chamberlain implored, "You never take my advice, I am aware. But if you do not *stop* this at once it will end in *hell*."[72]

The Chamberlains did not divorce, and after a time of separation, they eventually patched up their relationship. What exactly to make of this incident is difficult to say, but at a minimum it shows the challenges Chamberlain faced in adjusting to his return home despite all the outward appearances of success. Chamberlain's public reputation was well secured by his wartime exploits and equaled (if not surpassed) that of any man in the state, but he had either never truly gained Fanny's respect or perhaps gained it but then subsequently lost it by his actions. Regardless, the war's impact on Chamberlain's relationship with his wife is clear.

Chamberlain was in the final year of his gubernatorial career when Andrew Tozier's case came before his desk, and given his private suffering, his old sergeant's plight must have pulled on the governor's heartstrings. Other former soldiers were in jail during Chamberlain's term—including two men from the Twentieth Maine—but Tozier's actions on Little Round Top had set him apart from the rest. For this man, Chamberlain was willing to go further than a pardon, which might offer only a temporary reprieve.

Joshua Chamberlain, 1871 (Collections of Maine Historical Society)

Chamberlain offered Tozier a job and a place to live. By the time the census taker appeared on August 1, 1870, the Toziers were living in Chamberlain's Brunswick house, with both Andrew and Lizzie identified as "domestic servant[s]." Pension forms that Tozier filed carried a "Brunswick" heading until 1875, evincing the period of Tozier's rehabilitation. Facing a hard time himself, Chamberlain likely boosted his own mood and outlook with his act of benevolence for his former color sergeant, but it was also undoubtedly another form of his continued leadership of the Twentieth Maine.[73]

Tozier was not the only Twentieth Maine man to turn to crime in the 1860s. Like Tozier, David Royal had been wounded twice during the war. At the Wilderness, a gunshot to his right hand required the amputation of

Andrew Tozier and family on balcony of Joshua Chamberlain's house, early 1870s
(Courtesy of Pejepscot History Center)

his ring finger, and another bullet broke his leg. While Royal's wound did
not send him home, he was transferred to the Veteran Reserve Corps in
1864 and received a half pension ($4/month) starting in 1866. As was the
case with Andrew Tozier, for one who truly could not labor that amount
was simply insufficient. The exact circumstances of his crime are unknown,
but on February 10, 1868, Royal pleaded guilty to larceny and was sentenced
to one year in state prison. Chamberlain did not see fit to pardon him.[74]

The third known criminal was Alden Litchfield, the Twentieth's former
quartermaster and a man who had shown a mean streak during the war that
earned the enmity of many of the enlisted men.[75] While Tozier definitely and
Royal possibly turned to crime due to financial desperation caused at least partly
by war wounds, Litchfield had no such excuse. "Robbery of the Lime Rock
Bank. $26,000 Stolen," reported the *Rockland Gazette* on May 6, 1870. Two
days earlier, a group of burglars entered the Western Union Office in the predawn hours and tore down the brick wall it shared with the adjacent bank. The
gang then pried the safe door open enough to allow them to place a charge of

dynamite inside. The subsequent explosion opened the safe, cracked the vault, and blew out the bank's windows. The inept robbers overlooked a box containing $12,000 in gold and escaped with only around $1,100 in cash and some bonds and securities that were easily canceled. The men behind the robbery made good their escape, but the entire plot unraveled within a few hours. Several of the burglars were spotted fleeing the scene in a wagon, and one was identified as a former member of the local police department named Addison Keiser. On questioning, that man implicated Alden Litchfield, "A well-known trader in this city." A safecracker out of New York named Joshua Adams was found hiding in Litchfield's house. Keiser shared with the authorities the location where the burglars planned to meet to divide the loot the following night, and subsequently a posse arrested eight men and recovered all that had been taken. This might not have been Litchfield's first crime. Nine months earlier, thieves had unsuccessfully tried to rob the same bank. Litchfield was sentenced to four years in prison. Unlike Tozier and Royal, the crime and punishment do not appear to have been a turning point in his life. After many years of estrangement, Litchfield divorced his wife and was subsequently admitted to the Government Hospital for the Insane in Washington, DC, where he died in 1911.[76]

Alden Litchfield (Collections of Maine Historical Society)

The stories of Andrew Tozier, David Royal, and Alden Litchfield offer a window into the increase in crime following the Civil War. In 1867, Maine state warden Warren Rice noted, "For the last two years, there has been an unusual number of convicts sentenced to State Prison in this as well as other states." In 1866, there were ninety-three people sent to the Maine State Prison, a marked increase from the forty-one who were dispatched to that place in 1860, the last year before the Civil War. Other nearby states also saw a rise: In Massachusetts, the increase was from 144 to 249, and in Vermont, it was from 41 to 51. In all three states, the incarceration numbers then declined. Of those jailed in Maine in 1866, Warden Rice noted that "three-fourths of them have served in the army." They were also overwhelmingly young men, nearly half of them less than twenty-three years old, and most "have had very poor, if any, common school." For all but five, this was their first conviction, and Rice was convinced these men were not hardened criminals but desperate former soldiers who had returned home after the war without economic prospects. The declining incarceration rates in the later part of the 1860s would suggest that he was correct and that temporary resorts to crime ended once these men fully reintegrated into their communities, a conclusion supported by the stories of both Andrew Tozier and David Royal.[77]

From the governor to the criminals, a substantial number of the veterans were living with wartime wounds of various severities.

The most visually evocative of the wounded was Calvin Bates. His transfer from the notorious prison at Andersonville to one in Florence, South Carolina, had done little to improve his condition. At Florence, he was not provided with any shelter and sought warmth and protection by "burrowing in the ground." In early January 1865, "he contracted 'Swamp' Fever + Scurvy accompanied by gangrene about the ankle joints so that the flesh was destroyed to the bones," he testified. As a result, his feet "sloughed off." Bates was finally paroled on March 1, 1865, and three days later was admitted to a Union hospital in Wilmington, North Carolina. The doctors determined they could not save his feet, and on March 12, 1865, they "were cut away with a pair of Scissors." A month later, Bates transferred to the U.S. General Hospital on David's Island in New York, where another surgery on April 25 amputated the bottom parts of his legs two inches above the ankle joints. On April 28, 1865, Bates's image was taken by a photographer capturing the horrors of Andersonville and became part of a larger display of those who had suffered severely at the infamous prison.[78]

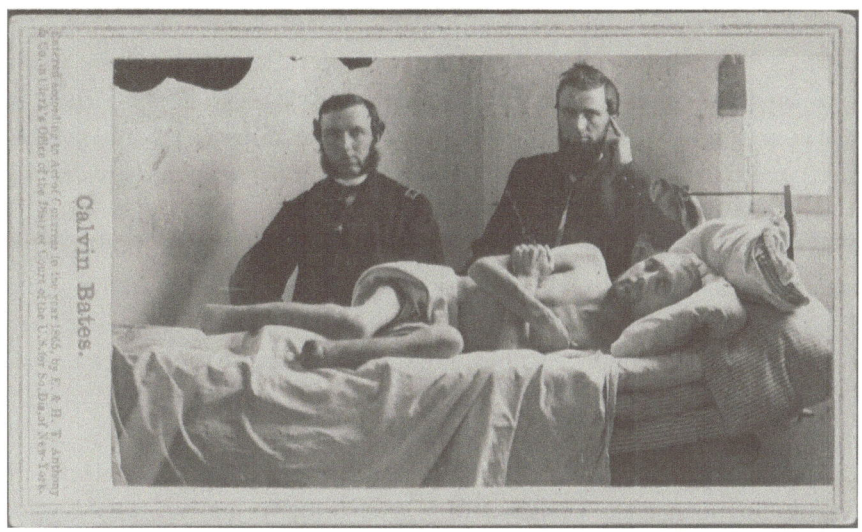

Calvin Bates, showing evidence of the privations of Andersonville (Library of Congress)

From 1829 until 1897, New York City's American Institute held an annual fair to showcase advances in agriculture, commerce, manufacturing, and the arts. With the Civil War having created an estimated forty-five thousand living amputees, four inventors of various prosthetic limbs attended the October 1865 fair to showcase their wares. John Austin, a Mr. Jewett, Gustavus Kirschmann, and A. A. Marks all exhibited varying forms of advanced artificial legs that offered far greater movement, hinging, and elasticity than the traditional wooden leg used for so long. The fair organizers sensed an opportunity beyond mere displays and announced in the *New York Times* "that a CRIPPLE RACE would be run in the evening." By 8:00 p.m., hundreds of people packed the venue. Calvin Bates, identified as "a two-legger," was one of three contestants and, like the others, was described as an "unabashed and incomplete gentleman."[79]

Bates was to walk five hundred feet on two artificial legs that he had worn for just a few weeks. The reporter described him as "a solemn, undertakerish-looking man, in a felt hat, gray sack, gray trowsers, and switching a cane." When the word was given, "He moodily started, and leisurely meandered in a waddling manner down the lane. He was not an entirely successful artificialist; not that he limped, but because he wiggled from side to side, or rather from leg to leg, and seemed rather glad, on the whole, when he finished his course, and was greeted with applause." The time elapsed was three minutes, a rate of around two miles per hour, approximately the marching pace Bates had used during his wartime service.[80]

The coverage of this "race" raises many unanswerable questions. Why did Bates volunteer to display his disability? Was he determined to prove something to himself? Was there a financial incentive for participating, either from the prosthetic manufacturer or from the fair organizers? Was his "undertakerish" demeanor his natural display, and was he in fact enjoying himself? At the time of the "race," Bates was still enlisted in the army but was discharged the following week on October 21, 1865.[81]

Calvin Bates filed for a pension a week after his discharge but did not immediately hear back. In April 1866, the adjutant general informed the pension office that Bates was "'Reported missing in action since May 5 1864' No evidence of discharge. No further record on file." No pension was granted. Bates pressed his case, writing in 1867, "I think it hard usage for a fellow to be in the army over three years and suffer the loss of his two feet and be obliged to crawl around on his knees to get a living." He submitted his discharge certificate, and after further investigation, he was pensioned at $20 a month, with a subsequent raise to $31.25 per month. In 1866, he married a widow named Elizabeth (Corey) Kelso. Calvin became stepfather to six-year-old Charles following the marriage. The 1870 census taker found the family of three living in New Hampshire, where Calvin listed his profession as "farmer" and claimed real estate values of $4,200 and personal property of $1,250—a comfortable sum. His life, however, was anything but comfortable. In 1875, his pension was increased to $50 a month because "he is so disabled as to be totally unable to do any work or to take care of himself, he is obliged to have the assistance and be under the care of one person all the time." His doctor noted, "The stump was prone to ulcerate and gave him trouble more or less, all of the time, he was anaemic had a bad cachexia [wasting syndrome] such is generally attributed to malaria." Bates lived for twenty-four pain-filled years beyond his captivity and double amputation, dying in 1889.[82]

Hiram Chesley spent his postwar years partially paralyzed. At Gettysburg, a bullet entered his neck on the left side and exited near his vertebrae. His spinal column and optical nerve were both injured, partially paralyzing his left arm and leg and severely impacting his vision. He was medically discharged on April 29, 1864, with the notation that "he cannot walk Stand, or feed himself." The paralysis in his left leg seems to have eased, though the pain remained and he frequently had to pace at night due to discomfort. For a time in the 1870s and 1880s, he was able to practice law, but by 1882, a doctor noted that the effects of his wound were worsening. There was "paralysis of whole left arm and hand. has no use and but slight control of it cant elevate of the left arm + the right arm is also disabled." Further, "I also find both eyes impaired as results of the GSW," resulting in an "almost entire loss of vision," with the prediction that it would "entirely fail in a short time." Chelsey lived until 1909, but with extreme limitations.[83]

Whereas many wounds grew increasingly debilitating over time, others went in the opposite direction, even if the veterans did not always want the Pension Bureau to know of their improved health. Former Second Maine man John Lynes Jr. had refused duty right up to Gettysburg but then picked up a rifle and fought with distinction, earning a promotion to corporal before being reduced to the ranks in August 1864 for unknown reasons. On March 29, 1865, Lynes was hit twice by musket balls. One bullet pierced his right leg, resulting in a minor wound the soldier described as an "inconvenience." The other was far more serious, hitting Lynes in the back, where it "entered at about the middle of base of right scapula [shoulder blade] + lodged." A probe sent into the wound shortly thereafter hit the missile about four and a half inches into the body, nearer to the right breast than the back. The bullet was not removed, and Lynes spent the rest of the war in the hospital before being discharged by General Order No. 77 on June 24, 1865. A month later, he applied for and received a pension of $8 a month for a full disability, the examiner noting that the loss of function was equal to a person who was missing a limb.[84]

Sometime in the latter part of 1868, Dr. E. F. Sanger of Bangor removed the bullet, leaving a three-inch scar below Lynes's right shoulder blade to mark the place where the ball had once rested. James Weston, the surgeon who had originally examined Lynes and recommended his rating for full disability, called the pensioner in for a reexamination in February 1869. Writing two days later, Weston explained, "I had been informed that the ball was removed more than a year ago, and expected, as sufficient time had elapsed for cicatrix [scar] to become sound, and as he looked well when I met him, to find sufficient improvement to authorize a reduction of the rate of disability." The wound site looked good, as did the patient's mobility. "He can move his arm freely and strike with his fist forcibly in all directions." Further, "There has been an improvement, since I made the examination March 7th, 1866, in the condition of the right lung. He has not spit blood since last spring, he has no cough today, neither have I heard him cough when I have occasionally met him." Denying that he was as fit as the doctor believed, Lynes "complains that it hurts him to put his arm behind him or to throw a stone forward, that it hurts him as much in the region of the wound or more than before the ball was removed," the doctor reported. But the protestations flew in the face of the evidence and were not credible, Weston concluded. He recommended a downgraded rating of three-quarters disabled or $6 per month. That rating went into effect two weeks later and then was further reduced to three-eighths disabled or $3 per month two years later. Lynes's health had improved with the operation, but his financial outlook had suffered.[85]

Henry Moore's adjustment to home life was also complicated. The one Second Maine mutineer who had refused to drop his dissent and join the ranks of the Twentieth Maine, Moore had been imprisoned at Fort Delaware from October 1863 until April 1864. In that month, authorities returned Moore to the Twentieth Maine to finish out his term of service, but almost immediately he was hit in the foot with a cannonball at Cold Harbor on June 3, 1864, losing part of his heel. Mustered out due to this wound, Moore was pensioned at $4 a month. Like Andrew Tozier, Joshua Chamberlain, and John Lynes Jr., Henry Moore also required a postwar surgery: "In 1865 was obliged to have wound re-opened and five pieces of bone removed, placing upon me an expense of $349 besides the loss of time. Am at times obliged to use crutches."[86]

Moore also had frequent spells of dizziness, and friends observed him falling down during those moments. It all became too much. "I have received a wound in my left side since the war," Moore told the Pension Bureau. "The wound received since the war was from a Bullet fired by my self with suicidal intention [in 1874 or 1875]. The bullet entered my side in the region of my former injury by shell as I have said . . . I was crazy at the time I shot myself as I have said. I was working hard and my head was bad and had been for some time. I have not been crazy since then, only have the blind staggers now and then." Reuben Bagley Jr., who had known Moore since before the war, testified, "When he worked for me in 1865–66 he had a fit or spasm and we had to bring him home with a team. He was working in the lumber woods at the time. He was unconscious for a time. . . . He has seemed to be queer in his head at times ever since then. Seemed to be sort of out of his mind. I remember of hearing of his shooting himself while in one of these crazy spells."[87]

Wounded twice, stricken by black measles, sentenced to execution, and then imprisoned for six months at hard labor, any one of several things could have led to Moore's mental breakdown and suicide attempt. That moment seems to have been a turning point. Despite continuing physical ailments—Moore's foot problems caused him to fall and break his leg in later years—mentally he seems to have found stable ground as he moved further away from the war. He lived until the age of seventy-five, dying in 1914 just months before World War I began.[88]

Others suffered war wounds and yet returned home to prosper. At the Wilderness, a bullet had hit William T. Livermore above his right elbow, passing through the muscle without hitting the bone. After a hospital stay and convalescence of three months, he returned to the regiment and remained there until mustered out in June 1865. A few weeks later, he applied for a pension. His former captain, Walter Morrill, endorsed his request, writing, "He was a good soldier and did his duty fearlessly, and is justly entitled to a pension." The examiners agreed, rating him at three-quarters disabled with the entitlement to $6 a month.[89]

Livermore returned to his hometown of Milo, Maine. His father passed away in 1867, and Will took over the family farm. The 1870 census lists him as managing a farm of 240 acres valued at $1,200. Three horses, two milk cows, and a single swine were valued at $450, while $75 worth of implements and machinery facilitated the work on the land. That year, Livermore's farm produced 580 bushels of oats, 350 bushels of potatoes, 200 pounds of butter, 20 tons of hay, $85 worth of forest products, and $100 in animals slaughtered or sold for slaughter. The total value of the farm's production was $898, the eighth-highest number of the seventy farms in Milo. All told, Livermore estimated his real estate to be worth $3,000 and his personal property $800.[90]

In 1862, he had been unimpressed with the women in Maryland, noting, "When I get a Woman I Shall get her just as near Katahdin as I can." He did just that, marrying eighteen-year-old Alice Stone of nearby Sebec—just fifty miles from Katahdin as the crow flies—on November 18, 1869. Besides Will and Alice, the 1870 census taker found four others in the household. Will's mother Sarah (age fifty-nine) lived with them after her husband's death. Will's beloved older brother Charles—his primary pen pal during the war—was a thirty-four-year-old "invalid" who would die in 1873. Younger brother Andrew (twenty-one years old) worked on the farm but soon received a portion of those lands and began his own operations. Finally, ten-year-old Fred Spearin was a local boy who worked on the farm.[91]

Will and Alice had six children from 1871 to 1891. Four lived long lives before passing away in the 1940s–1960s. Sadie, born in 1876, lived for just eight months, while Percy passed away at eighteen years of age. Will's family later described him as "a kind and indulgent husband and father." In the 1880s, he requested a pension increase due to stiffness and general disability resulting from his gunshot wound that made manual labor difficult and painful. By the end of his life, he suffered from trouble with his heart, as did many of his former comrades, and it was angina pectoris that killed him on August 29, 1911, at the age of seventy-one.[92]

Livermore exemplifies the many veterans who came home and led quiet lives. It is tempting to say that the three years of wartime service was but an interruption in the life Livermore led before and after the conflict, and while the experience and consequences of that term would be with him forever, the broader trajectory of his life was little impacted by his time with the Twentieth Maine. But that is too sweeping of a generalization, for it is impossible to know what personal thoughts a very private man like Will Livermore harbored. His former comrades implored him to publish parts or all of the wartime diary he had kept, but he only agreed to do so once, printing his account of Gettysburg in 1883, otherwise keeping his experiences largely to himself. But those who mattered knew all about Will Livermore, and Walter Morrill was not the only former officer to sing his praises. In his 1899 Memorial Day address in Milo, Joshua Chamberlain told all in the audience, "William T. Livermore of your town was the bravest man I ever saw."[93]

Like Will Livermore, most of the men remained in Maine after the war, but not all. Despite a national population growth of more than 22 percent, Maine saw a decrease of 1,364 people (0.2 percent) from 1860 to 1870 as its residents sought opportunity elsewhere. Of the 390 Gettysburg men who returned home after the war, the final burial place is known for 365. Of those, 269 rest in Maine cemeteries. At least seven of those men passed elsewhere but were returned to the Pine Tree State for burial. Some men left the state for a period before returning and eventually dying within its borders, but ninety-six moved permanently and, when they died, were buried in one of twenty-four other states or Washington, DC. Massachusetts and New Hampshire led the way with twenty-four and eleven, respectively. Seventeen relocated to and are buried in Michigan, Wisconsin, and Minnesota. Eight ended up in California. A dozen states have just one man from the Twentieth. The men tended to avoid the states of the former Confederacy. Leaving out Albert Titus, who was killed in Texas and buried by the army in Louisiana, plus four men buried at Arlington National Cemetery in Virginia, just a single man each was buried in Florida and Tennessee. Adding the four "Border States" of the Civil War era increases that count by only one, with Henry Carpenter lying in Missouri. In summary, 103 of the 365 men for whom a death or burial place is known either died or are buried outside of Maine, suggesting that roughly 28 percent of the soldiers made a postwar life for themselves elsewhere, while 72 percent remained in Maine.[94]

The 1862 Homestead Act allowed anyone over the age of twenty-one who had never borne arms against the government to claim 160 acres of land for either the sum of $1.25 per acre or a registration fee of $10 plus a commitment to live on and improve the land for five years. That five-year term was reduced for veterans by the amount of time they had served in the military, providing a nearly free way for veterans to acquire a 160-acre farm within two years. Edwin Morrill was one of the men who seized this opportunity. After working in a woolen mill in Maine in the early postwar years, he headed for Iowa in 1870 and secured 320 acres of government land. He prospered in the developing state, becoming a bank vice president and later a player in an electric and power company.[95]

Thomas Wyman moved to Coos, Oregon, shortly after the war. Census records show he and his family went back and forth between Oregon and Maine over the ensuing years, but in 1891 he took a job as the assistant lighthouse keeper at Cape Argo in Oregon. The lighthouse was four hundred feet offshore, and the treacherous currents capsized many boats and destroyed the bridges and walkways leading out to its location. Finally, the government installed a cable tramway to transport the attendants to the lighthouse. In July 1898, Wyman, his twenty-two-year-old daughter Mary, and two other men were all in the tramway when the cable snapped and dropped the group more than sixty feet. Mary and the other men survived without injuries, likely falling into the water below, but Thomas was dashed on the rocks, breaking both legs. Thirty-five years after Gettysburg, Wyman's leg was amputated due not to a Rebel bullet but to a faulty cable.[96]

Whether they remained in Maine or left for greener pastures, in the ten years after the war ended, twenty-two of the men who had been on Little Round Top perished. The first was Andrew Roberts, who died on December 2, 1865, from chronic diarrhea contracted while in the service. Christopher Pennington died twelve days later of the same cause, also a remnant of his war service. For Andrew Smith, who died in early 1867, it was tuberculosis picked up during the war. John Breen's wound and amputated arm caused frequent lung infections, including the final fatal one in 1869. Horace Monroe never fully recovered from the leg amputation he underwent in June 1864. Although Monroe married and started a family after his return home, his widow asserted that his health declined steadily until he died in 1870. Elijah Carr's widow believed the pneumonia that killed him in 1873 resulted from his exposure to the elements and disease in late 1862, from which he never fully recovered. Most of those twenty-two deaths in the first decade were directly attributable to wartime service, showing the longer-term impacts on the health of even those who returned home.[97]

Milton Davis returned home without a scratch and passed the first dozen years after the war peacefully until he disappeared on the night of December 7, 1878. Born in 1842, Davis became a fisherman in his home of Friendship, Maine. He was present with the Twentieth throughout the war except for a hospital stint in the spring of 1864 due to diphtheria. He was promoted to corporal in late 1864 and mustered out with the unit in June 1865. Back home he married Evelyn Guyer—a cousin—in September 1866. In 1878, the couple lived on Harbor Island, a tiny piece of land in Casco Bay just a mile in length and only a fraction of that in width. On December 7, 1878, "He went to Bremen for a load of wood and produce," four friends later recollected, adding ominously that Davis was "in an open boat." In Bremen, Davis purchased the wood and some cabbage, loaded up with the help of Will Nash, and headed back for Harbor Island. Davis had, it seems, overloaded his boat, a problem that became a nightmare when a squall kicked up while he was en route back to Harbor Island. Oscar Bickmore later testified, "He was last seen between Bremen Long Island and Jonses Garden exactly in the way of the tide and blowing very heavy." Davis never made it back to Harbor Island, and the following day search parties braved the ongoing weather to look for signs of Davis, his boat, or the cargo. Eventually, a single oar washed up on shore along with some of the cabbage, confirming everyone's worst fears. Evelyn was widowed, and two sons, aged ten and eight, were left without a father. Many years later, Evelyn secured a pension, but only after filing a mountain of paperwork to establish that Davis had died at sea despite the lack of an eyewitness.[98]

Will Owen also drowned. Or at least that is how it first appeared. Wounded at the Wilderness in 1864, Owen was hit a second time that year at Peebles' Farm on September 30. A surgeon examining the wound the following year noted, "He was shot between the third and fourth ribs on the left side the ball emerging near the anterior border of the scapular passing through the lung and affecting the action of the heart so much as to render active exercise dangerous." Owen was mustered out at war's end by General Order No. 77 and applied for a pension based on his latter wound. The examiners recommended a full pension of $8 a month due to his "incapability for manual labor." Incapacitated for manual labor but certainly not for brain work, Will worked as a druggist, town clerk, and postmaster in Milo, becoming one of the town's most prominent citizens. Will married Clara Johnson on July 4, 1864, while home on furlough from his first wound, and they had eight children—five of whom lived to adulthood.[99]

After the forenoon church service on August 31, 1884, Will went to bathe in the Sebec Stream, something he had been doing since childhood. Soap and towel in hand, Will walked to his usual spot, removed his clothes, and headed into the water. When he had not returned home after two hours, Clara grew concerned, and the town's residents began looking for their friend. Abial Leonard, who had been on Little Round Top with Will, was one of the many who joined the search. Finally, Frank Perkins "found his body in Sebec Stream about five rods from a stump upon which his clothing was lying in a depth of about eight feet of water." Perkins continued, "When I found him he was lying upon his face his hands beneath his body his features regular not distorted with no symptoms of having made any struggle for life."[100]

Local doctor Hannibal H. Hamlin, distant cousin to the former vice president, knew Will well and was present as the body was recovered from the stream. He wrote, "There are no signs of death by suffocation or drowning the lungs were not filled [with] water nor was the face livid or purple showing congestion." So what caused the veteran's death? "In my opinion," the doctor speculated, "death was not produced by drowning (suffocation) but by a sudden paralysis of the heart action due to the sending of the blood from the surface toward the heart upon plunging into the water." Dr. Lewis Ford concurred in the diagnosis. J. P. Kittredge, whose own place of business was across the street from Owen's, noted that a week before the fateful day he had observed Will have "a bad spell with his heart so bad that he should have fallen to the floor had he not grasped the counter." While the local *Piscataquis Observer* titled their news of the affair "Sad Case of Drowning at Milo," Clara soon claimed a widow's pension on the basis that her husband's death was not an accidental drowning; rather, it was directly attributable to the heart condition brought on by his war wound. Owen's death was a reminder that some of those who had made it home in 1865 still suffered severely from their wounds and could even die of those wartime afflictions twenty or more years after the conflict's end.[101]

Sometimes it was not the veteran but their spouse who passed away. In early 1874, Ellis Spear lost his wife, Susie, at the age of just thirty-seven. As was common in those days, he did not remain single for long. During the war he had made the acquaintance of Sarah Keene, wife of Captain Samuel Keene of Company F. In the winter of 1864, Susie Spear and Sarah Keene had made the trip from Maine to Virginia together to spend time with their husbands. "Capt. K. & wife were much in my Hd. Qrs. in the winter & we were in happy ignorance of the future & enjoyed passing the days, without apprehension of the future." Sam Keene had been killed in June 1864 outside Petersburg, just a few months after the happy times Spear chronicled. Now, having lost his wife, Spear proposed marriage to Sarah Keene. She accepted, and the couple were married on December 20, 1875. Each brought a child from their first marriage and, together, had two more.[102]

On leaving the governorship, Joshua Chamberlain returned to his beloved Bowdoin and assumed the presidency of that institution. Before the war such a position would have been the pinnacle of his dreams, but the war had changed his perspective. Chamberlain would likely have echoed the sentiment of James Whitehorne of the Twelfth Virginia, who wondered, "How can we get interested in farming or working in a store or warehouse when we have been interested day and night for years in keeping alive, whipping the invaders, and preparing for the next fight?"[103]

As president of Bowdoin, Chamberlain led a capital campaign that improved the physical facilities at the institution. He moved the curriculum away from the strictly classical to introduce additional liberal arts and science programs and founded four new professorships. The result was a doubling of Bowdoin's enrollment in Chamberlain's first year as president. Successful in many ways, Chamberlain's reign was tarnished by his dogged attempt to introduce a military drill requirement for the students. When they rebelled, he threatened to expel them all. The students backed down, but the college soon abolished the requirement and made participation in the military department strictly voluntary. Both Chamberlain's attempts to bring an air of the military to Bowdoin and his 1870 letter to the king of Prussia offering his services in that nation's war against France show a man desperate to return to a setting in which he had so excelled.[104]

Joshua Chamberlain's library (Courtesy of Pejepscot History Center)

Such an opportunity came in early 1880. The Maine State Constitution stipulated that if there was a plurality but no majority for any one gubernatorial candidate, then the state's House of Representatives would narrow the field to two candidates, with the State Senate then selecting one of those two people to become the next governor. The rise of a third party, the Greenbacks, led to that scenario in 1878, when a House dominated by Democrats and Greenbackers picked a candidate from each party to put forward, and the Republican-majority Senate had decided that Democrat Alonzo Garcelon was the lesser of two evils and appointed him governor.[105]

In 1879, Alonzo Garcelon ran again as the Democratic incumbent, this time against Daniel Davis (Republican) and Joseph Smith (Greenbacker). National eyes were on Maine: Would Democrats again carry a northern state? Would Maine Republican senator James G. Blaine (a possible presidential candidate in 1880) be able to flex his muscles and hold the state for his party? Even before election day, there were charges of corruption and irregularities.[106]

The election took place on Chamberlain's birthday, September 8. Republican Daniel Davis garnered 49.5 percent of the vote, falling just half a percentage point (or 493 votes) short of a majority. Democrats and Greenbackers had already agreed to work together on a "Fusion" ticket to gain control of the state legislature, but early returns suggested they had fallen short, with the Republicans holding a 90–61 advantage in the House and a 19–12 edge in the Senate. Before the state legislators could be seated and subsequently pick the next governor, town clerks had to certify the vote and send their complete lists to the Maine secretary of state in early December ahead of the formal seating of the new legislature on January 7, 1880.[107]

Oddly, Governor Garcelon ordered the Committee on Elections to begin examining the votes in late October, which raised suspicions. The *Bangor Whig & Courier* cried:

The Conspiracy!
The Revolution Actually Afoot!
Only Awaiting the Final Act!
Will They Dare Commit to the Monstrous Crime?

They did, as it turned out. Joshua Chamberlain later explained, "When the Governor and Council came to canvass these returns, they took occasion, on account of various alleged irregularities, to throw out many votes." In some cases, the committees erased, altered, and even forged records. In another, they refused to acknowledge that George S. Hill and G. S. Hill were the same candidate, effectively splitting his vote total in half by "counting out" certain votes. The result was a Fusion legislature with a majority of 78–58 in the House and 20–11 in the Senate—an inversion of the people's will.[108]

Republicans were furious, and James Blaine publicly implored that only "a great popular uprising will avert these evils and restore honest government to Maine." Blaine organized "indignation meetings" around the state whereby reliable Republicans were encouraged to make it known that they would not accept the rigged results without a fight. He wrote to Chamberlain, requesting assistance in organizing such an event in Brunswick. Chamberlain refused, saying that the proper course of action was to refer the matter to the state supreme court. He further counseled, "What we now need to do is not to add to popular excitement which is likely to result in disorder and violence." Doing so, he feared, would have disastrous consequences: "I cannot bear to think of our fair and orderly state plunged into the horrors of a civil war."[109]

Governor Garcelon saw a situation that was spiraling out of control and feared that a resort to arms by one or more parties was just around the corner. Having received only 15 percent of the votes in the election, the governor also questioned whether the state militia would follow his orders during the emergency, a fear exacerbated by rumors that a company of men from Dexter was heading for the capital. He gathered a force of one hundred men loyal to him and planned to arm them with weapons from the state's arsenal in Bangor, but the men he sent to secure those weapons were turned back by one thousand citizens outraged at the attempt. With two rival legislatures—the "counted out" and the "counted in" factions—both planning to physically occupy the capital on January 5, Garcelon saw only one way forward. He sent an urgent telegram asking Joshua Chamberlain to take charge of the state militia—a position to which he had been appointed but had not accepted—and "protect the public property and institutions of the state."[110]

Arriving in the capital on January 3, Chamberlain was sworn in as a major general of the state militia. He ordered the state's militia units to remain at home and immediately dismissed Garcelon's private army, trying to reduce the possibility of armed conflict. Chamberlain drew on his preexisting relationship with Augusta mayor Charles Nash, a former captain in the Nineteenth Maine and a confidant and political ally whom Chamberlain considered "a level-headed and independent man." Nash placed Augusta's police at the general's disposal should he need support.[111]

As the days ticked by and Chamberlain waited for the Supreme Court to make their ruling, he became the military governor of the state on January 7 when the terms of the previous officials expired without a new legislature having been seated that could pick the next governor. With each passing day, the situation grew more tense. On January 7, he wrote Fanny, "Everything is confusion here yet." He continued, "What vexed me is that some of our own people (Republicans) do not like to have me straight[en] things." Indeed, he was castigated by both sides, with the Republican papers referring to him as a "Renegade" and "Fusionist Sympathizer," while Democratics called him a "Lawless Usurper" and a "Traitor." Private citizens also wrote to him, and while some offered threats, many referred to him as a Moses guiding his people.[112]

Recognizing Chamberlain's pivotal role, both sides sought to control his actions. Republicans tried to seize the state house by subterfuge, and then by force, while the Fusionists attempted to arrest the former general— a plan that he refuted by simply refusing to acquiesce. Also, "There was a well-laid plot to kidnap him by night and take him off to an obscure town in the 'back country,' and hold him until the game was over," he recollected. Fortunately, his son Wyllys had feared for his safety and appeared with "two pistols that had been well tested in the 'civil' war." One of those pistols was likely the one that then-Colonel Chamberlain had captured during the bayonet charge at Gettysburg. With that deterrent, and by changing his sleeping location frequently, Chamberlain foiled the plot.[113]

With the threat of violence having proved unsuccessful, both parties turned to bribery. James Blaine's Senate seat was due up the following year, and the Fusionists offered to work together to oust James Blaine and place Chamberlain in the position if the current election went their way. Blaine himself offered to vacate the seat and pave the way for a grateful Republican legislature to elevate their former governor to the Senate, if only Chamberlain were to put his finger on the scale in their favor. The general, of course, refused both entreaties.[114]

While the court considered the matter, there was one last attempt to carry the day by force. On January 14, Chamberlain was alerted that a group of twenty-five to thirty men had gained entrance to the capitol rotunda and were intent on harming him. Striding out to the crowd, he addressed the mob: "Men, you wish to kill me, I hear. Killing is no new thing to me. I have offered myself to be killed many times when I no more deserved it than I do now. Some of you, I think, have been with me in those days." He continued, "I am here to preserve the peace and honor of this State, until the rightful government is seated,—whichever it may be, it is not for me to say. But it is for me to see that the laws of this state are put into effect, without fraud, without force, but with calm thought and sincere purpose. I am here for that, and I shall do it. If anybody wants to kill me for it, here I am. Let him kill!" With that, Chamberlain threw open his coat, baring his chest. He had judged his audience well, for a "grisly old veteran . . . a soldier still, in heart," pushed his way to the front and declared, "By god, old General, the first man that dares to lay a hand on you, I'll kill him on the spot!" With that, the crowd melted away. It had been, Chamberlain recounted to Fanny the next day, "Another Round Top."[115]

The anonymous veteran in the crowd was not the only one to offer assistance. Hearing of the commotion, Franklin Ward of Skowhegan, formerly one of Chamberlain's Little Round Top men, wrote the next day offering his support: "At a very short notice we can raise a Company here for you (mostly Veterans) that can be relied upon + that would stand by you as we of the old 20th did at Round Top. I lost one Leg in that Charge + if you require it am ready + willing to risk the other in either your defense or that of our rights . . . I remain as ever awaiting my old Commanders orders."[116]

It must have heartened Chamberlain to hear that the men who had stood by him in 1863 still backed him. Fortunately, he did not need to call on the proffered services, for the next day the state supreme court ruled in favor of the Republicans, and on January 17, the newly seated legislature selected Daniel Davis as the governor. Chamberlain immediately resigned his position, having guided the state through arguably the most testing two weeks in its history.[117]

If his wartime service had been the pinnacle of Chamberlain's life, and Gettysburg the particular height of those three years, then the "Count Out" crisis was the singular moment of his postwar life. His time as governor and president of Bowdoin offered some satisfaction, but he always yearned for a more active role leading in a crisis. The "Count Out" crisis was a fleeting moment, just two weeks from start to finish, but it was everything he had missed over the previous fifteen years. On January 17, Ellis Spear wrote to his old commander, "Your will and firm action has saved the state." He continued, "I laughed when I saw and heard the threats against you. The men who made them did not see you in the hell-fire of Petersburg." Chamberlain remained the man who knew what to do in a moment of crisis.[118]

Returning to Bowdoin after the "Count Out" affair, Chamberlain's heart was simply no longer in academia. Twice before the college's trustees had rebuffed his attempts to resign as president, but they accepted his third resignation in 1883. Chamberlain underwent surgery that year to address ongoing issues from his Petersburg wound, and a newspaper article in the aftermath of that procedure revealed to the public for the first time the extent of his daily suffering. Looking for a place to put his energies, Chamberlain accepted a position as the vice president of the Florida West Coast Improvement Company. Over the next several years, Chamberlain spent much of his time in New York City raising capital for the real estate venture, though ultimately without a great deal of success.[119]

Other veterans of the Twentieth also engaged in business. James Rundlett served with the Twentieth through the war's end and then enlisted as a captain in the 128th United States Colored Infantry and served until late 1866. What he did in the next few years is unknown, but by 1875, he and two brothers were in business together manufacturing chewing gum. A decade later they opened "Dirigo Mineral Springs," and James had additional property holdings in Maine, Virginia, and North Carolina.[120]

At the war's close Holman Melcher had wondered, "What is to be my life business?" As it turned out, business was to be his life business. His 1905 obituary noted, "Major Melcher has long been identified with the business interests of the city." He formed H. S. Melcher & Co. after the war, later reorganizing as H. S. Melcher Company in 1896. The firm advertised as "wholesale dealers in Groceries Flour and Provisions." Melcher's business success brought him to civic prominence, and he served two terms on the Portland City Council in the early 1880s and then two terms as the mayor of Maine's largest city from 1889 to 1891.[121]

Walter Morrill pursued a different line of business. He initially returned to the slate mines before moving to Dexter in 1876, where he helped run the Exeter Hotel. But that year he purchased a racetrack, and on the nation's centennial, he organized and promoted his first horse race, something he did for the next fifty-five years. He owned nearly forty horses himself at one point and would be known as the father of Maine's racing industry.[122]

For those who had not found riches in business, a change to the pension laws in 1890 brought financial relief. At the war's outbreak, around $1 million a year was distributed to the 10,700 people on the pension rolls. The existing statutes were unfit for an event such as the Civil War, and on July 14, 1862, Congress passed a new law providing pensions for anyone who incurred permanent bodily injury or disability arising directly from their service, as well as to the dependents of soldiers who had died due to either wounds or disease directly traceable to their war experiences. Under that law, a full pension for a private was $8 a month, while lieutenant colonels and higher received $30. Additions over the course of the war set specific rate increases for various disfigurements. The key aspects of these laws were that the injury or disability had to arise as a direct consequence of the war-time service, and in a practical sense, it could be difficult to prove the effects of a bout with disease versus the more obvious impact of a bullet. Even so, by 1870 there were nearly two hundred thousand invalids or dependents pensioned at an annual cost of $28 million. By 1885, that number had risen to almost 325,000 pensioners at $63 million a year.[123]

Throughout the 1880s, the call grew louder for *service*-based pensions rather than *disability*-based benefits. Many soldiers believed they had missed out on economic opportunity during their time in the army and saw more liberal pensions as at least partial compensation for that sacrifice. Issues of respect also played into these calls. Many veterans found it unseemly to have to demonstrate their physical maladies and testify to their decreased capability in order to secure a few dollars per month. Pensions based on service rather than disability would show greater respect to the veterans and allow them to preserve their dignity. Democrats opposed the expansion, with Grover Cleveland repeatedly blocking such measures, while Republicans were in favor. The election of Benjamin Harrison to the presidency in 1888 turned the tide, with the Civil War veteran telling his commissioner of pensions to "be liberal with the boys."[124]

The new pension law passed on June 27, 1890, stated that any honorably discharged soldier who had served ninety or more days and was now incapable of manual labor was eligible for a pension. The two critical caveats were that the disability did not have to result directly from the Civil War and that the soldier only had to prove they were incapable of *manual* labor, not all labor. The result was a rapid expansion, with the number of pensioners rising to 530,000 by 1891 with an expenditure of $105 million per year, or around 25 percent of the federal budget.[125]

The enlarged pension law accounted for something that was known at a macro level but difficult to prove on the individual level: Veterans were suffering from a variety of maladies at much higher rates than those who had not served. In 1892, veteran John Billings examined the census data for Massachusetts seeking to understand the relative disease rates between the veterans and non-veteran white males over forty. He found that the overall disease rate was nearly five times higher among the veterans. Consumption was twice as likely, heart issues seven times as likely, kidney and urinary issues almost four times as likely, respiratory issues more than three times as likely, and rheumatism five times as likely. Diarrhea had been the second most prevalent killer of men during the war, and veterans were fifty-five times more likely to suffer from that affliction than those who had not served. Proving that those afflictions *resulted* from their wartime service had been difficult, if not impossible, for many veterans, whereas showing that they *existed* at later times was often a matter of a simple doctor's examination combined with affidavits from neighbors and friends who had seen them struggle to labor in the postwar years.[126]

David Patten offers an interesting case study. Wounded at Gettysburg, Patten was pensioned at $2 a month (one-quarter disability) in the immediate postwar years. Patten passed away in 1891, but in 1897 his widow applied for an increase to her pension with the claim that the sunstroke David had suffered roughly a week before the Battle of Gettysburg led to rheumatism that permanently affected his ability to labor.[127]

William Davis was wounded in the left shoulder by an artillery shell at Spotsylvania Court House on May 8, 1864, but in 1902 applied for a pension based on sickness. While on picket duty near Antietam in November 1862, he fell ill with measles. Returning to camp, "He laid on the cold wet ground without sufficient clothing or shelter" for four days before being taken to the field hospital and eventually removed to the U.S. General Hospital at McKim's Mansion in Baltimore. The bout with measles had left his vision impaired, and in the ensuing years his eyesight worsened. He was granted a pension of $12 a month. In Davis's case, his battle wound caused fewer postwar problems than his bout with disease. Davis passed away in 1910 at the National Home for Disabled Volunteer Soldiers at Togus. His cause of death was listed as "Cirrhosis of the Liver," hinting at other challenges he faced in the postwar years.[128]

The pension laws allowed widows to continue receiving pensions as long as they did not remarry. John Lenfest was captured during the skirmish on July 10, 1863, and died in a Richmond prison the following January. In October 1867, John's widow, Lavinia, was granted a pension of $8 a month backdated to July 11, 1863, with an additional $2 a month for each of their six minor children. Things took a turn when Lavinia married John's second cousin, William, on September 27, 1870. Her remarriage meant Lavinia could no longer draw the widow's pension of $8 a month, though she continued to receive payments for the remaining minor children until they turned sixteen. The second marriage did not last long, however. In 1877, pension special agent John Mason reported that Lavinia had "been divorced in order to draw a pension." Despite her plan, it does not appear that Lavinia's widow's pension was reinstated.[129]

By the time the Pension Law of 1890 was enacted, seventy of the Gettysburg veterans who had returned home from war had passed away, leaving 320 alive. The veterans' longevity thoroughly dispels the oft-heard assumption that a nineteenth-century man was fortunate to live past his forties. Of the men who returned home and for whom a death date is known, the average age at death (mean) was sixty-eight years, while the median was seventy-one. In fact, just 53 of those 378 veterans died short of their fiftieth birthday, with a handful of those succumbing to their war wounds. A surprising 75 percent of the men died in their sixties, seventies, and eighties. Thirteen men lived into their nineties. Research into historic life expectancy funded by the National Institutes of Health suggests that a white male born in the 1830s and 1840s who attained the age of twenty had a life expectancy of fifty-nine years, roughly a decade less than these veterans of Little Round Top. The veterans came home with a host of medical issues, and yet their longevity was greater than that expected for the general population. Perhaps having survived the first ten months of their military service showed these men to be particularly hardy, or maybe the pensions many received after the war allowed access to better medical care or less burdensome physical labor. Whatever the cause, it is clear these men lived for a long time.[130]

By 1900, half of the men who stood on Little Round Top were gone, while 1908 marked the point at which half the men who had returned home from the war had passed away. Joshua Chamberlain finally succumbed to his Petersburg wound in 1914, dying of a bladder infection fifty years after his death was first announced in the nation's newspapers and becoming—officially, anyway—the last Civil War soldier to die of his wounds. Remarkably, 143 of his men were still alive.

Eighteen men lived until the 1930s. Of the officers, Walter Morrill had the greatest longevity. He flew in an airplane at the age of ninety-three, an experience that left him less than enthused. In the early days of the Great Depression, the Pension Bureau decreased his monthly allotment from $100 a month to $90, a cut that he found offensive and railed against to no avail. He finally passed in 1935.[131]

Edward Light died at ninety-three on April 11, 1938, leaving Leonard Cummings as the unit's sole remaining survivor. Eighteen years old at the time of his enlistment and a farmer living in Albany, Maine, Cummings had survived the war without injury, though he had been hospitalized in late 1862 and again for two weeks near the war's close for chronic diarrhea. Will Livermore later attested that the soldier had been "badly Run down" by 1865, and a neighbor described him as "emaciated" on his return home. The 1870 census found Cummings attending Wesleyan University in Connecticut, and following his time there, he became a teacher. In 1873, he married Ella Francella Cole, and they had three children. In 1886, he was pensioned at $2 a month for mass pharyngeal catarrh—a tumor in the back of his throat that interfered with drainage from his nasal passages and caused a persistent runny nose. Cummings's requests for a pension increase in 1891 and 1895 were denied despite "liver and heart trouble results of diarrhea; rheumatism; stomach troubles; dull aches in head; insomnia."[132]

Though Cummings was largely unsuccessful in securing a disability-based pension, his longevity eventually qualified him for an age-based pension of $12 a month when he turned sixty-two, followed by increases to $18 a month at age sixty-seven, $24 a month at age seventy, and $30 a month at age seventy-five. In 1930, any living veterans were pensioned at $100 a month, an amount that decreased by 10 percent during the Great Depression.[133]

Cummings spent most of his postwar life in Massachusetts, and the 1910 census taker found Leonard and Ella living on their own in Boston with Leonard employed as a representative for a gas company. By 1920, they had moved in with daughter Mae and her husband, Arthur J. Bean, the financial editor of the *Boston Post* and author of a treatise on investing. Leonard, age seventy-six, was employed as a bond salesman. In 1938, a pension field examiner visited Cummings and reported, "This veteran lives in a pretentious home in Melrose with his daughter and son-in-law . . . Mr. Cummings states that he is able to furnish himself with all of his needs with his pension. He is ninety-two years of age [he was ninety-four], but retains his faculties to a remarkable degree, and his only complaint physically, at the present time, is the partial loss of the use of his legs. There is every indication that Mr. Cummings is very comfortable in his passing years."[134]

Cummings died on February 7, 1939, the last of the 506 men who stood on Little Round Top to succumb to time.

Though Gettysburg would always be the touchstone of the Twentieth Maine's experience, and the battle in which they suffered the greatest casualties, they lost more men in combat in 1864 than they had the previous year. Thirty-eight men had been killed or succumbed to their wounds received at Gettysburg, but another seventy-eight perished before the war ended. When the men finally returned home, the vast majority had been shot or suffered through serious illness or disease. Though they displayed remarkable longevity, the impact of the wartime service is evident in their biographies. Some longed to return to the military, while others could not wait to get away. Some were open about their wounds and disabilities, while others tried to keep them from the public. Some excelled in business and politics, while others turned to crime. At least one attempted suicide, and several struggled with alcoholism. Many returned to the farms from which they had come and led quiet, productive lives, marrying and raising families. After three years of living in close proximity to men they had to rely on in the heat of battle, demobilization in 1865 scattered these men back to their prewar homes and turned a collective band of brothers into a group of individual civilians once again. Joshua Chamberlain noted sorrowfully, "And we are left alone, and lonesome . . . and we lose interest." But soon they found one another again as they reunited to make sense of their wartime experiences, commemorate their deeds, and secure their unit's reputation.[135]

6

"What you did, the world knows"

From History to Memory

THE NORMALLY UNFLAPPABLE WILL LIVERMORE WAS ANNOYED. IT WAS May 1899, and the fifty-eight-year-old former member of the color guard put down the book he was reading and took up his pen. "I have just received Maine at Gettysburg and carefully read the discription of the battle," he wrote to Joshua Chamberlain, his former colonel and the author of the narrative that caught Livermore's attention, "and while it is so vivid and acurate in the maine, I was surprised to read . . . that 'all the Color Guards were cut away, but Andrew J. Tozier was standing his ground defending his Colors with bullet bayonet and butt alone.'" Livermore noted that he must "protest against this" for his comrades "may ask as they read this history Where Livermore who was not wounded was at this critical time when the Sergt. was Alone defending the Colors." In seeking to praise the embattled Andrew Tozier, Chamberlain had unintentionally called into question the steadfastness of others, and Will Livermore wanted to make sure his "distinguished and honored Col." did not let that description become part of the accepted narrative of the fight on Little Round Top. He was successful: Joshua Chamberlain accepted Livermore's perspective and corrected his future narratives.[1]

The exchange between William T. Livermore and Joshua Chamberlain is symbolic of dozens, maybe hundreds of similar ones throughout the postwar period as the men of the Twentieth Maine engaged with each other and with their former opponents as they put forth their memories and accounts of what happened at Gettysburg on July 2, 1863. With the publication of each account, others came forth to correct small details, add further information, or ask clarifying questions. Their intentions were twofold. First, they were attempting to gain a full understanding of the what and why of their actions on July 2, 1863, a perspective that no man possessed on his own. Second, their early experiences during the war had shown that even worthy regiments could be ignored if a person or group of people did not advocate for them and tell their story. As other units began to publish accounts and place monuments at Gettysburg, the veterans of the Twentieth worried that the reputation they had fought so hard to win would simply fade away if they did not take action to ensure their deeds were well documented in ink and granite.

In examining their exchange of accounts and ideas, it is clear that the men did not always agree with each other on events that had happened twenty or even fifty years earlier, but over time a coherent narrative of their part in the great battle emerged. This chapter is the story of how and why that process unfolded, the controversies that arose, and how the final narrative emerged. Though built on and brought to broader attention by writers and filmmakers in the twentieth century, the story and reputation of the Twentieth Maine and Joshua Chamberlain on Little Round Top was fully developed by the veterans themselves from 1863 to 1939.

Joshua Chamberlain was the first man from the Twentieth Maine to return to and tour the Gettysburg battlefield, and he did so before the war had even ended. In the spring of 1864, the colonel was assigned to court-martial duty in Washington, a post in which he could recuperate from the sickness that had plagued him since before Gettysburg. Fanny joined him in the capital, and the couple journeyed to Gettysburg in early April. On April 9, 1864, Holman Melcher of Company F told his brother, "We expect Col. Chamberlain back to the Regiment Tuesday. He is at Gettysburg now to look over the battlefield." Five days later, Fanny wrote to her cousin, Deborah Folsom, "We have been to Gettysburg. I shall have much to tell you about our visit there." Shortly after the great battle the previous year, Joshua had written to his wife of the role he played, a letter that reads as a triumphant telling of heroic deeds from a man who perpetually felt like he had not yet fully earned Fanny's respect. He was devastated to discover that she was in New York, had not received his letters, and was long unaware of the honors he had won. Now he had the chance to show her himself. Unfortunately, neither Fanny nor Joshua, who added his own note to Cousin Deborah, revealed anything about their itinerary or responses to seeing the battlefield, but we do know what would have been possible for them to see.[2]

Chamberlain would have been drawn to the Soldiers' National Cemetery. Burial crews had completed the task of removing the bodies of Union soldiers from the battlefield gravesites and reinterring them in the cemetery just a few weeks earlier. Of the thirty-eight men in Chamberlain's command who had been killed or mortally wounded on Little Round Top, at least twenty-five were now resting near one another in the Maine section. Fifteen of those men were identified, but ten were marked as "Unknown" beyond their affiliation with the regiment. Twenty months later, Chamberlain told an audience in Portland, Maine, of his reaction to seeing the "Unknown" graves. "In the National Cemetery at Gettysburg are many graves marked—'Unknown, supposed Me. 20th.' Better to have left them in their graves on the rocky sides of Little Round Top, where it was known the Regiment fought than thus to have removed them and marked them 'unknown.'" Chamberlain may have lingered over the grave of Warren Kendall, who he mentioned in his reports and called "one of my finest Lieuts." Melville Day of the color guard had been standing just a few feet away from Chamberlain when he was hit by five bullets. Frank Curtis, Elfin Foss, Benjamin Grant, and William Hodgdon had been stationed directly in front of their colonel as members of Company F, and Chamberlain likely saw them as they were shot or soon after and may have remembered their last moments. His letters to Fanny had always downplayed the personal risks he faced—after Gettysburg, he told her a Confederate "insisted on presenting me with a fine pistol as a reward" rather than admit he had taken it at sword point after the man fired at him from mere inches away—and it is likely Chamberlain would not have dwelled on the possibility of death or disfigurement in front of his wife. He may instead have focused on the cemetery as the site of President Abraham Lincoln's Gettysburg Address, a speech that would have resonated with the former professor of rhetoric.[3]

Though Cemetery and Culp's Hill were more popular tourist spots in the early days than Little Round Top, at least in part due to their location on the edge of town and within walking distance of the train station, even by early 1864 visitors were making their way to the southern end of the battlefield and the Round Tops, as evidenced by a late 1863 woodcut in *Frank Leslie's Newspaper* of tourists viewing the sites. Less than a year after the battle, and with such prominent geographic features present, Chamberlain would have had no trouble narrating the battle's ebb and flow for Fanny. He likely showed her where he stood during the battle, as well as where the Confederates were positioned, and explained the moment when he ordered the bayonet charge. If Fanny had not previously understood the significance of her husband's actions on July 2, 1863, she must have after their visit to Little Round Top.[4]

On January 16, 1865, almost exactly nine months after the Gettysburg trip, the Chamberlains welcomed a baby girl to their family. They named her Gertrude. She lived just seven months, dying on August 14, 1865.

In *Embattled Courage*, his landmark work on the soldiers' experience in combat, historian Gerald Linderman argues that, in the first fifteen years after the war, most veterans were "uncertain that they could describe accurately what they had gone through or could speak of such things in ways those at home could understand," and thus ensued a period of "hibernation." The 1870s saw the publication of the fewest Civil War novels of any decade, while between 1869 and 1876 the *North American Review* published just a single article on the Civil War. The lone voice from the Twentieth Maine speaking during this period was Joshua Chamberlain, but he typically stuck to general or political themes rather than offering an account of the bullets he had faced and the death and destruction he had seen (or even ordered).[5]

In August 1865, at their first meeting after the end of the Civil War, the Board of Trustees of Pennsylvania (now Gettysburg) College voted to award Joshua Chamberlain an honorary degree of LLD. In notifying Chamberlain of this honor, board president David Buehler noted, "It may be interesting to you to know that this Institution, although in existence for over thirty years, has never conferred this degree until this occasion although repeated nominations have been made." In acknowledging the honor, Chamberlain noted, "it is with peculiar pleasure that I associate this honor with a place not only endeared to me by the most thrilling memories, but one forever precious in the heart of the Country and immortal in History." That Chamberlain received this honor at such an early date shows the reach of his reputation in the immediate aftermath of the war, and the honor extended to him by a college in Gettysburg evinces the widespread belief that he and the Twentieth Maine had played a critical role in the battle in that town.[6]

On December 15, 1865, Chamberlain spoke before the Portland Freedmen's Aid Association and offered a twenty-three-hundred-word account of the Twentieth's fight on Little Round Top. While the Battle of Gettysburg was "an old and perhaps to many a too familiar story," the Twentieth's "services on that occasion have not been fully understood before," the former colonel explained; thus, "I feel that it is my own duty to give some distinct account of their conduct." He credited captains Atherton Clark, Ellis Spear, and Walter Morrill for their performance; cited Andrew Tozier's bravery; and said that his men "rushed forward at the order 'charge.'" The basic facts Chamberlain established in this first lecture on Gettysburg formed the backbone of his speeches and writings on the topic for the next fifty years, though he would incorporate the various recollections of his men as they emerged in the 1880s and 1890s. Four days later, he delivered essentially the same lecture, this time for the Bangor Freedmen's Aid Association.[7]

Two months later, on February 22, 1866, Chamberlain was the speaker at the first meeting of the Military Order of the Loyal Legion of the United States (MOLLUS), an organization of Civil War officers formed at the time of Abraham Lincoln's assassination for the purpose of preventing future threats to the government. Chamberlain's selection as the speaker reveals the high esteem his fellow officers had for him and demonstrates his reputation as an orator. Speaking in Philadelphia, he did not talk about military tactics and actions but pondered the theme of "Loyalty." Chamberlain's Civil War–era reports were voluminous but written in plain and direct language, as was most of the battle narrative he offered in the late 1865 speeches on Gettysburg. This meditation on "Loyalty," however, was rooted in Chamberlain's background as a professor of rhetoric, complete with a dissection of the roots of the word *loyalty* from ancient Rome. It was a speech more fundamentally about the future than the past and what loyalty should mean during "the world's advancing age."[8]

The speech must have been well received. Three years later, Chamberlain was invited to be the inaugural speaker at the organizing event for the Society of the Army of the Potomac on July 4, 1869. His speech blended the two styles employed previously: a fact- and narrative-based history of the Army of the Potomac, but one that used literary flourishes such as the posing of rhetorical questions in order to defend the record of that oft-maligned body of men. Again the speech must have resonated, for the Society had it reprinted, and twenty years later its members selected Chamberlain as their president.[9]

The year 1876 marked a turning point and laid the groundwork to fully document and commemorate the Twentieth's wartime exploits. The previous fall, prominent veterans had gathered in Portland and established the Association of Maine Soldiers and Sailors, with Joshua Chamberlain as the first president. The association called for a reunion the following year and eventually organized an event in Portland for August 9 and 10. Nearly two thousand men representing most of Maine's Civil War units gathered in the state's largest city. Forty-six members of the Twentieth Maine attended, twenty-one of whom were at the Battle of Gettysburg. The ongoing impact of the economic Panic of 1873 likely prevented many who might have otherwise made the trip from coming. Nonetheless, "Men who had not met since their muster-out in 1865," the *Portland Daily Press* reported, "Found it difficult to recognize the comrades whose elbows they had touched in those days of toil, danger, devotion and glory. Eleven years had wrought changes." But soon, "The old fields were fought o'er again during the day and the old memories revived." Speech after speech was given until 2:00 a.m., before "the balance of the night was spent in 'howling.'" The men relished the opportunity to rekindle the bonds they had created during three years of glorious and torturous wartime service.[10]

On the reunion's second day, the Twentieth formed a regimental association, a critical body that organized future reunions and led the drive for a monument to be placed at Gettysburg honoring the regiment. Holman Melcher was selected as the first president, James Wescott as the vice president, and Samuel Miller as the secretary and treasurer.[11]

Though some had hoped the reunions would become annual affairs, the next gathering came as a part of another state-wide event five years later. An estimated two thousand veterans were again present, but the 137 Twentieth Maine men who registered at the regiment's headquarters tent represented a threefold increase over those who had attended in 1876. In fact, the Twentieth was one of just three units that required two headquarters tents. Most of the men arrived by train, with the Maine Central bringing twelve hundred veterans in nineteen crowded cars.[12]

On August 24, the *Portland Daily Press* announced that the Twentieth Maine Regimental Association invited the public to their meeting that night and that there would be music and then addresses by Samuel Miller and Joshua Chamberlain. "This is the regiment," the paper reminded any who had forgotten, "which under the command of Chamberlain, then colonel, held 'Little Round Top,' the key of the position at Gettysburg, against an overwhelming force of the enemy July 2, 1863."[13]

"The chief event of the evening was the reunion of the Twentieth Regiment, the gallant body of men which Chamberlain led to Little Round Top, and whose obstinate hold of that important position baffled the plans of Lee and made the battle of Gettysburg a Union victory," the *Portland Daily Press* reported on August 25. The Seventeenth Maine had come from Portland and had also played a significant role on July 2 at Gettysburg, so the local paper's decision to highlight the Twentieth Maine reveals how well established the unit's reputation was by 1881. The reporter noted that the tent was well filled long before the appointed hour with spectators eager to hear from the men of the Twentieth, and the report of the Regimental Association claimed there were two thousand in attendance when the program began at 7:30 p.m. Holman Melcher presented the unit's Gettysburg flag, which had previously resided with Adelbert Ames but was now entrusted to Elisha Coan for safekeeping. Samuel Miller then gave a history of the unit that the *Portland Daily Press* praised as "full without being verbose, and eloquent without being pretentious."[14]

Miller had been working on his address for some time and had corresponded with other veterans to present a story that was as accurate as possible. On August 6, 1881, Elisha Coan wrote to Miller, "I hear from Maj. Melcher that you are preparing an historical address to be delivered at the reunion of the Maine Veterans before the Twentieth Me. Association and I am very glad to hear it." He continued, "I have a few items that might not be out of place . . . I will send the items and if you have no place for them you can lay them aside and no harm will be done by either of us." The reason for Coan's letter was quite simple: "I send these as Genl Chamberlain states in his lectures on the 'Twentieth Maine at Gettysburg' that the Color Guards were all killed or wounded at that battle and as Corporal W. T. Livermore and myself but went through that firy ordeal without receiving a scratch I thought the statement ought to be corrected if by chance it should enter into the subject matter of your address." Like many, Coan wanted to ensure that the regiment's story was told in a way that enhanced both its reputation and his own. Miller's subsequent account shows Coan's influence: "The colors of the regiment were carried by Sergt. Tozier and although exposed on the angle of the line the sergeant and two of the four guards escaped without even a scratch."[15]

Miller's account marked the moment when the story of the Twentieth Maine's fight on Little Round Top moved from a series of individual accounts and recollections into the realm of a collective narrative fashioned and stitched together by the comparison and integration of multiple, sometimes conflicting, perspectives. After a brief, off-the-cuff address by Joshua Chamberlain, the association "*Voted*, That the LINCOLN COUNTY NEWS be made the organ of the Association," and "*Voted*, That the Secretary be instructed to have the historical address published in pamphlet form." These two stipulations ensured a fruitful decade for documenting the Twentieth's Gettysburg story.[16]

Lincoln County News editor Samuel Miller took his charge seriously, and the prominence he gave to the Twentieth Maine—and, to a lesser extent, the Civil War in general—provided the platform for nearly all the regiment's activities in the 1880s and 1890s. Throughout this period Miller ran a column titled "Veteran Department," with this description: "This column is specially devoted to the interests of the veterans of the Twentieth Regiment of Maine Infantry, and will be continued so long as comrades assist in sustaining it. War anecdotes and scraps of history solicited. Enquiries promptly answered." For other regiments that came from a particular region, the veterans encountered each other in person at the local Grand Army of the Republic (GAR) Post or in the course of their daily lives. Because the Twentieth's soldiers came from all over the state, they had no such meeting place, and the *Lincoln County News* effectively became the local store or GAR Post where they swapped stories and planned events.[17]

Samuel Miller, editor of the *Lincoln County News* (Collections of Maine Historical Society)

The year 1882 proved particularly momentous. That spring, now-Reverend Theodore Gerrish published *Army Life: A Private's Reminiscences of the Civil War*. Not a unit history, but rather a personal account of the war, Gerrish's work was unique at the time of its publication in that it was written by a mere private. The work came out in an economy and an illustrated edition, though the text was the same in both. The publisher claimed that five thousand copies were sold by pre-order, and the number still in existence today makes that quantity plausible. Additionally, Gerrish gave speeches throughout the state on "The Battle of Gettysburg." On February 1, 1883, he lectured in Searsport. Summarizing the event afterward, Belfast's *Republican Journal* noted, "Gettysburg was the most important battle of the war, and its story has been so frequently told that all must be familiar with it. But when told by one who participated in it, especially by one who fought on Little Round Top, the key to the whole position, the narrative has additional interest." Gerrish spoke on Gettysburg again a month later, this time before the GAR Post in Ellsworth. In previewing the event, the *Ellsworth American* editor opined that anyone who had already read Gerrish's *Army Life* "will have no doubt that his description of a battle in which he took part, and so important a battle as the one at Gettysburg, cannot fail of being both faithful and brilliant." Gerrish's lectures were likely brilliant—the prose in *Army Life* is outstanding—but "faithful" is another matter. Gerrish was not present at the Battle of Gettysburg but was instead sick in a Philadelphia hospital. It is notable that Gerrish drops his first-person point of view for his unit's most famous battle, instead adopting a third-person perspective. Regardless, many men in the Twentieth either read Gerrish's book or the parts of the work published in periodicals. The Gettysburg chapter was reprinted in the *Portland Advertiser* in March of that year and in the *National Tribune* in November, giving his battle account a vast readership. Most readers and listeners—including the editors of the two aforementioned papers—were unaware that Gerrish was absent from Gettysburg, a fact that his low rank helped obscure. Major Charles Gilmore, for example, was conspicuous by his absence and could never have claimed to be on Little Round Top.[18]

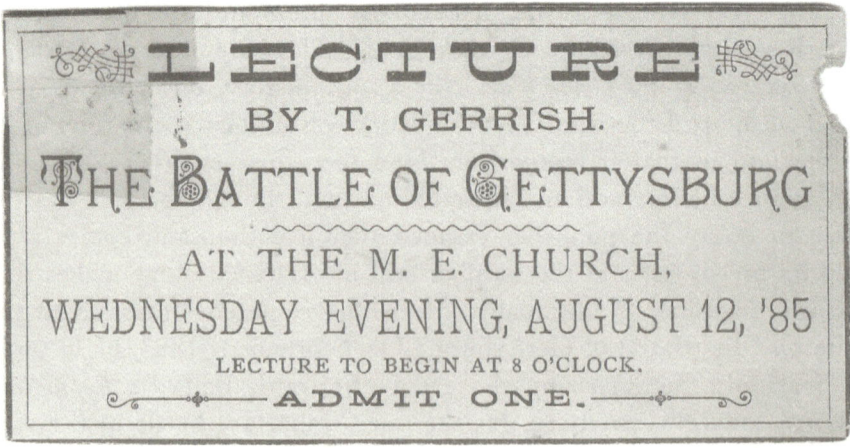

Ticket for Theodore Gerrish lecture (Author's collection)

When Nathan Clark penned his "army journal," he relied on Gerrish's description of the George Buck–Alden Litchfield incident, incorporating the reverend's words into his text verbatim. But others raised questions. Jim Nichols, former commander of Company K, felt Gerrish had slighted his company and offered a public rebuke that was published by the *Lincoln County News* in both April 1882 and December 1883 and the *Portland Press* in December 1883. Nichols claimed no complaint with *Army Life* "as a work of fiction, or as a history of perhaps one or two companies" but had "decided objections" to it as a history of the entire regiment. "Without entering into any detailed statement of the many errors, more perhaps of omission than commission," Nichols stated, "I propose to confine my objections to the important omissions relative to the history of Company K, with which I was connected." Unsurprisingly, it was at Gettysburg that Nichols was most concerned his unit should receive its proper due. "Take as the first illustration the battlefield at Gettysburg, where the general good conduct of Company K should have at least entitled them to some kind of recognition in the book purporting to be a history of the regiment." For a specific example of Company K's overlooked service, Nichols offered, "Making the discovery that the regiment was being surrounded by the enemy, and promptly communicating this discovery to the commanding officer, thus enabling him to meet the emergency, find no place in your history." Even more important, when "the companies on our right wavered and broke to the rear, Company K held its ground, firm as the rocks on which it stood; not one foot or one inch or for one moment, did they waver or yield." And most important, "You state in your history that when the order to charge was given, there was a disposition on the part of the regiment to hesitate, and a reluctance to obey. This is an imputation of cowardice which I respectfully deny." Cutting viciously, Nichols denied what he viewed as the charge of cowardice against his men and turned it on Gerrish himself: "It may have been true of that part of the line where you were, and of this I will admit you are better informed." Key in this passage is Nichols's assumption that Gerrish was writing from firsthand experience, whereas he must have pieced together the narrative from long-shared campfire stories of the event after he had rejoined the unit in the battle's aftermath. Nichols had the last word in this argument: Gerrish could have offered a rebuttal only by citing firsthand experience and evidence. He had none and would have been keen to ensure that his absence from the great battlefield was not highlighted.[19]

At any rate, the men were now quite publicly in conversation with one another, detailing blow by blow what exactly had happened on Little Round Top.

Whether it was because of the reunion in 1881 or the appearance of Gerrish's work and the questions it raised, the Twentieth's survivors soon took a greater public interest in their wartime service. In the summer of 1882, Atherton Clark and Elisha Coan each penned accounts for the *Lincoln County News* covering the war's final campaign.[20]

Ellis Spear and Howard Prince both lived in Washington and had risen to prominence. After serving as the U.S. commissioner of patents in the 1870s, Spear was now working as an attorney. Prince was the clerk of the city police. In early June, the two men joined approximately two hundred Union and Confederate veterans who journeyed to Gettysburg to mark the positions of various units on the field. Painter-turned-historian John Bachelder, who had recently secured $50,000 from Congress to write a history of the Battle of Gettysburg, met the group and walked with them around the field, collecting the information that flowed freely from their reminiscences. Six weeks later, Spear's account of that trip took up half of the first page of the *Lincoln County News*. He painted the picture well. "A narrow carriage way now runs down the crest of [Little Round Top], winding among the trees," Spear reported. "But excepting this and the increased size of the trees and perhaps that the western slope is more clear of bushes, the famous hill is precisely as it was on the 2d day of July 1863." The old veterans could probably imagine Little Round Top, even then, just as they had seen it nearly twenty years earlier.[21]

Spear concluded: "Before closing I wish to repeat a suggestion made by Capt. Prince, that the Twentieth set up a shaft to mark the place where they fought at Gettysburg. Other organizations have marked their positions, and while members of the regiment are living, it would be well to have the places marked." There had already been a dozen Civil War monuments erected in Maine, with the one in Sherman unveiled on July 4, 1882, just before the appearance of this story in the *Lincoln County News*. But no Maine unit had yet placed a monument on the great battlefield itself. In fact, relatively few units had put up the permanent stone markers that remain to this day, though, as Spear indicated in his article, many had marked their lines with temporary signs. On September 1, the *Lincoln County News* reported, "A movement has been started among the officers of the Twentieth Maine Volunteers to erect a monument to indicate the position occupied by that regiment at the battle of Gettysburg. In connection with the erection of the monument it is probable that arrangements will be made for a reunion of comrades on the battle-field about the middle of October."[22]

Thus, the Twentieth Maine Regiment Association held their reunion and business meeting in Gettysburg on October 18–20, 1882, with headquarters at the Eagle Hotel.

The train that brought the men down from Maine skirted Harrisburg before coming into Hanover, one of the towns the Twentieth had passed through on July 1, 1863, on their way to Gettysburg. The men arrived around 1:30 p.m., ate lunch, and then went out on the battlefield with John Bachelder. They toured the entire field before following in their own footsteps: "We rode over to the point where the Fifth Corps rested after crossing Rock Creek and thence traced our line of march to the front. Nineteen years have made but few changes. There stands Trostle's house near which we filed to the left with the shells bursting over us, and then passed to the rear of the 'wheat field,' crossed the low ground drained by Plum Run, and approached Little Round Top just as we did in 1863." For most of the men, this was their first time back to Gettysburg and Little Round Top, and seeing the sight of the flag they had fought under unfurled on Little Round Top again must have been a moving experience.[23]

That night they reconvened at the hotel for their business meeting, where association president Holman Melcher "stated that the object of the meeting was to consider a proposal to erect a monument on 'Little Round Top.'" Their timing could not have been better, for "a few weeks before our visit the Gettysburg Battle-field Association succeeded in purchasing Little Round Top from the owner, who was about to cut off the timber," Samuel Miller reported. Knowing that the land was now in the hands of preservationists, Ellis Spear and Joe Land offered ideas on the monument's cost, location, and design. Bachelder joined the meeting and suggested that the unit compile a list of all the men present and those who had become casualties, providing that list to any who contributed to the monument fund. The association voted to appoint Ellis Spear, Albert

Fernald, and Theodore Gerrish to "procure and place on Little Round Top such a monument as the Association may determine upon." The broader association decided "to inscribe upon the monument the names of the killed." While touring the field, they viewed the newly erected (1879) monument to the Second Massachusetts on Culp's Hill. The monument clearly made an impression, for Miller reflected, "Perhaps no better idea of a regimental monument can be given than a description of one already erected. . . . In the edge of the field the survivors have placed, upon a large flat boulder, a cubic granite monument." That monument contained a description of the unit's actions at Gettysburg, plus a complete list of all the men who had been killed or mortally wounded during the fighting. It was this design that the Twentieth Maine copied in nearly identical fashion.[24]

At the following evening's business meeting, Joe Land and Howard Prince were added to the monument committee—a logical decision given the interest both had shown in the project previously. By this time Joshua Chamberlain had arrived, and he participated in the ensuing discussion over the monument's potential design, suggesting, "An inscription upon one of the boulders which God had placed in that position and which witnessed the battle; but admitted that if no boulder was suitable for the purpose, the next best thing was a block of Maine granite." Chamberlain wished that the monument be completed quickly and dedicated the following summer on the twentieth anniversary of the battle, a timeline that proved unrealistic.[25]

"The next morning," Samuel Miller wrote, "the members who remained at Gettysburg visited Little Round Top and established the positions of the lines occupied by the regiment on the 2d of July, 1863. A very large and prominent boulder near the point occupied by the left of the regiment in the commencement of the attack and also near the salient angle of the line when the charge was made, was selected as the most suitable position for the monument." In addition to marking the unit's primary position, they "visited and marked the stone-wall occupied by Capt. Morrill's company and climbed Big Round Top where a board engraved by Capt. A. E. Fernald was nailed to a tree. The inscription was as follows: 'Advanced position 20th Me. Eve 2d Day.'" The next step was to secure permanent markers to replace those temporary signs.[26]

Selecting the monument location (From the Twentieth Maine Regimental Association stationery; Library of Congress)

Six months later, on April 13, 1883, the *Lincoln County News* informed its readers that the monument committee now had in hand potential designs and that the executive committee had "decided to take immediate steps to collect contributions from the survivors of the regiment" to fund the monument. Two months later, the treasurer reported contributions totaling $58, including $10 from former commander Adelbert Ames and $1 from William T. Livermore. A further $39 was promised, including $25 from the prosperous grocer and Regimental Association president Holman Melcher. "The prospects are good for the success of the undertaking," Miller opined. "But there is no possibility of dedicating July 2, 1883 as proposed last fall."

Periodically the *News* provided an updated list of subscribers and the amounts they donated. An initial flurry of donations slowed in late 1883, and in July 1884, Miller, in his capacity as treasurer of the association, noted, "An additional effort is now being made to raise the balance of the amount required to build the monument, and it is earnestly desired that all, who have not already done so, will contribute now." By the end of August 1884, a total of $334 had been received or pledged. By late 1885, the project neared completion. Having decided to follow the example of the Second Massachusetts and inscribe the names of those killed or mortally wounded on Little Round Top, the association wanted to ensure "that the list be absolutely correct" and asked for anyone who spotted mistakes with their list of thirty-nine names to contact Holman Melcher or Samuel Miller. Someone realized that Oliver French died not of his Gettysburg wounds but of an 1864 injury, and the list was reduced to the thirty-eight names that are emblazoned on the monument.[27]

On April 20, 1883, a week after he had begun soliciting donations to the monument fund, editor Miller devoted much of the *Lincoln County News'* front page to reprinting a five-year-old account from Colonel William Oates of the Fifteenth Alabama titled "Gettysburg—The Battle on the Right." This was likely the first time most of the Twentieth's veterans read Oates's account and understood the battle from the Confederate perspective. Between their own recollections, the pamphlet containing Miller's history of the unit from 1881 that so many had bought, and now the account from their foe, a more complete story of the fight on Little Round Top was emerging than most individual men had possessed previously.[28]

Oates's primary purpose in publishing his account was to point out the leadership failings on July 2 that, in his mind, had cost his men the chance to win the battle and the war for the Confederacy. In July 1863, Oates had tried to persuade his superiors to allow him to fortify Big Round Top and place cannon on its summit, but they had refused. Fifteen years later, Oates lamented, "It is manifest that if Gen. Longstreet had crowned Round top with his artillery any time that afternoon . . . he would have won the battle." To Longstreet's claim that the smaller of the two Round Tops was the key to the battle, Oates concluded, "In this he is evidently in error."[29]

Little interested in the internal squabbling of the former Confederates, editor Miller instead saw Oates's work as providing further evidence of the "distinct and signal service claimed for the Twentieth Maine at Gettysburg," while italicizing the portions of Oates's narrative dealing with the Twentieth Maine that he found problematic. Specifically, Miller dismissed Oates's claim that by the end of the fight "*Federal reinforcements had completely enveloped my right*," another "*two regiments* were coming up behind us," and there were "dismounted cavalry to the left." The record shows, Miller stated accurately, that no reinforcements arrived to support the Twentieth Maine, and the troops behind Oates and those he misidentified as dismounted cavalry were Captain Morrill's Company B reinforced by a dozen sharpshooters. Purporting to show what his unit had suffered, Oates claimed, "Its effectives numbered nearly 700 officers and men. *Now 225 answered at roll call.*" Though modern estimates place Oates's actual effective force closer to parity with the Twentieth Maine, the veterans reading this statement in 1883 were not to know that. Miller editorialized, "The manner in which the three hundred and fifty-eight men of the Twentieth Maine surrounded and nearly annihilated the seven hundred men of the Fifteenth Alabama, is a subject for the thoughtful consideration of the military student."[30]

The publication of Oates's account in the *Lincoln County News* brought an outpouring of responses—not from men seeking to disagree with their former foe but in working out the small details that had previously eluded them. "Rear Rank" wrote two weeks later asking Miller why the Twentieth Maine ended up on the far left of the brigade—and therefore the entire army—when the order of march would have led to the Sixteenth Michigan occupying that position. On the same day, William T. Livermore penned a short note praising "The Battle on the Right" as "about as correct as any account I have ever read" while agreeing with Miller's analysis of the errors. "I have never seen any account that agreed with my diary, or recollection, exactly," the former corporal concluded.[31]

Two weeks later, a "Reply to Rear Rank" was authored by "C," who was likely Elisha Coan. In addition to clearing up the question around the order of march and position, Coan took issue with Oates's assertion that "We drove the Federals from their strong defensive position; five times they rallied and charged us." He noted, "The reader would infer from the above that the troops opposed to the Fifteenth Alla. were completely routed and driven from the field, and but for the 'long blue lines of Federal infantry,' (which must have been the ghosts of those who lost their lives on the battlefield of Bull Run, the Peninsula, Antietam, Fredericksburg and Chancellorsville—truly an invincible host.)" This question—to what extent the Twentieth Maine was driven back—cropped up time and again in Oates's accounts over the next twenty years. He always claimed to have pushed the Twentieth to the brink, even to have forced their left so far back as to be fighting the Eighty-Third Pennsylvania, while the men in the unit remembered more modest ebbs and flows within their original position.[32]

"Reply to Rear Rank" was not the only Twentieth Maine item that day, for below ran "Still Another," a note by Holman Melcher that cleared up *how* the units had been placed on Little Round Top, but with the request "*Why* this was done, let someone tell us who *knows*." As president of the Twentieth Maine Regiment Association, Melcher clearly approved the outpouring of accounts and interest in the unit and tried to stoke the fire. "Why can [William T. Livermore] not be induced to give us the benefit of that diary and his recollections? His prominent position in the centre of the regiment, by the colors, enabled him to see and know more of that fierce fight than most members of the Twentieth."[33]

One senses a playful public banter between the two comrades, for Melcher could have just as easily sent a private letter to his old friend. Livermore, for his part, played along. A week later, he addressed an epistle not to Melcher but to "*Mr. Editor*," explaining, "The reason why I cannot be induced to write an account of the 20th Maine at Gettysburg is that so many thrilling and interesting accounts have already been written." He continued, "Should anything more be called for, there are many of my comrades who participated in that memorable battle that are better qualified to write than I am. I could only daub the pictures that have been so skillfully painted."[34]

If Livermore was reluctant to jump into the fray (or at least pretending to be), Howard Prince showed no such reservations. On June 1, he offered "A Probable Theory," which both suggested that the Sixteenth Michigan had been moved from the brigade's left to right due to the perceived danger in the latter position and put forth an explanation for Oates's belief that reinforcements had assisted the Twentieth. Prince noted that Fisher's Brigade of Pennsylvania Reserves arrived after the fighting had concluded but surmised that perhaps Oates, from his vantage point on Little Round Top, had seen that unit hurrying to the scene. When Captain Morrill's

Company B eventually increased their rate of fire from the occasional pot-shot to full-on volleys, Oates may have believed that the Pennsylvanians were now on his flank. Piece by piece, the men were testing out theories and explanations that allowed them to knit together varied, sometimes contrasting accounts into something that approached a coherent whole.[35]

All the accounts published thus far were postwar creations, subject to the tricks of time and collective remembering. That changed on June 22, when Will Livermore finally consented to make public his diary entries for July 1–5, 1863. Editor Miller explained the particular significance of this account: "Having been written upon the battlefield, of course it is nearly accurate and is a valuable addition to the history of the Twentieth." Indeed, few published accounts in this period offered such a raw look at battle from one who had carried a rifle rather than a sword, a man of the ranks rather than an officer. Livermore's admission that the unit had "giv[en] those too far away to be captured deadly shots in the back" was a rare public acknowledgment of the violence and savagery of Civil War combat.[36]

Seeking to fill in more of the story, Howard Prince forwarded to the *Lincoln County News* a letter he had received "from an ex-Confederate in Alabama" who offered "that if the Twentieth Maine would like to hear from the sentinel who challenged them on Round Top, he would tell his story." Prince responded affirmatively and, on June 29, 1883, published the letter from P[hinias]. K. McMiller, a Fourth Alabama veteran who claimed to have been in charge of a skirmish detail of approximately fifteen men sent onto Big Round Top that had possession of the summit while the fight raged below on Little Round Top. After the Twentieth's bayonet charge, McMiller gathered in another dozen or so stragglers, adding them to his defensive force. Time passed. "It was now very dark," McMiller recollected, "and I went back down my slim line, to see if everything was alright. When I came near the rocks on my return I heard men moving." McMiller assumed these were reinforcements coming to his aid, but after issuing a challenge, he noted, "Imagine my feelings when the reply came '20th Maine!' To fire was simply suicidal, so I answered 'All right 20th Maine!'" McMiller gathered his men and beat a hasty retreat. With the publication of this letter, another small piece of the puzzle was now completed.[37]

Joshua Chamberlain still lectured throughout this period. In December 1884, he spoke in Richmond, Maine, before a crowd that included Cyrus

Osborn, formerly of Company G. On Little Round Top, Osborn had heard Chamberlain's order "Fix bayonets; forward!" just before he was struck by a bullet that shattered his arm below the elbow. He was discharged at the beginning of 1864, likely due to his Gettysburg wound, and this was the first time he had seen his former commander since the Battle of Gettysburg.[38]

Theodore Gerrish was also a frequent speaker on the lecture circuit, and Holman Melcher entered the fray in December 1885. Praising his speech, editor Miller remarked, "Maj. Melcher displayed great gallantry in that battle and has visited the battlefield twice since. He knows whereof he speaks."[39]

As the Twentieth's veterans were trying to compile and record their unit history, the U.S. government was doing the same at the macro level. The result was the 128-volume *Official Records of the War of the Rebellion*, a vast documentary record of military affairs during the Civil War published between 1880 and 1901. By 1884, the adjutant general was working on the three volumes covering the Gettysburg Campaign and discovered that Joshua Chamberlain's official report of the battle was missing. Without the original report, the deeds of the Twentieth Maine at Gettysburg would be entirely left out of the *Official Records* apart from passing references by others. When he was alerted to the potentially catastrophic news for the regiment's long-term reputation, Chamberlain quickly wrote to the adjutant general with a proposal: "I filed away in my papers a copy of my report made at the time the report was sent forward. I beg now to inquire if this copy, without alteration of course, would be received at your office." The plan was approved, and twelve days later Chamberlain forwarded the account with the statement, "I hereby certify on honor that this written 'copy' is the draft from which the original Report of the Battle of Gettysburg was made." The report Chamberlain submitted, and which was subsequently published in the *OR*, carries the date of July 6, 1863, but references the deaths of Charles Billings and Arad Linscott, officers who did not succumb to their wounds until after that date. This report, with twenty years of hindsight and the benefit of the type of information that had recently filled the pages of the *Lincoln County News*, was no doubt more detailed than the ones he had written and sent to others in 1863.

On the essential questions, however, the narrative was no different. Some have criticized Chamberlain for not dating his report to 1884, but it was the editors in the adjutant general's office who decided to print the report with a date of July 6, 1863, and without any explanation as to its creation.[40]

Not content just to correspond with one another through the pages of the *Lincoln County News*, the veterans also began to gather with increasing frequency. In August 1884, the men of Company E planned a "reunion of the survivors of that company" whereby they would take a trip to the home of Charles Bickmore on the steamer *Blonde* the following month.[41]

The National Encampment of the GAR was held in Portland in June 1885, with fifteen thousand veterans from across the nation descending on the Pine Tree State. The parade of the veterans stretched out more than three miles and took more than two and a half hours to pass. Thirty-eight bands and forty drum corps provided music. Of those fifteen thousand veterans, 150 were from the Twentieth Maine, and this event represented their third official reunion following the ones in 1876 and 1881. As old acquaintances were renewed, Samuel Miller and Thomas Little spoke for the first time since Miller had wrapped a handkerchief around the nasty head wound Little had received at Gettysburg twenty-two years earlier before sending him off to the aid station for further assistance. Miller cheekily asked for his handkerchief back.[42]

On May 14, 1886, the *Lincoln County News* announced that the regimental monument was completed "and will be placed on Little Round Top at an early day." By summer, plans were afoot for even more monuments. Charles Hamlin, a veteran of the Battle of Gettysburg and one of the sons of the wartime vice president, explained, "Agitation of the project of having monuments to Maine regiments began in Maine at regimental reunions and in Grand Army posts in the summer of 1886, and steps were taken to bring the matter before the next legislature." Hamlin himself introduced the subject in January 1887, and a month later an appropriation was made of $2,500 for land purchase and $12,500 for monuments. The bill also called for the appointment of a Maine Gettysburg Commission, with a representative from each regiment who had fought at the battle. Not surprisingly, Joshua Chamberlain was picked as the Twentieth's representative.[43]

The commission met in Gettysburg in May 1887. Their main purpose was to "designate upon the field and agree upon the location of the monuments." Commissioner Benjamin Harris, formerly of the Sixth Maine, was appalled by what he found. "Maine troops were on all the famous places in the field and earned the places . . . their monuments will occupy," he reported in comments carried by the *Lincoln County News* on May 19, 1887. "But that cannot be said of the regiments of other States. They have been crowding their monuments into the famous places, and if Maine had delayed her appropriation a while longer the other States would have had all the locations that our boys made historic." He noted that another had claimed the position of the Seventeenth Maine in the Wheatfield and that the ground on Big Round Top that the Twentieth had taken possession of and held on the night of July 2, 1863, featured a large monument to the 119th Pennsylvania, a unit that had merely "slept there" once the battle was over. Editor Miller noted, "The Twentieth Maine has a monument on Little Round Top, but the 'advanced position' on Round Top itself is only marked by a piece of board nailed to a tree. It is hoped the Commission will decide to place the State monument to mark the advanced position."[44]

While the Twentieth's role in defending Little Round Top was well known, others had sought credit for securing Big Round Top as soon as the battle ended. Within a week of the action, Colonel Joseph Fisher, commanding one of the Pennsylvania Reserve brigades in the Fifth Corps, claimed in his official report to have seen the value in Big Round Top and, at his own initiative, secured the position with two of his regiments. In addition to his own units, he "took" the Twentieth, relegating the Mainers to a subordinate, passive role in the action. Samuel Crawford, commanding the division that included Fisher's brigade, echoed his subordinate in his official report, noting, "To Colonel Fisher, commanding the Third Brigade, great credit is also due in early realizing the importance of the occupation of the Round Top and in promptly and successfully occupying it. The enemy would undoubtedly have occupied it during the night."[45]

If there had been any doubt about placing the monuments before, there could be none after seeing the injustice done to the Seventeenth and Twentieth Maine. The monuments could not go up soon enough. Soon after arriving home from Gettysburg, the commission issued a circular to each unit's association directing them to submit proposals for monument designs to the commission, which would then have the memorials con-structed and placed on the field. In June, the commission's executive com-mittee notified each unit association that $830 was allotted for their monument. However, more elaborate monument designs were acceptable provided the survivors contributed the additional funds. The hope was to have all the monuments ready for placement in 1888, the twenty-fifth anni-versary of the great battle.[46]

Not surprisingly, the monuments took more time and money than anticipated, with the state contributing an additional $10,000 and delaying the dedication of the monuments by a year. By March 1889, the *Lincoln County News* reported that the inscription for the Twentieth's Big Round Top monument "has substantially been agreed upon" and would read, "The 20th Maine regiment, Colonel Joshua L. Chamberlain, captured and held this position, pursuing the enemy from their front on the line marked by the monument below on the evening of July 2nd, 1863. This monument marks the extreme left of the Union line during the battle of the 3rd day." A month later, the inscription was modified at the suggestion of the Gettysburg Battlefield Memorial Association to include the regiment's place within the order of battle, the number of men engaged, and the casualties.[47]

The monuments were finished in the spring of 1889 and awaited the warmer weather that would dry out the roads in Gettysburg and allow them to be transported from the train station to their various positions around the field. At their meeting in April 1889, the executive committee set October 3, 1889, as the date to dedicate all the Maine monuments and tapped Joshua Chamberlain as "President" to preside over the ceremonies.[48]

By early September, the Twentieth's survivors received information about the dedicatory ceremonies and the arrangements to transport them to Gettysburg if they wished to go. Train travel had been secured from Portland to Gettysburg and back, departing on October 1 and returning October 5 at a cost of roughly $20 per person. Ultimately, four hundred Maine veterans made the journey, including thirty-three veterans of the Twentieth Maine. Seven of the men brought their wives, Albert Fernald brought his son, and Howard Prince brought two ladies in addition to his wife. Former vice president Hannibal Hamlin also made the journey. While most men left Maine on October 1, others joined along the way, includ-ing Joshua Chamberlain, who met the group as they transited New York.

Arriving at 5:00 p.m. on October 2, the Twentieth made their headquarters at the Springs Hotel on the first day's battlefield at Herr Ridge. That evening the regimental association held their annual meeting. Sadly, the time had come when the veterans felt it necessary to establish a "committee on necrology" to keep a list of deaths and publish obituaries, with Elisha Coan, Albert Fernald, and Ruel Thomas appointed to fulfill the task. The other business was routine and primarily concerned the following day's events.[49]

The next morning the men departed the hotel in carriages and first visited the nearest monuments that honored the units who had fought earliest in the battle, including the Second Maine Battery, the Sixteenth Maine, and the Fifth Maine Battery, before journeying east to see where the First Maine Cavalry fought on July 3. Returning to town, they visited the Soldiers' National Cemetery. Former bugler Joseph Tyler then called for the group to assemble by playing their old brigade's unique tune, "Dan, Dan, Dan, Butterfield, Butterfield," and the group "drove to Little Round Top where some time was spent looking over the position of the Twentieth's greatest achievement."[50]

Soon the men assembled for a "memorial service at the monument on Little Round Top." Association president Holman Melcher opened the proceedings and then introduced historian Howard Prince, "who delivered an eloquent and interesting address minutely describing the desperate and bloody fight which took place there July 2, 1863." Prince began by acknowledging that he was the regimental quartermaster in 1863 and, as such, "was within hearing of the guns of Gettysburg" but not present on Little Round Top. Rather than relying solely on his own experiences then, it was clear that his account of the battle would be a synthesis of what others had told him over the years. It was no easy task "to speak of great deeds in the presence of the actors themselves, and to air my feeble periods in the face of one [Joshua Chamberlain] whose eloquence has made the '20th Maine at Gettysburg' a classic scarcely less renowned than his own brilliant career."[51]

Prince's narrative of the Twentieth Maine at Gettysburg was the most complete account of the unit's actions on Little Round Top yet and remained so until John Pullen's 1957 history of the unit. Much of the account was straightforward, but there were many areas that touched on controversy. Earlier in the decade, Prince tried to establish the how and why of Vincent's placement of the units on Little Round Top, and he offered the full explanation in this text. He also incorporated the actions of Confederate scout and skirmisher Phinias McMiller. Prince spent a great deal of time explaining the Confederate approach to Little Round Top, possibly because he knew that part of the story was less familiar to his audience than what happened once the Confederates began their attacks on the Mainers. In describing Oates's hesitation on the summit of Big Round Top, Prince mused, "Maj. Melcher has elsewhere stated that this delay was a fatal one, as it enabled Vincent's brigade to become established on the Spur. I do not think this is correct," explaining that the Twentieth was in position for more than ten minutes before the Confederates appeared. This was no more than a minor quibble among the unit's survivors, but the fact that it was included in the speech dedicating the monument and subsequently reprinted shows the different memories and perspectives the men held more than a quarter of a century after the event.[52]

Prince soon addressed those varying perspectives, noting that there were at least two different memories of when the unit had refused or bent back its line to meet a Confederate flanking force: "It is probable that both statements are correct from different points of view. It is not believed to be possible to reconcile all the theories and beliefs of the actors, even in so small a space as the front of a regiment, and when we fail, as sometimes we must, we must conclude, that as there is a substantial agreement on the main features of the action, these disputed details were seen from different points, or were viewed at different stages as parts of a whole." Another such example was which officer had first called Chamberlain's attention to the Fifteenth Alabama's presence on the extreme left, a valuable act that both Jim Nichols and Ellis Spear had claimed as their own. Countering Theodore Gerrish's claim in *Army Life* that the men had briefly hesitated when Chamberlain ordered them forward, Prince recounted, "The die is thrown, and the one word 'bayonets' rings from Chamberlain's lips like a bugle note. . . . The lines were in motion before the word of command was completed, and Col. Chamberlain does not know whether he ever finished that order."[53]

Prince's thorough account ran to nineteen pages when subsequently printed and must have taken an hour or more to deliver. When he finished, Joshua Chamberlain stood to add his own remarks, which ran to just a quarter the length of his former quartermaster's and stuck to broader themes rather than minute details. Much of Chamberlain's speech concerned the various divergences in the men's accounts, and while he sought to correct the record in a few places, he primarily acted as the peacemaker.[54]

1889 reunion and monument dedication on Little Round Top (Collections of Maine Historical Society)

Chamberlain began by emphasizing their actions' importance: "Far greater was the result of the action taken than any statistical description of it could import. You were making history. The world has recorded for you more than you have written." But in a testament to how confusing battle could be and the mistakes that could creep into human memory after the passage of a quarter century, Chamberlain asserted, "I am certain that the position of this monument is quite to the left of the centre of our regimental line when the final charge was ordered. Our original left did not extend quite to the great rock which now supports this memorial of honor." Rather, with its position beyond the regiment's lines, the rock on which the monument now sat "became so conspicuous an object during the terrible struggle—the centre and pivot of the whirlpool that raged around."[55]

Having thrown one piece of the story into contention, Chamberlain then sought to bring harmony to others. Noting the claims that various officers made to have alerted Chamberlain to the Confederates' flanking maneuvers, the colonel explained, "As well might be believed of such gentleman and soldiers, they are all right; no one of them is wrong." They had simply alerted him at different times to different movements, he explained.[56]

To Gerrish's assertion that some men had paused before complying with the order to fix bayonets and charge: "I am sorry to have heard it intimated that any hesitated when that order was given." He continued, "That was not so. No man hesitated." After explaining the situation's physics and the hill's topography, he reiterated, "Nobody hesitated to obey the order. In fact, to tell the truth, the order was never given, or but imperfectly"—an acknowledgment that the men had started moving as soon as he shouted "bayonets" and that he may have never shouted "charge," or, if he did, it is possible few heard him do so. Having set the record straight, he also tried to ameliorate all: "There may be stories apparently not consistent with each other, yet all of them true in their time and place, and so far as each actor is concerned." Just as he had a quarter century earlier, Chamberlain continued to lead his men. Now, instead of forming the individuals into a single unit, he was forming their story into a single narrative that would sustain the reputation they had earned.[57]

Later that night Chamberlain addressed even broader themes as the keynote speaker dedicating all the Maine monuments, but here at the scene of his and his unit's greatest glory, he offered one last summation of what their fight on Little Round Top had meant: "The lesson impressed on me as I stand here and my heart and mind traverse your faces, and the years that are gone, is that in a great momentous struggle like this commemorated here, it is character that tells." He continued, "No man becomes suddenly different from his habit and cherished thought. We carry our accustomed manners with us. And it was the boyhood you brought from your homes which made you men, which braced your hearts, which shone upon your foreheads, which held you steadfast in mind and body, and lifted those heights of Gettysburg to immortal glory."[58]

Former bugler Joe Tyler then played Taps, following which the group moved a few hundred yards to the east to place a small marker denoting Company B's position during the battle. The veterans then made the strenuous hike to the summit of Big Round Top to dedicate their third

Gettysburg monument. Samuel Miller offered a controversy-free short history of the unit's second position on the bigger hill.[59]

That evening, the Maine State Monument Commission held ceremonies to formally dedicate and then turn over all the Maine monuments to the Gettysburg Battlefield Memorial Association. As "president" for the day, Joshua Chamberlain employed all the elements of rhetoric in making a speech appropriate to the more formal occasion. Whereas earlier in the day he had talked specifically of the Twentieth Maine, at the evening ceremonies in the courthouse he meditated on the broader cause and sacrifices made to save the Union and the concepts of service. In perhaps the second most quoted commemorative speech to come out of the Civil War—trailing only the Gettysburg Address—Chamberlain closed:

> *In great deeds, something abides. On great fields, something stays. Forms change and pass; bodies disappear; but spirits linger, to consecrate ground for the vision-place of souls. And reverent men and women from afar, and generations that know us not and that we know not of, heart-drawn to see where and by whom great things were suffered and done for them, shall come to this deathless field, to ponder and dream; and lo! the shadow of a mighty presence shall wrap them in its bosom, and the power of the vision pass into their souls.[60]*

The men left for home the next morning, most of them never to return to Gettysburg again. Their positions were as well marked as any unit on the field, and Chamberlain's prediction that future generations would come to the "deathless field" to see and hear what the men had done proved accurate.

The dedication of the monuments on October 3, 1889, marked both the apex and the end of the most important decade in the creation of the Twentieth Maine's narrative of their fight on Little Round Top. While some men, notably Chamberlain and Ellis Spear, had spoken publicly before the 1880s and continued to do so over the ensuing quarter century, the 1880s was the era when most of the accounts published by other men appeared in print. These accounts propelled interest in marking their position at Gettysburg, and the monuments that resulted, in turn, led to the proliferation of additional firsthand accounts as well as works (such as that by Howard Prince) that drew on both Union and Confederate narratives to create a synthesis of what happened on Little Round Top. In the short term, most controversies seemed to have been reconciled.

"Understanding that you are awarding Medals of Honor for special acts of service or conduct, performed in the late war," New York lawyer Thomas Hubbard wrote to the secretary of war on February 15, 1893, "I desire, while confessing my personal ignorance of the act of Congress which authorizes the awards, to call special attention to the case of my friend General Joshua L. Chamberlain."[61]

In the early 1890s, the number of Medals of Honor awarded jumped dramatically. In 1890, there were just thirty-three awarded, but then from 1891 to 1897 roughly five hundred medals were bestowed on Civil War veterans. Hubbard was clearly aware of this uptick and wanted to ensure that Chamberlain, whose "service during the war was exceptionally meritorious and brilliant," was not overlooked, particularly as there was no time to waste: "He has been suffering from the wounds received in battle, wounds that have prostrated him at intervals ever since the war and that have now, I fear, brought his life near its close." A pension examination the following month revealed that Chamberlain was bedridden a quarter of the time because of his war wounds, and Hubbard was rightly fearful that his friend could succumb at any time.[62]

There were "three battles in which he bore a part more honorable than literal obedience of orders would require and where the results of his acts were such as to call for special commendation from his commanding officers," Hubbard relayed. Those three were Gettysburg, White Oak Road, and Appomattox. Hubbard reminded the secretary of war that at Gettysburg, "When almost overwhelmed by the enemy, with nearly half of his command killed or wounded and ammunition exhausted, General Chamberlain—then Colonel—made a countercharge with the bayonets, which checked, or broke, the enemy's attempt to turn the left of the Union line on Round Top."[63]

Soon letters of support arrived from Fitz John Porter, former commander of the Fifth Corps; Alexander Webb, a brigade commander at Gettysburg; and Maine governor Henry Cleaves. Webb, who had himself received the Medal of Honor in 1891, offered perhaps the most significant support, asserting, "I know of no one whose designation by yourself, as Secretary of War, as a proper recipient of this Medal, who would be more acceptable to the whole Army of the Potomac."[64]

A Medal of Honor had to be awarded for a specific action, and it was Gettysburg, of course, that was the choice. On August 11, 1893, Chamberlain was awarded the Medal of Honor for his "daring heroism and great tenacity in holding his position on the Little Round Top against repeated assaults, and carrying the advance position on the Great Round Top." He was the second man in the unit so honored, following Albert Fernald, but would not be the last.[65]

"Major C. J. House, one of the members of the State House staff in Augusta, is preparing a list of Maine men who participated in the battle of Gettysburg and the casualties suffered by Maine troops which will appear in the report of the Maine Gettysburg commission," the *Lincoln County News* reported on March 5, 1896. As an accompaniment to the monuments, the Maine State Monument Commission decided to publish a report—eventually called *Maine at Gettysburg*—that featured images of the monuments, histories of the units before and during the battle, and complete rosters of all the soldiers who fought at Gettysburg. The men who had been on Little Round Top were desperate to ensure that their names were included. Reuel Thomas had written to Chamberlain the previous year to remind him of the role he played in the battle and to make certain that he was listed as one of the men in the heat of the battle and not serving on detached duty, as he had been right up until the battle began. "Gen'l you remember I had charge of the Pioner Corps until we arrived at Little Round Top. and then you gave orders each man to report to his Co. and I said to you where shall I go and you said Sergt. I want you to come with me. And I never left yr side only to obey orders until the fight was over. Now I dint care where I am in that fight only want the Wourld to know it."[66]

Holman Melcher knew that the monument on Little Round Top gave a specific strength for the Twentieth Maine at Gettysburg: 358 men plus 28 officers. But now, "The names of the 358 men that participated in that battle will be a delicate as well as a difficult task to prepare." They took the muster rolls of June 30 as their basis—which gave a strength of 511 men—but knew that it overestimated the number of combatants, as some men dropped out along the march and were not present during the battle. In November, the *Lincoln County News* published a preliminary list, and the men were "requested to carefully scrutinize these names and report to Gen. Chamberlain, Brunswick, Me., any additions or omissions that should be made." Indeed, "It is known that there are many more names in the list than were engaged in the battle," the commissioners admitted, asking for help in weeding out those who dropped out on the march to Gettysburg. Reuel Thomas's name appeared on the list, with the note that he was "detailed as special Orderly for Colonel." Not surprisingly, few men wrote in to remove themselves from the list, and thus the total number of men on the final roster was 509, which was 123 more than the total given on the unit's monument at Gettysburg. Chamberlain was so frustrated that stragglers who had not actually participated in the battle might appear on the printed list and forever be credited with glory they had not earned that he suggested withholding the entire list and leaving it out of *Maine at Gettysburg*. Charles Hamlin cautioned that "justice to your brave fellows" would not permit such an action, and Chamberlain acquiesced.[67]

During this process, if not earlier, Chamberlain became aware that Theodore Gerrish, author of the only full-length book on the Twentieth Maine, had not been present at the unit's most famous battle. On March 4, 1897, Albert Fernald told Chamberlain, "Gerrish is not reported in Co H at Gettysburg. I have just looked over again." Despite that information, Gerrish's name remained on the roster. Whether that was a decision made to protect Gerrish the individual or to ensure that no scandal arose over the regiment and its best-selling chronicler that might damage the reputation of all is unclear.[68]

Throughout the spring and summer of 1896, three men worked on the portion of *Maine at Gettysburg* concerning the Twentieth: Major House worked on the roster, Ellis Spear began drafting a history of the unit's participation in the entire war, and Joshua Chamberlain refined his oft-told account of their actions at Gettysburg. As they were doing so, an article appeared in the *Lincoln County News* on July 2, 1896, offering a synthesis of the fighting on Little Round Top. The author was George L. Kilmer, who was not a veteran of the Twentieth Maine but may have been the same person who served in the Twenty-Seventh New York before Gettysburg and then the Fourteenth New York Heavy Artillery later in the war. Based on the speeches delivered by Howard Prince and Samuel Miller at the monument dedications in 1889 and William Oates's 1878 account, Kilmer identified Holman Melcher as the "hero of the bayonet charge."[69]

Though he had sought to harmonize any differences in the recollections and accounts the men had put forth when speaking at the dedication of the monuments in 1889, Joshua Chamberlain was annoyed at what he perceived to be these late-breaking accounts that threatened his own reputation. In late November, Ellis Spear sent a draft of the unit history he had compiled, and Chamberlain responded with some suggestions and critiques but with the overall comment that he had made few edits and that the account was "of utmost value." Chamberlain spent most of the letter, however, letting off steam. "As to Gettysburg itself," he told his former subordinate, "Quite a number of things have been put in distorted perspective lately." William Oates spoke of the Twentieth as only having fought against the Fifteenth Alabama, which was both inaccurate and vastly limited the scope of their activities, and far too many were following their former opponents' lead. Further, "The Melcher incident is also magnified. He is now presented to the public as having suggested the charge." Importantly, Chamberlain accurately placed that last sentence in the third person, for Holman Melcher himself never claimed credit for the charge; rather, outsiders—many of whom had not even been on Little Round Top or served in the Twentieth Maine—had claimed that honor for him. "I have been trying," Chamberlain confided, "to reconcile the several accounts of the battle . . . and it is the hardest work I ever did in the literary line." Chamberlain went so far as to reach out to Colonel Oates to help clarify the narrative, and the two men exchanged letters on the ebb and flow of the battle in early 1897.[70]

As the Maine at Gettysburg Commission continued to work on their final report, two soldiers from the Twentieth Maine came to their particular attention. The executive chairman of the committee, Charles Hamlin, wrote the history of the Sixth Maine that appeared in the volume. In detailing the unit's "brilliant charge" at Rappahannock Station, he also gave credit to the men from the Twentieth who had joined them, particularly Captain Walter Morrill, who "was by his almost unexampled courage and gallantry of the greatest assistance in the achievement which followed." Hamlin was struck by this act of volunteer courage and surprised that Morrill had not already been awarded a Medal of Honor. Hamlin wrote to Congressman Edwin Burleigh on January 7, 1898, suggesting, "Here is a good opportunity for you to do a good thing for your constituent by obtaining for him a medal of honor." Burleigh agreed and visited the secretary of war on January 18 to make the recommendation, following up with a formal letter the next day. The process moved quickly, and Morrill was awarded the Medal on March 28, 1898, the third unit member to be so honored.[71]

A fourth followed in quick succession. As Joshua Chamberlain mentally refought the Battle of Gettysburg and tried to construct a coherent narrative to be included in *Maine at Gettysburg* that gave all their proper due while batting away the claims of some that he felt were unworthy of the reputations they sought, he realized that he had perhaps not gone far enough in his post-battle recognition of one soldier: Color Sergeant Andrew Tozier, the man who had lived with Chamberlain in the 1870s as he tried to reform his life and get back on the straight and narrow. "At the crisis of the engagement," Chamberlain wrote to Secretary of War Russell Alger in March 1898, "when our whole center was for a moment broken and the enemy seemed about to overpower us, I saw, as a thick cloud of smoke lifted, Sergeant Tozier standing alone at his advanced post,—the two center companies having lost nearly half their members, and the Color guard entirely cut away,—the color-staff rested on the ground and supported in the hollow of his shoulder, while with a musket and cartridge-box he had picked up at his feet he was defending his color; presenting a figure which seemed to have paralyzed the enemy in front of him, who might otherwise have captured the color. This was the object around which I made the rallying point for the Regiment, and the center guide for the following charge." Chamberlain had made no mention of Tozier in his official report because, he stated, "I thought then that no one there had done more than a soldier's duty." But the intervening years had changed his mind. "I feel now, however, that his conduct was somewhat beyond what could have been required and expected as a part of duty," and thus he recommended Tozier for the Medal of Honor. On August 5, 1898, the assistant secretary of war notified Tozier that President William McKinley, himself a Civil War veteran, had awarded him the medal, a remarkable turnaround for the former inmate.[72]

Finally, *Maine at Gettysburg* was completed in the late summer of 1898. Of the two thousand copies printed, one was given to the nearest surviving relative of each of the 225 Mainers killed at Gettysburg, with the rest distributed to the regimental associations at the various reunions over the ensuing year. In the spring of 1899, William T. Livermore, a former member of the color guard, secured a copy of *Maine at Gettysburg*, and, not surprisingly, he was particularly interested in the passage that covered the actions of Andrew Tozier and the color guard that Chamberlain had largely copied in his letter recommending his former color sergeant for the Medal of Honor. In *Maine at Gettysburg*, Chamberlain wrote, "At one moment, it looked as if the colors of the Twentieth Maine must be lost. Buried from sight in smoke, when the black cloud lifted for a moment the colors were seen almost alone. All the Color-Guard and the flanks of the companies on its right and left were cut away; but the Color-Sergeant, Andrew J. Tozier, was standing his ground, the staff planted on the earth, and supported within his left arm, while he had picked up a musket and was defending his colors with bullet, bayonet, and butt, alone!" Livermore picked up his pen and wrote a remarkable four-page letter to his former colonel, a letter worthy of reprinting in full.[73]

Milo May 22nd 1899
Gen J. L. Chamberlain
Brunswick

Dear General. As Memorial day draws near and you are to deliver the address and in the evening deliver your lecture on the battle on Little Round Top it awakens a deep interest and I look back with pride and satisfaction to that eventful day when our Regt. had the opportunity and valor to erect July 2 1863 a monument more enduring than the Survivors of the Regt. and a greatful State has since erected.

I have just received Maine at Gettysburg and carefully read the discription of the battle and while it is so vivid and acurate in the maine, I was surprised to read on Page 256 That at one time the colors was almost alone that "all the Color Guards were cut away, but Andrew J. Tozer was standing his ground defending his Colors with bullet bayonet and butt alone."

As I am the only survivor of that guard I must in justice to myself and Company and now especially my lamented Comrade Coan protest against this. If Coan was living he would have something to say. I was detailed by Adjutant Brown as Color Guard soon after the battle of Fredericksburg and the Colors was never unfirled in camp on the march or in battle when I was not under its folds up to May 5, 1864 in the Wilderness here I was wounded on the right of the Colors in the front rank, where I Steped when Charles H. Reed was wounded on Little Round Top. When we went into the fight there were four of us Reed was wounded on the right of the Colors and I Steped into his place Melville Day on the left was Killed and Coan Steped into his place. There was not a minute when we were not on the right and left of the Colors and had Tozier been Shot the Colors would not have Struck the ground. As I was the Senior guard I expected every minute to go down or See the Sergt. fall Sergt. Tozier did his duty bravely and I would not detract from the honor so richly earned. But why Special mention is made of him defending the Colors alone when he was not and the guard represented as absent when the Colors was in such peril I cannot understand. Neither of us was wounded if "cut away" it must have been by smoke or fright. All the Survivors of the Center Companies Know that the two remaining guards were always under the Colors and were not behind the Colors in the Charge. Any of Co. B who was on the skirmish line at this time may ask as they read this history Where Livermore who was not wounded was at this critical time when the Sergt. was Alone defending the Colors. It is true the center was reduced to a Skirmish line as the two small companies + guard had lost in killed and wounded 43 men, but there was no time when there was not Several Guards between the Colors and the enemy. and there was realy no occasion for the guards to use either "bayonet or butt." I have always supposed and as far as I know others claim that the charge started in the center.

No man in the Regt. had more interest in the flag than E. S. Coan and no man was among the prisoners sooner than he. He took five to the rear and I believe it was the first Squad Started in that direction.

Five years ago I attended the department of Maine G.A.R. in Bangor, and being in a group of GAR boys I was asked which Regt. I said 20th Maine and a man said I belonged to the 20th and was wounded on Little Round Top carrying the Colors I said you must be mistaken. Sergt. Tozier carried the Colors and I was one of the guards.

*He said Yes that is right. Sergt. Tozier said Reed you take the colors
and let me shoot and we exchanged and I was wounded. Tozier fired
Several Shots but I think they were from Reeds musket while Reed held
the Colors. There was glory enough earned on Little Round Top for
every participant from our distinguished and honored Col. to the humble
private who did his duty.*

*Personaly I claim no distinction it is enough to be credited with being
one of the Color Guard and Standing by them in that trying ordeal and
a member of Co B 20th Maine Vols.*

*Hoping a kind providence will allow us to meet and greet you on
Memorial day I remain*

    Yours Truly
      W. T. Livermore Sergt Co "B" 20th Maine Vols.[74]

In trying to honor Tozier, Chamberlain had gone too far. A return letter from Chamberlain to Will Livermore is not in existence, but after Livermore's death in 1911 the author of his obituary noted, "The writer remembers at one time of hearing Major General Joshua L. Chamberlain say in a Memorial day address in this town 'William T. Livermore of your town was the bravest man that I ever saw.'" But Chamberlain did not just offer a short-term platitude to smooth things over with Livermore; he also changed his accounts going forward. In 1913, Chamberlain penned an article on Gettysburg that appeared in *Hearst's Magazine* on the battle's fiftieth anniversary. Now Chamberlain described the situation thus: "The cross-fire had cut keenly; the center had been almost shot away; only two of the color guard had been left, and they fighting to fill the whole space; and in the center, wreathed in battle smoke, stood the Color-Sergeant, Andrew Tozier."[75]

In his excellent work, *Belligerent Muse: Five Northern Writers and How They Shaped Our Understanding of the Civil War*, author Stephen Cushman argues, "Imperfection or flaw in recollection actually may be a sign of authenticity rather than falsehood, whereas exact, undeviating repetition of precisely the same details over fifty years could characterize the rigidly rehearsed consistency of a liar."[76] Given Chamberlain's rank and role, he could be expected to have a more holistic and yet less detailed perspective than the soldiers on the front lines who were loading and firing their weapons and seeing the intimate details of what was occurring in their field of vision but were unaware of much that was not in immediate orbit. Chamberlain's accounts of Gettysburg changed over the years as he gained new information, such as that submitted by William T. Livermore, a man he greatly respected and whose account he trusted. In Chamberlain's papers at the Library of Congress are copies of the *Lincoln County News* containing Will Livermore's diary, William C. Oates's "Gettysburg: The Battle on the Right," and others, all showing evidence of a man trying to acquire more knowledge and a deeper understanding of the nuances of the fight on Little Round Top. That the colonel was willing to change—to correct and perfect—his oft-told narrative suggests not some character flaw but a man with a growth mentality who sought a more accurate narrative rather than dogmatically holding on to outdated views.[77]

The last great controversy arose in 1903 and pitted Joshua Chamberlain and the Twentieth Maine against their old foes, the Fifteenth Alabama and, more specifically, their former commander, William C. Oates. In August of that year, the Gettysburg National Park Commission notified Joshua Chamberlain that Oates had submitted "a proposition to place a monument on Chamberlain Avenue in front of the position of the 20th Maine," a marker delineating the Confederate unit's supposed farthest point of advance during the battle. In 1903, tablets marked Confederate brigade, division, and corps positions, but there was just a single regimental marker—one to the Second Maryland erected in 1884. Oates's request inaugurated what historian Timothy B. Smith has called Gettysburg's biggest controversy of the era.[78]

It had all begun with a letter from William C. Oates to William Robbins on April 1, 1902. When Congress passed the legislation to create the National Military Parks in the 1890s—legislation backed by then-congressman William C. Oates—they established a system whereby each park was run by three commissioners—two Union veterans and one Confederate veteran. Robbins, the former Confederate on the Gettysburg Commission, also happened to be a veteran of the Fourth Alabama, which had served in Law's brigade alongside the Fifteenth Alabama and had fought on Little Round Top on July 2, 1863. In his letter to "My dear old Comrade and Friend," Oates noted his intent to place a monument at the point of the Fifteenth Alabama's farthest advance. The monument's intended inscription showed that the spot was particularly meaningful: "To the Memory of Lt. John A. Oates and his gallant Comrades who fell here July 2nd, 1863."[79]

Oates had assumed that Robbins would be supportive of his plan, but the opposite was true. Robbins did not respond to Oates's original letter, and finally, after returning from a trip to Europe, Oates followed up in September. Now forced to take a position, Robbins shared with his fellow commissioners "the delicacy I feel in regard to a proposal to single out any one regiment in my brigade for special honors." He also worried that singling out one regiment set a bad precedent, a position he knew was shared by the other commissioners. The "special honors" that Robbins referenced concerned the location of the monument, for the park's regulations stipulated that "the monument must be on the line of the battle held by the Brigade unless the Regiment was detached," and that line was nowhere near the advanced position that Oates had identified. When Robbins's own Fourth Alabama—a unit that was separated from the Fifteenth Alabama on July 2, 1863, by only the seven companies of the Forty-Seventh Alabama—put up their monument in 1903, they placed it back along the brigade line just off the Emmitsburg Road and nearly a mile west of Oates's proposed location. Robbins wrote to Oates to share these concerns on September 27, 1902.[80]

Oates was furious with the commission's take on the matter and fired off a lengthy response to Robbins five days later. He argued that requiring monuments to be placed "at the point where formed for beginning the attack, will simply prevent any from being erected to the Confederates." Thus, "I intend to place the matter before Congress and will write it up in the newspapers for I consider it a great wrong to our side." If there was any doubt as to Oates's fury, he concluded, "I shall never visit Gettysburg if I am not allowed to erect a little simple monument to the memory of my comrades who died on that spot."[81]

Robbins continued trying to persuade Oates to place the monument along Confederate Avenue on the brigade line, but to no avail. In January 1903, Oates wrote to the commissioners, "I do not feel like I ought to apply to the Secretary of war, nor to Congress, until I have applied to your board, and failed to obtain permission." The threat was clear. The commission chairman, John Nicholson, wrote back on February 9, asking for more details as to Oates's request and encouraging him to come to Gettysburg to see the work that had been done on the field and to clarify where he wanted his monument placed. While maintaining a largely cordial tone, Nicholson concluded, "I do not quite understand your reference to Congress."[82]

Oates was in no mood to negotiate and just two days later informed Nicholson, "I have forwarded an application to Congressman A. A. Wiley, to be submitted to the secretary of war for permission to erect a little monument or marker which I wish to place on the east side of Little Round Top, at or about the point to which my command advanced." He noted that the location he desired was "125 or 150 yards or probably a little more east from the N.Y. monument on the side of Little Round Top." Noting that he had charge of his own Fifteenth Alabama plus the seven companies of the Forty-Seventh Alabama that were on his left, Oates asserted, "My command was wholly disconnected from the Brigade and guessing at the distance, was at least 200 yards, and maybe more, separated from the 4th Ala. which was the next regiment in the line of the brigade to my left." This was a critical distinction, for the park's stipulation that a regimental marker must be placed on the brigade line "unless the Regiment was detached" offered Oates a potential opening. But Oates's letter was full of imprecise language that suggested a weak grasp of the battlefield and the various units' positions, and acceding to his wish in terms of the monument's location and inscription might perpetuate a falsehood. Oates referred to the spot he had identified for the monument as "at or about the point my regiment . . . advanced." In another passage, he admitted, "(I am guessing at the distance)," and then described the position of the Fourth Alabama "as I understand it" before acknowledging, "I may not state the direction correctly." He noted that he hoped during some future visit "to get more accurate information than I have in regard to direction and distance," but that would occur only after the monument was placed, for he would not return before and until his wishes were granted.[83]

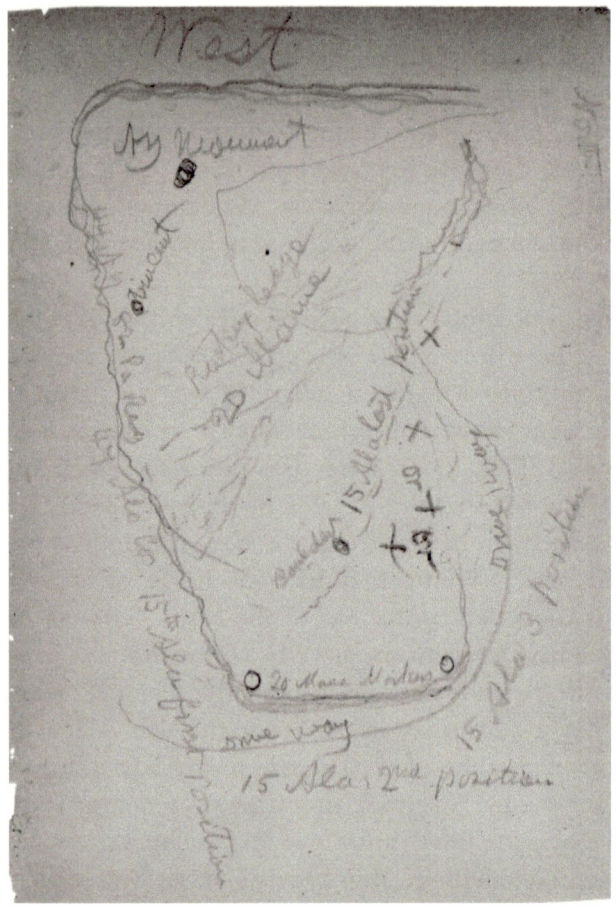

Sketch of Little Round Top by William C. Oates indicating location for a proposed monument to the Fifteenth Alabama (National Park Service, Gettysburg National Military Park)

In the interim, Oates corresponded directly with William Robbins, offering a battle narrative to buttress his argument that he had been detached from the brigade during the fight. He noted that brigade commander Evander Law had ordered the seven companies of the Forty-Seventh Alabama to operate under his authority if they became detached from the rest of the brigade and that, in pursuing the sharpshooters over Big Round Top, the Fifteenth and Forty-Seventh Alabama become separated from the rest of the brigade by "a quarter of a mile perhaps much more." Thus, when the battle came, "We [the Fifteenth Alabama] were confronting the 20th Me. and 83rd Pa. The 47th was terribly enfiladed by the fire of the 44th N.Y." Oates's letter argued that his "command" had been detached from the brigade and implied that his Fifteenth Alabama had fought against two regiments.[84]

Rather than clarify anything, Oates's letter exasperated Robbins, who protested Oates's assertion that he was "far off to himself in the fight there" in a letter to John Nicholson just five days later: "Gen. O. is very considerably in error as to the relative position of the Confed. Regts. and their distances from each other, or rather, their nearness to each other . . . I'm sure I was within about 100 yards of where Gen. O. must have been. I being at the right flank of the 4th Ala. and only the 7 small companies of the 47th Ala. Between me and the left of the 15th Ala."[85]

At the end of February, Robbins explained where Oates's interpretation of the battle was flawed: "Col. Chamberlain stood on the large boulder I've shown you—& it is scarcely over 50 yards from where I was—and he told me all about the fight. . . . Oates really fought the left battalion of that Regt: the 47th Ala (7 Co's only) fought its center; and the 4th Ala fought its right, [and] the 87th [83rd] Pa." Robbins continued, "All the regiments on both sides were in close touch with each other and it is a mistake to say that either regiment on either side fought a separate fight off to itself or excelled the others in achievement or gallantry." That last statement was the crux of the matter and the source of Robbins's opposition to the plan for a monument that singled out the Fifteenth Alabama at the expense of others, including his own Fourth Alabama.[86]

On February 19, 1903, Oates filed a petition with the secretary of war to place his monument on Little Round Top. On May 23, 1903, Secretary of War Elihu Root wrote to Oates suggesting that he "visit Gettysburg and go over the situation fully with the Commission on the spot." In responding to the secretary, Oates noted that he had already visited the field three times: once as a congressman, once when he was the governor of Alabama, and finally when he was serving as a brigadier general during the Spanish-American War. In detailing his visits, Oates clearly intended to draw attention to his political power and the positions of prominence he had held previously. Oates then tried to advance his cause by invoking reconciliation, asking, "Cannot one humble shaft be erected on that field where a so-called Rebel command fought? If not, then, Mr. Secretary, it shows that the bitterness of feeling engendered by the Civil War has not completely subsided."[87]

When the secretary of war referred the application to the Gettysburg commissioners, they knew they needed reinforcements. Oates's invocation of his past positions of authority and his comments about sectional bitterness raised the stakes. On August 6, 1903, John Nicholson wrote to Joshua Chamberlain, passing along Oates's letters and his "proposition to place a monument on Chamberlain Avenue in front of the position of the 20th Maine." Nicholson shared the commission's view that the marker should be placed on the brigade front along Confederate Avenue, and the explanation, "Some of the statements are so much at variance with the records that we thought we would ask your opinion on the subject."[88]

Chamberlain's response came quickly. After opening niceties, he laid out his position quite clearly: "I should feel no objection to the erection of a monument to the honor of a regiment that had pushed its way so far around the flank of the Union line and made so gallant an attack; but I should expect it to be placed on ground where it actually stood at some time during the battle,—at the extreme point of its advance, if desired,—so that it might not only represent the valor of a regiment but the truth of history." The problem was that Oates's statements in his petition to the secretary of war "differ widely from the established record of facts in the case, and very materially from former statements of his in papers published by him and in personal letters in the course of a correspondence with me." Chamberlain listed five issues with Oates's account of the fight, but the central one was that no part of Oates's line ever made it anywhere near the spot now proposed for a monument, and to locate a marker there would be to place it on "ground never seen by the 15th Alabama during the battle." For the Fifteenth Alabama to have reached that spot, Chamberlain argued, they must have "run entirely over the 20th Maine and annihilated it" before encountering the Eighty-Third Pennsylvania. "The relatively small loss in the 83rd,—8 killed and 38 wounded,—is enough to show that it was never struck by the fierce onset of the 15th Alabama." In short, Chamberlain argued that he was perfectly sanguine with placing a monument to the Fifteenth Alabama on Little Round Top, but putting one where Oates demanded would solidify in granite form a narrative of the battle that was simply untrue and one that would forever damage the Twentieth Maine's reputation.[89]

In various letters Oates described his advanced point as it related to the Forty-Fourth New York memorial, the Strong Vincent marker, Chamberlain Avenue, and the Twentieth Maine's 1886 monument. Perhaps due to Chamberlain's stance on the matter, the commission was willing to consider casting aside their regulation that the monument must be placed on the brigade line and instead put it at the advanced point if only that spot could be identified. With that in mind, Nicholson wrote to Oates in the fall of 1903, inviting him to come to Gettysburg to identify the location. On November 4, 1903, Oates responded that such a visit would "give me pleasure" but then noted that he would undertake the visit only after he had been assured that he had permission to place the marker. That was a challenge, of course, for as Nicholson soon after wrote to the secretary of war, Oates continued to insist that it would not be until after he received permission to place the monument that "he would select the exact position he desired."[90]

Oates finally visited Gettysburg in July 1904, but he announced that visit only a few days in advance and then moved the exact date at the last minute, meaning he visited Little Round Top with William Robbins but not with John Nicholson, and certainly not with Joshua Chamberlain. Nicholson was able to be present that evening and shared Chamberlain's letter from the previous year. In April 1905, Oates wrote directly to Chamberlain. He began by pointedly disavowing Chamberlain's assertion to Nicholson that the two men had corresponded previously—but the fourteen-page 1897 letter from Oates to Chamberlain on "State of Alabama, Executive Office" stationery and carrying the identical signature of "WmC Oates" as the 1905 missive still exists and raises questions about Oates's mindset. In the 1905 letter, Oates asserted that it did not matter whether the right flank or left flank of his attack reached the point proposed for the monument; he was sure that someone had. "You, unintentionally I presume, misrepresented what you understand me to have claimed, to wit: that I drove back your right and advanced up the slope a good distance. That letter of yours was what did the work and caused my application to be turned down." But Oates had written to William Robbins a letter that the commissioners had no doubt shown to Chamberlain, which stated, "I tell you Major the claim of Chamberlain that he was never driven from the ledge of rock where his markers are placed will not do. Just as sure as your name is Robbins and mine Oates my regiment not only overlapped his left flank but drove the 20th Maine from that position back to where I showed you and his right as well as his left was forced back but not so far."[91]

Chamberlain was exasperated with the whole affair but wrote to Oates on May 18, 1905, assuring his former foe, as he had the commissioners, of "my complete and cordial willingness to have the monument of the 15th Alabama placed within my lines on the slope of Little Round Top, on ground actually reached by portions of that regiment in the sharp passages of the fight. As to the exact location, I cannot say from mere description what was the extreme point to which my left was driven by you." To remedy their conflicting accounts, Chamberlain offered, "I should be glad to meet you again," suggesting a trip to Gettysburg.[92]

That meeting never came to pass, and the Oates monument was never erected. Over the years, Chamberlain has sometimes been portrayed as jealously protecting the Twentieth's reputation in this matter—as well as his own—by refusing to admit that the unit had wavered in the position, but the correspondence makes it clear that was not the case. Chamberlain's objection, and that of the Gettysburg National Park commissioners (including former Confederate William Robbins, who also fought on Little Round Top), was that Oates wanted to place his monument in a position his unit never reached. Throughout the postwar period, Chamberlain and the men of the Twentieth Maine eagerly sought Confederate accounts of their fight, seeing them as helping to fill in the gaps and move the overall story closer to the full history. But in this case, placing a monument to their foe's extreme advance on ground that those Alabamians had not actually occupied would forever perpetuate a falsehood.

The Fifteenth Alabama statue was not the only monument that Joshua Chamberlain opposed in the early 1900s. He also scuttled a proposal to build one honoring himself on Little Round Top. The details remain somewhat murky, but by late 1909, Maine state historian Henry Burrage had secured permission from the Gettysburg National Park Commission to place a monument to Chamberlain within the Twentieth Maine's lines. On November 22, he wrote to the former colonel recommending a spot on a boulder near the unit's left flank marker. At least two further pieces of correspondence appear to be missing—a response from Chamberlain and a note from Burrage to John Nicholson of the Gettysburg National Park Commission—for the next letter on record is dated December 15, 1909. In that note, John Nicholson wrote to Burrage, "If he has not interest enough in the matter why should be push him. Let it go." The proposed location of the monument was awfully close to where Oates had wanted to put his marker—perhaps even the same boulder—and Chamberlain may have balked at the optics of securing a monument for himself so soon after denying one to his opponent. Either way, Chamberlain's less than enthusiastic response to plans for a personal monument offers a further counter to claims that he tried to seize all the glory for himself.[93]

By the early 1900s, the basic narrative of the fight on Little Round Top had taken shape. It was a relatively quiet period in many ways, with the annual reunions now more about comradery than establishing the unit's history and record of deeds. Roughly one hundred attended the 1896 reunion in Waldoboro, but the numbers were dwindling. By 1907, only fifty-two attended, including survivors of the unit and their "ladies." In that year, only 196 of those who had been at Gettysburg were still among the living.[94]

In 1908, the Commonwealth of Pennsylvania began preparing to host a fiftieth-anniversary commemoration of the Battle of Gettysburg in 1913. While the idea may have originated with Henry Huidekoper, formerly of the 150th Pennsylvania, Gettysburg National Park commissioner John Nicholson got the ball rolling with a planning meeting in late 1908 at Gettysburg's Eagle Hotel. Ultimately, planning this massive event took longer than the war itself and became, for many, the trip of a lifetime. Not surprisingly, Joshua Chamberlain served on the organizing committee and spent a great deal of time helping to plan the reunion.[95]

All veterans were invited to attend, not just those who had been present at Gettysburg. Some states offered no financial support to veterans who wanted to make the journey, but Maine made an appropriation that would fully fund the cost of railroad transportation and meals for anyone who had actually participated in the battle before allocating any leftover money to other veterans. Those wishing to foot their own bill had to pay $20.95 for the railroad fare from Portland to Gettysburg, plus extra for meals. Once in Gettysburg, all lodging and meals were covered. As veterans indicated their interest in attending, Maine's adjutant general cross-checked their names against the roster printed fifteen years earlier in *Maine at Gettysburg* to see whether they were eligible to have their expenses paid. At least three men whose names were not in that publication made an application and engaged in a lengthy back-and-forth pleading their case for having been on Little Round Top and thus deserving of traveling at state expense, but none succeeded.[96]

In mid-June, Maine's commissioner for the reunion sent a voucher for a railroad ticket and detailed information to all of those who were planning to attend. He also noted that "the commissioners feel it their duty to call the attention of aged and decrepit comrades to the necessity of carefully considering their condition, as no one who has any doubt as to his ability to stand the strain should venture the journey." Ultimately, Joshua Chamberlain did not attend due to poor health, despite having taken such a part in the preparations, while Ellis Spear backed out at the last minute because of his own medical issues.[97]

The arrangements called for a special train to leave Portland at 7:00 p.m. on June 28 and arrive in Gettysburg roughly twenty-four hours later. The men would have five full days in Pennsylvania before departing for home at 7:30 a.m. on July 5. Event organizers anticipated between forty thousand and fifty thousand attendees, but the final tally was fifty-five thousand. A tent city was set up on the southern edge of Gettysburg on the fields between Confederate Avenue and the Emmitsburg Road.[98]

On the second day of the reunion, July 2, 1913, the fiftieth anniversary of the Twentieth Maine's stand on Little Round Top, fifty-eight members of the unit assembled on that very ground to hold their annual reunion. Four men had fallen ill and remained behind in their tents. Most of the men who had come to the reunion were veterans of the great battle, and fifty of the fifty-eight men on Little Round Top on July 2, 1913, had been there fifty years earlier. They represented slightly more than a third of the Twentieth Maine's 144 living veterans of the Battle of Gettysburg. Those assembled on the rocky hill had brought from Maine "the same dear, though battered old flag which waved over them on that crucial day." There were speeches and songs, but mostly the men just talked with one another. The association's secretary and treasurer, Osgood Martin, noted, "The reunion was one of great enthusiasm, mingled with tender memories." The reunion's best chronicler, Thomas Flagel, concludes, "The Reunion's most bountiful outcome was its ability to successfully combat loneliness. The isolation in which many lived was temporarily yet profoundly absolved by the encounter of thousands who endured similar experiences, and who longed to form new memories through that intrinsic support."[99]

Concurrent with the battle's fiftieth anniversary, *Hearst's Magazine* published "Through Blood and Fire at Gettysburg," Joshua Chamberlain's final account of the fight on Little Round Top. Chamberlain had agreed to write two articles, one on Fredericksburg (which appeared in *Cosmopolitan* in January 1913 right after the semi-centennial of that battle) and the one for *Hearst's*. Both magazines were owned by William Randolph Hearst, the sensationalist newspaperman and icon of the "yellow journalism" era, and both of Chamberlain's articles were sensationalized by the editors.

In the Gettysburg story, there is a full letter purportedly from a Confederate, which reads:

Dear Sir: I want to tell you of a little passage in the battle of Round Top, Gettysburg, concerning you and me, which I am now glad of. Twice in that fight I had your life in my hands. I got a safe place between two rocks, and drew bead fair and square on you. You were standing in the open behind the center of your line, full exposed. I knew your rank by your uniform and your actions, and I thought it a mighty good thing to put you out of the way. I rested my gun on the rock and took steady aim. I started to pull the trigger, but some queer notion stopped me. Then I got ashamed of my weakness and went through the same motions again. I had you, perfectly certain. But that same queer something shut right down on me. I couldn't pull the trigger, and, gave it up—that is, your life. I am glad of it now, and hope you are. Yours Truly.

The letter seems preposterous and does not appear in any of the collections of Chamberlain papers. Historian Thomas Desjardin suggests that *Hearst's* editors may well have taken a brief reference to an Alabama soldier firing at Chamberlain but hitting another man who stepped in the way and turned it into the letter above. "The Hearst Editors mutilated and 'corrected' my 'Gettysburg' so that I have not tried to get copies," Chamberlain lamented to a correspondent who had offered their congratulations on the publication. "It is much curtailed and changed by the insertion of 'connective tissue' by the Editor."[100]

Before these two accounts were published, Ellis Spear was one of Chamberlain's biggest supporters. As previously detailed, Spear wrote one of the first public accounts of the battle in late July 1863, telling the readers of the *Portland Daily Press*, "In the hottest part of the fight, when it was perhaps uncertain whether we should hold the place assigned us or be driven back, the Colonel ordered a charge! Nothing could have been more opportune." In 1864, he and Tom Chamberlain sought out and oversaw the medical care that saved a grievously wounded Joshua Chamberlain. In 1880, he had written Chamberlain congratulating him on his handling of the disputed gubernatorial election: "Your will and firm action has saved the state . . . I laughed when I saw and heard the threats against you. The men who made them did not see you in the hell-fire of Petersburg." In 1899, Spear advocated for Chamberlain to be appointed collector of the Port of Portland, a patronage job that would have eased his former commander's tenuous financial condition. Writing to Maine congressman Amos Allen, Spear noted that Chamberlain was "relied upon" by his superior officers during the war, making him the "most conspicuous in the state." He added, "I was with him when he was wounded, and I know how severely it was." In late 1910, Spear invited Chamberlain to visit him in Washington and conversed freely and in a friendly manner with his old commander. But his blood boiled when Spear read Chamberlain's Fredericksburg and then Gettysburg stories. He wrote in a personal critique of the Fredericksburg article soon after, "The word painting is extraordinary, but one notices that all the pictures, more or less directly, illustrate Chamberlain."[101]

Spear was always a rather taciturn man, and one—as evidenced by his reaction to the death of John West at Middleburg in June 1863—whose overriding concept of war was one of brutality and loss. Chamberlain's earlier accounts of the war in general and Gettysburg in particular had been well written and dramatic but largely without literary flourishes. These two accounts, however, took on a far more romantic tone. Some of the change was due to the not-fully-known work of the editors at *Cosmopolitan* and *Hearst's*, and some of it was no doubt Chamberlain's own attempt to write in a more literary style that he thought the magazines' readers desired. Spear went through the Fredericksburg account nearly line by line. To an assertion that the musketry fire of the Rebels blended with the setting sun, Spear pointed out that the Union soldiers faced south and their foes north, making such a scene impossible. Chamberlain described his horse as a majestic steed, while Spear asserted it was "a 'chunky,' clumsy old stallion of the County Fair variety." Spear contended that the image of Chamberlain sleeping between two bodies on the battlefield was ludicrous and never happened. Perhaps most damaging, Ames "should have been more prominent in the 'Story,'" which led to Spear's belief that Chamberlain was seeking too much of the glory.[102]

When Chamberlain's "Through Blood and Fire at Gettysburg" appeared in the June 1913 issue of *Hearst's*, the title alone was enough to prompt a response from Spear. On June 12, 1913, Spear's "The Left at Gettysburg" was published in the *National Tribune*, the publication of the Grand Army of the Republic. Spear never mentioned Chamberlain's name or even referred to him by his rank, and early on he called Strong Vincent "the true hero of Little Round Top (if any officer is to have that honor)." It is difficult to narrate a story of the Twentieth's fight without mentioning Chamberlain, which led Spear to use the passive voice extensively. Spear said he had barely returned to the left flank after walking along the unit's line when "I heard a shout of 'Forward!' on the right and progressing to the left, and, looking saw the center advancing. Wondering for an instant what this might mean (as I received no orders), the next impulse was that if any part of the regiment was charging all must." It was not an officer— not Chamberlain certainly, Spear implied without saying—who began the charge, but rather the common soldiers who, of their own volition, moved forward to cover their comrades who had fallen in their front and were now in the ground between the two units. This action "helps illustrate the common saying that 'the battle of Gettysburg was fought by the men.'" Spear's initial statement that he "heard a shout of 'Forward'" and then the admission that he wondered what it meant makes clear that his later narration of the origins of the charge was not an eyewitness account. It also directly contradicts what he had written in 1863. Spear concluded, "I do not mean to disparage the officers, high or low. They shared in the battle fully and honorably," but there was only one worth singling out: "Its first

Colonel, Adelbert Ames, though young, was a trained soldier, with the original instincts of a soldier, and his firm and made skillful discipline and instruction had made out of the original town-meeting enlisted men of the 20th Me. a regiment which was always ready to charge."[103]

Chamberlain was dead within a year, while Spear lived only until 1917. It is lamentable that these two former comrades and colleagues, men who had once been close and had relied on each other in battle, went to their deathbeds as friends no more. We will never know to what extent that controversy was manufactured by the sensationalist editing of others who twisted Chamberlain's words and which of the passages that offended Spear were not actually from his former commander's pen. By 1913 Chamberlain's health was failing, however, and he missed the fiftieth anniversary of the battle due to that ill health. He had to know the end was near and realize these two articles were among the last things he would ever write. Perhaps it was not just the magazine editors who sensationalized things but also Chamberlain who sought to secure his place in history by playing up his own role in both battles. Many Chamberlain detractors have invoked the Spear-Chamberlain controversy in recent years as evidence of the colonel's self-centeredness, but the story is more complex than that simple interpretation.

When Joshua Chamberlain passed away on February 24, 1914, the greatest champion of the Twentieth Maine's story and legacy was gone. The death of Leonard Cummings in 1939, the last living member of the Twentieth Maine who had stood on Little Round Top, meant there would be no new accounts of the battle by an eyewitness who had felt the bullets, seen the charge, and lived to talk about the "great deeds" on that July afternoon.

The men of the Twentieth might have worried that their story would be lost and their reputation in endangered once the last member of the unit had passed, but they had little to fear. The year before Leonard Cummings died, Maine author Kenneth Roberts published a short meditation titled "Maine Stories I'd Like to Write" in his *Trending into Maine*. After offering a few vignettes on the remarkable activities of various Maine regiments during the Civil War, Roberts noted, "But of all those regiments, the one that should be longest remembered is the Twentieth Maine—and certainly no commander in any army at any period of the world's history was more worthy of admiration and emulation than the colonel of that regiment, Joshua Lawrence Chamberlain of Brewer, Maine."[104]

Roberts never wrote the story of the Twentieth Maine and Joshua Chamberlain, but soon others were doing so. In 1957, John Pullen's *The Twentieth Maine* was published by J. B. Lippincott Company. One of the first books on a Civil War regiment not to be written by a veteran, Pullen's work, along with Alan Nolan's on the Iron Brigade four years later, sparked the unit history era of Civil War writing. A journalist by profession, Pullen writes with exceptional skill, and his storytelling ability is nearly unmatched. In the 1950s, most writers were still telling history through the eyes of great men, but Pullen gave voice to the soldiers in the ranks and introduced the world to people like William T. Livermore and Will Owen. Three years later, Willard Wallace published the first full-length biography of Joshua Chamberlain, *Soul of the Lion*, with the result that there were books on both the unit and its most famous commander available for the Civil War Centennial.

Ironically, the most influential book to use the Twentieth Maine and Chamberlain as significant characters is a work of fiction. English professor Michael Shaara penned *The Killer Angels* in the early 1970s and featured Joshua Chamberlain as one of his main characters in an epic on the Battle of Gettysburg. *The Killer Angels* is a beautifully written book, so much so that it won the Pulitzer Prize for Fiction in 1975. Despite that honor, the book sold slowly until it was turned into the movie *Gettysburg* in 1993.

Presenting the three-day Battle of Gettysburg in a bit over four hours on the big screen, the final act before *Gettysburg*'s intermission portrays the defense of Little Round Top on the second day of that battle, with the climactic scene dramatizing the Mainers' bayonet charge. Despite a cast of more established names, Jeff Daniels stole the show with his portrayal of Joshua Chamberlain. Some have critiqued *The Killer Angels* and *Gettysburg* for how they interpret certain events and characters, but when it comes to the Twentieth Maine and Joshua Chamberlain, both get more right than wrong.

The success of *Gettysburg* dramatically increased visitation to the Gettysburg National Military Park and sparked a Chamberlain mania. Nearly every visitor to Gettysburg wanted to see the spot where Chamberlain and the Twentieth Maine made their stand, and many then went into the town to find T-shirts with "Don't Call Me Lawrence" emblazed on them. They could purchase those shirts with a credit card that displayed a Mort Kunstler image of the Twentieth's advance, allowing them to "charge with Chamberlain." Then, if so inclined, they could retire to a nearby watering hole and drink a Chamberlain Pale Ale courtesy of Shipyard Brewing Company.

On the academic front, more than a dozen books on the Twentieth Maine or Chamberlain were published before the millennium. Some were reprints of earlier works, such as Oliver Norton's *Attack and Defense of Little Round Top*. Norton had been Strong Vincent's bugler and was upset by the focus on Chamberlain over Vincent in the early 1900s. He would likely have been mortified that the reprint of his book in 1992 featured a painting of Chamberlain and the Twentieth Maine on its cover. Somewhat predictably, all the public adulation of the Twentieth Maine and Joshua Chamberlain eventually prompted a backlash. The unit performed admirably, nearly everyone admits, but critics argue that writers and speakers who overemphasize their contributions diminish other units that were just as important or even more so.

Most of the backlash has been against Chamberlain. In his 2002 work on the Fifteenth Alabama at Gettysburg, *Storming Little Round Top*, historian Phillip Thomas Tucker contends, "The reality that Chamberlain's own versions of Gettysburg were self-serving and exaggerated has been conveniently overlooked and ignored by most of today's historians." Over the past several years, many writers and interpreters of the battlefield have referenced Theodore Gerrish's account of the battle to suggest that the charge was not solely Chamberlain's idea and have invoked Ellis Spear's bitter post-1913 writings to "show" that it was not only outsiders but even members of the unit who were unhappy with their former colonel. Writing an appendix titled "The Hero of Little Round Top?" in *Don't Give an Inch*, Ryan Quint notes Spear's "vitriolic" comments on Chamberlain and then references Gerrish's argument that it was Melcher who led the charge as proof that "there were other soldiers in the 20th Maine who did not quite agree with Chamberlain's narrative of the Mainers' bayonet charge." In a review of Ronald C. White's 2023 biography of Chamberlain, eminent Civil War historian Allen Guelzo pans both the book and its subject:

"Apart from the notoriety Chamberlain has won from being at the center of a marvelous novel and an epic motion picture, it is not clear why Chamberlain deserves to be the object of so much bouquet-throwing." Guelzo also invokes Spear, employing his 1916 line that Chamberlain was "absolutely unable to tell the truth." Chamberlain had his flaws, but the bulk of the arguments by his critics are easily disproved, while many of the sources they invoke are so completely lacking in context that using them reveals more about their own overeagerness to tear him down than it does anything about the man himself. Arguing that his reputation was a twentieth-century creation is verifiably untrue. Quoting Theodore Gerrish to cast aspersions on Chamberlain's leadership on Little Round Top conveniently overlooks the fact that *he was not there*. Ellis Spear clearly soured on his old commander late in life, but his post-1913 accounts that diminished Chamberlain directly contradicted almost everything he had written up until that year.[105]

But among the general public, the admiration for both the Twentieth and its most famous commander remains. In 2019, "Ballad of the 20th Maine" by a band named the Ghost of Paul Revere was named Maine's official ballad by Governor Janet Mills. Told from the perspective of Andrew Tozier, the song narrates the fight on Little Round Top and that pivotal moment: "And then appeared our lion, he was roaring bayonets / And we charged on down the mountain with what forces we had left."

Military staff rides and leadership development programs spend extensive time studying Joshua Chamberlain and the Twentieth Maine, often vying for space along the thin ridge known as Vincent's Spur. Due to this popularity and the incredible foot traffic it has brought to Little Round Top, the hill was closed to the public from July 2022 to June 2024 for a nearly two-year-long rehabilitation that restored old and created new pathways in the name of sustainability and protecting the site. The park took the opportunity to install additional interpretive markers at the same time. Four new displays titled "Hold to the Last," "The Tenacious 20th Maine," "Bayonets," and "Chamberlain Avenue" offer visitors much to ponder. The display titled "Bayonets" includes brief accounts of the bayonet charge by Chamberlain, Oates, Gerrish, and Spear with this instruction: "Read them as if you were a historian. Which accounts would you believe? Whose version of events were correct?"

The short answer is this: None of them. Not by themselves. The men in the Twentieth Maine understood this in the postwar years, and so did their commander. They spent nearly fifty years publicly offering their reminiscences of what happened on that fateful day, hearing the input and reactions of their comrades, and adding or correcting details. Over time, they added to their individual memories of what happened in their immediate vicinity an understanding of the broader experiences of their comrades, the other units in their brigade, and even those on the other side of the battle lines. From these many individual battle recollections in the 1880s there emerged larger narratives of the unit's fight put together by Samuel Miller for their reunion in 1881, by Howard Prince for the dedication of their monument in 1889, and by Joshua Chamberlain for *Maine at Gettysburg* (1898). Their story was written and their reputation established long before *The Killer Angels* or *Gettysburg*. Some small points of contention remain, and some details are lost to history, but the work the veterans did to tell and correct their stories of what happened on Little Round Top means that, as Joshua Chamberlain said in 1889, "what you did, the world knows."

Conclusion

Fourteen-year-old Mildred Grant wanted to know about the Battle of Gettysburg. Her grandfather, Captain Samuel Keene of Company F, Twentieth Maine, had been in the thickest of the fighting and suffered a severe wound in his side as a result, but he had been killed a year later outside of Petersburg, Virginia, and she could not ask him. A decade after the war's end, however, her grandmother had married Ellis Spear, the unit's second-in-command at Gettysburg—so Mildred wrote to ask her step-grandfather for his memories. On March 14, 1910, he responded.[1]

"Dear Mildred," he began, "I was much surprised to learn from your letter that you were not at the battle of Gettysburg. So many people were there that I do not fully understand how you missed it. It is not unreasonable, therefore, that you should wish to know something about it. I fear that you will never know all about it. Nobody does, and nobody ever did or ever will. It was a very mixed up and extensive affair." After explaining the arrival of the Confederates, he offered a caveat: "I did not see the whole of the battle; but I saw enough, and was quite satisfied with that. Nor did I hear anybody complain of lack; there was enough to go around." He narrated the back-and-forth fight, focusing on the actions in front of Sam Keene's Company F and highlighting Andrew Tozier's stand. And then there were things that occurred in the heat of the battle that were inexplicable.

> One of our men who had a very long gun and a long bayonet fixed on the end ran through one Confederate, and then another and another until he had six, like a string of fish, and then he put the gun over his shoulder & marched off, satisfied that he had done his share while six pairs of legs were wriggling behind him. Another man, instead of returning his ramrod to the gun after loading, ran it down his throat, to save time

and then held it until he wanted to load again. The Colonel got off his horse, seized a rail in both hands & rushed at the enemy. . . . I should not forget to add that the Colonel's horse, emulating the spirit of the Colonel, rushed after him & fell upon the enemy biting and kicking.

But, he cautioned, those tales may all have been made up. "A great many deeds of valor were performed, but in the excitement of the time and the mental occupation & close attention to the business, they were not noticed; but may have been invented since, after much reflection and in an amplified form—It is much easier to tell about a battle than to fight it; and safer, especially after a lapse of 47 years and the witnesses have become few and scattered."[2]

By the time Ellis Spear penned this remarkable letter, there had been dozens of accounts of the Twentieth Maine's stand on Little Round Top, and yet he recognized that no one person had the whole picture. Each man had experienced the combat and its aftermath in very personal, very different ways and, in some cases, contradictory to what others perceived. But one thing was nearly universal: a continued disbelief in what they had done and accomplished. Almost fifty years later, Spear could only describe the bayonet charge and its stunning success in the language of the supernatural: From the soldier bayoneting Confederates as though they were fish to Chamberlain swinging a fence rail to the colonel's horse joining in the fight, the men of the Twentieth Maine became mythical heroes.

But there may have been another reason. Describing those momentous actions in a nonsupernatural way would have meant reliving the brutality of that firefight: the death or mortal wounding of thirty-eight men; the severe side wound suffered by Mildred's grandfather, Samuel Keene; and the visuals of the man bayoneted in the head while trying to grab the Fifteenth Alabama's flag. Like most of the Twentieth's veterans, Ellis Spear talked about his experiences in the postwar years—but always at a distance.

Throughout the letter to Mildred, Ellis Spear's sense of pride in belonging to such a regiment as the Twentieth Maine permeates. And well it should. In ten short months, they had transformed from a bunch of untrained civilians into a fighting force that had held its ground "at all hazards" on Little Round Top, contributing substantially to the Union's victory in the war's pivotal battle and earning a reputation that persists to this day. "In the hour of battle they knew the meaning of 'Dirigo' on your State escutcheon," Joshua Chamberlain reflected in 1865. "May their memory be as green as your Pines."[3]

Notes

Abbreviations
CMSR Compiled Military Service Record
GNMP Gettysburg National Military Park Library
JLC Joshua Lawrence Chamberlain
LOC Library of Congress
MeAGR *Annual Report of the Adjutant General of the State of Maine*
MSA Maine State Archives
NA National Archives
OR *The War of the Rebellion: A Compilation of the Official Records of the Union and Confederate Armies*
PHC Pejepscot History Center
UMO University of Maine at Orono
WCO William C. Oates

Dedication
1. "The Maine 20th at Gettysburg," *Eastern Argus*, December 20, 1865.

Introduction
1. Report of Joshua L. Chamberlain, July 6, 1863, in *OR*, Ser. I, Vol. 27, Pt. 1, 623.
2. Gerrish, *Army Life*, 107; Holman Melcher, "The Twentieth Maine at Gettysburg," *Lincoln County News*, March 13, 1885.
3. Report of Joshua L. Chamberlain, July 6, 1863, in *OR*, Ser. I, Vol. 27, Pt. 1, 623; William T. Livermore, "Extracts from a Veteran's Diary," *Lincoln County News*, June 22, 1883; Gerrish, *Army Life*, 108.
4. Chapter 6 of the present work further explains the process by which that roster was created.

Chapter 1
1. Spear, "The Civil War Recollections," in Spear et al., *The Civil War Recollections of General Ellis Spear*, 9; Nathan Clark Journal, September 8, 1862, MSA.

2. Joseph Bartlett to John Hodsdon, November 10, 1864, 20th Maine Regimental Correspondence, MSA.

3. Spear, "The Civil War Recollections," in Spear et al., *The Civil War Recollections of General Ellis Spear*, 4–5; Nathan Clark Journal, [undated entry on p. 2], MSA.

4. *MeAGR 1861*, Appendix A, 14, 20, 45.

5. *MeAGR 1862*, Appendix A, 9, 30, 31.

6. Lysander Hill to Israel Washburn, August 23, 1862, 20th Maine Regimental Correspondence, MSA. It is unclear what, if any, action was taken against Hiram Bliss Jr. The twenty-six-year-old never enlisted, lived until 1898, and is buried in Washington, Maine.

7. Charles Greenleaf to Israel Washburn, August 21, 1862, 20th Maine Regimental Correspondence, MSA.

8. Samuel Keene Diary, August 13, 1862, PHC; Pullen, *The Twentieth Maine*, 9; Spear, "The Civil War Recollections," in Spear et al., *The Civil War Recollections of General Ellis Spear*, 6; Henry Pero Pension File, NA. Both Glazier Estabrook and Jeremiah Stevens were forty-nine years old at the time of their enlistment, and either may be the person to whom Spear refers. Stevens's wife died on June 25, 1862, which may have prompted his enlistment.

9. *MeAGR 1862*; Clark and Plant, *Of Age*, 1.

10. *MeAGR 1862*.

11. Desjardin, *Stand Firm Ye Boys from Maine*, 169–80. The information on the professions does not come from all of the enlistees in 1862, but rather from those who were with the unit at Gettysburg; Glatthaar, "A Tale of Two Armies," 329.

12. William T. Livermore Pension File, NA; William T. Livermore Diary, UMO; Glatthaar, "A Tale of Two Armies," 317.

13. *MeAGR 1862*; Desjardin, *Stand Firm Ye Boys from Maine*, 169–80. The information on the professions does not come from all of the enlistees in 1862, but rather from those who were with the unit at Gettysburg. On the social advantages of height, see Judge and Cable, "The Effect of Physical Height on Workplace Success and Income."

14. *MeAGR 1861*; *MeAGR 1862*.

15. JLC, *The Passing of the Armies*, 13; Gallagher, *The Union War*, 2; William Owen to Abbie Owen, May 26, 1863, Milo Historical Society.

16. Goodheart, *1861*, 121.

17. U.S. Census Bureau, "Population of the United States in 1860," iv, xiii; William T. Livermore Diary, September 7, 1862, UMO.

18. Glatthaar, "A Tale of Two Armies," 317, 330; U.S. Census Bureau, *Statistics of the United States in 1860*, 512; *MeAGR 1862*, 7, 15, Appendix A, 32, 45: William T. Livermore Diary, August 29, 1862, UMO.

19. *MeAGR 1861*, 43; Hezekiah Long to Sarah Long, April 4, 1863, in Richardson's, *Hard Times*, 34; Giuseppe Garibaldi quoted in Rable, *Fredericksburg! Fredericksburg!*, 7.

20. William Lamson to Jennie Lamson, August 10, 1862, in Engert, *Maine to the Wilderness*, 16; Spear, "The Story of the Raising," 7.

21. William Lamson to Jennie Lamson, August 20, 1862, in Engert, *Maine to the Wilderness*, 18; William T. Livermore Diary, September 7, 1862, UMO.

22. Spear, "The Story of the Raising," 8–9.

23. Ames, *Adelbert Ames*, 1, 4, 59; Morrison, *The Best School in the World*, 63, 69, 91, 98, 114, 117, 120.

24. Report of Charles Griffin, July 23, 1861, in *OR*, Ser. I, Vol. 2, 394; Adelbert Ames to Parents, December 4, 1861, in Ames, *Chronicles from the Nineteenth Century*, 1:2–3.

25. Adelbert Ames to Parents, December 4, 1861, in Ames, *Chronicles from the Nineteenth Century*, 1:3; Adelbert Ames to Parents, December 21, 1861, in Ames, *Chronicles from the Nineteenth Century*, 1:3; Adelbert Ames to Parents, April 18, 1862, in Ames, *Chronicles from the Nineteenth Century*, 1:10.

26. Adelbert Ames to Parents, December 4, 1861, in Ames, *Chronicles from the Nineteenth Century*, 1:2; Adelbert Ames to Parents, January 21, 1862, in Ames, *Chronicles from the Nineteenth Century*, 1:6.

27. Report of George W. Getty, July 8, 1862, in *OR*, Ser. I, Vol. 11, Pt. 2, 253; Ames, *Adelbert Ames*, 88, 93.

28. Spear, "The Civil War Recollections," in Spear et al., *The Civil War Recollections of General Ellis Spear*, 9.

29. Spear, "The Story of the Raising," 11.

30. Spear, "The Civil War Recollections," in Spear et al., *The Civil War Recollections of General Ellis Spear*, 6–7.

31. Spear, "The Civil War Recollections," in Spear et al., *The Civil War Recollections of General Ellis Spear*, 6–7; Adelbert Ames to JLC, October 18, 1864, Joshua Lawrence Chamberlain Papers, Box 1, Manuscript Division, LOC; *MeAGR 1862*.

32. Ames quote in Ames, *Adelbert Ames*, 171.

33. Nathan Clark Journal, September 3, 6, 1862, MSA; William T. Livermore Diary, September 5, 6, 1862, UMO; Spear, "The Civil War Recollections," in Spear et al., *The Civil War Recollections of General Ellis Spear*, 10.

34. Gerrish, *Army Life*, 18; William T. Livermore Diary, September 7, 1862, UMO.

35. Gerrish, *Army Life*, 19; James Rundlett to Cyrus Rundlett, September 9, 1862, in Wells, *Rundlett's War*, 11; Hezekiah Long to Sarah Long, September 19, 1862, in Richardson's, *Hard Times*, 6; Krick, *Civil War Weather in Virginia*, 71.

36. James Rundlett to Elizabeth Rundlett, August 31, 1862, in Wells, *Rundlett's War*, 7; Spear, "The Civil War Recollections," in Spear et al., *The Civil War Recollections of General Ellis Spear*, 11.

37. *MeAGR 1861*, 48; Spear, "The Civil War Recollections," in Spear et al., *The Civil War Recollections of General Ellis Spear*, 7.

38. Holman Melcher to Nathaniel Melcher, September 10, 1862, in Styple, *With a Flash of His Sword*, 3; Samuel Keene Diary, September 12, 1862, PHC.

39. Harlan Bailey to Maria Bailey, September 23, 1862, Vertical File Collection 6—20th ME, GNMP.

40. Gordon, *A Broken Regiment*, 27, 31–34.

41. Rafuse, *McClellan's War*, 333.

42. Spear, "The Civil War Recollections," in Spear et al., *The Civil War Recollections of General Ellis Spear*, 14; William T. Livermore Diary, September 24, 1862, UMO; *MeAGR 1862*; 20th Maine Consolidated Morning Reports, MSA.

43. William Lamson to Jennie Lamson, October 12, 1862, in Engert, *Maine to the Wilderness*, 31; William Lamson to Jennie Lamson, November 10, 1862, in Engert, *Maine to the Wilderness*, 37; William Lamson to Jennie Lamson, February 24, 1863, in Engert, *Maine to the Wilderness*, 57; William T. Livermore Diary, September 17, 1862, UMO.

44. Holman Melcher to Nathaniel Melcher, October 23, 1862, in Styple, *With a Flash of His Sword*, 7; Hezekiah Long to Sarah Long, December 28, 1862, in Richardson's, *Hard Times*, 21; Brennan, "The Civil War Diet," 39, 99, 106, 108.

45. Oates, *A Woman of Valor*, 309; Charles Francis Adams Jr. to Charles Francis Adams, September 5, 1863, in Ford, *A Cycle of Adams Letters*, 2:79.

46. Gerrish, *Army Life*, 66; Samuel Keene Diary, December 16, 1862, and January 9, 1863, PHC.

47. Hezekiah Long to Sarah Long, December 7, 1862, in Richardson's, *Hard Times*, 18; James Rundlett to Elizabeth Rundlett, February 8, 1863, in Wells, *Rundlett's War*, 65; Tom Chamberlain quote in Pullen, *The Twentieth Maine*, 39.

48. Gerrish, *Army Life*, 47; 20th Maine Consolidated Morning Reports, MSA; *MeAGR 1862*; *MeAGR 1863*; JLC to Fanny Chamberlain, November 3, 1862, Joshua Lawrence Chamberlain Papers, Box 4, Manuscript Division, LOC; *Dedication of the Twentieth Maine Monuments at Gettysburg*, 16.

49. Adelbert Ames to Parents, October 10, 1862, in Ames, *Chronicles from the Nineteenth Century*, 1:14.

50. Hezekiah Long to Sarah Long, January 9, 1863, in Richardson's, *Hard Times*, 21; Samuel Keene Diary, September 25–December 4, 1862, PHC.

51. Hess, *Civil War Infantry Tactics*, xiii, 80; Stiles, *Custer's Trials*, 29.

52. Rice, *Reminiscences of Abraham Lincoln*, 218–19.

53. Hess, *Civil War Infantry Tactics*, xx, 139.

54. Spear, "The Personal Memoranda," in Spear et al., *The Civil War Recollections of General Ellis Spear*, 296; Morrison, *The Best School in the World*, 87.

55. Gerrish, *Army Life*, 45–46.

56. Foote, *The Gentlemen and the Roughs*, 10; Hezekiah Long to Sarah Long, October 26, 1862, in Richardson's, *Hard Times*, 10; Spear, "The Civil War Recollections," in Spear et al., *The Civil War Recollections of General Ellis Spear*, 9; Samuel Keene Diary, September 26, 1862, PHC.

57. Spear, "The Civil War Recollections," in Spear et al., *The Civil War Recollections of General Ellis Spear*, 9, 14; *MeAGR 1862*; *MeAGR 1863*; Adelbert Ames to Abner Coburn, March 10, 1863, 20th Maine Correspondence, MSA; Adelbert Ames to Parents, January 10, 1863, in Ames, *Chronicles from the Nineteenth Century*, 1:17; Correspondence all in 20th Maine Infantry Regimental Letter, Endorsement, and Order Book, vol. 2 of 7, RG 94, Records of the Adjutant General's Office, NA.

58. Hezekiah Long to Sarah Long, October 26, 1862, in Richardson's, *Hard Times*, 10; Holman Melcher to Nathaniel Melcher, February 11, 1863, in Styple, *With a Flash of His Sword*, 20; William Lamson to Jennie Lamson, December 16, 1862, in Engert, *Maine to the Wilderness*, 45; James Rundlett to Elizabeth Rundlett, December 2, 1862, in Wells, *Rundlett's War*, 41; William T. Livermore Diary, October 5, 1862, UMO.

59. Adelbert Ames to Israel Washburn, October 28, 1862, 20th Maine Regimental Correspondence, MSA; JLC to Fanny Chamberlain, October 26, 1862, Joshua Lawrence Chamberlain Papers, Box 4, Manuscript Division, LOC; Hezekiah Long to Sarah Long, October 26, 1862, in Richardson's, *Hard Times*, 10.

60. U.S. Census Bureau, "Population Schedule," 1860; U.S. Census Bureau, *Statistics of the Population of the United States in 1870*, 397; Gerrish, *Army Life*, 68; Holman Melcher to Nathaniel Melcher, October 23, 1862, in Styple, *With a Flash of His Sword*, 7. Many studies cite 90 percent as the literacy rate of Union soldiers, but an examination of the census shows there to have been 167,724 white males over the age of twenty in Maine in 1860, of whom only 4,282 were identified as unable to read and write, giving a literacy rate of 97.447 percent.

61. William Lamson to Jennie Lamson, October 12, 1862, in Engert, *Maine to the Wilderness*, 32; William Lamson to Jennie H. Lamson, November 5, 1862, in Engert, *Maine to the Wilderness*, 34; William T. Livermore Diary, March 28, 1863, UMO.

62. Samuel Keene Diary, January 5, 1863, PHC; JLC to Joseph Badger, January 6, 1863, in Desjardin, *Joshua L. Chamberlain*, 187.

63. James Rundlett to Elizabeth Rundlett, September 23, 1862, in Wells, *Rundlett's War*, 17.

64. William T. Livermore Diary, October 5, 1862, UMO; Confederate soldier quote from Krick, "The Army of Northern Virginia in September 1862," 41.

65. James Rundlett to Cyrus Rundlett, October 13, 1862, in Wells, *Rundlett's War*, 26.

66. Nathan Clark Journal, September 11, 1862, MSA.

67. Holman Melcher to Nathaniel Melcher, September 14, 1862, in Styple, *With a Flash of His Sword*, 5; Gerrish, *Army Life*, 55, 56, 59.

68. William T. Livermore Diary, May 6, 1863, UMO.

69. Gerrish, *Army Life*, 53; James Rundlett to Elizabeth Rundlett, November 10, 1862, in Wells, *Rundlett's War*, 35; Samuel Keene Diary, February 24, March 3, and March 12, 1863, PHC; William T. Livermore Diary, June 10, 1863, UMO.

70. Abraham Lincoln to George McClellan, October 25, 1862, in Basler, Pratt, and Dunlap, *Collected Works*, 5:474; McPherson, *Battle Cry of Freedom*, 570.

71. Nathan Clark Journal, October 29, October 30, November 8, November 16, 1862, MSA; James Rundlett to Elizabeth Rundlett, November 25, 1862, in Wells, *Rundlett's War*, 37; McPherson, *Battle Cry of Freedom*, 570.

72. McPherson, *Battle Cry of Freedom*, 571; James Rundlett to Elizabeth Rundlett, December 8, 1862, in Wells, *Rundlett's War*, 45.

73. Rable, *Fredericksburg! Fredericksburg!*, 162, 168, 170, 176; Gerrish, *Army Life*, 74.

74. Holman Melcher to Nathaniel Melcher, December 19, 1862, in Styple, *With a Flash of His Sword*, 11; Rable, *Fredericksburg! Fredericksburg!*, 191, 219.

75. Rable, *Fredericksburg! Fredericksburg!*, 216, 255–56.

76. JLC to Fanny Chamberlain, December 17, 1862, in Desjardin, *Joshua L. Chamberlain*, 179; Gerrish, *Army Life*, 76.

77. Rable, *Fredericksburg! Fredericksburg!*, 260; Holman Melcher to Nathaniel Melcher, December 19, 1862, in Styple, *With a Flash of His Sword*, 13; JLC to Fanny Chamberlain, December 17, 1862, in Desjardin, *Joshua L. Chamberlain*, 179.

78. Carter, "Four Brothers in Blue," 236; Gerrish, *Army Life*, 77.

79. Spear, "The Civil War Recollections," in Spear et al., *The Civil War Recollections of General Ellis Spear*, 20.

80. Gerrish, *Army Life*, 77–78.

81. JLC to Fanny Chamberlain, December 17, 1862, in Desjardin, *Joshua L. Chamberlain*, 180; Rable, *Fredericksburg! Fredericksburg!*, 272. The man from Company B killed at Fredericksburg was Seth Woodward.

82. JLC, "My Story of Fredericksburg," 156–58.

83. McPherson, *Battle Cry of Freedom*, 575; Rable, *Fredericksburg! Fredericksburg!*, 325; Adelbert Ames to John Hodsdon, December 28, 1862, 20th Maine Regimental Correspondence, MSA; *MeAGR 1863*; Silliker, *The Rebel Yell & the Yankee Hurrah*, 60; Gerrish, *Army Life*, 79–80; JLC to Fanny Chamberlain, December 17, 1862, in Desjardin, *Joshua L. Chamberlain*, 182.

84. Gerrish, *Army Life*, 79–80; Spear, "The Civil War Recollections," in Spear et al., *The Civil War Recollections of General Ellis Spear*, 24; James Rundlett to Elizabeth Rundlett, December 29, 1862, in Wells, *Rundlett's War*, 49.

85. Adelbert Ames to Parents, undated letter [likely from late December 1862], in Ames, *Chronicles from the Nineteenth Century*, 1:16.

86. Adelbert Ames to Parents, January 10, 1863, in Ames, *Chronicles from the Nineteenth Century*, 1:17.

87. JLC to Fanny Chamberlain, October 26, 1862, Joshua Lawrence Chamberlain Papers, Box 4, Manuscript Division, LOC.

88. 20th Maine Officers to Abner Coburn, February 6, 1863, 20th Maine Regimental Papers, MSA. The letter was signed by nineteen of the regiment's company officers, and only the names of Prentiss Fogler and Mattson Sanborn did not appear. Possibly these men were away from the unit at the time. Sanborn had not joined the unit until November 16, 1862, so he may not have felt credible signing a document about matters of which he had no firsthand knowledge.

89. *MeAGR 1862*.

90. JLC to Abner Coburn, February 26, 1863, 20th Maine Regimental Correspondence, MSA.

91. Hezekiah Long to Sarah Long, March 1, 1863, in Richardson's, *Hard Times*, 25.

92. Holman Melcher to Nathaniel Melcher, February 11, 1863, in Styple, *With a Flash of His Sword*, 21.

93. William Lamson to Jennie Lamson, March 29, 1863, in Engert, *Maine to the Wilderness*, 61; Hess, *The Rifle Musket*, 68; Guelzo, *Gettysburg*, 38.

94. Hess, *The Rifle Musket*, 107–8.

95. William T. Livermore Diary, March 27, 1863, UMO.

96. Hezekiah Long to Sarah Long, April 4, 1863, in Richardson's, *Hard Times*, 33; Nathan Clark Journal, [undated entry on p. 9], MSA; Gerrish, *Army Life*, 86; Pullen, *The Twentieth Maine*, 73–74; Hezekiah Long to Sarah Long, April 30, 1863, in Richardson's, *Hard Times*, 39.

97. James Rundlett to Elizabeth Rundlett, April 26, 1863, in Wells, *Rundlett's War*, 75; Hezekiah Long to Sarah Long, April 17, 1863, in Richardson's, *Hard Times*, 35; Hezekiah Long to Sarah Long, April 30, 1863, in Richardson's, *Hard Times*, 39.

98. JLC to Abner Coburn, May 25, 1863, in 20th Maine Regimental Correspondence, MSA; Holman Melcher to Nathaniel Melcher, April 21, 1863, in Styple, *With a Flash of His Sword*, 23.

99. Hezekiah Long to Sarah Long, May 16, 1863, in Richardson's, *Hard Times*, 46; Holman Melcher to Nathaniel Melcher, May 21, 1863, in Styple, *With a Flash of His Sword*, 28; Hezekiah Long to Sarah Long, May 22, 1863, in Richardson's, *Hard Times*, 47; *Reunions of the Twentieth Maine*, 13; Addison Ames Pension File, NA.

100. *Reunions of the Twentieth Maine Regiment Association*, 20.

CHAPTER 2

1. JLC to Israel Washburn, July 14, 1862, 20th Maine Correspondence, MSA.

2. Adelbert Ames to JLC, July 5, 1863, Joshua L. Chamberlain Letters and Reports, General Order Book, PHC.

3. JLC, *Blessed Boyhood!*, 3–5.

4. Trulock, *In the Hands of Providence*, 5.

5. JLC, *Blessed Boyhood!*, 4.

6. Trulock, *In the Hands of Providence*, 26; Borneman, *1812*, 116–18.

7. JLC, *Blessed Boyhood!*, 7; JLC, "Joshua as a Military Commander," *Sunday School Times* (Philadelphia), December 1, 1883, Joshua Lawrence Chamberlain Papers, Box 9, Manuscript Division, LOC.

8. JLC, *Blessed Boyhood!*, 13, 15.

9. JLC, *Blessed Boyhood!*, 8.

10. JLC, *Blessed Boyhood!*, 15, 20–22, 43–45.

11. JLC, *Blessed Boyhood!*, 25.

12. McKinney, *Brandy Station*, 63, fn275.

13. JLC, *Blessed Boyhood!*, 25–27.

14. JLC, *Blessed Boyhood!*, 28, 36.

15. JLC, *Blessed Boyhood!*, 36–38.

16. JLC, *Blessed Boyhood!*, 42.

17. JLC, *Blessed Boyhood!*, 39.

18. JLC, *Blessed Boyhood!*, 46; Trulock, *In the Hands of Providence*, 36.

19. JLC, *Blessed Boyhood!*, 49; Kalandarov, "Bowdoin Confederates," 1, 3. Beyond Bowdoin, the other three institutions of higher learning were Colby College (founded 1813, still open), Bangor Theological Seminary (1814–2013), and Westbrook College (1831–1996); Bowdoin College, *Bowdoin College Catalogue*, 1848.

20. JLC to "My dear Pastor," May 5, 1848, Joshua Chamberlain Collection, Correspondence, Bowdoin College.

21. JLC to "My dear Pastor," May 5, 1848, Joshua Chamberlain Collection, Correspondence, Bowdoin College; JLC, *Blessed Boyhood!*, 56.

22. JLC, *Blessed Boyhood!*, 62.

23. JLC, *Blessed Boyhood!*, 64.

24. Reynolds, *Mightier Than the Sword*, 56, 122.

25. JLC, *Blessed Boyhood!*, 65; Reynolds, *Mightier Than the Sword*, 128.

26. Reynolds, *Mightier Than the Sword*, 88; JLC, "Despotisms of Modern Europe," March 22, 1852, in Desjardin, *Joshua L. Chamberlain*, 13; JLC, *Blessed Boyhood!*, 65, 67.

27. Desjardin, *Joshua L. Chamberlain*, 73; JLC to Fanny Adams, October 23, 1853, in Desjardin, *Joshua L. Chamberlain*, 95; JLC to Fanny Adams, January 18, 1854, in Desjardin, *Joshua L. Chamberlain*, 98.

28. JLC to Fanny Adams, July 6, 1854, in Desjardin, *Joshua L. Chamberlain*, 100; JLC, *Blessed Boyhood!*, 68; JLC to Fanny Adams, July 23, 1854, in Desjardin, *Joshua L. Chamberlain*, 103.

29. JLC to Fanny Adams, April 26, 1853, in Desjardin, *Joshua L. Chamberlain*, 79; JLC to Fanny Adams, May 4, 1853, in Desjardin, *Joshua L. Chamberlain*, 81.

30. Chamberlain, *Blessed Boyhood!*, 70, 72; Wellington Newell to JLC, December 8, 1855, in, Desjardin, *Joshua L. Chamberlain*, 113; C. Chelsey to JLC, March 27, 1856, in Desjardin, *Joshua L. Chamberlain*, 135–36; E. Beaman to JLC, May 13, 1856, in Desjardin, *Joshua L. Chamberlain*, 137–38; Desjardin, *Joshua L. Chamberlain*, 129; Bowdoin College, *Bowdoin College Catalogue*, Fall 1855.

31. Bowdoin College, *Bowdoin College Catalogue*, Fall 1855, Spring 1856, Fall 1856; JLC to Nehemiah Cleveland, October 14, 1859, Joshua Chamberlain Collection, Correspondence, Bowdoin College; [Twelve students] to JLC, November 19, 1855, Joshua Chamberlain Collection, Correspondence, Bowdoin College.

32. JLC to Sarah Chamberlain, January 31, 1860, Joshua Chamberlain Collection, Correspondence, Bowdoin College; Smith, *Fanny & Joshua*, 96.

33. Fanny Chamberlain to JLC, May 4, 1852, in Desjardin, *Joshua L. Chamberlain*, 42; Fanny Chamberlain to JLC, October 10, 1852, in Desjardin, *Joshua L. Chamberlain*, 58; Desjardin, *Joshua L. Chamberlain*, 6–7.

34. JLC to Thomas Chamberlain, March 4, 1861, Joshua Chamberlain Collection, Correspondence, Bowdoin College.

35. Hatch, *History of Bowdoin College*, 119–20; Curtis, "Bowdoin Under Fire," in Minot and Snow, *Tales of Bowdoin*, 268–69.

36. JLC to Israel Washburn, July 14, 1862, 20th Maine Correspondence, MSA; undated speeches, Joshua Chamberlain Collection, Lecture Notes, Recruitment, Bowdoin College.

37. Bowdoin College, *Bowdoin College Catalogue*, 1862–1863.

38. Smith, *Fanny & Joshua*, 106; JLC to Sarah Chamberlain, February 4, 1861, Joshua Chamberlain Collection, Correspondence, Bowdoin College; JLC, *Blessed Boyhood!*, 74.

39. JLC to Israel Washburn, July 14, 1862, 20th Maine Correspondence, MSA; JLC, *Blessed Boyhood!*, 76.

40. *MeAGR 1862*, Appendix A, 9; JLC to Israel Washburn, July 14, 1862, 20th Maine Correspondence, MSA.

41. JLC to Israel Washburn, July 17, 1862, 20th Maine Correspondence, MSA; *MeAGR 1862*, Appendix D; JLC to Israel Washburn, July 22, 1862, 20th Maine Correspondence, MSA.

42. JLC to Israel Washburn, July 14, 1862, 20th Maine Correspondence, MSA; Trulock, *In the Hands of Providence*, 10–11; undated speeches, Joshua Chamberlain Collection, Lecture Notes, Recruitment, Bowdoin College.

43. Newspaper clipping in Joshua L. Chamberlain Letters and Reports, General Order Book, PHC; JLC to Israel Washburn, July 22, 1862, 20th Maine Correspondence, MSA.

44. Josiah Drummond to Israel Washburn, July 21, 1862, 20th Maine Correspondence, MSA; JLC, *Blessed Boyhood!*, 75; JLC to Fanny Chamberlain, October 26, 1862, Joshua Lawrence Chamberlain Papers, Box 4, Manuscript Division, LOC. It is possible that the "Professor Smyth" Chamberlain referenced was Egbert C. Smyth, but it seems more likely it was William Smyth.

45. Higgins, *A Sketch*, 12; JLC to Israel Washburn, August 8, 1862, 20th Maine Correspondence, MSA; JLC, *Blessed Boyhood!*, 75.

46. Father quoted in Trulock, *In the Hands of Providence*, 25; Fanny Chamberlain to JLC, November 27, 1862, quoted in Golay, *To Gettysburg and Beyond*, 107.

47. Trulock, *In the Hands of Providence*, 23–25.

48. JLC to Adelbert Ames, August 15, 1862, 20th Maine Correspondence, MSA; Spear, "The Civil War Recollections," in Spear et al., *The Civil War Recollections of General Ellis Spear*, 7.

49. "Presentation to Lt. Col. Chamberlain," *Portland Daily Press*, September 2, 1862.

50. JLC to Fanny Chamberlain, September 4, 1862, Joshua L. Chamberlain Research Files, Correspondence 1862, PHC.

51. JLC, *The Passing of the Armies*, xiii–xiv.

52. JLC to Fanny Chamberlain, September 9, 1862, Joshua L. Chamberlain Research Files, Correspondence 1862, PHC.

53. JLC to Fanny Chamberlain, September 9, 1862, Joshua L. Chamberlain Research Files, Correspondence 1862, PHC.

54. Holman Melcher to Nathaniel Melcher, September 14, 1862, in Styple, *With a Flash of His Sword*, 5.

55. John Chamberlain Journal, 4, Joshua Chamberlain Research Files, PHC.

56. JLC to Fanny Chamberlain, September 21, 1862, Navarro College Archives, photocopy in Joshua L. Chamberlain Research Files, Correspondence 1862, PHC; list of horses in Joshua L. Chamberlain Letters and Reports, General Order Book, PHC.

57. JLC to Fanny Chamberlain, September 29, 1862, Joshua L. Chamberlain Research Files, Correspondence 1862, PHC.

58. William T. Livermore Diary, October 5, 1862, UMO; "Army Correspondence," October 23, 1862, newspaper clipping, Joshua L. Chamberlain Letters and Reports, General Order Book, PHC; JLC to Fanny Chamberlain, October 12, 1862, in Desjardin, *Joshua L. Chamberlain*, 170.

59. JLC to Fanny Chamberlain, October 10, 1862, Joshua Lawrence Chamberlain Papers, Box 4, Manuscript Division, LOC; JLC to Fanny Chamberlain, October 26, 1862, Joshua Lawrence Chamberlain Papers, Box 4, Manuscript Division, LOC.

60. JLC to Fanny Chamberlain, October 26, 1862, Joshua Lawrence Chamberlain Papers, Box 4, Manuscript Division, LOC.

61. Jomini, *The Art of War*, xi–xiv; Morrison, *The Best School in the World*, 96; Reardon, *With a Sword in One Hand*, 5.

62. JLC to Fanny Chamberlain, November 4, 1862, Joshua Lawrence Chamberlain Papers, Box 4, Manuscript Division, LOC; JLC to Fanny Chamberlain, November 27, 1862, in Desjardin, *Joshua L. Chamberlain*, 177.

63. JLC to Fanny Chamberlain, November 3, 1862, Joshua Lawrence Chamberlain Papers, Box 4, Manuscript Division, LOC; JLC to Fanny Chamberlain, November 22, 1862, in Desjardin, *Joshua L. Chamberlain*, 173.

64. JLC to Fanny Chamberlain, December 17, 1862, in Desjardin, *Joshua L. Chamberlain*, 178.

65. JLC to Fanny Chamberlain, December 17, 1862, in Desjardin, *Joshua L. Chamberlain*, 179.

66. Holman Melcher to Nathaniel Melcher, December 19, 1862, in Styple, *With a Flash of His Sword*, 13; George Carleton letter quoted in Trulock, *In the Hands of Providence*, 95.

67. JLC, "My Story of Fredericksburg," 154; JLC to Fanny Chamberlain, December 17, 1862, in Desjardin, *Joshua L. Chamberlain*, 180.

68. JLC, "My Story of Fredericksburg," 156.

69. JLC, "My Story of Fredericksburg," 158; Desjardin, "A Broken Bond?" 24, 27.

70. JLC to Fanny Chamberlain, December 17, 1862, in Desjardin, *Joshua L. Chamberlain*, 182; Adelbert Ames to Parents, undated letter [likely from late December 1862], in Ames, *Chronicles from the Nineteenth Century*, 1:16; James Rundlett to Elizabeth Rundlett, January 15, 1863, in Wells, *Rundlett's War*, 58.

71. Little, *Genealogical and Family History of the State of Maine*, 1:134.

72. JLC to Joseph Badger, January 6, 1863, in Desjardin, *Joshua L. Chamberlain*, 187; JLC to Fanny Chamberlain, January 5, 1863, in Desjardin, *Joshua L. Chamberlain*, 186; JLC to Fanny Chamberlain, January 11, 1863, in Desjardin, *Joshua L. Chamberlain*, 187–88.

73. JLC, *The Passing of the Armies*, xiv; JLC to Abner Coburn, February 26, 1863, 20th Maine Correspondence, MSA.

74. *MeAGR 1864*, 331; JLC to Daniel Butterfield, April 20, 1863, Joshua Lawrence Chamberlain Papers, Box 5, Manuscript Division, LOC.

75. JLC to Fanny Chamberlain, March/April 1863, in Desjardin, *Joshua L. Chamberlain*, 194; JLC to Fanny Chamberlain, May 5, 1863, in Desjardin, *Joshua L. Chamberlain*, 196.

76. *Dedication of the Twentieth Maine Monuments at Gettysburg*, 30.

CHAPTER 3

1. JLC to John Chamberlain, May 22, 1863, Joshua Lawrence Chamberlain Papers, Box 11, Manuscript Division, LOC.

2. 20th Maine Consolidated Morning Reports, MSA; Henry Moore Pension File, NA.

3. U.S. Laws, Statutes, etc., *An Act to Provide for Calling Forth the Militia*; U.S. Laws, Statutes, etc., *An Act Giving Eventual Authority to the President of the United States*.

4. *MeAGR 1861*, 5; Gould, *History of the First-Tenth-Twenty-Ninth Maine Regiment*, 9; 2nd Maine Enlistment Papers, MSA.

5. Basler, Pratt, and Dunlap, *Collected Works*, 4:353–54; Gould, *History of the First-Tenth-Twenty-Ninth Maine Regiment*, 22; *MeAGR 1861*, 6, Appendix A, 8–9.

6. Stanley and Hall, *Eastern Maine and the Rebellion*, 51–55. Today, Willets Point is partially covered by Citi Field, home of baseball's New York Mets.

7. *MeAGR 1861*, 18; Stanley and Hall, *Eastern Maine and the Rebellion*, 56.

8. *MeAGR 1861*, Appendix D, 61–118.

9. *MeAGR 1861*, Appendix D, 61–118; Blanton, "Women Soldiers of the Civil War."

10. *MeAGR 1861*, Appendix D, 61–118. See *MeAGR 1862–1864* to track progress of Scribner; *MeAGR 1863*, 64, for number of battles for the Second Maine.

11. Charles Roberts to Israel Washburn, August 15, 1861, 2nd Maine Correspondence, MSA; 2nd Maine Officers to Israel Washburn, August 14, 1861, 2nd Maine Correspondence, MSA.

12. Gould, *History of the First-Tenth-Twenty-Ninth Maine Regiment*, 15, 65.

13. *MeAGR 1861*, 10.

14. Whitman and True, *Maine in the War*, 41–43; Charles Jameson to Israel Washburn, August 13, 1861, 2nd Maine Correspondence, MSA.

15. Charles Roberts to Israel Washburn, August 15, 1861, 2nd Maine Correspondence, MSA.

16. Mundy, *Second to None*, 96–97.

17. 2nd Maine Officers to Israel Washburn, August 14, 1861, 2nd Maine Correspondence, MSA; *MeAGR 1861*, Appendix D, 61–120; Mundy, *Second to None*, 97–98.

18. S. W. Hoskins to Israel Washburn, August 26, 1861, 2nd Maine Correspondence, MSA.

19. Samuel Nash to John Hodsdon, January 30, 1863, 2nd Maine Correspondence, MSA; H. F. Gould to John Hodsdon, February 9, 1863, 2nd Maine Correspondence,

MSA. The inference of Gould having signed a three-year enlistment is based on the fact that he was mustered out on June 9, 1863, rather than on June 4, 1863. The renewed request was by G. P. Brown. G. P. Brown to John Hodsdon, April 16, 1863, 2nd Maine Correspondence, MSA.

20. Leonard Carver to Dear Sir [John Hodsdon?], March 12, 1863, 2nd Maine Correspondence, MSA.

21. See, for example, William Waid to John Hodsdon, March 19, 1863, and L. W. Atkins to John Hodsdon, March 23, 1863, both in 2nd Maine Correspondence, MSA; George Varney to John Hodsdon, April 18, 1863, 2nd Maine Correspondence, MSA.

22. George I. Brown to Abner Coburn, April 22, 1863, 2nd Maine Correspondence, MSA.

23. James Rundlett to Elizabeth Rundlett, April 26, 1863, in Wells, *Rundlett's War*, 75; William T. Livermore Diary, April 27, 1863, UMO; Nathan Clark Journal, April 28, 1863, MSA.

24. James Bacon Pension File, NA.

25. Stephen Fowler Court Martial File, NA; Nehemiah Doe Court Martial File, NA.

26. Nehemiah Doe Court Martial File, NA.

27. James Bacon Court Martial File, NA.

28. James Bacon Court Martial File, NA.

29. William Fowler Court Martial File, NA.

30. Nehemiah Doe Court Martial File, NA; Stephen Fowler Court Martial File, NA.

31. James Bacon Court Martial File, NA; Nehemiah Doe Court Martial File, NA; Stephen Fowler Court Martial File, NA; William Fowler Court Martial File, NA; Charles H. Plummer Court Martial File, NA; Lewis Snow Court Martial File, NA.

32. James Bacon Court Martial File, NA.

33. James Bacon Court Martial File, NA.

34. William Owen to Abbie Owen, May 12, 1863, Milo Historical Society.

35. Joseph Hooker to J. C. Kelton, May 28, 1863, in *OR*, Ser. I, Vol. 25, Pt. 2, 532.

36. William T. Livermore Diary, May 16, 1863, UMO.

37. William T. Livermore Diary, May 18–20, 1863, UMO; Holman Melcher to Nathaniel Melcher, May 21, 1863, in Styple, *With a Flash of His Sword*, 28.

38. Frank Grindle to J. B. Wilson, May 22, 1863, 2nd Maine Correspondence, MSA.

39. On the relative safety of the artillery versus infantry, the Third Massachusetts Battery brought 124 men to Gettysburg and had just six wounded.

40. J. B. Wilson to Abner Coburn, June 2, 1863, 2nd Maine Correspondence, MSA; JLC to John Chamberlain, May 22, 1863, Joshua Lawrence Chamberlain Papers, Box 11, Manuscript Division, LOC.

41. William T. Livermore Diary, May 23, 1863, UMO; Samuel Keene Diary, May 23, 1863, PHC; JLC to John Hodsdon, November 15, 1865, Joshua L. Chamberlain Letters and Reports, General Order Book, PHC. Also in *MeAGR 1864–1865*, 331–32.

42. JLC to John Hodsdon, November 15, 1865, Joshua L. Chamberlain Letters and Reports, General Order Book, PHC. Also in *MeAGR 1864–1865*, 331–32; JLC to Abner Coburn, May 25, 1863, 20th Maine Correspondence, MSA.

43. JLC, "Through Blood and Fire at Gettysburg," 900, *Hearst's Magazine*, June 1913; JLC to John Hodsdon, November 15, 1865, Joshua L. Chamberlain Letters and Reports, General Order Book, PHC. Also in *MeAGR 1864–1865*, 331–32.

44. JLC to Abner Coburn, May 25, 1863, 20th Maine Correspondence, MSA; 20th Maine Consolidated Morning Reports, May 23, 1863, MSA.

45. Whitman and True, *Maine in the War*, 54–55.

46. 20th Maine Consolidated Morning Reports, May 26, 1863, MSA; Circular, May 26, 1863, 20th Maine Infantry Regimental Letter, Endorsement, and Order Book, vol. 4 of 7, RG 94, Records of the Adjutant General's Office, NA.

47. Henry Moore Court Martial File, NA.

48. Henry Moore Court Martial File, NA.

49. U.S. Census Bureau, "Population Schedule," 1850 and 1860; Henry Moore CMSR, NA.

50. Henry Moore Court Martial File, NA; Henry Moore CMSR, NA.

51. Henry Moore Pension File, NA.

52. Benjamin Coombs CMSR, NA. Because court-martial charges were made out against Coombs, but no trial was ever held, the papers are found in his CMSR rather than in a court-martial file.

53. JLC to Abner Coburn, May 27, 1863, 20th Maine Correspondence, MSA.

54. 20th Maine Consolidated Morning Reports, MSA; Thomas Townsend CMSR, NA; Henry Moore Court Martial File, NA.

55. Charles Billings to Dear Father, May 31, 1863, transcript of letter posted online in author's possession.

56. William T. Livermore Diary, June 3, 1863, UMO; "An Act for Establishing Rules and Articles for the Government of the Armies of the United States," in U.S. Congress, *Acts of the Ninth Congress of the United States (1805–1807)*, Session I, Chapter 20, 360.

57. Henry Moore Court Martial File, NA.

58. Henry Moore Court Martial File, NA.

59. Henry Moore Court Martial File, NA.

60. 20th Maine Consolidated Morning Reports, MSA; John O'Connell Memoir, 41, in Box 87, Folder 7 & 9, Civil War Document Collection, U.S. Army Heritage and Education Center; Edwin Witherell, "Men Loved Gen Chamberlain," *Springfield Republican*, February 26, 1914; Affidavit from Samuel Veazie, January 27, 1890, in Thomas Chamberlain Pension File, NA.

61. Hezekiah Long to Sarah Long, June 13, 1863, in Richardson's, *Hard Times*, 54.

62. JLC to John M. Clark, July 30, 1863, 20th Maine Infantry Regimental Letter, Endorsement, and Order Book, vol. 2 of 7, RG 94, Records of the Adjutant General's Office, NA.

63. Henry Moore Court Martial File, NA; Foote, *The Gentlemen and the Roughs*, 155; Carmichael, *The War for the Common Soldier*, 55; Henry Moore CMSR, NA.

64. *MeAGR 1863*; JLC to John M. Clark, July 30, 1863, 20th Maine Infantry Regimental Letter, Endorsement, and Order Book, vol. 2 of 7, RG 94, Records of the Adjutant General's Office, NA.

65. Elisha Coan to Samuel Miller, August 6, 1881, Elisha Coan Collection, Box 1, Folder "Letters, 1857–1955," Bowdoin College.

66. Hatch, *History of Bowdoin College*, 131.

CHAPTER 4

1. *Dedication of the Twentieth Maine Monuments at Gettysburg*, 26, 29–30.

2. *Dedication of the Twentieth Maine Monuments at Gettysburg*, 29. Among those who suggest that Little Round Top was never really in danger, Twentieth Maine or no, is Thomas Desjardin, the author of an entire book on the regiment during the Gettysburg Campaign. See Desjardin, "Last Resort?"

3. William T. Livermore Diary, May 28–30, 1863, UMO; James Rundlett to Elizabeth Rundlett, June 6, 1863, in Wells, *Rundlett's War*, 83.

4. William T. Livermore Diary, June 2–3, 1863, UMO; Ellis Spear Diary, June 3, 1863, in Spear et al., *The Civil War Recollections of General Ellis Spear*, 211.

5. Jedediah Hotchkiss Diary, February 23, 1863, in McDonald, *Make Me a Map of the Valley*, 116.

6. Guelzo, *Robert E. Lee*, 292.

7. Nathan Clark Journal, June 4, 1863, MSA; Ellis Spear Diary, June 4, 1863, in Spear et al., *The Civil War Recollections of General Ellis Spear*, 211; William T. Livermore Diary, June 5, 1863, UMO; Albert Fernald Diary, June 5, 1863, PHC; James Rundlett to Elizabeth Rundlett, June 6, 1863, in Wells, *Rundlett's War*, 83.

8. James Rundlett to Elizabeth Rundlett, June 6, 1863, in Wells, *Rundlett's War*, 83; Holman Melcher to Nathaniel Melcher, June 6, 1863, in Styple, *With a Flash of His Sword*, 30–31.

9. Joseph Hooker to Abraham Lincoln, June 5, 1863, 11:30 a.m., in *OR*, Ser. I, Vol. 27, Pt. 1, 30; Joseph Hooker to Henry Halleck, June 6, 1863, 3:00 p.m., in *OR*, Ser. I, Vol. 27, Pt. 1, 33; Joseph Hooker to Abraham Lincoln, June 5, 1863, 9:15 p.m., in *OR*, Ser. I, Vol. 27, Pt. 1, 32–33.

10. Joseph Hooker to Abraham Lincoln, June 5, 1863, 11:30 a.m., in *OR*, Ser. I, Vol. 27, Pt. 1, 30; Abraham Lincoln to Joseph Hooker, June 5, 1863, 4:00 p.m., in *OR*, Ser. I, Vol. 27, Pt. 1, 31; Henry Halleck to Joseph Hooker, June 5, 1863, 4:40 p.m., in *OR*, Ser. I, Vol. 27, Pt. 1, 31–32.

11. Samuel Keene Diary, June 9, 1863, PHC; Coddington, *The Gettysburg Campaign*, 65.

12. Ellis Spear Diary, June 10, 1863, in Spear et al., *The Civil War Recollections of General Ellis Spear*, 212; Samuel Keene Diary, June 10, 1863, PHC; Albert Fernald Diary, June 10, 1863, PHC; William T. Livermore Diary, June 10, 1863, UMO; Holman Melcher to Nathaniel Melcher, June 12, 1863, in Styple, *With a Flash of His Sword*, 32.

13. William T. Livermore Diary, June 12, 1863, UMO; Hezekiah Long to Sarah Long, June 13, 1863, in Richardson's, *Hard Times*, 54.

14. Joseph Hooker to Henry Halleck, June 13, 1863, 7:00 p.m., in *OR*, Ser. I, Vol. 27, Pt. 1, 38.

15. William T. Livermore Diary, June 13 and June 14, 1863, UMO; Joseph Hooker to Edwin Stanton, June 14, 1863, 5:30 p.m., in *OR*, Ser. I, Vol. 27, Pt. 1, 38; Ellis Spear Diary, June 13, 1863, in Spear et al., *The Civil War Recollections of General Ellis Spear*, 212; James Rundlett to Elizabeth Rundlett, June 16, 1863, in Wells, *Rundlett's War*, 87; Samuel Keene Diary, June 14, 1863, PHC; Albert Fernald Diary, June 14, 1863, PHC.

16. Ellis Spear Diary, June 15, 1863, in Spear et al., *The Civil War Recollections of General Ellis Spear*, 212–13; Samuel Keene Diary, June 15, 1863, PHC; Albert Fernald Diary, June 15, 1863, PHC; James Rundlett to Elizabeth Rundlett, June 16, 1863, in Wells, *Rundlett's War*, 87; Krick, *Civil War Weather in Virginia*, 101; William T. Livermore Diary, June 15, 1863, UMO.

17. William T. Livermore Diary, June 15, 1863, UMO; Albert Fernald Diary, June 15, 1863, PHC.

18. Samuel Keene Diary, June 16, 1863, PHC; Ellis Spear Diary, June 16, 1863, in Spear et al., *The Civil War Recollections of General Ellis Spear*, 213; Nathan Clark Diary, June 16, 1863, MSA.

19. James Rundlett to Elizabeth Rundlett, June 24, 1863, in Wells, *Rundlett's War*, 89; William T. Livermore Diary, June 17, 1863, UMO; Alfred Pleasonton to Seth Williams, June 20, 1863, 7:00 a.m., in *OR*, Ser. I, Vol. 27, Pt. 3, 224; "Return of Casualties in the Union Forces at Aldie, Va., June 17, 1863," in *OR*, Ser. I, Vol. 27, Pt. 1, 171.

20. Krick, *Civil War Weather in Virginia*, 101; James Rundlett to Elizabeth Rundlett, June 24, 1863, in Wells, *Rundlett's War*, 89; William T. Livermore Diary, June 17, 1863, UMO; Ellis Spear Diary, June 18, 1863, in Spear et al., *The Civil War Recollections of General Ellis Spear*, 213; Adney Boothby Diary, June 18, 1863, Vertical File Collection 6—20th ME, GNMP.

21. Samuel Keene Diary, June 19, 1863, PHC; William T. Livermore Diary, June 19, 1863, UMO.

22. Samuel Keene Diary, June 20, 1863, PHC; Ellis Spear Diary, June 20, 1863, in Spear et al., *The Civil War Recollections of General Ellis Spear*, 213; William T. Livermore Diary, June 19–20, 1863, UMO; Albert Fernald Diary, June 20, 1863, PHC; "Return of Casualties in the Union Forces at Aldie, Va., June 17, 1863," in *OR*, Ser. I, Vol. 27, Pt. 1, 171. On despising Gilmore, see Spear, "The Civil War Recollections," in Spear et al., *The Civil War Recollections*, 30, 48, 54–56.

23. Alfred Pleasonton to Seth Williams, June 20, 1863, 12:30 p.m., in *OR*, Ser. I, Vol. 27, Pt. 1, 911; Daniel Butterfield to Alfred Pleasonton, June 20, 1863, 5:20 p.m., in *OR*, Ser. I, Vol. 27, Pt. 3, 227–28.

24. William T. Livermore Diary, June 21, 1863, UMO; Nathan Clark Journal, June 21, 1863, MSA; Report of Strong Vincent, June 22, 1863, in *OR*, Ser. I, Vol. 27, Pt. 1, 614.

25. William T. Livermore Diary, June 21, 1863, UMO; Samuel Keene Diary, June 21, 1863, PHC; O'Neill, "The Fight for the Loudoun Valley," 50; Alfred Pleasonton to David Gregg, June 20, 1863, 11:15 p.m., in *OR*, Ser. I, Vol. 27, Pt. 3, 229–30.

26. Report of Strong Vincent, June 22, 1863, in *OR*, Ser. I, Vol. 27, Pt. 1, 614; O'Neill, "The Fight for the Loudoun Valley," 50.

27. Holman Melcher to Nathaniel Melcher, June 27, 1863, in Styple, *With a Flash of His Sword*, 33; William T. Livermore Diary, June 21, 1863, UMO; Report of Strong Vincent, June 22, 1863, in *OR*, Ser. I, Vol. 27, Pt. 1, 614.

28. Hezekiah Long to Sarah Long, June 23, 1863, in Richardson's, *Hard Times*, 55; Report of Strong Vincent, June 22, 1863, in *OR*, Ser. I, Vol. 27, Pt. 1, 614; Holman Melcher to Nathaniel Melcher, June 27, 1863, in Styple, *With a Flash of His Sword*, 34; William T. Livermore Diary, June 21, 1863, UMO.

29. Samuel Keene Diary, June 21, 1863, PHC; Spear, "The Personal Memoranda," in Spear et al., *The Civil War Recollections of General Ellis Spear*, 310; John P. West Pension File, NA; James Rundlett to Elizabeth Rundlett, June 24, 1863, in Wells, *Rundlett's War*, 89.

30. Report of Strong Vincent, June 22, 1863, in *OR*, Ser. I, Vol. 27, Pt. 1, 614; O'Neill, "The Fight for the Loudoun Valley," 53.

31. Report of Strong Vincent, June 22, 1863, in *OR*, Ser. I, Vol. 27, Pt. 1, 615.

32. Nathan Clark Journal, June 21, 1863, MSA.

33. William T. Livermore Diary, June 21, 1863, UMO.

34. "Return of Casualties in the Union Forces at Upperville, Va., June 21, 1863," in *OR*, Ser. I, Vol. 27, Pt. 1, 171–72; Spear, "The Civil War Recollections," in Spear et al., *The Civil War Recollections of General Ellis Spear*, 30; Spear, "The Personal Memoranda," in Spear et al., *The Civil War Recollections of General Ellis Spear*, 310, Albert Robinson Pension File, NA; Holman Melcher to Nathaniel Melcher, June 27, 1863, in Styple, *With a Flash of His Sword*, 33–34. Those slightly wounded who would be at Gettysburg were Holman Melcher of Company F and Samuel Gray and Edwin Keating of Company K. Asbury Dickinson of Company G and James Miller of Company K would miss the fighting on July 2. One of the casualties was identified as "William Runkins" of Company F, but no such man appears on the Twentieth's roster. "Losses in the Maine Twentieth," *Bangor Daily Whig and Courier*, July 4, 1863; *MeAGR 1863*.

35. John Chamberlain Journal, 9, PHC.

36. Samuel Keene Diary, June 23–25, 1863, PHC; George Meade to O. O. Howard, June 22, 1863, in *OR*, Ser. I, Vol. 27, Pt. 3, 255; Holman Melcher to Dear Brother, June 27, 1863, in Styple, *With a Flash of His Sword*, 35; Joseph Hooker to Henry Halleck, June 24, 1863, in *OR*, Ser. I, Vol. 27, Pt. 1, 55–56; G. H. Sharpe to Dan Butterfield, June 23, 1863, 12:15 a.m., in *OR*, Ser. I, Vol. 27, Pt. 3, 266.

37. Holman Melcher to Nathaniel Melcher, June 27, 1863, in Styple, *With a Flash of His Sword*, 33-35; Samuel Keene Diary, June 26, 1863, PHC; William T. Livermore Diary, June 26, 1863, UMO; Hezekiah Long to Sarah Long, June 28, 1863, in Richardson's, *Hard Times* 56; Guelzo, *Gettysburg*, 106–8.

38. Samuel Keene Diary, June 27, 1863, PHC; William T. Livermore Diary, June 27, 1863, UMO; Holman Melcher to Nathaniel Melcher, June 27, 1863, in Styple, *With a Flash of His Sword*, 33; John Chamberlain Journal, 9, PHC.

39. Albert Fernald Diary, June 28, 1863, PHC; Ellis Spear Diary, June 28, 1863, in Spear et al., *The Civil War Recollections of General Ellis Spear*, 214.

40. Brown, *Meade at Gettysburg*, 35–38.

41. William T. Livermore Diary, June 29, 1863, UMO; Samuel Keene Diary, June 29, 1863, PHC; Nathan Clark Journal, June 29, 1863, MSA; Elisha Coan to Samuel L. Miller, August 6, 1881, Elisha Coan Collection, Box 1, Folder "Letters, 1857–1955," Bowdoin College.

42. Andrew Tozier Pension File, Department of Veterans Affairs; U.S. Census Bureau, "Population Schedule," 1850, 1860.

43. Andrew Tozier Pension File, Department of Veterans Affairs.

44. Andrew Tozier Pension File, Department of Veterans Affairs; "Alphabetical List of the Members Absent from the 2nd Maine Regiment," June 30, 1862, 2nd Maine Correspondence, MSA.

45. Andrew Tozier CMSR, NA.

46. Andrew Tozier Pension File, Department of Veterans Affairs.

47. William T. Livermore Diary, June 30, 1863, UMO.

48. William T. Livermore, "Extracts from a Veteran's Diary," *Lincoln County News*, June 22, 1883.

49. William Lamson to William Lamson Sr., July 1–6, 1863, in Engert, *Maine to the Wilderness*, 70.

50. Longstreet, *From Manassas to Appomattox*, 364–65.

51. Longstreet, *From Manassas to Appomattox*, 362, 363, 365; Robert E. Lee Official Report, July 31, 1863, in *OR*, Ser. I, Vol. 27, Pt. 2, 308.

52. James Longstreet Official Report, July 27, 1863, in *OR*, Ser. I, Vol. 27, Pt. 2, 358.

53. George Meade Official Report, October 1, 1863, in *OR*, Ser. I, Vol. 27, Pt. 1, 116.

54. Oates, *War Between*, 207, 210.

55. Norton, *Attack and Defense*, 263; Nathan Clark Journal, July 2, 1863, MSA.

56. Norton, *Attack and Defense*, 263–64.

57. Norton, *Attack and Defense*, 265–66.

58. Norton, *Attack and Defense*, 265; Report of Joshua L. Chamberlain, July 6, 1863, 1863, in *OR*, Ser. I, Vol. 27, Pt. 1, 623.

59. U.S. Congress, *Report of the Joint Committee*, 332.

60. Vermilyea, "Meade's Pipe Creek Line"; Brown, *Meade at Gettysburg*; Harmon, *All Roads Led to Gettysburg*.

61. James Rice Official Report, July 31, 1863, in *OR*, Ser. I, Vol. 27, Pt. 1, 617; Law, "Round Top and the Confederate Right at Gettysburg," 300; Oates, *War Between*, 214.

62. Walter Morrill to JLC, July 8, 1863, in Ladd and Ladd, *The Bachelder Papers*, 2:1029–30.

63. *Dedication of the Twentieth Maine Monuments at Gettysburg*, 17.

64. JLC to Abner Coburn, October 28, 1863, 20th Maine Correspondence, MSA; JLC to Abner Coburn, August 7, 1863, 20th Maine Correspondence, MSA; JLC to John M. Clark, July 30, 1863, 20th Maine Infantry Regimental Letter, Endorsement, and Order Book, vol. 4 of 7, RG 94, Records of the Adjutant General's Office, NA.

65. JLC to John M. Clark, July 30, 1863, 20th Maine Infantry Regimental Letter, Endorsement, and Order Book, vol. 4 of 7, RG 94, Records of the Adjutant General's Office, NA.

66. Nathan Clark Journal, July 2, 1863, MSA; William T. Livermore, "Extracts from a Veteran's Diary," *Lincoln County News*, June 22, 1883; Ellis Spear to Mildred Grant, March 14, 1910, in Styple, *With a Flash of His Sword*, 300–301; Spear, "The Civil War Recollections," in Spear et al., *The Civil War Recollections of General Ellis Spear*, 34.

67. Walter Morrill to JLC, July 8, 1863, in Ladd and Ladd, *The Bachelder Papers*, 2:1029–30; Allen, *The 2nd U.S. Sharpshooters at Gettysburg*, 14, 149.

68. *Maine at Gettysburg*, 255.

69. Faust, *Fighting Fifteenth*, 36, 41, 52, 62.

70. Faust, *Fighting Fifteenth*, 36, 41, 52, 62.

71. Faust, *Fighting Fifteenth*, 61, 65; LaFantasie, *Gettysburg Requiem*, xviii, 9, 11, 13, 16.

72. Faust, *Fighting Fifteenth*, 77–79; Oates, *War Between*, 212.

73. Oates, *War Between*, 212; Henry Jacobs, "Meteorology of the Battle," *Star and Sentinel*, July 30, 1885.

74. Oates, *War Between*, 213–14.

75. Oates, *War Between*, 214.

76. *Dedication of the Twentieth Maine Monuments at Gettysburg*, 27.

77. JLC to James Barnes, undated [cover letter September 3, 1863], Vertical File Collection 5—Participants Accounts—Joshua L. Chamberlain, GNMP.

78. Pullen, *Twentieth Maine*, 117–18; *The Civil War*, 1990 documentary produced by Ken Burns and Florentine Films.

79. Hess, *Civil War Infantry Tactics*, 139, 163.

80. JLC to James Barnes, undated [cover letter September 3, 1863], Vertical File Collection 5—Participants Accounts—Joshua L. Chamberlain, GNMP.

81. William T. Livermore, "Extracts from a Veteran's Diary," *Lincoln County News*, June 22, 1883; Oates, *War Between*, 218.

82. Hess, *Union Soldier in Battle*, 11, 4; Ellis Spear, "The 20th Maine at Gettysburg," *Portland Daily Press*, July 24, 1863.

83. Hess, *Rifle Musket*, 5–7, 108; Grossman, *On Killing*, 10, 12. In his wonderfully insightful work *The Rifle Musket in Civil War Combat*, Earl Hess discusses the various studies by Paddy Griffith, Mark Grimsley, and himself. Dave Grossman's *On Killing* is also a thought-provoking study into combat, referencing many other classic studies on the subject.

84. Lord, *Civil War Collector's Encyclopedia*, 1:242.

85. Grossman, *On Killing*, 180.

86. Eugene Kelleran to Dear Brother M&W, July 12, 1863, Vertical File Collection 6—20th ME, GNMP; Nathan Clark Journal, July 2, 1863, MSA.

87. JLC to James Barnes, undated [cover letter September 3, 1863], Vertical File Collection 5—Participants Accounts—Joshua L. Chamberlain, GNMP; Oates, *War Between*, 218; *Dedication of the Twentieth Maine Monuments at Gettysburg*, 28.

88. Oates, *War Between*, 218; WCO to JLC, March 8, 1897, Vertical File Collection 7—15th AL, GNMP (original in Schoff Civil War Collection, University of Michigan); JLC to James Barnes, undated [cover letter September 3, 1863], Vertical

File Collection 5—Participants Accounts—Joshua L. Chamberlain, GNMP; Oates, *War Between*, 218; Jordan, *Some Events and Incidents*, 43.

89. Gerrish, *Army Life*, 69–70.

90. JLC to John Hodsdon, July 13, 1863, 20th Maine Correspondence, MSA; Elisha Coan to Samuel L. Miller, August 6, 1881, Elisha Coan Collection, Box 1, Folder "Letters, 1857–1955," Bowdoin College; Albert Fernald Diary, July 2, 1863, PHC.

91. JLC to John Hodsdon, July 13, 1863, 20th Maine Correspondence, MSA; *Dedication of the Twentieth Maine Monuments at Gettysburg*, 21; E. S. Coan, "The Twentieth Maine: The Color Guard's Story," undated newspaper clipping in Elisha Coan Collection, Box 1, Folder "Clippings," Bowdoin College; Hezekiah Long to Sallie [Sarah Long], March 30, 1864, in Richardson's, *Hard Times*, 110.

92. Judson, *History of the Eighty-Third Regiment Pennsylvania Volunteers*, 68; JLC to John Nicholson, August 14, 1903, Archival Box B-6—Col. William C. Oates Correspondence, GNMP.

93. William T. Livermore to JLC, May 22, 1899, Joshua Lawrence Chamberlain Correspondence, Box 10, Folder 1—1856–1879, Maine Historical Society; Elisha Coan, undated account of Gettysburg, Elisha Coan Collection—Box 1, Folder "Articles and Addresses," Bowdoin College; Spear, "The Civil War Recollections," in Spear et al., *The Civil War Recollections of General Ellis Spear*, 34. The Livermore letter mentioned in this quote has been previously misdated to 1877, thus its placement in a folder covering the earlier period.

94. James Stanwood to JLC, July 30, 1863, 20th Maine Correspondence, MSA; Henry Sidelinger to JLC, July 30, 1863, 20th Maine Correspondence, MSA; "The Maine 20th at Gettysburg," *Eastern Argus*, December 20, 1865; JLC to John Hodsdon, July 13, 1863, 20th Maine Correspondence, MSA.

95. JLC to James Barnes, undated [cover letter September 3, 1863], Vertical File Collection 5—Participants Accounts—Joshua L. Chamberlain, GNMP; William T. Livermore, "Extracts from a Veteran's Diary," *Lincoln County News*, June 22, 1883; Oates, *War Between*, 218–19.

96. *Dedication of the Twentieth Maine Monuments at Gettysburg*, 28; JLC to Lieut. [George Herendeen], July 6, 1863, 20th Maine Correspondence, MSA.

97. William T. Livermore, "Extracts from a Veteran's Diary," *Lincoln County News*, June 22, 1883; Ellis Spear, "The 20th Maine at Gettysburg," *Portland Daily Press*, July 24, 1863.

98. Holman Melcher, "The Twentieth Maine at Gettysburg," *Lincoln County News*, March 13, 1885; Oates, *War Between*, 220.

99. Hess, *Civil War Infantry Tactics*, 165; Stewart, *Pickett's Charge*, 267; McWhiney and Jameson, *Attack and Die*, 79–80; Melcher, "An Experience in the Battle of the Wilderness," 80; Judson, *History of the Eighty-Third Regiment Pennsylvania Volunteers*, 96.

100. Nathan Clark Journal, July 2, 1863, MSA; William T. Livermore, "Extracts from a Veteran's Diary," *Lincoln County News*, June 22, 1883; JLC to James Barnes, undated [cover letter September 3, 1863], Vertical File Collection 5—Participants Accounts—Joshua L. Chamberlain, GNMP.

101. JLC, "Through Blood and Fire at Gettysburg," 907.

102. JLC to Fanny Chamberlain, July 17, 1863, Joshua Lawrence Chamberlain Papers, Box 4, Manuscript Division, LOC.

103. Spear, "The Personal Memoranda," in Spear et al., *The Civil War Recollections of General Ellis Spear*, 311, 314.

104. Holman Melcher, "The Twentieth Maine at Gettysburg," *Lincoln County News*, March 13, 1885.

105. Ellis Spear, "The Left at Gettysburg," *National Tribune*, June 12, 1913.

106. Walter Morrill to JLC, July 8, 1863, in Ladd and Ladd, *The Bachelder Papers*, 2:1029–30; Oates, *War Between*, 220–21; Ellis Spear to Mildred Grant, March 14, 1910, in Styple, *With a Flash of His Sword*, 300–301.

107. Judson, *History of the Eighty-Third Regiment Pennsylvania Volunteers*, 68.

108. Ellis Spear to Mildred Grant, March 14, 1910, in Styple, *With a Flash of His Sword*, 300–301; William T. Livermore, "Extracts from a Veteran's Diary," *Lincoln County News*, June 22, 1883; William Lamson to William Lamson Sr., July 1–6, 1863, in Engert, *Maine to the Wilderness*, 70.

109. Elisha Coan to Samuel L. Miller, August 6, 1881, Elisha Coan Collection, Box 1, Folder "Letters, 1857–1955," Bowdoin College.

110. William T. Livermore to JLC, May 22, 1899, Joshua Lawrence Chamberlain Correspondence, Box 10, Folder 1—1856–1879, Maine Historical Society.

111. JLC to James Barnes, undated [cover letter September 3, 1863], Vertical File Collection 5—Participants Accounts—Joshua L. Chamberlain, GNMP; JLC to Abner Coburn, July 21, 1863, 20th Maine Correspondence, MSA; Nathan Clark Journal, July 2, 1863, MSA; Adney Boothby to Dear Folks at Home, July 4, 1863, Vertical File Collection 6—20th ME, GNMP; Oates, *War Between*, 225–26.

112. JLC to Fanny Chamberlain, July 4, 1863, Joshua Lawrence Chamberlain Papers, Box 4, Manuscript Division, LOC; Albert Fernald Diary, July 2, 1863, PHC; Adney Boothby to Dear Folks at Home, July 4, 1863, Vertical File Collection 6—20th ME, GNMP.

113. Elisha Coan to Samuel L. Miller, August 6, 1881, Elisha Coan Collection, Box 1, Folder "Letters, 1857–1955," Bowdoin College.

114. JLC to James Barnes, undated [cover letter September 3, 1863], Vertical File Collection 5—Participants Accounts—Joshua L. Chamberlain, GNMP; JLC to Lieut. [George Herendeen], July 6, 1863, 20th Maine, MSA; JLC to John Hodsdon, July 13, 1863, 20th Maine Correspondence, MSA; Fox, *Regimental Losses*, 38.

115. JLC to John P. Nicholson, January 25, 1884, in Goulka, *Grand Old Man*, 118; JLC to Lieut [George Herendeen], July 6, 1863, 20th Maine Correspondence, MSA; William T. Livermore, "Extracts from a Veteran's Diary," *Lincoln County News*, June 22, 1883.

116. JLC to Lieut [George Herendeen], July 6, 1863, 20th Maine Correspondence, MSA; William Lamson to William Lamson Sr., July 1–6, 1863, in Engert, *Maine to the Wilderness*, 70, 72; William T. Livermore, "Extracts from a Veteran's Diary," *Lincoln County News*, June 22, 1883.

117. William Lamson to William Lamson Sr., July 1–6, 1863, in Engert, *Maine to the Wilderness*, 70, 72; William T. Livermore, "Extracts from a Veteran's Diary," *Lincoln County News*, June 22, 1883.

118. William T. Livermore, "Extracts from a Veteran's Diary," *Lincoln County News*, June 22, 1883.

119. William T. Livermore, "Extracts from a Veteran's Diary," *Lincoln County News*, June 22, 1883.

120. William Lamson to William Lamson Sr., July 1–6, 1863, in Engert, *Maine to the Wilderness*, 73; William T. Livermore, "Extracts from a Veteran's Diary," *Lincoln County News*, June 22, 1883.

121. William T. Livermore to Charles Livermore, July 6–9, 1863, Vertical File Collection 6—20th ME, GNMP.

122. J. B. Wescott to JLC, February 1896, Joshua Lawrence Chamberlain Papers, Box 3, Manuscript Division, LOC.

123. William T. Livermore to Charles Livermore, July 6–9, 1863, Vertical File Collection 6—20th ME, GNMP.

124. JLC to John Hodsdon, July 13, 1863, 20th Maine Correspondence, MSA; JLC to John M. Clark, July 30, 1863, 20th Maine Infantry Regimental Letter, Endorsement, and Order Book, vol. 4 of 7, RG 94, Records of the Adjutant General's Office, NA.

125. Adelbert Ames to JLC, July 3, 1863, Joshua L Chamberlain Letters and Reports, General Order Book, PHC.

126. James Rice to William P. Fessenden, September 8, 1863, 20th Maine Correspondence, MSA; James Barnes to JLC, September 1, 1863, 20th Maine Correspondence, MSA; JLC to Fanny Chamberlain, July 4, 1863, Joshua Lawrence Chamberlain Papers, Box 4, Manuscript Division, LOC.

127. Adney Boothby to Dear Folks at Home, July 4, 1863, Vertical File Collection 6—20th ME, GNMP; John Lenfest to Lavinia Lenfest, July 9, 1863, PHC; Sylvester Baker to Emily Baker, July 9, 1863, MSA; William T. Livermore, "Extracts from a Veteran's Diary," *Lincoln County News*, June 22, 1883.

128. JLC to Abner Coburn, July 21, 1863, 20th Maine Correspondence, MSA; L. L. Crounse, "Further Details of the Battle of Gettysburgh," *New York Times*, July 9, 1863.

129. Ellis Spear, "The 20th Maine at Gettysburg," *Portland Daily Press*, July 24, 1863.

130. Hezekiah Long to Sarah Long, April 30, 1863, in Richardson's, *Hard Times*, 39; *Dedication of the Twentieth Maine Monuments at Gettysburg*, 16; Useem, *The Leadership Moment*, 53.

131. James Rice to William P. Fessenden, September 8, 1863, 20th Maine Correspondence, MSA.

132. U.S. Congress, *Report of the Joint Committee*, 332.

133. JLC, "Through Blood and Fire at Gettysburg," 897.

134. Pfanz, *Gettysburg*, xv.

Chapter 5

1. Andrew Tozier Pension File, Department of Veterans Affairs, St. Louis, MO; U.S. Census Bureau, "Population Schedule," 1870.

2. Hezekiah Long to Sarah Long, July 19, 1863, in Richardson's, *Hard Times*, 64; Holman Melcher to Nathaniel Melcher, July 28, 1863, in Styple, *With a Flash of His Sword*, 148.

3. JLC to T. F. Locke, July 27, 1863, 20th Maine Infantry Regimental Letter, Endorsement, and Order Book, vol. 4 of 7, RG 94, Records of the Adjutant General's Office, NA.

4. William Lamson to Jennie Lamson, July 28, 1863, in Engert, *Maine to the Wilderness*, 77; Hezekiah Long to Sallie [Sarah Long], August 2, 1863, in Richardson's, *Hard Times*, 65–66; Hezekiah Long to Sarah Long, September 3, 1863, in Richardson's, *Hard Times*, 73.

5. JLC to Abner Coburn, August 25, 1863, 20th Maine Correspondence, MSA.

6. Holman Melcher to Editor of the *Portland Press*, November 13, 1863, in Styple, *With a Flash of His Sword*, 155–56; *MeAGR 1863*, 71; Hezekiah Long to Sarah Long, November 12, 1863, in Richardson's, *Hard Times*, 82; Fox, *Regimental Losses*, 20.

7. James Rundlett to Harriett Rundlett, December 13, 1863, in Wells, *Rundlett's War*, 131; William T. Livermore Diary, December 20, 1863, UMO; Fernald estimate of furloughs costing $75 relayed in Hezekiah Long to Sarah Long, January 29, 1865, in Richardson's, *Hard Times*, 190.

8. *MeAGR1864–1865*, 33, 37, 927; Hess, *Union Soldier*, 89.

9. Hezekiah Long to Sarah Long, January 29, 1864, in Richardson's, *Hard Times*, 97.

10. William Ward Jr. to John Hodsdon, December 12, 1863, 20th Maine Correspondence, MSA; William Ward Jr. Court Martial File, NA.

11. Andrew Tozier CMSR, NA; *MeAGR 1864–1865*, 2:470.

12. Hezekiah Long to Sarah Long, February 12, 1864, in Richardson's, *Hard Times*, 99; James Rundlett to Elizabeth Rundlett, April 17, 1864, in Wells, *Rundlett's War*, 143.

13. Hezekiah Long to Sarah Long, March 19, 1864, in Richardson's, *Hard Times*, 107; Ellis Spear Diary, March 24, 1864, in Spear et al., *The Civil War Recollections of General Ellis Spear*, 237; Holman Melcher to Nathaniel Melcher, April 9, 1864, in Styple, *With a Flash of His Sword*, 163; William T. Livermore Diary, March 26, 1864, and April 26, 1864, UMO.

14. Holman Melcher to Nathaniel Melcher, April 22, 1864, in Styple, *With a Flash of His Sword*, 164; William Lamson to Jennie Lamson, May 3, 1864, in Engert, *Maine to the Wilderness*, 95; Fox, *Regimental Losses*, 541.

15. Rhea, *The Battle of the Wilderness*, 108, 434, 440.

16. Melcher, "An Experience in the Battle of the Wilderness," 75–78; Gerrish, *Army Life*, 160–63.

17. Melcher, "An Experience in the Battle of the Wilderness," 77–81; Holman Melcher to Nathaniel Melcher, May 3, 1864, in Styple, *With a Flash of His Sword*, 167.

18. *MeAGR 1864–1865*, 284; William T. Livermore Diary, May 12, 1864, UMO.

19. Gerrish, *Army Life*, 175; Fox, *Regimental Losses*, 135.

20. Samuel Keene Diary, 239, PHC.

21. Smith, *Chamberlain at Petersburg*, 16, 32; JLC, "The Charge at Fort Hell," in Smith, *Chamberlain at Petersburg*, 48–50.

22. JLC, "The Charge at Fort Hell," in Smith, *Chamberlain at Petersburg*, 48, 52, 56, 60–65.

23. Harmon and McAllister, "The Lion of the Union," 715; JLC, "The Charge at Fort Hell," in Smith, *Chamberlain at Petersburg*, 69.

24. Harmon and McAllister, "The Lion of the Union," 713, 715.

25. Calvin Bates Pension File, NA.

26. William T. Livermore Diary, September 12, 1864, UMO; "The Maine Election," *New York Times*, September 14, 1864.

27. Gerrish, *Army Life*, 215–18; *MeAGR 1864–1865*, 286; Vicent Pinhorn Pension File, NA; Hezekiah Long to Sarah Long, September 24, 1864, in Richardson's, *Hard Times*, 148.

28. William T. Livermore Diary, November 8, 1864, UMO; Holman Melcher to Nathaniel Melcher, December 20, 1864, in Styple, *With a Flash of His Sword*, 185; Holman Melcher Diary, February 17, 1865, in Styple, *With a Flash of His Sword*, 198.

29. William T. Livermore Diary, January 29, 1865, UMO. For deserters, see William T. Livermore Diary entries for February 25, February 28, and March 3, all in 1865, UMO.

30. William T. Livermore Diary, March 15, 1865, UMO; Holman Melcher to Nathaniel Melcher, March 2, 1865, in Styple, *With a Flash of His Sword*, 204; Holman Melcher Diary, February 3, 1865, in Styple, *With a Flash of His Sword*, 194; Gerrish, *Army Life*, 230.

31. Gerrish, *Army Life*, 230–44; William T. Livermore Diary, April 1, 1865, UMO.

32. Holman Melcher to Nathaniel Melcher, April 2, 1865, in Styple, *With a Flash of His Sword*, 212; William T. Livermore Diary, April 9, 1865, UMO; Holman Melcher to Nathaniel Melcher, April 9, 1865, in Styple, *With a Flash of His Sword*, 217.

33. William T. Livermore Diary, April 12, 1865, UMO; JLC, *The Passing of the Armies*, 248–49, 260–61.

34. Holman Melcher to Nathaniel Melcher, May 17, 1865, in Styple, *With a Flash of His Sword*, 228–30.

35. Holman Melcher to Nathaniel Melcher, May 17, 1865, in Styple, *With a Flash of His Sword*, 228–30.

36. William T. Livermore Diary, May 11, 1865, UMO; Fox, *Regimental Losses*, 135.

37. *Reunions of the Twentieth Maine Regiment Association at Portland*, 2–7.

38. Holman Melcher Diary, April 26, 1865, in Styple, *With a Flash of His Sword*, 225; Holman Melcher Diary, January 16, 1865, in Styple, *With a Flash of His Sword*, 190.

39. William T. Livermore Diary, June 4–10, 1865, UMO; Gerrish, *Army Life*, 306.

40. Gerrish, *Army Life*, 307–8.

41. Gerrish, *Army Life*, 308; William T. Livermore Diary, June 14, June 15, June 22, all in 1865, UMO.

42. John O'Connell CMSR, NA; Charles Avery CMSR, NA; Willian Whitney Pension File, NA.

43. George Bowman Pension File, NA; Oscar Thomas Pension File, NA.

44. Fox, *Regimental Losses*, 46, 132–35, 526.

45. U.S. Census Bureau, "Population Schedule," 1870.

46. "Turns Up After Many Years," *Lincoln County News*, September 8, 1887.

47. *MeAGR 1861–1865*; "Death of Lieut. Sanbourne," *Helena Weekly Herald*, January 16, 1873.

48. John O'Connell Pension File, NA; John O'Connell CMSRs for 2nd, 20th, and 11th Maine, NA.

49. Lewis Merriam Pension File, NA.

50. Albert Titus Pension File, NA.

51. Albert Titus CMSR, NA; Albert Titus Pension File, NA.

52. Albert Titus Pension File, NA; "Texas Items," *South-Western* (Shreveport, LA), August 7, 1867; Bill O'Neal, "Swamp Fox of the Sulphur," 18–19.

53. Albert Titus Pension File, NA; "Texas Items," *South-Western* (Shreveport, LA), August 7, 1867; Bill O'Neal, "Swamp Fox of the Sulphur," 18–19.

54. Andrew Tozier Pension File, Department of Veterans Affairs, St. Louis, MO.

55. Andrew Tozier CMSR, NA.

56. Andrew Tozier Pension File, Department of Veterans Affairs, St. Louis, MO.

57. *State v. Tozier*, in *Androscoggin County Supreme Judicial Court Record* 12 (January 1870–April 1871): 135–36, MSA, available at FamilySearch.org; *State v. Jerry Riggs*, in *Androscoggin County Supreme Judicial Court Record* 8 (1864–1865): 516, MSA, available at FamilySearch.org.

58. "Justice Finally Triumphs," *Lewiston Journal*, February 9, 1870; "The Maine 20th at Gettysburg," *Eastern Argus*, December 20, 1865.

59. Andrew Tozier Pension File, Department of Veterans Affairs.

60. *State v. Tozier*, in *Washington County Supreme Judicial Court Record* 21 (April 1868–October 1870): 232–33, MSA; "Justice Finally Triumphs," *Lewiston Journal*, February 9, 1870.

61. *State v. Tozier*, in *Washington County Supreme Judicial Court Record* 21 (April 1868–October 1870): 232–33, MSA; "Justice Finally Triumphs," *Lewiston Journal*, February 9, 1870.

62. *State v. Tozier*, in *Washington County Supreme Judicial Court Record* 21 (April 1868–October 1870): 232–33, MSA.

63. "Justice Finally Triumphs," *Lewiston Journal*, February 9, 1870; "State News: Androscoggin County," *Portland Daily Press*, May 19, 1869.

64. "Justice Finally Triumphs," *Lewiston Journal*, February 9, 1870.

65. Maine, *Revised Statutes of the State of Maine*, 672; *State v. Tozier*, in *Androscoggin County Supreme Judicial Court Record* 12 (January 1870–April 1871): 135–36, MSA.

66. Maine, *Reports of the Warden and Inspectors of the Maine State Prison*, 2–4.

67. Maine, *Reports of the Warden and Inspectors of the Maine State Prison*, 4.

68. JLC Pension File, NA.

69. Pullen, *Joshua Chamberlain*, 37–48; John Bachelder to JLC, October 29, 1865, Joshua Lawrence Chamberlain Papers, Box 1, Manuscript Division, LOC.

70. Pullen, *Joshua Chamberlain*, 37–48.

71. White, *On Great Fields*, 258–59.

72. JLC to Fanny Chamberlain, November 20, 1868, in Goulka, *Grand Old Man*, 26–28.

73. U.S. Census Bureau, "Population Schedule," 1870.

74. David Royal Pension File, NA; "Local and Maine Items," *Bangor Whig and Courier*, February 11, 1868; Maine, *Reports of the Warden and Inspectors of the Maine State Prison, and of the Physician and Chaplain, 1868*, 14.

75. Gerrish, *Army Life*, 69–71.

76. "Robbery of the Lime Rock Bank," *Rockland Gazette*, May 6, 1870; Alden Litchfield Pension File, NA.

77. Maine, *Reports of the Warden and Inspectors of the Maine State Prison, and of the Physician and Chaplain, 1867*, 5; Maine, *Reports of the Warden and Inspectors of the Maine State Prison, and of the Physician and Chaplain, 1860*, 5; Abbott, "The Civil War and the Crime Wave of 1865–1870," 217.

78. Calvin Bates Pension File, NA; Barnes, *Medical and Surgical History of the War of the Rebellion*, 12:671; Calvin Bates Photograph, LOC, https://www.loc.gov/item /2012650230/.

79. "American Institute Fair," *New York Times*, October 15, 1865.

80. "American Institute Fair," *New York Times*, October 15, 1865.

81. Calvin Bates Pension File, NA.

82. Calvin Bates Pension File, NA; U.S. Census Bureau, "Population Schedule," 1860–1880.

83. Hiram Chesley Pension File, NA.

84. John Lynes Jr. CMSR, NA; John Lynes Jr. Pension File, NA.

85. John Lynes Jr. Pension File, NA.

86. Henry Moore Pension File, NA.

87. Henry Moore Pension File, NA.

88. Henry Moore Pension File, NA.

89. William T. Livermore Pension File, NA.

90. U.S. Census Bureau, "Population Schedule," 1870; U.S. Census Bureau, "Non-Population Schedule," 1870.

91. William T. Livermore Diary, October 5, 1862, UMO; William T. Livermore Pension File, NA; U.S. Census Bureau, "Population Schedule," 1870.

92. William T. Livermore Pension File, NA.

93. William T. Livermore Pension File, NA.

94. U.S. Census Bureau, "Population Schedule," 1860 and 1870. The burial locations are as follows: Maine (269), Unknown (25), Massachusetts (24), New Hampshire (11), Wisconsin (9), California (8), Minnesota (6), Illinois (4), Iowa (4), Pennsylvania (4), Connecticut (3), Kansas (2), Michigan (2), and Oregon (2). The following had one

each: Colorado, Florida, Louisiana, Missouri, Montana, North Dakota, Nevada, New York, South Dakota, Tennessee, Washington, and Washington, DC.

95. "Homestead Act (1862)," NA, https://www.archives.gov/milestone-documents/homestead-act; Hart, *History of Butler County, Iowa*, 2:72–76.

96. Kerner Smith, "Gettysburg Survivor Loses Leg in Oregon Accident," Jefferson Public Radio, January 5, 2016, https://www.ijpr.org/show/as-it-was/2016-01-05/gettysburg-survivor-loses-leg-in-oregon-accident.

97. Andrew Roberts Pension File, NA; Christopher Pennington Pension File, NA; Andrew Smith Pension File, NA; John Breen Pension File, NA; Horace Monroe Pension File, NA; Elijah Carr Pension File, NA.

98. Milton Davis Pension File, NA.

99. William Owen Pension File, NA.

100. William Owen Pension File, NA; "Sad Case of Drowning at Milo," *Piscataquis Observer*, September 4, 1884.

101. William Owen Pension File, NA; "Sad Case of Drowning at Milo," *Piscataquis Observer*, September 4, 1884.

102. Spear, "The Personal Memoranda," in Spear et al., *The Civil War Recollections of General Ellis Spear*, 336–37; Samuel Keene Pension File, NA; Ellis Spear Pension File, NA.

103. Whitehorne quoted in Holberton, *Homeward Bound*, 147.

104. Higgins, *A Sketch*, 25–27; JLC to Wilhelm I, King of Prussia, July 20, 1870, Joshua Chamberlain Research Files, Correspondence—1869–1870, PHC.

105. Pullen, *Joshua Chamberlain*, 77–78.

106. Pullen, *Joshua Chamberlain*, 77–78.

107. Pullen, *Joshua Chamberlain*, 79–80.

108. Pullen, *Joshua Chamberlain*, 80–82; "The Conspiracy!" *Bangor Whig and Courier*, November 17, 1879; JLC, *The Twelve Days*, 3.

109. "The Great Crime," *Bangor Whig and Courier*, December 20, 1879; JLC to James G. Blaine, December 29, 1879, in Goulka, *Grand Old Man*, 91–92.

110. Pullen, *Joshua Chamberlain*, 86–89.

111. Pullen, *Joshua Chamberlain*, 90–93; JLC, *The Twelve Days*, 6; Charles Nash to JLC, January 14, 1879, and Charles Nash to JLC, October 14, 1879, Joshua Lawrence Chamberlain Papers, Box 2, Manuscript Division, LOC.

112. JLC, *The Twelve Days*, 7, 18; JLC to Fanny Chamberlain, January 7, 1880, in Goulka, *Grand Old Man*, 94. For letters invoking the Moses analogy, see Calvin Leavey to JLC, January 11, 1880, in Desjardin, *A Life in Letters*, 241, Mary Clark to JLC, January 11, 1880, in Desjardin, *Joshua L. Chamberlain*, 244, and Sewall Brackett to JLC, January 13, 1880, in Desjardin, *Joshua L. Chamberlain*, 249.

113. JLC, *The Twelve Days*, 19.

114. Pullen, *Joshua Chamberlain*, 95.

115. JLC, *The Twelve Days*, 24–25; JLC to Fanny Chamberlain, January 15, 1880, in Goulka, *Grand Old Man*, 96.

116. Franklin Ward to JLC, January 15, 1880, Joshua Lawrence Chamberlain Papers, Box 2, Manuscript Division, LOC.

117. Pullen, *Joshua Chamberlain*, 99.
118. Ellis Spear to JLC, January 17, 1880, in Desjardin, *Joshua L. Chamberlain*, 263.
119. White, *On Great Fields*, 322.
120. Wells, *Rundlett's War*, 159.
121. Holman Melcher Diary, April 26, 1865, in Styple, *With a Flash of His Sword*, 225; Styple, *With a Flash of His Sword*, 292–93.
122. Vickery, "Walter G. Morrill," 127, 149.
123. Glasson, *Federal Military Pensions*, 124–30, 144.
124. Glasson, *Federal Military Pensions*, 126, 226–27; Marten, *Sing Not War*, 61.
125. Glasson, *Federal Military Pensions*, 125, 144, 234; Browning and Silver, *An Environmental History*, 158.
126. Billings, "The Health of the Survivors of the War," 652–58.
127. David Patten Pension File, NA.
128. William H. Davis Pension File, NA.
129. John Lenfest Pension File, NA; information about remarriage and lineage comes from Ancestry.com.
130. Hacker, "Decennial Life Tables for the White Population of the United States, 1790–1900," 44.
131. Walter Morrill Pension File, NA; Vickery, "Walter G. Morrill," 127.
132. Leonard Cummings Pension File, NA; Census data from Ancestry.com. Thanks to Gettysburg Licensed Battlefield Guides—and former medical professionals—Fran Feyock and Rick Schroeder—who provided the layman's description of this particular issue.
133. Leonard Cummings Pension File, NA.
134. U.S. Census Bureau, "Population Schedule," 1920 and 1930; Leonard Cummings Pension File, NA.
135. JLC, *The Passing of the Armies*, 272.

CHAPTER 6

1. William T. Livermore to JLC, May 22, 1899, Joshua Lawrence Chamberlain Correspondence, Box 1 Folder 1—1856–1879, Maine Historical Society. For an example of the change, see JLC, "Through Blood and Fire at Gettysburg," 904.
2. Holman Melcher to Nathaniel Melcher, April 9, 1864, in Styple, *With a Flash of His Sword*, 163; Fanny Chamberlain to Deborah Folsom, April 14, 1864, Joshua Lawrence Chamberlain Correspondence, Box 3, Folder 2, Maine Historical Society.
3. *Revised Report of the Select Committee*, 14, 41–43, 149, 152; "The Maine 20th at Gettysburg," *Eastern Argus*, December 20, 1865; JLC to Fanny Chamberlain, July 17, 1863, Joshua Lawrence Chamberlain Papers, Box 4, Manuscript Division, LOC.
4. Weeks, *Gettysburg*, 19.
5. Linderman, *Embattled Courage*, 266, 268, 271.
6. David Buehler to JLC, August 9, 1866, Joshua L. Chamberlain Letters and Reports, General Order Book, PHC; JLC to D. A. Buehler, August 21, 1866, GCVFM-29, Gettysburg College Special Collections. Many thanks to Meggan Smith

and Amy Lucadamo at Gettysburg College, who helped track down both the original letters and the context of the Board of Trustees meeting minutes.

7. "The Maine 20th at Gettysburg," *Eastern Argus*, December 20, 1865; "Local and Other Items," *Bangor Whig and Courier*, December 20, 1865.

8. JLC, "Loyalty," Joshua Chamberlain Collection, Box 9, Folder 13—Articles and Addresses, Bowdoin College. Also available in the published papers of MOLLUS, reprinted by Broadfoot in 1992.

9. MOLLUS, "In Memoriam: Joshua Lawrence Chamberlain."

10. "The Veteran," *Portland Daily Press*, August 10, 1876; *Reunions of the Twentieth Maine Regiment*, 3–5.

11. *Reunions of the Twentieth Maine Regiment*, 5.

12. *Reunions of the Twentieth Maine Regiment*, 6, 9; "In Camp," *Portland Daily Press*, August 24, 1881.

13. "In Camp," *Portland Daily Press*, August 24, 1881.

14. "Camp Berry," *Portland Daily Press*, August 25, 1881; *Reunions of the Twentieth Maine*, 9.

15. Elisha Coan to Samuel L. Miller, August 6, 1881, Elisha Coan Collection, Box 1, Folder "Letters, 1857–1955," Bowdoin College; *Reunions of the Twentieth Maine*, 18.

16. *Reunions of the Twentieth Maine*, 18.

17. "Veteran Department," *Lincoln County News*, September 1, 1882.

18. "New Publications," *Lincoln County News*, August 18, 1882; "The Town," *Lincoln County News*, February 2, 1883; "Searsport," *Republican Journal* (Belfast, ME), February 8, 1883; "City and County," *Ellsworth American*, March 1, 1883; Desjardin, *Stand Firm Ye Boys from Maine*, 127; Theodore Gerrish, "Battle of Gettysburg," *National Tribune*, November 23, 1882.

19. "Veteran Department: Company K at Round Top," *Lincoln County News*, December 21, 1883.

20. "The Town," *Lincoln County News*, June 23, 1882; "Veteran Department," *Lincoln County News*, August 25, 1882.

21. "A Visit to Gettysburg," *Lincoln County News*, July 28, 1882; "The Blue and the Gray," *Lancaster* (PA) *Daily Intelligencer*, June 8, 1882; Desjardin, *From These Honored Dead*, 83–84.

22. "A Visit to Gettysburg," *Lincoln County News*, July 28, 1882; "Lincoln County News," *Lincoln County News*, September 1, 1882.

23. "Veteran Department: Twentieth Maine Regiment Association," *Lincoln County News*, November 3, 1882; "Original Sketch: The Invasion of Pennsylvania," *Lincoln County News*, December 1, 1882.

24. "Veteran Department: Twentieth Maine Regiment Association," *Lincoln County News*, November 3, 1882; "Original Sketch: The Invasion of Pennsylvania," *Lincoln County News*, December 1, 1882.

25. "Veteran Department: Twentieth Maine Regiment Association," *Lincoln County News*, November 3, 1882.

26. "Veteran Department: Twentieth Maine Regiment Association," *Lincoln County News*, November 3, 1882.

27. "Twentieth Maine," *Lincoln County News*, April 13, 1883; "The Gettysburg Monument," *Lincoln County News*, June 15, 1883; "Gettysburg Monument," *Lincoln County News*, July 25, 1884; "Gettysburg Monument," *Lincoln County News*, August 29, 1884; "Twentieth Maine Monument," *Lincoln County News*, November 13, 1884.

28. "Veteran Department: Gettysburg—The Battle on the Right," *Lincoln County News*, April 20, 1883.

29. "Veteran Department: Gettysburg—The Battle on the Right," *Lincoln County News*, April 20, 1883.

30. "Veteran Department: Editorial Remarks," *Lincoln County News*, April 20, 1883.

31. "Veteran Department," *Lincoln County News*, May 4, 1883.

32. "Veteran Department: Reply to Rear Rank," *Lincoln County News*, May 18, 1883.

33. "Veteran Department: Still Another," *Lincoln County News*, May 18, 1883.

34. "One of the Color-Guard," *Lincoln County News*, May 25, 1883.

35. "Veteran Department: A Probable Theory," *Lincoln County News*, June 1, 1883.

36. "Veteran Department: Extract from a Veteran's Diary," *Lincoln County News*, June 22, 1883.

37. "Veteran Department: The Confederate Sergeant Who Challenged the 20th Maine," *Lincoln County News*, June 29, 1883.

38. "Two Old Comrades Meet," *Lincoln County News*, December 19, 1884.

39. "Twentieth Maine," *Lincoln County News*, December 11, 1885.

40. JLC to Adjutant General, March 3, 1884, and March 17, 1884, Vertical File Collection 5—Participants Accounts—Joshua L. Chamberlain, GNMP; Report of Joshua L. Chamberlain, July 6, 1863, in *OR*, Ser. I, Vol. 27, Pt. 1, 622–26. For an example of who castigates Chamberlain for dating his official report to 1863, see Myers, *The Lion of Round Top*, 151.

41. "The Town," *Lincoln County News*, August 29, 1884.

42. "G. A. R.," *Lincoln County News*, June 26, 1885; "After Twenty-Two Years," *Lincoln County News*, July 10, 1885.

43. "The 20th Maine's Monument," *Lincoln County News*, May 14, 1886; *Maine at Gettysburg*, 586–87.

44. *Maine at Gettysburg*, 588; "Maine at Gettysburg," *Lincoln County News*, May 19, 1887.

45. Joseph Fisher Report, July 9, 1863, in *OR*, Ser. I, Vol. 27, Pt. 1, 658; Samuel Crawford Report, July 10, 1863, in *OR*, Ser. I, Vol. 27, Pt. 1, 655–56.

46. *Maine at Gettysburg*, 589; "The Gettysburg Commission," *Lincoln County News*, June 23, 1887.

47. *Maine at Gettysburg*, 589; "Regimental Monuments," *Lincoln County News*, March 21, 1889; "Regimental Monuments," *Lincoln County News*, April 18, 1889.

48. "Regimental Monuments," *Lincoln County News*, April 18, 1889; *Maine at Gettysburg*, 590.

49. "Excursion of the 20th Maine to Gettysburg," *Lincoln County News*, September 12, 1889; "Gettysburg," *Lincoln County News*, October 10, 1889.

50. "Gettysburg," *Lincoln County News*, October 10, 1889.

51. "Gettysburg," *Lincoln County News*, October 10, 1889; *Dedication of the Twentieth Maine Monuments at Gettysburg*, 8.

52. *Dedication of the Twentieth Maine Monuments at Gettysburg*, 12–14.

53. *Dedication of the Twentieth Maine Monuments at Gettysburg*, 18, 23.

54. *Dedication of the Twentieth Maine Monuments at Gettysburg*, 26.

55. *Dedication of the Twentieth Maine Monuments at Gettysburg*, 26–27.

56. *Dedication of the Twentieth Maine Monuments at Gettysburg*, 27.

57. *Dedication of the Twentieth Maine Monuments at Gettysburg*, 28–29.

58. *Dedication of the Twentieth Maine Monuments at Gettysburg*, 29.

59. "Gettysburg," *Lincoln County News*, October 10, 1889; *Dedication of the Twentieth Maine Monuments at Gettysburg*, 7.

60. *Maine at Gettysburg*, 558–59.

61. JLC Medal of Honor File, NA.

62. Mollan, "The Army Medal of Honor"; JLC Medal of Honor File, NA; JLC Pension File, NA.

63. JLC Medal of Honor File, NA.

64. JLC Medal of Honor File, NA.

65. JLC Medal of Honor File, NA.

66. "The State," *Lincoln County News*, March 5, 1896; *Maine at Gettysburg*, 590; Reuel Thomas to JLC, March 23, 1896, Joshua Lawrence Chamberlain Correspondence, Box 1, Folder 3—1882–1897, Maine Historical Society.

67. Holman Melcher to JLC, March 4, 1895, Joshua Lawrence Chamberlain Papers, Box 3, Manuscript Division, LOC; "Who Were in the Battle," *Lincoln County News*, November 5, 1896; "Twentieth Maine at Gettysburg," *Lincoln County News*, November 5, 1896; Charles Hamlin to JLC, July 7, 1896, Joshua Lawrence Chamberlain Papers, Box 3, Manuscript Division, LOC.

68. Albert Fernald to JLC, March 4, 1897, Joshua Chamberlain Collection, Box 6—Correspondence, Bowdoin College.

69. "Crisis on Round Top," *Lincoln County News*, July 2, 1896.

70. JLC to Ellis Spear, November 27, 1896, in Goulka, *Grand Old Man*, 154–55; JLC to WCO, February 27, 1897, Joshua Chamberlain Collection, Box 6—Correspondence, Bowdoin College; WCO to JLC, March 8, 1897, copy in Vertical File Collection 7—15th AL, GNMP (original in Schoff Civil War Collection, University of Michigan).

71. *Maine at Gettysburg*, iii, 420; Walter Morrill Medal of Honor File, NA.

72. Andrew Tozier Medal of Honor File, NA.

73. "Interesting War Book," *Lincoln County News*, August 18, 1898; *Maine at Gettysburg*, 256.

74. William T. Livermore to JLC, May 22, 1899, Joshua Lawrence Chamberlain Correspondence, Box 1, Folder 1—1856–1879, Maine Historical Society.

75. Clipped obituary among photocopies of William T. Livermore Diary at UMO; JLC, "Through Blood and Fire at Gettysburg," 904.

76. Cushman, *Belligerent Muse*, 158.

77. For examples of the newspaper clippings referenced, see Joshua Lawrence Chamberlain Papers, Box 9, Manuscript Division, LOC.

78. John P. Nicholson to JLC, August 6, 1903, Archival Box B-6—William C. Oates Correspondence, GNMP; Smith, *Golden Age*, 167.

79. Smith, *Golden Age*, xiii; WCO to William Robbins, April 1, 1902, Archival Box B-6—William C. Oates Correspondence, GNMP.

80. William Robbins to John Nicholson, September 27, 1902, Archival Box B-6—William C. Oates Correspondence, GNMP; GNMP Park Commissioners to WCO, March 5, 1903, Archival Box B-6—William C. Oates Correspondence, GNMP.

81. WCO to William Robbins, October 2, 1902, Archival Box B-6—William C. Oates Correspondence, GNMP.

82. William Robbins to WCO, December 16, 1902, Archival Box B-6—William C. Oates Correspondence, GNMP; WCO to Gettysburg Commissioners, January 21, 1903, Archival Box B-6—William C. Oates Correspondence, GNMP; John Nicholson to WCO, February 9, 1903, Archival Box B-6—William C. Oates Correspondence, GNMP.

83. WCO to John Nicholson, February 11, 1903, Archival Box B-6—William C. Oates Correspondence, GNMP.

84. WCO to William Robbins, February 14, 1903, Archival Box B-6—William C. Oates Correspondence, GNMP.

85. William Robbins to John Nicholson, February 19, 1903, Archival Box B-6—William C. Oates Correspondence, GNMP.

86. William Robbins to John Nicholson, February 26, 1903, Archival Box B-6—William C. Oates Correspondence, GNMP.

87. WCO to Secretary of War, February 19, 1903, Archival Box B-6—William C. Oates Correspondence, GNMP; WCO to Secretary of War, June 2, 1903, Archival Box B-6—William C. Oates Correspondence, GNMP.

88. John Nicholson to JLC, August 6, 1903, Archival Box B-6—William C. Oates Correspondence, GNMP.

89. JLC to John Nicholson, August 14, 1903, Archival Box B-6—William C. Oates Correspondence, GNMP.

90. WCO to John Nicholson, November 4, 1903, Archival Box B-6—William C. Oates Correspondence, GNMP; Gettysburg Commissioners to Secretary of War, January 18, 1904, Archival Box B-6—William C. Oates Correspondence, GNMP.

91. WCO to JLC, April 4, 1905, Archival Box B-6—William C. Oates Correspondence, GNMP; WCO to William Robbins, September 4, 1904, Archival Box B-6—William C. Oates Correspondence, GNMP. Regarding their correspondence in 1897, see WCO to JLC, March 8, 1897, Vertical File Collection 7—15th AL, GNMP (original in Schoff Civil War Collection, University of Michigan).

92. JLC to WCO, May 18, 1905, Archival Box B-6—William C. Oates Correspondence, GNMP.

93. Christopher Gwinn, "Joshua Chamberlain, Little Round Top, and the Memorial That Never Was."

94. "Invasion of Waldoboro," *Lincoln County News*, August 27, 1896; "The Twentieth Maine," *Lincoln County News*, September 5, 1907.

95. Flagel, *War, Memory, and the 1913 Gettysburg Reunion*, 16.

96. Flagel, *War, Memory, and the 1913 Gettysburg Reunion*, 20; Maine Adjutant General to O. P. Martin, April 5, 1913, 1913 Gettysburg Reunion Records, Box 6, Folder—"Twentieth Maine Regimental Association," MSA; Unknown to J. F. Fuller, May 9, 1913, 1913 Gettysburg Reunion Records, Box 6, Folder—"Twentieth Maine Regimental Association," MSA.

97. Circular—"To the Veterans of the Civil War," June 16, 1913, 1913 Gettysburg Reunion Records, Box 6, Folder—"Twentieth Maine Regimental Association," MSA.

98. Circular—"To the Veterans of the Civil War," June 16, 1913, 1913 Gettysburg Reunion Records, Box 6, Folder—"Twentieth Maine Regimental Association," MSA.

99. "Twentieth Maine Reunion," *Piscataquis Observer*, July 24, 1913; Flagel, *War, Memory, and the 1913 Gettysburg Reunion*, 166.

100. Desjardin, "A Broken Bond?" 24, 27; JLC, "Through Blood and Fire at Gettysburg," 905.

101. Ellis Spear, "The 20th Maine at Gettysburg," *Portland Daily Press*, July 24, 1863; Ellis Spear to JLC, January 17, 1880, in Desjardin, *Joshua L. Chamberlain*, 263; Ellis Spear to Amos Allen, December 4, 1899, Joshua Chamberlain Collection, Box 6—Correspondence, Bowdoin College; Ellis Spear to JLC, December 24, 1910, Joshua Chamberlain Collection, Box 6—Correspondence, Bowdoin College; Spear and Spear, *The 20th Maine at Fredericksburg*, 40.

102. Spear and Spear, *The 20th Maine at Fredericksburg*, 40, 42, 49.

103. Ellis Spear, "The Left at Gettysburg," *National Tribune*, June 12, 1913.

104. Roberts, *Trending into Maine*, 42–43.

105. Tucker, *Storming Little Round Top*, 9; Quint, "The Hero of Little Round Top?" in Mackowski, White, and Davis, *Don't Give an Inch*, 149; Allen Guelzo, "The Legend from Little Round Top," *Free Beacon*, February 4, 2024, https://freebeacon.com/culture/the-legend-from-little-round-top/.

Conclusion

1. Ellis Spear to Mildred Grant, March 14, 1910, in Styple, *With a Flash of His Sword*, 300.

2. Ellis Spear to Mildred Grant, March 14, 1910, in Styple, *With a Flash of His Sword*, 300.

3. "The Maine 20th at Gettysburg," *Eastern Argus*, December 20, 1865.

Bibliography

Primary Sources: Manuscripts

Bowdoin College Special Collections and Archives
Elisha Coan Collection—M36
Joshua Lawrence Chamberlain Collection—M27

Gettysburg National Military Park Library

Vertical File Collection

5—Participants Accounts—Joshua Chamberlain
6—Union Regiment Files—20th ME
7—Confederate Regiment Files—15th AL

Archival Box Collection

B-6—William C. Oates Correspondence

Library of Congress
Joshua Lawrence Chamberlain Papers
Photograph Collection

Maine Historical Society
Joshua Lawrence Chamberlain—Collection 10

Maine State Archives
Nathan Clark Diary
1913 Gettysburg Reunion Records
2nd Maine Correspondence

2nd Maine Enlistment Papers
Supreme Judicial Court Records
    Androscoggin County
    Washington County
Sylvester Baker Letters
20th Maine Consolidated Morning Reports
20th Maine Correspondence

Milo Historical Society
William Owen Papers
William T. Livermore Diary Transcription

National Archives
Compiled Military Service Records (CMSR)
Court Martial Records
Medal of Honor Files
Pension Files
20th Maine Infantry Regimental Letter, Endorsement, and Order Book

Pejepscot History Center
Joshua Chamberlain Research Files
Albert Fernald Diary—Cabinet 1, Drawer 2
John Chamberlain Journal—Cabinet 1, Drawer 3
John Lenfest Letters—Cabinet 1, Drawer 2
Samuel Keene Diary (photocopy)—Cabinet 1, Drawer 2
Joshua L. Chamberlain Letters and Reports—General Order Book

University of Maine at Orono
William T. Livermore Diary Photocopy—MS 1394

U.S. Army Heritage and Education Center
Civil War Document Collection
    John O'Connell Memoir

Primary Sources: Published

Ames, Blanche. *Chronicles from the Nineteenth Century: Family Letters of Blanche Butler and Adelbert Ames, Married July 21st, 1870.* 2 vols. Privately printed, 1957.

Barnes, Joseph K. *The Medical and Surgical History of the War of the Rebellion (1861–65).* 15 vols. Washington, DC: Government Printing Office, 1870–1888.

Basler, Roy P., Marion Dolores Pratt, and Lloyd A. Dunlap, eds. *The Collected Works of Abraham Lincoln.* 9 vols. New Brunswick, NJ: Rutgers University Press, 1953–1955.

Bowdoin College. *Bowdoin College Catalogues.* https://digitalcommons.bowdoin.edu/course-catalogues.

Carter, Robert G. "Four Brothers in Blue: The Battle of Fredericksburg." *Maine Bugle*, July 1898.

Chamberlain, Joshua. *"Blessed Boyhood!" The "Early Memoir" of Joshua Lawrence Chamberlain*, annotated by Thomas A. Desjardin and David K. Thomson. Brunswick, ME: Bowdoin College, 2013.

———. "My Story of Fredericksburg." *Cosmopolitan Magazine*, January 1913.

———. *The Passing of the Armies: An Account of the Final Campaign of the Army of the Potomac, Based upon Personal Reminiscences of the Fifth Army Corps.* New York: Putnam, 1915.

———. "Through Blood and Fire at Gettysburg. *Hearst's Magazine*, June 1913.

———. *The Twelve Days at Augusta 1880.* Portland, ME: Smith and Sale, 1906.

Dedication of the Twentieth Maine Monuments at Gettysburg, October 3, 1889, with Report of Annual Reunion, Oct. 2d, 1889. Waldoboro, ME: New Steam Job Print, 1891.

Desjardin, Thomas, ed. *Joshua L. Chamberlain: A Life in Letters.* Long Island City, NY: Osprey, 2012.

———, ed. *The Major Writings: The Autobiography of Joshua Chamberlain.* Camden, ME: Downeast Books, 2024.

Engert, Roderick M., ed. *Maine to the Wilderness: The Civil War Letters of Pvt. William Lamson, 20th Maine Infantry.* Orange, VA: Publisher's Press, 1993.

Ford, Worthington Chauncey. *A Cycle of Adams Letters, 1861–1865.* 2 vols. Boston: Houghton Mifflin, 1920.

Gerrish, Theodore. *Army Life: A Private's Reminiscences of the Civil War.* Portland, ME: Hoyt, Fogg & Donham, 1882.

Gould, John M. *History of the First-Tenth-Twenty-Ninth Maine Regiment in Service of the United States from May 3, 1861, to June 21, 1866.* Portland, ME: Stephen Berry, 1871.

Goulka, Jeremiah E. *The Grand Old Man of Maine: Selected Letters of Joshua Lawrence Chamberlain, 1865–1914.* Chapel Hill: University of North Carolina Press, 2004.

Hatch, Louis C. *The History of Bowdoin College.* Portland, ME: Loring, Short & Harmon, 1927.

Higgins, Brian, ed. *A Sketch: The Original 1905 Biography of Joshua Larwence Chamberlain.* Bangor, ME: Bangor Letter Shop, 1995.

Jomini, Baron Antoine Henri de. *The Art of War.* Philadelphia: Lippincott, 1862. Restored ed. Kingston, ON: Legacy, 2008.

Jordan, William C. *Some Events and Incidents During the Civil War.* Montgomery, AL: Paragon, 1909.

Judson, Amos M. *History of the Eighty-Third Regiment Pennsylvania Volunteers.* Erie, PA: Lynn, 1865.

Ladd, David L., and Audrey J. Ladd, eds. *The Bachelder Papers: Gettysburg in Their Own Words.* 2 vols. Dayton, OH: Morningside, 1994.

Law, Evander. "Round Top and the Confederate Right at Gettysburg." *Century Magazine* 33, no. 2 (December 1886): 296–305.

Longstreet, James. *From Manassas to Appomattox: Memoirs of the Civil War in America.* Philadelphia: Lippincott, 1895.

Maine. *Annual Report of the Adjutant General of the State of Maine.* Augusta, ME: Stevens & Sayward, 1861–1866.

———. *Reports of the Warden and Inspectors of the Maine State Prison, and of the Physician and Chaplain, 1860.* Augusta, ME: Stevens & Sayward, 1861.

———. *Reports of the Warden and Inspectors of the Maine State Prison, and of the Physician and Chaplain, 1867.* Augusta, ME: Stevens & Sayward, 1867.

———. *Reports of the Warden and Inspectors of the Maine State Prison, and of the Physician and Chaplain, 1868.* Augusta, ME: Owen & Nash, 1868.

———. *Reports of the Warden and Inspectors of the Maine State Prison, and of the Physician and Chaplain, 1870.* Augusta, ME: Sprague, Owen & Nash, 1871.

———. *Revised Statutes of the State of Maine, Passed April 17, 1857.* Bangor, ME: Wheeler & Lynde, 1857.

Maine at Gettysburg: Report of Maine Commissioners Prepared by the Executive Committee. Portland, ME: Lakeside, 1898.

McDonald, Archie, ed. *Make Me a Map of the Valley: The Civil War Journal of Stonewall Jackson's Topographer.* Dallas, TX: Southern Methodist University Press, 1973.

McWhiney, Grady, and Perry D. Jameson. *Attack and Die: Civil War Military Tactics and Southern Heritage.* Tuscaloosa: University of Alabama Press, 1982.

Melcher, Holman S. "An Experience in the Battle of the Wilderness." *War Papers Read Before the Commandery of the State of Maine, Military Order of the Loyal Legion of the United States,* 1:73–84. Portland, ME: Thurston Print, 1898. Reprint, Wilmington, NC: Broadfoot, 1992.

Minot, John C., and Donald F. Snow, eds. *Tales of Bowdoin: Some Gathered Fragments and Fancies of Underground Life in the Past and Present.* Augusta, ME: Press of Kennebec Journal, 1901.

MOLLUS. "In Memoriam: Joshua Lawrence Chamberlain." Circular 5, Series of 1914, Whole Number, 328. https://digitalcommons.library.umaine.edu/mainehistory/263/.

Nesbitt, Mark, ed. *Through Blood and Fire: Selected Civil War Papers of Major General Joshua Chamberlain.* Mechanicsburg, PA: Stackpole Books, 1996.

Norton, Oliver Wilcox. *The Attack and Defense of Little Round Top, Gettysburg, July 2, 1863.* New York: Neale, 1913. Reprint, Gettysburg, PA: Stan Clark Military Books, 1992.

Oates, William C. *The War Between the Union and the Confederacy and Its Lost Opportunities.* New York: Neale, 1905.

Reunions of the Twentieth Maine Regiment Association at Portland. Waldoboro, ME: Press of Samuel L. Miller, 1881.

Revised Report of the Select Committee Relative to the Soldiers' National Cemetery Together with the House of Representatives and the Commonwealth of Pennsylvania. Harrisburg, PA: Singerly & Myers, 1865.

Rice, Allen Thorndike. *Reminiscences of Abraham Lincoln by Distinguished Men of His Time.* New York: North American, 1886.

Richardson's Civil War Round Table, eds. *Hard Times, Hard Bread, and Harder Coffee: The Civil War Correspondence of Hezekiah Long Company F 20th Maine Infantry.* Northport, ME: Richardson's Civil War Round Table, 2008.

Silliker, Ruth, ed. *The Rebel Yell & the Yankee Hurrah: The Civil War Journal of a Maine Volunteer.* Camden, ME: Down East Books, 1984.

Spear, Abbott, Andrea C. Hawkes, Marie H. McCosh, Craig L. Symonds, and Michael H. Alpert, eds. *The Civil War Recollections of General Ellis Spear.* Orono: University of Maine Press, 1997.

Spear, Ellis. "The Story of the Raising and Organization of a Regiment of Volunteers in 1862." Military Order of the Loyal Legion of the United States. War Paper 46, 1903.

Stanley, R. H., and Geo. O. Hall. *Eastern Maine and the Rebellion: Being an Account of the Principal Local Events in Eastern Maine During the War.* Bangor: Stanley, 1887.

Stewart, George R. *Pickett's Charge: A Microhistory of the Final Attack at Gettysburg, July 3, 1863.* Revised ed. Dayton, OH: Press of Morningside Bookshop, 1980.

Styple, William B., ed. *With a Flash of His Sword: The Writings of Major Holman S. Melcher, 20th Maine Infantry.* Kearny, NJ: Bell Grove, 1994.

U.S. Census Bureau. "Non-Population Schedule." 1870–1880. Ancestry.com.

———. "Population of the United States in 1860." http://www2.census.gov/prod2/decennial/documents/1860a-02.pdf.

———. "Population Schedule." 1850–1930. Ancestry.com.

———. *Statistics of the Population of the United States in 1870.* Washington, DC: Government Printing Office, 1872.

———. *Statistics of the United States in 1860.* Washington, DC: Government Printing Office, 1866.

U.S. Congress. *Acts of the Ninth Congress of the United States (1805–1807).* Session I, Chapter 20. https://tile.loc.gov/storage-services/service/ll/llsl//llsl-c9/llsl-c9.pdf.

———. *Report of the Joint Committee on the Conduct of the War at the Second Session Thirty-Eighth Congress. Army of the Potomac. Battle of Petersburg.* Washington, DC: Government Printing Office, 1865.

U.S. Laws, Statutes, etc. *An Act Giving Eventual Authority to the President of the United States to Augment the Army, 2 March 1799.* https://maint.loc.gov/law/help/statutes-at-large/5th-congress/session-3/c5s3ch31.pdf.

———. *An Act to Provide for Calling Forth the Militia to Execute the Laws of the Union, Suppress Insurrections, and Repel Invasions and to Repeal the Act Now in Force for Those Purposes.* Philadelphia, 1795. https://www.loc.gov/item/2020769638/.

U.S. War Department. *The War of the Rebellion: A Compilation of the Official Records of the Union and Confederate Armies.* 128 volumes. Washington, DC: Government Printing Office, 1880–1901.

Wells, Carlotta, ed., assisted by John W. Wells and James C. Rundlett II. *Rundlett's War: Civil War Letters of James C. Rundlett, 20th Maine Volunteers, Company G.* Privately printed, 1999.

Whitman, William E. S., and Charles H. True. *Maine in the War for the Union: A History of the Part Borne by Maine Troops in the Suppression of the American Rebellion.* Lewiston, NY: Nelson Dingley Jr., 1865.

SECONDARY SOURCES: BOOKS

Adams, Michael C. C. *Living Hell: The Dark Side of the Civil War*. Baltimore: Johns Hopkins University Press, 2014.

Allen, Mark W. *The 2nd U.S. Sharpshooters at Gettysburg: Like a Perfect Hornet's Nest*. Jefferson, NC: McFarland, 2024.

Ames, Blanche. *Adelbert Ames: General Senator Governor 1835–1933*. London: Macdonald, 1965.

Bledsoe, Andrew S. *Citizen-Officers: The Union and Confederate Volunteer Junior Officer Corps in the Civil War*. Baton Rouge: Louisiana State University Press, 2015.

Borneman, Walter R. *1812: The War That Forged a Nation*. New York: Harper Perennial, 2004.

Brown, Kent Masterson. *Meade at Gettysburg: A Study in Command*. Chapel Hill: University of North Carolina Press, 2021.

Browning, Judkin, and Timothy Silver. *An Environmental History of the Civil War*. Chapel Hill: University of North Carolina Press, 2020.

Carmichael, Peter S. *The War for the Common Soldier: How Men Thought, Fought, and Survived in Civil War Armies*. Chapel Hill: University of North Carolina Press, 2018.

Clarke, Frances M., and Rebecca Jo Plant. *Of Age: Boy Soldiers and Military Power in the Civil War*. New York: Oxford University Press, 2023.

Coddington, Edwin B. *The Gettysburg Campaign: A Study in Command*. New York: Scribner, 1968.

Cushman, Stephen. *Belligerent Muse: Five Northern Writers and How They Shaped Our Understanding of the Civil War*. Chapel Hill: University of North Carolina Press, 2014.

Dean, Eric T., Jr. *Shook Over Hell: Post-Traumatic Stress, Vietnam, and the Civil War*. Cambridge, MA: Harvard University Press, 1997.

Deans, Sis. *His Proper Post: A Biography of Gen. Joshua Lawrence Chamberlain*. Kearny, NJ: Belle Grove, 1996.

Desjardin, Thomas A. *From These Honored Dead: How the Story of Gettysburg Shaped American Memory*. New York: Da Capo, 2003.

———. *Stand Firm Ye Boys from Maine: The 20th Maine and the Gettysburg Campaign*. Gettysburg, PA: Thomas, 1995.

Faust, James P. *The Fighting Fifteenth Alabama Infantry: A Civil War History and Roster*. Jefferson, NC: McFarland, 2015.

Flagel, Thomas. *War, Memory, and the 1913 Gettysburg Reunion*. Kent: Kent State University Press, 2019.

Foote, Lorien. *The Gentlemen and the Roughs: Violence, Honor, and Manhood in the Union Army*. New York: New York University Press, 2010.

Fox, William F. *Regimental Losses in the American Civil War 1861–1865*. Albany, NY: Albany Publishing, 1889.

Gallagher, Gary. *The Union War*. Cambridge, MA: Harvard University Press, 2011.

Glasson, William H. *Federal Military Pensions in the United States*. New York: Oxford University Press, 1918.

Golay, Michael. *To Gettysburg and Beyond: The Parallel Lives of Joshua Lawrence Chamberlain and Edward Porter Alexander*. Rockville Centre, NY: Sarpedon, 1994.

Goodheart, Adam. *1861: The Civil War Awakening*. New York: Knopf, 2011.

Gordon, Lesley. *A Broken Regiment: The 16th Connecticut's Civil War*. Baton Rouge: Louisiana State University Press, 2014.

Guelzo, Allen C. *Gettysburg: The Last Invasion*. New York: Knopf, 2013.

———. *Robert E. Lee: A Life*. New York: Knopf, 2021.

Grossman, Dave. *On Killing: The Psychological Cost of Learning to Kill in War and Society*. New York: Little, Brown, 1995.

Handley-Cousins, Sarah. "The Disabled Lion of the Union." In *Bodies in Blue: Disability in the Civil War*, 71–94. Athens: University of Georgia Press, 2019.

Harmon, Troy D. *All Roads Led to Gettysburg: A New Look at the Civil War's Pivotal Campaign*. Essex, CT: Stackpole Books, 2022.

Hart, Irving H. *History of Butler County, Iowa: A Record of Settlement, Organization, Progress and Achievement*. 2 vols. Chicago: Clarke, 1914.

Hasegawa, Guy R. *Mending Broken Soldiers: The Union and Confederate Programs to Supply Artificial Limbs*. Carbondale: Southern Illinois University Press, 2012.

Hess, Earl J. *Civil War Infantry Tactics: Training, Combat, and Small-Unit Effectiveness*. Baton Rouge: Louisiana State University Press, 2015.

———. *The Rifle Musket in Civil War Combat: Reality and Myth*. Lawrence: University Press of Kansas, 2008.

———. *The Union Soldier in Battle: Enduring the Ordeal of Combat*. Lawrence: University Press of Kansas, 1997.

Holberton, William B. *Homeward Bound: The Demobilization of the Union and Confederate Armies, 1865–1866*. Mechanicsburg, PA: Stackpole Books, 2001.

Jordan, Brian Matthew. *Marching Home: Union Veterans and Their Unending Civil War*. New York: Liveright, 2014.

Krick, Robert K. "The Army of Northern Virginia in September 1862: Its Circumstances, Its Opportunities, and Why It Should Not Have Been at Sharpsburg." In *Antietam: Essays on the 1862 Maryland Campaign*, edited by Gary Gallagher, 35–55. Kent, OH: Kent State University Press, 1989.

———. *Civil War Weather in Virginia*. Tuscaloosa: University of Alabama Press, 2007.

LaFantasie, Glenn W. *Gettysburg Requiem: The Life and Lost Causes of Confederate Colonel William C. Oates*. New York: Oxford University Press, 2006.

———. *Twilight at Little Rond Top: July 2, 1863—the Tide Turns at Gettysburg*. Hoboken, NJ: Wiley, 2005.

Linderman, Gerald F. *Embattled Courage: The Experience of Combat in the American Civil War*. New York: Free Press, 1987.

Little, George T. *Genealogical and Family History of the State of Maine*. 4 vols. New York: Lewis Historical Publishing, 1909.

Longacre, Edward G. *Joshua Chamberlain: The Solider and the Man*. Conshohocken, PA: Combined, 1999.

Lord, Francis A. *Civil War Collector's Encyclopedia: Arms, Uniforms, and Equipment of the Union and Confederacy*. 4 vols. Secaucus, NJ: Castle Books, 1977. First published in 1963.

Loski, Diana Halderman. *The Chamberlains of Brewer*. Gettysburg, PA: Thomas, 1998.

Marten, James. *Sing Not War: The Lives of Union & Confederate Veterans in Gilded Age America*. Chapel Hill: University of North Carolina Press, 2011.

McKinney, Joseph W. *Brandy Station, Virginia, June 9, 1863: The Largest Cavalry Battle of the Civil War.* Jefferson, NC: McFarland, 2013.

McPherson, James. *Battle Cry of Freedom: The Civil War Era.* New York: Oxford University Press, 1987.

Morrison, James L., Jr. *The Best School in the World: West Point, the Pre-Civil War Years, 1833–1866.* Kent, OH: Kent State University Press, 1986.

Mundy, James H. *Second to None: The Story of the 2d Maine Volunteers "The Bangor Regiment."* Scarborough, ME: Harp, 1992.

Myers, H. G. *The Lion of Round Top: The Life and Military Service of Brigadier General Strong Vincent in the American Civil War.* Havertown, PA: Casemate, 2022.

Oates, Stephen B. *A Woman of Valor: Clara Barton and the Civil War.* New York: Free Press, 1994.

Perry, Mark. *Conceived in Liberty: Joshua Chamberlain, William Oates, and the American Civil War.* New York: Viking, 1997.

Pfanz, Harry W. *Gettysburg: The Second Day.* Chapel Hill: University of North Carolina Press, 1987.

Prokopowicz, Gerald J. *All for the Regiment: The Army of the Ohio, 1861–1862.* Chapel Hill: University of North Carolina Press, 2001.

Pullen, John J. *Joshua Chamberlain: A Hero's Life and Legacy.* Mechanicsburg, PA: Stackpole Books, 1999.

———. *The Twentieth Maine: A Volunteer Regiment in the Civil War.* Philadelphia: Lippincott, 1957.

Quint, Ryan. "The Hero of Little Round Top?" In *Don't Give an Inch: The Second Day at Gettysburg, July 2, 1863—from Little Round Top to Cemetery Ridge,* by Chris Mackowski, Kristopher D. White, and Daniel T. Davis, 147–51. El Dorado Hills, CA: Savas Beatie, 2016.

Rable, George C. *Fredericksburg! Fredericksburg!* Chapel Hill: University of North Carolina Press, 2002.

Rafuse, Ethan. *McClellan's War: The Failure of Moderation in the Struggle for the Union.* Bloomington: Indiana University Press, 2005.

Reardon, Carol. *With a Sword in One Hand & Jomini in the Other: The Problem of Military Thought in the Civil War North.* Chapel Hill: University of North Carolina Press, 2012.

Reynolds, David S. *Mightier Than the Sword: Uncle Tom's Cabin and the Battle for America.* New York: Norton, 2011.

Rhea, Gordon C. *The Battle of the Wilderness, May 5–6, 1864.* Baton Rouge: Louisiana State University Press, 1994.

Roberts, Kenneth. *Trending into Maine.* Boston: Little, Brown, 1938.

Shaara, Michael. *The Killer Angels: A Novel.* New York: McKay, 1974.

Smith, Diane Monroe. *Chamberlain at Petersburg: The Charge at Fort Hell, June 18, 1864.* Gettysburg, PA: Thomas, 2004.

———. *Fanny & Joshua: The Enigmatic Lives of Frances Caroline Adams and Joshua Larwence Chamberlain.* Gettysburg, PA: Thomas, 1999.

Smith, Mac. *Siege at the State House: The 1879 Coup That Nearly Plunged Maine into Civil War.* Lanham, MD: Down East Books, 2022.

Smith, Timothy B. *The Golden Age of Battlefield Preservation: The Decade of the 1890s and the Establishment of America's First Five Military Parks.* Knoxville: University of Tennessee Press, 2008.

Spear, Abbott, and Ellis Spear. *The 20th Maine at Fredericksburg: The Conflicting Accounts of General Joshua L. Chamberlain and General Ellis Spear*. Union, ME: Union Publishing, 1989.

Stiles, T. J. *Custer's Trials: A Life on the Frontier of a New America*. New York: Knopf Doubleday, 2015.

Swartz, Brian F. *Passing Through the Fire: Joshua Lawrence Chamberlain in the Civil War*. El Dorado Hills, CA: Savas Beatie, 2021.

Trulock, Alice Rains. *In the Hands of Providence: Joshua L. Chamberlain and the American Civil War*. Chapel Hill: University of North Carolina Press, 1992.

Tucker, Phillip Thomas. *Storming Little Round Top: The 15th Alabama and Their Fight for the High Ground, July 2, 1863*. Cambridge, MA: Da Capo, 2002.

Useem, Michael. *The Leadership Moment: Nine True Stories of Triumph and Disaster and Their Lessons for Us All*. New York: Crown, 1998.

Vickery, James B. "Walter G. Morrill: The Fighting Colonel of the Twentieth Maine." In *A Handful of Spice: A Miscellany of Maine Literature and History*, edited by Richard Sprague, 127–51. Orono: University of Maine Press, 1968.

Wallace, Willard M. *Soul of the Lion: A Biography of General Joshua L. Chamberlain*. New York: Nelson, 1960.

Weeks, Jim. *Gettysburg: Memory, Market, and an American Shrine*. Princeton, NJ: Princeton University Press, 2009.

White, Ronald C. *On Great Fields: The Life and Unlikely Heroism of Joshua Lawrence Chamberlain*. New York: Random House, 2023.

Wongsrichanalai, Kanisorn. *Northern Character: College-Educated New Englanders, Honor, Nationalism, and Leadership in the Civil War Era*. New York: Fordham University Press, 2016.

SECONDARY SOURCES: ARTICLES

Abbott, Edith. "The Civil War and the Crime Wave of 1865–1870." *Social Service Review*, June 1927: 212–34.

Billings, John Shaw. "The Health of the Survivors of the War." *Forum*, January 1892: 652–58.

Blanton, DeAnne. "Women Soldiers of the Civil War." *Prologue Magazine*, Spring 1993. https://www.archives.gov/publications/prologue/1993/spring/women-in-the-civil -war-1.html.

Desjardin, Tom. "A Broken Bond? The Little Round Top Feud Between Joshua Chamberlain and Ellis Spear." *America's Civil War*, July 2017: 20–27.

———. "Last Resort? Historian Sheds New Light on the 20th Maine's Epic Bayonet Charge Down Little Round Top." *America's Civil War*, Autumn 2022: 22–29.

Glatthaar, Joseph T. "A Tale of Two Armies: The Confederate Army of Northern Virginia and the Union Army of the Potomac and Their Cultures." *Journal of the Civil War Era* 6, no. 3 (September 2016): 315–46. http://www.jstor.org/stable/26070428.

Gwinn, Christopher. "Joshua Chamberlain, Little Round Top, and the Memorial That Never Was." *The Blog of the Gettysburg National Military Park*, January 30, 2014. https://npsgnmp.wordpress.com/2014/01/30/joshua-chamberlain-little-round-top -and-the-memorial-that-never-was/.

Hacker, J. David. "Decennial Life Tables for the White Population of the United States, 1790–1900." *Historical Methods* 43, no. 2 (2010): 45–79. https://doi.org/10.1080/01615441003720449.

Harmon, William J., and Charles K. McAllister. "The Lion of the Union: The Pelvic Wound of Joshua Lawrence Chamberlain." *Journal of Urology* 163, no. 3 (March 2000): 713–16. https://doi.org/10.1016/S0022-5347(05)67789-0.

Judge, T. A., and D. M. Cable. "The Effect of Physical Height on Workplace Success and Income: Preliminary Test of a Theoretical Model." *Journal of Applied Psychology* 89, no. 3 (June 2004): 428–41. https://doi.org/10.1037/0021-9010.89.3.428.

Kalandarov, Arthur. "Bowdoin Confederates: Why Maine Students Fought for the South During the Civil War." *Journal of Undergraduate Research and Scholarly Excellence* 11 (2022): 1–9.

Mollan, Mark C. "The Army Medal of Honor: The First Fifty-Five Years." *Prologue*, Summer 2001. https://www.archives.gov/publications/prologue/2001/summer/medal-of-honor-1.html.

O'Neal, Bill. "Swamp Fox of the Sulphur: Tennessee-Born Killer Cullen Baker Hits His Stride After the Civil War." *Wild West*, October 2016: 18–19.

O'Neill, Robert. "The Fight for the Loudoun Valley—Aldie, Middleburg and Upperville, Va.: Opening Battles of the Gettysburg Campaign." *Blue & Gray Magazine*, October 1993: 12–21, 46–48, 50–61.

SECONDARY SOURCES: THESES/DISSERTATIONS/PAPERS

Brennan, Matthew. "The Civil War Diet." Master's thesis, Virginia Tech, 2005.

Vermilyea, Peter C. "Meade's Pipe Creek Line." Paper presented at the Civil War Institute, Gettysburg College, June 2022.

www.ingramcontent.com/pod-product-compliance
Ingram Content Group UK Ltd.
Pitfield, Milton Keynes, MK11 3LW, UK
UKHW041828270526
6060IPUK00001B/1